Fill in Your Important Internet

Information Here

Your e-mail address: _____
@ _____

Your Internet provider's data phone number (the number your software dials):

_____

Your Internet provider's technical-support phone number (if you want to talk to a human being):

_____

Your Internet provider's technical-support department's e-mail address:

_____

For SLIP and PPP accounts:

Your Internet hostname (you may not have one assigned):

_____

Your IP address (you may not have one assigned):
_____._____._____._____

Your Internet provider's DNS (domain name server):
_____._____._____._____

Your Internet provider's mail gateway (for outgoing mail): _____

Your Internet provider's POP mail server (for incoming mail): _____

Your Internet provider's news server (for Usenet newsgroups): _____

Hostname Zones

(Three-letter last word of Internet hostnames; for two-letter country codes, see the appendix in this book.)

com	Company or individual
edu	Educational institution
gov	Government
mil	Military
net	Network organization
int	International organization
org	Nonprofit or other noncommercial organization

Acronyms to Know

BTW	By the way
RTFM	Read the manual
IMHO	In my humble opinion
ROFL	Rolling on floor, laughing
TIA	Thanks in advance
YMMV	Your mileage may vary

IDG BOOKS WORLDWIDE™

Internet For Dummies, 3rd Edition

COMPUTER BOOK SERIES FROM IDG

Cheat Sheet

E-mail Addresses

To Send To	With This Address	Type This:
AOL	SteveCase	stevecase@aol.com
AT&T Mail	agbell	agbell@attmail.com
BITNET	user@node	user@node.bitnet or user%node.bitnet @cunyvm.cuny.edu
CompuServe	77777,7777	77777.7777@compuserve.com
Delphi	jsmith	jsmith@delphi.com
Easylink	1234567	1234567@eln.attmail.com
FIDONET	MarySmith 1:2/3.4	mary.smith@p4.f3.n2.z1.fidonet.org
GEnie	J.SMITH7	J.SMITH7@genie.geis.com
MCI Mail	555-2468	5552468@mcimail.com
MSN	BillGates	billgates@msn.com
Prodigy	ABCD123A	abcd123a@prodigy.com

Useful Web Pages

http://www.yahoo.com/	Yahoo index to the Web
http://www.infoseek.com	
http://www.cis.ohio-state.edu/hypertext/ faq/usenet/FAQ-List.html	List of Usenet FAQs
http://cws.wilmington.net/	Stroud's Consummate WinSock Applications
http://hoohoo.ncsa.uiuc.edu/archie.html	Archie request form (to search FTP archives for a file)
http://www.unitedmedia.com/comics/dilbert	Dilbert
http://att.net/dir800	AT&T 800-number directory
http://www.usps.gov/ZIP4Form.html	U.S. Postal Service ZIP codes
http://www.uwm.edu/Mirror/inet.services.html	Yanoff's List
http://rs.internic.net/scout_report-index.html	InterNIC Scout Report
http://dummies.com/	Updates to this book

Usenet News Hierarchies

alt	Alternative newsgroups
comp	Computer-related topics
misc	Miscellaneous topics
news	Usenet-related topics
rec	Recreational topics
sci	Scientific topics
soc	Social and societal topics
talk	Discussions and arguments

Types of URLs

file://pathname	File stored on local computer
ftp://hostname/pathname	File on FTP server
http://hostname/pathname	World Wide Web page
gopher://hostname/pathname	Gopher menu
mailto:address	E-mail
telnet:hostname	Telnet to log in to system

. . . For Dummies: #1 Computer Book Series for Beginners

References for the Rest of Us!®

COMPUTER BOOK SERIES FROM IDG

Are you intimidated and confused by computers? Do you find that traditional manuals are overloaded with technical details you'll never use? Do your friends and family always call you to fix simple problems on their PCs? Then the *. . . For Dummies*® computer book series from IDG Books Worldwide is for you.

. . . For Dummies books are written for those frustrated computer users who know they aren't really dumb but find that PC hardware, software, and indeed the unique vocabulary of computing make them feel helpless. *. . . For Dummies* books use a lighthearted approach, a down-to-earth style, and even cartoons and humorous icons to diffuse computer novices' fears and build their confidence. Lighthearted but not lightweight, these books are a perfect survival guide for anyone forced to use a computer.

> *"I like my copy so much I told friends; now they bought copies."*
>
> **Irene C., Orwell, Ohio**

> *"Quick, concise, nontechnical, and humorous."*
>
> **Jay A., Elburn, Illinois**

> *"Thanks, I needed this book. Now I can sleep at night."*
>
> **Robin F., British Columbia, Canada**

Already, hundreds of thousands of satisfied readers agree. They have made *. . . For Dummies* books the #1 introductory level computer book series and have written asking for more. So, if you're looking for the most fun and easy way to learn about computers, look to *. . . For Dummies* books to give you a helping hand.

IDG BOOKS WORLDWIDE

THE INTERNET FOR DUMMIES®

3RD EDITION

THE INTERNET FOR DUMMIES®

3RD EDITION

by John R. Levine, Carol Baroudi,
and Margy Levine Young

Foreword by Paul McCloskey,
Executive Editor, *Federal Computer Week*

IDG Books Worldwide, Inc.
An International Data Group Company

Foster City, CA ♦ Chicago, IL ♦ Indianapolis, IN ♦ Braintree, MA ♦ Dallas, TX

The Internet For Dummies,® 3rd Edition

Published by
IDG Books Worldwide, Inc.
An International Data Group Company
919 E. Hillsdale Blvd.
Suite 400
Foster City, CA 94404

Library of Congress Catalog Card No.: 95-81433

ISBN: 1-56884-620-7

Printed in the United States of America

10 9 8 7 6 5 4 3 2 1

3A/QX/RS/ZV

Distributed in the United States by IDG Books Worldwide, Inc.

Distributed by Macmillan Canada for Canada; by Computer and Technical Books for the Caribbean Basin; by Contemporanea de Ediciones for Venezuela; by Distribuidora Cuspide for Argentina; by CITEC for Brazil; by Ediciones ZETA S.C.R. Ltda. for Peru; by Editorial Limusa SA for Mexico; by Transworld Publishers Limited in the United Kingdom and Europe; by Al-Maiman Publishers & Distributors for Saudi Arabia; by Simron Pty. Ltd. for South Africa; by IDG Communications (HK) Ltd. for Hong Kong; by Toppan Company Ltd. for Japan; by Addison Wesley Publishing Company for Korea; by Longman Singapore Publishers Ltd. for Singapore, Malaysia, Thailand, and Indonesia; by Unalis Corporation for Taiwan; by WS Computer Publishing Company, Inc. for the Philippines; by WoodsLane Pty. Ltd. for Australia; by WoodsLane Enterprises Ltd. for New Zealand.

For general information on IDG Books Worldwide's books in the U.S., please call our Consumer Customer Service department at 800-762-2974. For reseller information, including discounts and premium sales, please call our Reseller Customer Service department at 800-434-3422.

For information on where to purchase IDG Books Worldwide's books outside the U.S., contact IDG Books Worldwide at 415-655-3021 or fax 415-655-3295.

For information on translations, contact Marc Jeffrey Mikulich, Director, Foreign & Subsidiary Rights, at IDG Books Worldwide, 415-655-3018 or fax 415-655-3295.

For sales inquiries and special prices for bulk quantities, write to the address above or call IDG Books Worldwide at 415-655-3200.

For information on using IDG Books Worldwide's books in the classroom, or ordering examination copies, contact Jim Kelly at 800-434-2086.

For authorization to photocopy items for corporate, personal, or educational use, please contact Copyright Clearance Center, 222 Rosewood Drive, Danvers, MA 01923, or fax 508-750-4470.

trademark under exclusive license to IDG Books Worldwide, Inc., from International Data Group, Inc.

About the Authors

John R. Levine was a member of a computer club in high school — before high school students, or even high schools, had computers. He met Theodor H. Nelson, the author of *Computer Lib/Dream Machines* and the inventor of hypertext, who reminded us that computers should not be taken seriously and that everyone can and should understand and use computers.

John wrote his first program in 1967 on an IBM 1130 (a computer roughly as powerful as your typical modern digital wristwatch, only more difficult to use). He became an official system administrator of a networked computer at Yale in 1975. He began working part-time, for a computer company, of course, in 1977 and has been in and out of the computer and network biz ever since. He got his company on to Usenet (see Chapter 9) early enough that it appears in a 1982 *Byte* magazine article in a map of Usenet, which then was so small that the map fit on half a page.

He used to spend most of his time writing software, but now he mostly writes books (including *UNIX For Dummies* and *Internet Secrets*, published by IDG Books Worldwide) because it's more fun and he can do so at home in the tiny village of Trumansburg, New York. He also teaches some computer courses and publishes and edits an incredibly technoid magazine called *The Journal of C Language Translation*. He holds a B.A. and a Ph.D in computer science from Yale University, but please don't hold that against him.

Carol Baroudi began playing with computers in 1971 at Colgate University, where two things were new: the PDP-10 and women. She was lucky to have unlimited access to the state of the-art PDP-10, where she learned to program, operate the machine, and talk to Eliza. She taught Algol and helped to design the curricula for computer science and women's studies. She majored in Spanish and studied French, which, thanks to the Internet, she can now use every day.

In 1975 Carol took a job doing compiler support and development, which was a perfect use for her background in languages. For six years she developed software and managed software development. For a while she had a small business doing high-tech recruiting (okay, she was a headhunter). Although she wrote her first software manuals in 1975, her *job* has been writing since 1984. She has described all kinds of software, from the memory-management system of the Wang VS operating system to e-mail products for the PC and Mac. For the past several years she has been writing books for ordinary people who want to use computers. *The Internet For Dummies,* 3rd Edition, marks her fourth collaborative effort with John Levine. *Internet Secrets* (IDG Books Worldwide, 1995) afforded Carol her first opportunity to use her French professionally.

The mother of a fantastic five-year-old, Carol loves acting and singing and will fly to France on any excuse. She believes that we are living in an interesting time when technology is changing faster than people can imagine. She hopes that as we learn to use new technologies, we don't lose sight of our humanity. She also feels that computers can be useful and fun but that they are no substitute for real life.

Margy Levine Young has used small computers since the 1970s. She graduated from UNIX on a PDP/11 to Apple DOS on an Apple II to MS-DOS and UNIX on a variety of machines. She has done all kinds of jobs that involve explaining to people that computers aren't as mysterious as they might think, including managing the use of PCs at Columbia Pictures, teaching scientists and engineers what computers are good for, and writing and co-writing computer manuals and books, including *Understanding Javelin PLUS* (Sybex, 1987), *The Complete Guide to PC-File* (Center Books, better known as Margy and her Dad, 1991), *UNIX For Dummies, MORE Internet For Dummies, WordPerfect For Windows For Dummies,* and *Internet FAQs: Answers to the Most Frequently Asked Questions.* Margy has a degree in computer science from Yale University and lives with her husband, two children, and chickens in Lexington, Massachusetts.

Acknowledgments

Many of the tables in *The Internet For Dummies,* 3rd Edition, were adapted from material provided *gratis* by people on the Internet. Some of the information about DOS and Windows TCP/IP packages in Chapter 21 was adapted from a list maintained by C.J. Sacksteder, at Pennsylvania State University.

John particularly thanks his editors at IDG, Mary Bednarek and Diane Steele, for believing him when he said that he was finishing the first edition of this book, despite considerable evidence to the contrary. (They were a little more skeptical for this third edition, but we can't blame them.) Carol and Margy thank them too and feel blessed to be in such fine company.

John thanks Tonia Saxon, for taking such good care of both him and The Bug during the often exciting process of revising this book.

Carol would also like to thank Joshua, whose spirit and good cheer lighten every day; and Philippe, whose friendship is the best thing she has found on the Internet. Special thanks to Arnold for the extra coverage in the extra innings.

Margy would like to acknowledge Barbara Begonis and the folks at Lexington Playcare, without whom she would have been typing with one hand while holding two kids. She would also like to thank Meg and Zac, the two kids in question, for being such extraordinary people.

Thanks to Rebecca Whitney, who did her usual superb job of producing an English translation of our natterings. Dennis Cox did the technical edit and caught lots of lies that we would otherwise have told you. (By mistake. Honest. Any remaining lies are of course our responsibility, not his.)

The entire contents of this book were submitted by the authors to the publisher over the Internet. Edited chapters were returned for review in the same way. We thank TIAC (Bedford, Massachusetts), CENTNet (Cambridge, Massachusetts), and Lightlink (Ithaca, New York), our Internet providers.

(The publisher would like to give special thanks to Patrick J. McGovern, without whom this book would not have been possible.)

Welcome to the world of IDG Books Worldwide.

IDG Books Worldwide, Inc., is a subsidiary of International Data Group, the world's largest publisher of computer-related information and the leading global provider of information services on information technology. IDG was founded more than 25 years ago and now employs more than 7,700 people worldwide. IDG publishes more than 250 computer publications in 67 countries (see listing below). More than 70 million people read one or more IDG publications each month.

Launched in 1990, IDG Books Worldwide is today the #1 publisher of best-selling computer books in the United States. We are proud to have received 8 awards from the Computer Press Association in recognition of editorial excellence and three from Computer Currents' First Annual Readers' Choice Awards, and our best-selling ...*For Dummies*® series has more than 19 million copies in print with translations in 28 languages. IDG Books Worldwide, through a joint venture with IDG's Hi-Tech Beijing, became the first U.S. publisher to publish a computer book in the People's Republic of China. In record time, IDG Books Worldwide has become the first choice for millions of readers around the world who want to learn how to better manage their businesses.

Our mission is simple: Every one of our books is designed to bring extra value and skill-building instructions to the reader. Our books are written by experts who understand and care about our readers. The knowledge base of our editorial staff comes from years of experience in publishing, education, and journalism — experience which we use to produce books for the '90s. In short, we care about books, so we attract the best people. We devote special attention to details such as audience, interior design, use of icons, and illustrations. And because we use an efficient process of authoring, editing, and desktop publishing our books electronically, we can spend more time ensuring superior content and spend less time on the technicalities of making books.

You can count on our commitment to deliver high-quality books at competitive prices on topics you want to read about. At IDG Books Worldwide, we continue in the IDG tradition of delivering quality for more than 25 years. You'll find no better book on a subject than one from IDG Books Worldwide.

John J. Kilcullen

John Kilcullen
President and CEO
IDG Books Worldwide, Inc.

IDG Books Worldwide, Inc., is a subsidiary of International Data Group, the world's largest publisher of computer-related information and the leading global provider of information services on information technology. International Data Group publishes over 250 computer publications in 67 countries. Seventy million people read one or more International Data Group publications each month. International Data Group's publications include: **ARGENTINA:** Computerworld Argentina, GamePro, Infoworld, PC World Argentina; **AUSTRALIA:** Australian Macworld, Client/Server Journal, Computer Living, Computerworld, Digital News, Network World, PC World, Publishing Essentials, Reseller; **AUSTRIA:** Computerwelt, PC TEST; **BELARUS:** PC World Belarus; **BELGIUM:** Data News; **BRAZIL:** Annuário de Informática, Computerworld Brazil, Connections, Super Game Power, Macworld, PC World Brazil, Publish Brazil, SUPERGAME; **BULGARIA:** Computerworld Bulgaria, Networkworld/Bulgaria, PC & MacWorld Bulgaria; **CANADA:** CIO Canada, ComputerWorld Canada, InfoCanada, Network World Canada, Reseller World; **CHILE:** Computerworld Chile, GamePro, PC World Chile; **COLUMBIA:** Computerworld Colombia, GamePro, PC World Colombia; **COSTA RICA:** PC World Costa Rica/Nicaragua; **THE CZECH AND SLOVAK REPUBLICS:** Computerworld Czechoslovakia, Elektronika Czechoslovakia, PC World Czechoslovakia; **DENMARK:** Communications World, Computerworld Danmark, Macworld Danmark, PC World Danmark, PC World Danmark Supplements, TECH World; **DOMINICAN REPUBLIC:** PC World Republica Dominicana; **ECUADOR:** PC World Ecuador, GamePro; **EGYPT:** Computerworld Middle East, PC World Middle East; **EL SALVADOR:** PC World Centro America; **FINLAND:** MikroPC, Tietoverkko, Tietoviikko; **FRANCE:** Distributique, Golden, Info PC, Le Guide du Monde Informatique, Le Monde Informatique, Reseaux & Telecoms; **GERMANY:** Computer Business, Computerwoche, Computerwoche Extra, Computerwoche Focus, Electronic Entertainment, GamePro, I/M Information Management, Macwelt, PC Welt; **GREECE:** GamePro, Macworld & Publish; **GUATEMALA:** PC World Centro America; **HONDURAS:** PC World Centro America; **HONG KONG:** Computerworld Hong Kong, PCWorld Hong Kong, Publish in Asia; **HUNGARY:** ABCD CD-ROM, Computerworld Szamitastechnika, PC & Mac World Hungary, PC-X Magazine; **INDIA:** Computerworld India, PC World India, Publish in Asia; **INDONESIA:** InfoKomputer PC World, Komputek Computerworld, Publish in Asia; **IRELAND:** ComputerScope, PC Live!; **ISRAEL:** PC World 32 BIT, People & Computers; **ITALY:** Computerworld Italia, Computerworld Italia Special Editions, Lotus Italia, Macworld italia, Networking Italia, PC Shopping, PC World Italia, PC World/Walt Disney; **JAPAN:** Macworld Japan, Nikkei Personal Computing, SunWorld Japan, Windows World Japan; **KENYA:** East African Computer News; **KOREA:** Hi-Tech Information/Computerworld, Macworld Korea, PC World Korea; **MACEDONIA:** PC World Macedonia; **MALAYSIA:** Computerworld Malaysia, PC World Malaysia, Publish in Asia; **MEXICO:** Computerworld Mexico, GamePro, Macworld, PC World Mexico; **MYANMAR:** PC World Myanmar; **NETHERLANDS:** Computable, Computer! Totaal, LAN Magazine, Macworld, Net Magazine; **NEW ZEALAND:** Computer Buyer, Computerworld New Zealand, MTB, Network World, PC World New Zealand; **NICARAGUA:** PC World Costa Rica/Nicaragua; **NIGERIA:** PC World Africa; **NORWAY:** Computerworld Norge, Computerworld Privat, CW Rapport Klient/Tjener, CW Rapport Nettverk & Telecom, CW Rapport Offentlig Sektor, IDG's KURSGUIDE, Macworld Norge, Multimedia World, PC World Ekspress, PC World Nettverk, PC World Norge, PC World's Produktguide, Windows Spesial; **PAKISTAN:** Computerworld Pakistan, PC World Pakistan; **PANAMA:** GamePro, PC World Panama; **PARAGUAY:** PC World Paraguay; **P. R. OF CHINA:** China Computerworld, China Infoworld, Computer & Communication, Electronic Product World, Electronics Today, Game Camp, PC World China, Popular Computer Week, Software World, Telecom Product World; **PERU:** Computerworld Peru, GamePro, PC World Profesional Peru, PC World Peru; **POLAND:** Computerworld Poland, Computerworld Special Report, Macworld, Networld, PC World Komputer; **PHILIPPINES:** Computerworld Philippines, PC Digest, Publish in Asia; **PORTUGAL:** Cerebro/PC World, Correio Informático/Computerworld, Mac•In/PC•In Portugal; **PUERTO RICO:** PC World Puerto Rico; **ROMANIA:** Computerworld Romania, PC World Romania, Telecom Romania; **RUSSIA:** Computerworld Rossiya, Network World Russia, PC World Russia; **SINGAPORE:** Computerworld Singapore, PC World Singapore, Publish in Asia; **SLOVENIA:** MONITOR; **SOUTH AFRICA:** Computing S.A., Network World S.A., Software World; **SPAIN:** Computerworld España, COMUNICACIONES WORLD, Dealer World, Macworld España, PC World España; **SWEDEN:** CAP&Design, Computer Sweden, Corporate Computing, MacWorld, Maxi Data, MikroDatorn, Nätverk & Kommunikation, PC/Aktiv, PC World, Windows World; **SWITZERLAND:** Computerworld Schweiz, Macworld Schweiz, PCtip; **TAIWAN:** Computerworld Taiwan, Macworld Taiwan, PC World Taiwan, Publish Taiwan, Windows World; **THAILAND:** Thai Computerworld, Publish in Asia; **TURKEY:** Computerworld Monitör, MACWORLD Turkiye, PC WORLD Turkiye; **UKRAINE:** Computerworld Kiev, Computers & Software Magazine, PC World Ukraine; **UNITED KINGDOM:** Acorn User, Amiga Action, Amiga Computing, Amiga, Appletalk, CD Powerplay, CD-ROM Now, Computing, Connexion, GamePro, Lotus Magazine, Macaction, Macworld, Open Computing, Parents and Computers, PC Home, PC Works, The WEB; **UNITED STATES:** Cable in the Classroom, CD Review, CIO Magazine, Computerworld, Computerworld Client/Server Journal, Digital Video Magazine, DOS World, Electronic, InfoWorld, I-Way, Macworld, Maximize, MULTIMEDIA WORLD, Network World, PC World, PUBLISH, SWATPro Magazine, Video Event, WebMaster; **URUGUAY:** PC World Uruguay; **VENEZUELA:** Computerworld Venezuela, GamePro, PC World Venezuela; and **VIETNAM:** PC World Vietnam   10/17/95

Credits

Senior Vice President and Publisher
Milissa L. Koloski

Associate Publisher
Diane Graves Steele

Brand Manager
Judith A. Taylor

Editorial Managers
Kristin A. Cocks
Mary Corder

Product Development Manager
Mary Bednarek

Editorial Executive Assistant
Richard Graves

Editorial Assistants
Constance Carlisle
Chris Collins
Stacey Holden Prince
Kevin Spencer

Acquisitions Assistant
Suki Gear

Production Director
Beth Jenkins

Production Assistant
Jacalyn L. Pennywell

Supervisor of Project Coordination
Cindy L. Phipps

Supervisor of Page Layout
Kathie S. Schnorr

Production Systems Specialist
Steve Peake

Pre-Press Coordination
Tony Augsburger
Patricia R. Reynolds
Theresa Sánchez-Baker

Media/Archive Coordination
Leslie Popplewell
Michael Wilkey

Project Editor
Rebecca Whitney

Technical Reviewer
Dennis Cox

Associate Project Coordinator
Sherry Gomoll

Graphic Coordination
Shelley Lea
Gina Scott
Carla Radzikinas

Production Page Layout
Shawn Aylsworth
Kerri Cornell
Anna Rohrer
Kate Snell
Michael Sullivan

Proofreaders
Kathy McGuinnes
Christine Meloy Beck
Gwenette Gaddis
Dwight Ramsey
Carl Saff
Robert Springer

Indexer
Liz Cunningham

Cover Design
Kavish + Kavish

Contents at a Glance

Table of Contents

• •

Part II: Using Your Internet Account 51

Chapter 4: Netscape, Mosaic, and the Wild, Wonderful, Wacky World Wide Web 53

Chapter 5: Stupid Netscape Tricks 67

Part V: The Part of Tens *297*

Foreword

A year ago I was the original Internet Dummy.

Although I had been covering technology in one form or another for 10 years as a journalist, I considered most computers to be typewriters on steroids. I just needed a good text editor, about 15 megabytes of storage, and a push-button phone.

Also, I thought most of my officer mates who actually did bury their heads in their personal computers were the newsroom equivalents of heating and air conditioning engineers. I had better things to do than marvel about "personal productivity tools" or "spreadsheet performance." Computing in a bubble, I thought.

Then while I was on vacation, a colleague ran some telephone wire into the back of my computer, loaded a communications package, and left me a note about how to launch the operation.

Readers, that note is now framed in my office. Eventually, that telephone wire led to the Internet and the single most amazing, entertaining, and educational experience of my career.

Quite simply, the Internet has revolutionized the way I interact with the outside world, altered my work habits, and burst the bubble around my PC. It has also challenged my thinking about the future of personal communications technology. And I believe that sooner — rather than later — those changes will be mapped onto society as a whole.

Consider this: My $1,000 PC is now a personal broadcasting station that reaches more people than the CBS affiliate in Washington D.C. I can get more local viewers with a single e-mail posting to the Internet than Sally Jessy Raphael can get in a sweeps month.

Or this: I'm going to send this piece to my editor for about a sixtieth of a cent — it will take roughly a sixth of a second. (Memo to the Letter Carriers Union: Invest in night schools, *now*.)

Or this: When Vice President Al Gore released his proposal for the National Information Infrastructure, his personal vision for the Information Superhighway, it was zapped to my e-mail box that very morning, courtesy of an Internet group I belong to that is interested in such matters. (Hey Washington Post! Poof! You're a newsletter!)

I've also had some amazing interactions on the Internet, the implications of which I am still trying to figure out. For instance, a few months ago I was logged on to the Internet's equivalent of a live on-line forum in which two other people were present. Now that's not so unusual, considering the popularity of similar forums running on the dressier, private on-line services. But then one of them handed me a photograph. Actually, it was a little more complicated than that — given the hardware and software being used, I had to execute some commands, download the file, and stomp on it a few times — but that is essentially what happened. Instead of exchanging text messages, we swapped graphics.

Although it was a simple transaction, given that I was in Washington, D.C. and the other two people possibly in Wheaton, Illinois, and Durban, South Africa, it was an amazing interaction. Wait until baseball card collectors get ahold of that one.

But that is one of the joys of the Internet. Its constantly evolving set of applications is being driven not so much by software developers but by its users, all crowding around, talking, and trying out new things.

And while the Internet has turned around the way I interact with the outside world, it has also made me more keen about the technology on my end of the wall jack. Those little pieces of software that make my personal computer more of a convenience have a whole new power and meaning when attached to the two million computers on the Internet.

I now run short digital motion pictures on my PC. The software and the graphics are tucked away in their proper places on the Internet. My PC is humming with software — Indiana Jones never saw more icons. My home and office are now wired together. And I no longer discredit the office PC tinkerers; I just urge them to get on the Internet.

I therefore urge you to read John Levine's *The Internet For Dummies*, 3rd Edition. It will guide you with patience and a refreshing sense of humor through the sometimes daunting job of getting going on the net. But you will be rewarded. And the rest is up to your imagination.

Paul McCloskey
Executive Editor
Federal Computer Week

Introduction

● ●

*W*elcome to *The Internet For Dummies,* 3rd Edition. Lots of books about the Internet are available , but most of them assume that you have a degree in computer science, would love to learn every strange and useless wart of the Internet, and enjoy memorizing unpronounceable commands and options. We hope that this book is different.

Instead, this book describes what you actually do to become an *Internaut* (someone who navigates the Internet with skill) — how to get started, what commands you really need, and when to give up and go for help. And we describe it in plain old English.

We've made many changes for this new, third edition. When we first wrote *The Internet For Dummies*, a typical Net user was a student who connected from school or a technical worker who had access through work. But now, two years later, the Net has grown like crazy to include millions of (dare we say it?) normal people, connecting on their own nickel from computers at home, along with students ranging from elementary school to adult education. Now we zero in on the parts of the Net that are of the most interest to typical users — electronic mail for person-to-person communications and the World Wide Web, including Netscape and Mosaic, the best-known Web programs, for visiting the wonders the Net has to offer.

About This Book

We don't flatter ourselves that you are interested enough in the Internet to sit down and read the entire book (although it should be a fine book for the bathroom). When you run into a problem using the Internet ("Hmm. . .I *thought* I ran a program that would log in to another computer, but it didn't respond with any message. . . ."), just dip into the book long enough to solve your problem.

Pertinent sections include:

- What the Internet is
- How to get connected to the Net
- Communicating with electronic mail
- Weaving through the World Wide Web

- ✔ Moving files and other data around
- ✔ Ways to find useful stuff on the Internet
- ✔ Common mistakes and how to correct them
- ✔ Where to find services and software

How to Use This Book

To begin, please read the first three chapters. They give you an overview of the Net and some important tips and terminology. Besides, we think that they're interesting. After that, use this book as a reference. Look up your topic or command in the table of contents or the index, which refers you to the part of the book in which we describe what to do and perhaps define a few terms (if absolutely necessary).

When you have to type something, it appears in the book like this:

```
cryptic command to type
```

Type it just as it appears. Use the same capitalization we do — many systems care very deeply about CAPITAL and small letters. Then press the Enter or Return key. The book tells you what should happen when you give each command and what your options are.

Who Are You?

In writing the book, we assumed that

- ✔ You have or would like to have access to the Internet.
- ✔ You want to get some work done with it. (We consider the term "work" to include the concept "play.")
- ✔ You are not interested in becoming the world's next great Internet expert, at least not this week.

How This Book Is Organized

This book has five parts. The parts stand on their own — you can begin reading wherever you like, but you should at least skim Part I first to get acquainted with some unavoidable Internet jargon and learn how to get your computer on the Net.

Here are the parts of the book and what they contain:

Part I "Welcome to the Internet." In this part you learn what the Internet is and why it's interesting (at least why we think it's interesting). Also, there's stuff about vital Internet terminology and concepts that will help you as you move through the later parts of the book. It discusses how you get on the Internet and gives some thoughts about children's use of the Net.

Part II "Getting Going on the Net." Part II looks at the two most important and useful Net services: electronic mail and the World Wide Web. You learn how to exchange electronic mail with people down the hall or on other continents and how to use electronic mailing lists to keep in touch with people of like interests. For the Web, we describe the two most popular Web programs: Netscape (for people whose computers have mice and graphics) and Lynx (for people whose computers don't.)

Part III "The Rest of the Net." We cover the other major Net services in this part. You learn about using Usenet news to keep in touch even better, and you even get some suggestions for checking out the thousands of topics that Usenet addresses. You learn how to log in to other computers, retrieve useful files from computers around the world, and figure out what to do with the files after you have them.

Part IV "Four Entrance Ramps." You learn about the four most popular "gateways" to the Net, including the popular on-line services America Online (AOL), CompuServe, Prodigy, and Microsoft Network. If you use a UNIX shell account, there's a chapter for you here, too.

Part V "The Part of Tens." This part is a compendium of ready references and useful facts (which, we suppose, suggests that the rest of the book is full of useless facts).

Part VI "Resource Reference." In this part you learn about where to find Internet providers, Internet software, and more sources of information about the Net.

Icons Used in This Book

Lets you know that some particularly nerdy, technoid information is coming up so that you can skip it if you want (on the other hand, you might want to read it).

Indicates that a nifty little shortcut or time-saver is explained.

 Arrrghhhh! Don't let this happen to you!

 Points out a resource on the World Wide Web that you can use with Netscape or other Web software.

Alerts you to particularly juicy information related to locating something or someone on the Net.

What Now?

That's all you need to know to get started. Whenever you hit a snag using the Internet, just look up the problem in the table of contents or index in this book. You'll either have the problem solved in a flash or you'll know whether you need to find some expert help.

Because the Internet has been evolving for more than 20 years, largely under the influence of some extremely nerdy people, it was not designed to be particularly easy for normal people to use. So don't feel bad if you have to look up a number of topics before you feel comfortable using the Internet. After all, most computer users never have to face anything as complex as the Internet.

Feedback, Please

We love to hear from our readers. If you want to contact us, please feel free to do so in care of IDG Books Worldwide, 7260 Shadeland Station, Suite 100, Indianapolis, IN 46256.

Better yet, send us Internet electronic mail at `ninternet @dummies.com` or visit our Web home page at `http://dummies.com`. These electronic addresses just contact the authors of this book; to contact the publisher or authors of other ...*For Dummies* books, send e-mail to `info@idgbooks.com` or write to the address just listed.

Part I
Welcome to
the Internet

The 5th Wave   By Rich Tennant

"Oh, that there's just something I picked up as a grab bag special from the 'Curiosities' Web Page."

In this part . . .

The Internet is a big and happening place. But because it's full of computers, nothing there is quite as simple as it should be. First we look at what the Internet is, how it got that way, and how to figure out how to get your computer in touch with the Net. Then we take a short but important detour about your kids and the Net.

Chapter 1

What Is the Net?

What Is the Internet?

The answer to this question depends a great deal on whom you ask. The Internet and its associated technologies are changing faster than anyone can keep track of. In this chapter we begin with the basics and tell you what it is and, just as important, what has changed during the past couple of years so that you can begin to have an understanding of what it's all about. If you are completely new to the Internet, and especially if you don't have much computer experience, *be patient with yourself.* Many of the ideas here are completely new. Allow yourself some time to read and reread. It's a brand-new world with its own language, and it takes some getting used to. Many people find it helpful to read through the entire book quickly one time to get a broader perspective of what we're talking about. Others plow through a page at a time. Whatever your style, remember that it's *new* stuff — you're not *supposed* to understand it already. And even for many experienced Internet users, it's a new world.

The Internet — also known as the *Net* — is the world's largest computer network, or network. "And what is a network?" you might ask. Even if you already know, you might want to read the next couple of paragraphs to make sure that we're speaking the same language.

A computer *network* is basically a bunch of computers hooked together somehow. (Here in the World of Computers, we like these crisp, precise definitions.) In concept, it's sort of like a radio or TV network that connects a bunch of radio or TV stations so that they can share the latest episode of "The Simpsons."

But don't take the analogy too far. TV networks send the same information to all the stations at the same time (it's called *broadcast* networking, for obvious reasons); in computer networks, each particular message is usually routed to a particular computer. Unlike TV networks, computer networks are invariably two-way, so that when computer A sends a message to computer B, B can send a reply back to A.

Some computer networks consist of a central computer and a bunch of remote stations that report to it (a central airline-reservation computer, for example, with thousands of screens and keyboards at airports and travel agencies). Others, including the Internet, are more egalitarian and permit any computer on the network to communicate with any other.

So, as we were saying, the Internet is the world's largest computer network. "So what?" you're probably saying. "I once saw the world's largest turnip on TV, and it didn't look very interesting — and I bet that it didn't taste so great either." With networks, unlike vegetables, size counts for a lot because the larger a network is, the more stuff it has to offer.

The Internet isn't really a network — it's a network of networks, all freely exchanging information. The networks range from the big and formal, like the corporate networks at AT&T, Digital Equipment, and Hewlett-Packard, to the small and informal, like the one in John's back bedroom (with a couple of old PCs bought through the *Want Advertiser*) and everything in between. College and university networks have long been part of the Internet, and now high schools and elementary schools are joining up too. In the past year or two, Internet usage has been increasing at a pace equivalent to that of television in the early '50s; the Net now has an estimated 35 million users, with growth rates adding another 16 million by the middle of 1996.

So What's All the Hoopla?

Everywhere you turn you hear people talking about the Net — like they're on a first-name basis. Radio shows give you their e-mail address, and strangers ask whether you have a home page. People are "going on-line and getting connected." Are they really talking about this same "network of networks?" Yes, *and* there's more.

The Internet is new communications technology that is affecting our lives on a scale as significant as the telephone and television. If you use a telephone, write letters, read a newspaper or magazine, or do business or any kind of research, the Internet can radically alter your entire world view.

When people talk about the Internet today, they're usually talking about what they can do and whom they've met. The Internet's capabilities are so expansive that we don't have room to give a complete list here (indeed, it would fill several books larger than this one), but here's a quick preview:

- ✔ **Electronic mail (e-mail):** This service is certainly the most widely used — you can exchange e-mail with millions of people all over the world. People use e-mail for anything they might use paper mail or the telephone for: gossip, recipes, rumors, love letters — you name it. (We hear that some people even use it for stuff related to work.) Electronic *mailing lists* enable you to join in group discussions with people who have similar interests and meet people over the Net. *Mail servers* (programs that respond to e-mail messages automatically) let you retrieve all sorts of information. See Chapters 6, 7, 8, and 17 for details.

- ✔ **The World Wide Web**: When people these days talk about surfing the Net, they often mean checking out sites on this (buzzword alert) multimedia hyperlinked database that spans the globe. The Web, unlike earlier Net services, combines text, pictures, sound, and even animation, and it lets you move around with a click of your computer mouse. New *Web sites* are growing faster than you can say "Big Mac with cheese," with new sites appearing every minute. The software used to navigate the Web is known as a *browser*. The most popular browsers today are Netscape and Mosaic, but new ones are appearing even as we type (see Chapters 4 and 5).

- ✔ **Information retrieval:** Many computers have files of information that are free for the taking. The files range from U.S. Supreme Court decisions and library card catalogs to the text of old books, digitized pictures (nearly all of them suitable for family audiences), and an enormous variety of software, from games to operating systems. Many of the tools discussed in this book help you to make sense of the mountain of information available on the Net and figure out what is available where. As mentioned in the Introduction, you'll see a Web icon here and there; it points to resources you can retrieve from the Net yourself (see Chapters 10 and 11).

- ✔ **Bulletin boards:** A system called *Usenet* is an enormous, distributed, on-line bulletin board with about 700 million characters of messages in more than 12,000 different topic groups flowing daily. Topics range from nerdy computer stuff to hobbies such as cycling and knitting to endless political arguments to just plain silliness. The most widely read Usenet group is one that features selected jokes, most of which *are* pretty funny (see Chapter 9).

- ✔ **Games and gossip:** A game called *MUD (Multi-User Dungeon)* can easily absorb all your waking hours — in it, you can challenge other players who can be anywhere in the world. *Internet Relay Chat (IRC)* is a party line over which you can have more or less interesting conversations with other users all over the place. IRC seems to be frequented primarily by bored college students, but you never know whom you'll encounter. Many Internet providers (the folks who get you connected to the Internet — see Chapter 2) have facilities for "chatting" that enable you to have on-line conversations with a bunch of people at the same time.

A Few Real-Life Stories

Seventh-grade students in San Diego use the Internet to exchange letters and stories with kids in Israel. Partly it's just for fun and to make friends in a foreign country, but a sober academic study reported that when kids have a real audience for their stuff, they write better. (Big surprise.)

In some parts of the world, the Internet is the fastest and most reliable way to move information. During the 1991 Soviet coup, a tiny Internet provider called RELCOM, which had a link to Finland and through there to the rest of the Internet world, found itself as the only reliable path to get reports in and out of Moscow because telephones were shut off and newspapers weren't being published. RELCOM members sent out stories that would have been in newspapers, statements from Boris Yeltsin (hand-delivered by friends), and their personal observations from downtown Moscow.

Medical researchers around the world use the Internet to maintain databases of rapidly changing data.

The Internet has more prosaic uses too. Here are some from our personal experience:

Last year when we began our megabook, *Internet Secrets*, we posted notices on the Net asking for contributions. We got responses from all over the world. Many of these contributors became our friends. Now we have people to visit all over the world. It could happen to *you*.

We get mail every day from all over the world from readers of ...*For Dummies* books and are often the happy recipients of a reader's first-ever e-mail message.

The Internet is its own best source of software. Whenever we hear about a new service, it usually takes only a few minutes to find software for one of our computers (a 486 laptop running Windows), download it, and start it up. And nearly all the software available on the Internet is free.

The Internet has local and regional parts as well. When John wanted to sell a trusty but tired minivan, a note on the Internet in a local for-sale area found a buyer within two days. Margy's husband sold his used computer within half an hour of posting a message in the relevant Usenet newsgroup.

Why Is This Medium Different?

The Internet is unlike all the other communications media we've ever encountered. People of all ages, colors, creeds, and countries freely share ideas, stories, data, and opinions.

Anybody can access it

One unusual thing about the Internet is that it's probably the most open network in the world. Thousands of computers provide facilities that are available to anyone who has Net access. This situation is unusual — most networks are very restrictive in what they allow users to do and require specific arrangements and passwords for each service. Although a few pay services exist (and more are added every day), the vast majority of Internet services are free for the taking. If you don't already have access to the Internet through your company, your school, or a friend's attic, you'll probably have to pay for access by using one of the Internet access providers. We talk about them in Chapter 2.

It's politically, socially, and religiously correct

Another unusual thing about the Internet is that it is what one might call "socially unstratified." That is, one computer is no better than any other, and no person is any better than any other. Who you are on the Internet depends solely on how you present yourself through your keyboard. If what you say makes you sound like an intelligent, interesting person, that's who you are. It doesn't matter how old you are or what you look like or whether you're a student, a business executive, or a construction worker. Physical disabilities don't matter — we correspond with people who are blind or deaf. If they hadn't felt like telling us, we never would have known. People become famous in the Net community, some favorably and some unfavorably, but they get that way through their own efforts.

Where Did the Internet Come From?

If you're not interested in Net history, just skip to the beginning of Chapter 2.

The ancestor of the Internet was the *ARPANET,* a project funded by the Department of Defense (DOD) in 1969, both as an experiment in reliable networking and to link DOD and military research contractors, including the large number of universities doing military-funded research. (*ARPA* stands for *Advanced Research Projects Administration,* the branch of Defense in charge of handing out grant money. For enhanced confusion, the agency is now known as *DARPA* — the added *D* is for *Defense,* just in case there was any doubt where the money was coming from.) The ARPANET started small, connecting three computers in California with one in Utah, but it quickly grew to span the continent.

Every continent?

Some skeptical readers, after reading the claim that the Internet spans every continent, may point out that Antarctica is a continent, even though its population consists largely of penguins, who (as far as we know) are not interested in computer networks. Does the Internet go there? It does. A few machines at the Scott Base on McMurdo Sound in Antarctica are on the Net, connected by radio link to New Zealand. The base at the South Pole is supposed to have a link to the U.S., but it doesn't publish its electronic address.

At the time of this writing, the largest Internet-free land mass in the world is apparently New Guinea. (Bali got on the Internet in 1994.)

The reliable networking part involved *dynamic routing*. If one of the network links became disrupted by enemy attack, the traffic on it could automatically be rerouted to other links. Fortunately, the Net rarely has come under enemy attack. But an errant backhoe cutting a cable is just as much of a threat, so it's important for the Net to be backhoe-resistant.

The ARPANET was wildly successful, and every university in the country wanted to sign up. This success meant that the ARPANET began getting difficult to manage, particularly with the large and growing number of university sites on it. So it was broken into two parts: *MILNET,* which had the military sites, and the new, smaller ARPANET, which had the nonmilitary sites. The two networks remained connected, however, thanks to a technical scheme called *IP (Internet Protocol),* which enabled traffic to be routed from one network to another as necessary. All the networks connected in the Internet speak IP, so they all can exchange messages.

Although there were only two networks at that time, IP was designed to allow for tens of thousands of networks. An unusual fact about the IP design is that every computer on an IP network is, in principle, just as capable as any other, so any machine can communicate with any other machine. (This communication scheme may seem obvious, but at the time most networks consisted of a small number of enormous central computers and a large number of remote *terminals,* which could communicate only with the central systems, not with other terminals.)

Meanwhile, back at the classroom

Beginning around 1980, university computing was moving from a small number of large *time-sharing* machines, each of which served hundreds of simultaneous users, to a large number of smaller desktop *workstations* for individual users. Because users had gotten used to the advantages of time-sharing systems, such

Can the Internet really resist enemy attack?

It looks that way. During the Gulf War in 1991, the U.S. military had considerable trouble knocking out the Iraqi command network. It turned out that the Iraqis were using commercially available network routers with standard Internet routing and recovery technology. In other words, dynamic routing really worked. It's nice to know that dynamic routing works, although perhaps this was not the most opportune way to find out.

as shared directories of files and e-mail, they wanted to keep those same facilities on their workstations. (They were perfectly happy to leave behind the disadvantages of time-shared systems. A sage once said, "The best thing about a workstation is that it's no faster in the middle of the night.")

Most of the new workstations ran a variety of *UNIX,* a popular (and, for many versions, free or close to it) kind of operating software that had been developed at AT&T and the University of California at Berkeley. The people at Berkeley were big fans of computer networking, so their version of UNIX included all the software necessary to hook up to a network. Workstation manufacturers began to include the necessary network hardware also, so all you had to do to get a working network was to string the cable to connect the workstations, something that universities could do for cheap because they usually could get students to do it.

Then, rather than have one or two computers to attach to the ARPANET, a site would have hundreds. What's more, because each workstation was considerably faster than an entire 1970s multiuser system, one workstation could generate enough network traffic to swamp the ARPANET, which was getting creakier by the minute. Something had to give.

Enter the National Science Foundation

The next event was that the National Science Foundation (NSF) decided to set up five supercomputer centers for research use. (A supercomputer is a really fast computer with a hefty price, like $10 million apiece.) The NSF figured that it would fund a few supercomputers, let researchers from all over the country use the ARPANET to send their programs to be "supercomputed," and then send back the results.

The plan to use the ARPANET didn't work out for a variety of reasons — some technical, some political. So the NSF, never shy about establishing a new political empire, built its own, much faster network to connect the supercomputing centers: the *NSFNET.* Then it arranged to set up a bunch of regional networks to connect the users in each region, with the NSFNET connecting all the regional networks.

The NSFNET worked like a charm. By 1990, in fact, so much business had moved from the ARPANET to the NSFNET that, after nearly 20 years, the ARPANET had outlived its usefulness and was shut down. The supercomputer centers the NSFNET was supposed to support turned out to be a fizzle: Some of the supercomputers didn't work, and the ones that did were so expensive to use that most potential customers decided that a few high-performance workstations would serve their needs just as well. Fortunately, by the time it became clear that the supercomputers were on the way out, the NSFNET had become so entrenched in the Internet that it lived on without its original purpose. By 1994, several large, commercial Internet networks had grown up within the Internet, some run by large, familiar organizations such as IBM and Sprint and others by such specialist Internet companies as Performance Systems International (always known as PSI) and Alternet. The NSFNET has been wound down, with its traffic taken over by commercial networks.

The NSFNET permitted traffic related only to research and education, but the independent, commercial IP network services can be used for other kinds of traffic. The commercial networks connect to the regional networks just like the NSFNET does, and they provide direct connections for customers. Chapter 22 lists many commercial IP providers.

Outside the United States, IP networks have appeared in many countries, either sponsored by the local telephone company (which is usually also the local post office) or run by independent national or regional providers. The first international connections were in 1973 with England and Norway. Nearly all countries are connected directly or indirectly to some U.S. network, meaning that they all can exchange traffic with each other.

The term Internet first appeared in 1982 with DARPA's launch of the Internet Protocol (IP).

Chapter 2

Internet, Here I Come

● ●

In This Chapter

▶ Connecting to the Net

▶ Determining whether you're on the Net already

▶ Learning about connection strategies

● ●

Which Way to the Internet?

"Great," you say, "How do I get to the Internet?" The answer is "It depends." The Internet isn't one network — it's 60,000 separate networks hooked together, each with its own rules and procedures, and you can get to the Net from any one of them. But readers of previous editions of this book pleaded (well, they did other things too, but this is a family-oriented book) for step-by-step directions for how to get on, so we'll be as step-by-step as we can.

So here are the basic steps:

1. Figure out what kind of computer you have or can use.
2. Figure out what kinds of Internet connections are available where you are.
3. Figure out how much you are willing to pay.
4. Set up your connection and decide whether you like it.

Do You Have a Computer?

There's really no way around this one. The Internet is a computer network, so the only way to hook up to it is by using a computer.

Nope!

If you don't have a computer, you still have some options. If you have a computer at work, particularly if it's already set up to handle electronic mail, you may already have an Internet connection. (See the nearby sidebar "Are you already on the Internet?")

If you don't have the work option, the next most likely place to find Net access is in your public library. This is particularly true if you have a local cable-TV company that thinks it wants to get into the Internet business — hooking up to the Internet over a TV cable turns out to be a technical nightmare, so the cable company often sets up one free connection at the library first to get the bugs out. (Because it's free, it's hard to complain when it doesn't work.) Many cities also have *freenets*, a kind of local community computer system that usually has a link to the Internet. Except in Los Angeles, freenets are indeed free (although they won't turn down a contribution if you want to support them).

Another possibility is your local community college or continuing-education center. (They go by different names; in New York, for example, our local one is called BOCES.) They often have a short and inexpensive "Introduction to the Internet" course. You may at this point be wondering "What kind of loser book tells people to go out and take a course?" There are two things you can get from a course that you can't possibly get from any book: A live demonstration of what the Internet is like and, more important, someone to talk to who knows the local Internet situation. You can certainly get on the Net without a class (we did, after all), but if an inexpensive class is available, take it.

Popping up with surprising speed are *cybercafes*. You can now surf the Net while sipping your favorite beverage and sharing your cyber experience. Cybercafes are a great place to "try before you buy" if you want to check out the Internet.

Are you already on the Internet?

If you have access to a computer or a computer terminal, you may already be on the Internet. Here are some ways to check.

If you have an account on an on-line service such as CompuServe, America Online (AOL), Microsoft Network (MSN), or MCI Mail, you already have a connection to the Internet. At the least, you can send mail, and some on-line services provide relatively complete Internet connections.

If you use a bulletin board system (BBS) that exchanges messages with other BBSs, again you can exchange e-mail with the Internet.

If your company or school has an internal e-mail system, it may also be connected to the Internet. Ask a local mail expert.

If your company or school has a local computer network, it may be connected directly or indirectly to the Internet, either just for mail or for a wider variety of services. Networks of workstations usually use the same kind of networking the Internet does, so connection is technically easy. Networks of PCs or Macs often use different kinds of network setups (most commonly Novell Netware or AppleTalk), so it's more difficult, but still possible, for the people who run the network to hook it to the Internet.

Yup!

Ah, you do have a computer. (Or maybe you're thinking of buying one.)

One approach (let's call it the "geek," or "deranged," approach) is to run network cables (held in place by duct tape, of course) all over your house, climb up on the roof, put up radio antennas, and fill up the attic with humming boxes full of routers and subnets and channel service units and heaven knows what else. This approach can be made to work (John has done it, in fact, more than once), but if you were the kind of geek who liked to do that sort of thing, you probably wouldn't be reading this book.

The other approach, the "normal" approach, is to use a computer and a phone line to dial in to an Internet service in which the geeks have already set things up for you. (Carol and Margy favor this approach.)

Let's Be Normal

To make the "normal" approach work, you need four pieces: a computer, a modem to hook your computer to the phone line, an account with an Internet provider, to give your modem someplace to call, and software to run on your computer. We'll look at each of these items in turn.

Any Computer Will Do

People argue at great length about the advantages and disadvantages of various kinds of computers. We're not going to do that here (although, if you'll buy the beer, we'll be happy to argue about it after work). Pretty much any personal computer made since 1980 is adequate for at least some kind of connection to the Internet, although some computers make it easier than others.

The leading contenders, fortunately, are the most popular: IBM-compatible computers running Windows, and Macintoshes. On either of those computers, you can get the spiffiest kind of Internet connection (known as a SLIP or PPP connection, but we'll worry about that later), which makes it possible to use the nicest point-and-click programs and get pictures, sounds, and even movies from the Net.

On any other kind of computer, you can still have a text-only Internet connection that isn't as cool as the fancy ones but that is still adequate for a great deal of Net surfing.

Modems, Ho!

A modem is the thing that hooks your computer to the phone line. Because the usual way to hook up to the Internet is over the phone, you need one. Modems come in all sorts of shapes and sizes. Some are separate boxes, known as *external* modems, with cables that plug in to the computer and the phone line with power cords. Some are inside the computer with just a cable for the phone, and some of the newest ones are tiny credit-card-size things you stuff into the side of your computer. (But they still have a cable for the phone — some things never change.)

Matching the variety of physical sizes is an equally wide variety of internal features. The speed at which the modem operates (that is, the rate at which it can stuff computer data into the phone line) ranges from a low of 2400 bits per second (bps, commonly but erroneously called baud) to 28,800 bps. Some modems can act as fax machines, and some can't. Some have even more exotic features, such as built-in answering machines.

Pretty much any modem made in the past ten years is adequate for an initial foray into the Net, so if you already have a modem, use it. If you don't have a modem, here's our suggestion about what you should buy:

Get an inexpensive 14,400 bps external modem that's intended for use with your kind of computer.

The nerdspeak term for a 14,400 bps modem is V.32*bis*, by the way, named after the official international standard that describes how that kind of modem is supposed to work. (*Bis* is, oddly, French for "and a half.") Ask for one at your computer store and they'll think that you're an expert.

We suggest 14,400 because anything slower isn't much cheaper. We prefer external modems because you can install them without opening up your computer and because external modems have indicator lights that can be useful when you're trying to get things going. There are differences between inexpensive modems and expensive ones (try throwing them up in the air and see what happens when they hit the floor), but they aren't of much importance unless you plan to be on-line 24 hours a day, you're an unusually violent computer user, or (the serious reason) you're on a noisy phone line way out in the country. You can get faster modems that run at up to 28,800 bps, known as V.34, but they cost much more and are less widely supported by Internet providers. Your Internet provider, whoever it is, has a modem at its end of the phone line as well, and the actual connection is made at the slower of the speeds of your modem and theirs.

Most 14,400 modems are also fax modems, which means that with a suitable program, usually included with the modem, you can send and receive faxes with your computer. We find that feature moderately useful, but not so much that we would pay extra for a fax feature.

Be sure to get a cable to connect the modem to your computer, and be sure that it has connectors which match the computer — there are three different kinds of plugs that might be on the back of the computer.

Note to laptop owners: If your computer has credit-card-size PCMCIA slots, get a PCMCIA modem that fits in a slot so that you don't have to carry around a separate modem when you take your computer on the road.

If you want to find out more about modems, check out Tina Rathbone's book *Modems For Dummies* (published by IDG Books Worldwide).

Normal Terminal Program: Is That Contagious?

You're going to need, to go along with your modem, some software to be able to use other people's computers. Most on-line services and many Internet providers give or sell you software for Windows and the Mac, but if you have some other kind of computer or want something simple, you can use a simpler software that usually comes with the computer or with the modem.

This simpler software is called *terminal-emulation software* because it makes your computer look like just another terminal (that is, a keyboard and a text-only screen) on that remote computer. *Modems For Dummies* describes this software and how to get it up and running on your computer. Figure 2-1 shows a typical terminal-emulator screen.

Windows users can use Windows Terminal, a rudimentary but usable terminal emulator that is a standard part of Windows 3.1.

Figure 2-1:
Your normal
terminal
emulator in
action.

```
The Fall Classic is back! An exclusive online tour of the new
World Series exhibit at the National Baseball Hall of Fame and
Museum. Ace baseball writer Roger Kahn celebrates the sport,
and takes you out to the ball game. Take a look at the News
Corp/MCI feature on the Internet at http://www.delphi.com, or
just type:  GO ENT DELPHI (and select #1)




MAIN Menu:

Business and Finance      News, Weather, and Sports
Computing Groups          Reference/Health/Education
Conference                Shopping
Custom Forums             Social Groups
ELECTROPOLIS (Games)      Travel and Leisure
Entertainment             UK DELPHI
Hobbies and Interests     Using DELPHI
Internet Services         Workspace
Mail                      HELP
Member Directory          EXIT

MAIN>What do you want to do? █
```

For Mac and Windows users who plan to use something fancier than a terminal emulator, we'll come back and talk some more about software after we've discussed the possible Internet providers, because the software and the provider have to match.

Providing That. . . .

You have to subscribe to a provider to give you your Internet connection. You use your computer and modem to call in to the provider's system, and the provider handles the rest of the details of connecting to the Internet.

There are (wait — no, how did you guess?) many different types of Internet providers, with a trade-off among ease of use, range of features, and price. Table 2-1 shows which on-line services support which Internet services.

Table 2-1	Internet Services Provided by the Major On-line Services				
Internet Service	*Internet SLIP or PPP account*	*Internet Shell Account*	*AOL*	*CompuServe*	*MSN*
E-mail	Yes (using Eudora or another mail program)	Yes (using Elm, Pine, or another mail program)	Yes (using Read New Mail icon on toolbar)	Yes (using the Mail command on the menu bar: surcharge for receiving mail)	Yes (using Microsoft Exchange)
World Wide Web	Yes (using Mosaic, Netscape, or another browser)	Yes (using Lynx)	Yes (after downloading extra software: keyword WEB)	Yes (using Spry Mosaic, after downloading NetLauncher and logging in as an Internet account)[1]	Yes (using Internet Explorer)
Host your own Web pages	Usually (ask your provider how: It may cost extra)	Usually (ask your provider how: It may cost extra)	Yes (keyword HTML: Includes Web-page builder)	No	No
Usenet news-groups	Yes (using Agent, NEWTNews, or another newsreader)	Yes (using trn, nn, tin, or another newsreader)	Yes (keyword NEWSGROUPS)	Yes (go NEWSGROUPS),	Yes (use Go word *usenet*)
FTP [2]	Yes (using WS_FTP, Fetch, or another FTP program)	Yes (using FTP)	Yes (keyword FTP)	Yes (go FTP)	Yes (click Internet Newsgroups icon in Internet Center window)

Internet Service	Internet SLIP or PPP account	Internet Shell Account	AOL	CompuServe	MSN
Gopher[3]	Yes (using Hgopher or other programs)	Yes (using gopher)	Yes (keyword GOPHER)	Yes (using Spry Mosaic)	Yes (using Internet Explorer)
Telnet	Yes (using a telnet program)	Yes (using telnet)	No	Yes (go TELNET)	No
Ping	Yes (using a ping program)	Yes (using ping)	No[4]	No	Yes
Finger	Yes (using a finger program)	Yes (using finger)	No[4]	No	No
IRC	Yes (using WS_IRC or mIRC)	Yes (using irc or ircii)	No[4]	No	No
WAIS	Yes (using WinWAIS or another client program)	Usually (using WAIS)	Yes (keyword WAIS)	Yes (using Spry Mosaic and WAIS gateway)	Yes (using Internet Explorer and Web gateway)
Whois[5]	Yes (using a whois program)	Yes (using whois)	Yes (using Web browser and InterNIC Directory Services Web page)	Yes (using Spry Mosaic and InterNIC Directory Web page)	Yes (using Internet Explorer and InterNIC Directory Services Web page)

Notes:

[1] Using CompuServe's NetLauncher package, you can use any WinSock-compatible programs with your CompuServe account, except for e-mail programs.

[2] Most Web browsers can retrieve files via anonymous FTP by using URLs of the form `ftp://hostname/directory/filename`.

[3] Any Web browser can view Gopher pages by using URLs of the form `gopher://hostname/pagename`.

[4] Using the AOL WINSOCK.DLL, you can use any WinSock-compatible programs with your AOL account.

[5] Any Web browser can do a whois search by going to the InterNIC Directory Services Web search page, at `http://rs.internic.net/cgi-bin/whos`.

Big ol' commercial providers

You can choose one of the big, commercial on-line services such as CompuServe, America Online (AOL), Microsoft Network (MSN), or Delphi. Each has its own software package that you run on your computer and that connects you to the service. The on-line services have versions of the packages for Windows, Mac, and, in most cases, DOS. You can still use CompuServe and Delphi with a terminal emulator if you have some other kind of computer, but AOL requires that you use its software, MSN requires that you have Windows 95, and even the services you can use via a terminal emulator look much nicer if

All the commercial providers started in business as "information utilities"; that is, they originally provided service to just their own users, without connecting to the outside. They all eventually connected to the Internet, but a large part of what each of the commercial providers offers is proprietary material specific to that provider.

Here are some good things about the big commercial services:

- ✔ They're relatively easy to get connected to and use.
- ✔ They have lots of helpful people you can call when you get stuck.
- ✔ They offer flashy screen- and mouse-oriented programs to help you use them.
- ✔ They offer proprietary services and information not available elsewhere on the Net. (If you want to use the Eaasy Sabre airline-reservation system, for example, you have to use one of the commercial providers.)
- ✔ Many give you a way to limit the material your kids can access.

And here are some bad things about the big commercial services:

- ✔ They limit you to whatever specific set of Internet services they choose to offer; if you want something else, you're out of luck.
- ✔ They make it more difficult or, in some cases, impossible to get to parts of the Net considered controversial. (Some people consider this restriction to be an advantage, of course.)
- ✔ They're relatively expensive if you spend more than a few hours a month on-line.

Figures 2-2 through 2-4 show typical screens from the major commercial services.

The Internet, the whole Internet, and nothing but the Internet, so help us. . . .

The next kind of provider to look at is an *Internet service provider,* often abbreviated *ISP.* (We computer types just love TLAs — three-letter acronyms.) An ISP is sort of like a commercial service, but with the important difference that its primary business is hooking people to the Internet. It turns out that nearly all ISPs buy their equipment and software from a handful of manufacturers, so the features and services offered by one ISP are much like those of another, with such important differences as price, service, and reliability. Think of it as the difference between a Ford and a Buick, with the differences between your local dealers being at least as important to the purchase decision as the difference between the cars.

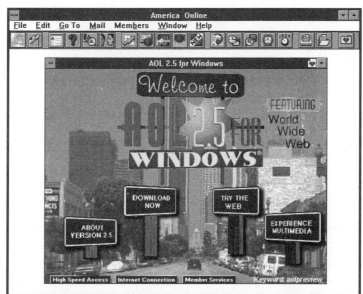

Figure 2-2:
America
Online is
on-screen.

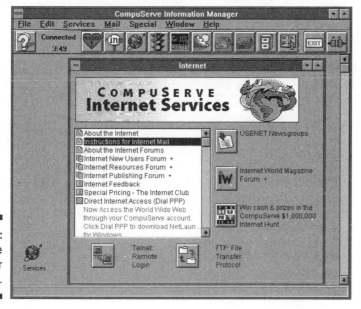

Figure 2-3:
CompuServe
at your
service.

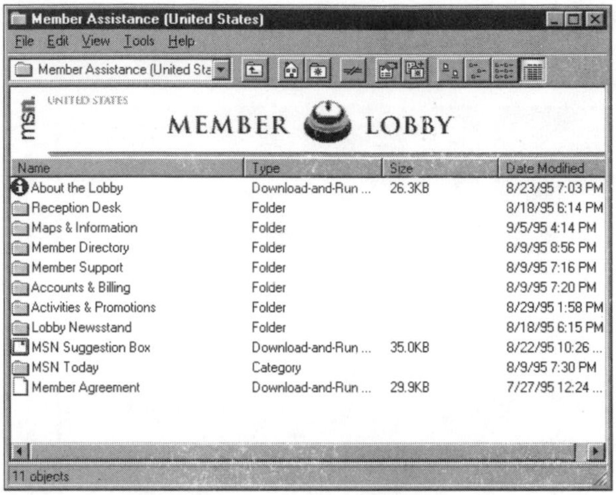

Figure 2-4:
Microsoft
Network at
work.

ISPs provide two different kinds of access: *shell* access and *SLIP/PPP* access. Most ISPs offer both kinds of access. Some offer both with a single account, and others require that you choose one or the other.

Shell-shocked

The older and usually cheaper kind of ISP account is *shell access.* It's less flexible than the other kind, but it's much easier to set up. For shell access, the only software you need on your computer is a terminal emulator, as you saw in Figure 2-1.

With shell access, your provider's computer is considered part of the Internet, but your computer is not. When you connect to your provider, you type commands to its system, which tell it what Internet or other functions you want to do. The program on your provider's computer that receives and acts on the commands is known as a *shell* (hence the name). The shell and the programs it runs for you send back to your computer some text that is displayed on your screen.

Almost without exception, shell access providers are running UNIX system software, so it will eventually help to learn a little about UNIX systems. Your shameless authors suggest *UNIX For Dummies,* 2nd Edition (IDG Books Worldwide, 1995).

How much does this all cost?

You can spend a great deal of money on your Internet connection. Or you can spend practically none. Here are a few things to look out for:

Provider charges

Pricing schemes vary all over the lot. Some providers charge you by the hour, and others have a flat rate per month. Many have "blended" schemes: For a monthly charge you get a set number of hours, and you pay by the hour if you use more than that. Major on-line services in the U.S. charge about $10 per month, which includes about five hours. If you use more than that, you pay $2 to $4 per extra hour. Most Internet service providers have flat-rate plans: For between $10 and $50 per month, you can use its service as much as you want. Others have blended plans: For your monthly fee you get enough hours for any but the most dedicated Internet fanatic. Studies have shown that average Internet use is about 18 hours per month.

A few providers charge more for daytime use than for nights and weekends, although that's much less common than it used to be.

Warning: If you or your kids become regular on-line users, you will find that time stands still while you're on-line and that you use much more on-line time than you think you do. Even if you think that you'll be on for only a few minutes a day, you may be surprised when the bill comes at the end of the month.

Phone charges

If you're not careful, you can end up paying more for the phone call than you do for your Internet service itself. One of the things you do when you sign up for an on-line service is to determine the phone number to call. *If at all possible, use a provider whose number is a free or untimed local call.* If you use a local or regional Internet service provider, that provider will have a short list of phone numbers you can use. Of the national providers, IBM Advantis and CompuServe have their own national networks of dial-in numbers, and the rest piggyback on other networks with such names as Sprintnet and Tymnet. (To add to the confusion, many providers other than CompuServe also use CompuServe's network.) If one national provider has a local number, therefore, they probably all do because it's a Sprintnet, Tymnet, or CompuServe number that will work for any of them.

If you cannot find a provider that is a local call for you, your options are limited. Some providers have 800 access, but that's rarely a good deal because you pay extra by the hour for using the 800 number. (Someone has to pay for that 800 call, and that someone is you.) If you have a long-distance plan such as Sprint's "The Most" or MCI's "Friends and Family," you can put your provider's phone number on your list of frequently called numbers and get a low rate that should be less than 10 cents per minute for nights and weekends. (But that's still more than $5 per hour.) Be sure to compare rates for in-state and out-of-state calls because in many cases an out-of-state call is cheaper even though it's farther away.

If you're a long, expensive toll call from anywhere, take a look at MCI Mail, described later in this chapter, which offers only one service (electronic mail), but which has 800 access from anywhere in the country at no hourly charge.

SLIPping up

The newer kind of connection to the Internet is known as *SLIP,* or *PPP,* access. (There are technical differences between SLIP and PPP, but they're not important to normal users, so we say SLIP/PPP to mean either.) With SLIP/PPP, when you connect to your provider, your computer becomes part of the Internet. You type directly to programs running on your computer, and those programs communicate over the Net to do whatever it is they do for you.

The biggest advantage of this type of access is that the programs running on your computer can take full advantage of your computer's facilities so that they can draw graphics, display windows, play sounds, receive mouse clicks, and otherwise do all the fancy stuff that modern computer programs do. (With shell access, remember that the Internet programs are running on your provider's computer and are restricted to sending text.) If your computer system can handle more than one running program at a time, as Macs and Windows can do, you can have several Internet applications running at a time, which can be quite handy. You might be reading your electronic mail, for example, and receive a message describing a cool, new home page on the World Wide Web. You can switch immediately to your Web program (Netscape, most likely), look at the page, and then return to the mail program and pick up where you left off.

Another advantage of SLIP/PPP access is that you're not limited to running programs your Internet provider gives you. You can download a new Internet application from the Net and begin using it immediately — your provider is just acting as a data conduit between your computer and the rest of the Net.

The disadvantages of SLIP/PPP access are that it's somewhat more difficult to set up because you have to get an Internet access package loaded and configured on your computer and in some cases ISPs charge more for SLIP/PPP access than for shell access.

Picking an ISP

After you've decided that you want to go with an ISP, the next question is *which* ISP. This question is relatively complicated because you have several thousand ISPs from which to choose. Many are listed in Chapter 20.

There are a few national ISPs, such as IBM Internet Connection, Netcom, Portal, and PSI. At the time we wrote this book, MCI and AT&T announced that they were getting into the Internet business, so by the time you read this, they may well have done so. National ISPs have lots of dial-in numbers across the country, which can be handy if you travel much and usually (but, sadly, not always) have extensive support staffs to help you. Their pricing varies, but it tends to be relatively high. (An exception is Netcom, which for years has offered unlimited shell access for $20 per month.)

You can usually get a better deal from a regional or local ISP. They tend to compete in price more than the national ones do, and in many cases, because they stick to one geographic area, they offer community-oriented on-line materials as well. When you're comparison shopping, consider the following:

- ✔ Price
- ✔ Support (call and talk to the support staff before you sign up)
- ✔ Load (the length of response time during peak hours)
- ✔ Modem speed (some providers haven't upgraded their equipment in a long time)

ISP odds and ends

A few Internet providers don't exactly fall into any of the categories we've discussed:

Pipeline: An all-in-one Internet access package from The Pipeline, an Internet provider in New York City. It has been licensed by several other providers around the country. It's a decent way to get on the Net, relatively easy to set up, and relatively complete.

Netcruiser: Another all-in-one package from Netcom. If you're using Netcom as your provider, give Netcruiser a try and see whether you like it, because the software is free.

UUCP: An antique dial-up system that offers only electronic mail and network news (which despite its name is more like a bulletin board). It's a "batch" system (your computer dials the provider, exchanges data with the provider at top speed, and then hangs up). You can then peruse, at your leisure, the stuff it received from your provider. If your provider is a toll call, UUCP access can be a way to keep your phone bills down, although it can't give you any of the fun, new interactive Internet services.

Back to Software

The kind of access you have is intimately related to the kind of software you need.

Commercial providers

Nearly all the commercial providers give you program disks with software that works with their particular systems. A few of them, including CompuServe and Delphi, still offer text-only access by using terminal-emulator software.

Part IV describes how to use the most popular commercial on-line services and how to get and install the software required to access them.

Shell access

If you use an ISP and pick shell access, you use a terminal emulator: software that makes your computer act as though it's just a screen and keyboard hooked up to your ISP's computer. This isn't something you usually have to think much about, but we tell you what you need to know in Chapter 15.

SLIP or PPP access

If you use an ISP with SLIP or PPP access, you need SLIP/PPP software. There are lots of alternatives:

- The most popular access software for Windows is Trumpet Winsock. It's shareware, and many ISPs give their customers disks with copies of it. (Unfortunately, most of them forget to mention that if you use the software on the disk, you owe a registration fee to the program's author in Tasmania.)

- A few free access software packages are available, most notably the Chameleon Sampler, which is packaged in the back of many Internet books (but not this one). It's an older, buggier, and unsupported version of the commercial Chameleon software package, but it works well enough for many users.

- Several commercial Windows packages are available too. Most are pricey, but two of the least expensive are the Spry, Inc. package, which you can get in Internet in a Box for about $100 (O'Reilly) and Internet Chameleon, available in, among other places, *The Internet For Windows For Dummies Starter Kit* (IDG Books Worldwide): 30 days free, $15 for a permanent license, plus the cost of the book.

- For Mac users, most of the necessary Internet software, called MacTCP, is a standard part of System 7. The missing parts are the dial-up access software and the applications, both of which are available from most ISPs and are also bound in the back of some books.

- If you use Linux or a workstation running some version of UNIX, all the necessary software is part of the standard system.

Chapter 21 describes how to find software to use with your SLIP/PPP account.

TECHNICAL STUFF

A few lines about Linux

Linux is a new, completely free, UNIX-style system that runs on PCs. Most servers on the Net run UNIX, so most server software runs on Linux or can be easily adapted for it by someone with a little programming experience. It can be a pain to get Linux installed, but if you find yourself wanting to put your computer on the Net many hours a day or to test out a set of interrelated Web pages you've written, Linux is the system to use. By using advanced system-software techniques known since about 1961 (but not yet fully implemented in Windows — even in Windows 95), Linux protects running programs from each other so that if one program crashes it almost never takes the system with it. Nobody thinks it at all unusual when a Linux system runs continuously for a month or more without having to be restarted.

You can download Linux from the Net if you are an extremely patient person (it takes several days), but the usual way to set up a Linux system is to buy or borrow some Linux CD-ROMs and install from there. The CD-ROMs are inexpensive (we got a set for $14.95), and because Linux is free, it's entirely legitimate to install one set of bought or borrowed CD-ROMs on as many computers as you want.

Linux is not as easy to set up as Windows, but it's considerably cheaper and much more reliable for use as a server.

On and off the Information Superhighway

There's a first time for everything. If it's the information superhighway you're looking for, just buckle up. If the computer you use is connected to a network, you're probably familiar with such terms as user ID and login name. If you're not, here's the scoop.

There are 35 million people on the Internet. Only one of them is you, so it would be nice if the other 34,999,999 weren't able to snoop through your files. No matter which kind of provider you use, you have to use a security procedure to prove that you are who you say you are.

Would you sign your name in, please?

Not so different from that prehistoric TV show "What's My Line," service providers of all sorts want to know who's on the system. To track usage, users are given an account, sort of like a bank account. The account has your name and a secret password associated with it.

Your account name may also be called your user ID or your login or logon name. Your name must be unique among all the names assigned to your provider's users.

Your password, just like those associated with ATM cards, should not be a common word or something easily guessed. Stay away from names and birthdays, unless you mix them up. We've heard that the most commonly used password in the world is "Sue." For best results, include both numbers and letters so that a bad guy using a dictionary won't find your password listed. You really don't want strangers using your account, and your password is your primary protection.

Please don't touch the crystal

After you begin exploring the Internet, you can find yourself in many far-off and not-so-far-off lands on many strange computers. Those computers have information that's available to every Sally and Sam, but usually these computers are also used for lots of other things. These other things are none of your business (nor ours, for that matter).

To protect information from the voyeurs, the ignorant, and the vile, an elaborate scheme of permissions is used. Permissions, also known as access control, determine who can do what to what. Each data file or other resource on computers on the Net has a set of permissions assigned that might say, for example, that anyone can look at the file but only the file's owner can change it. Or, for more private data, it might say that no one except the file's owner can even look at it. When you're wandering around the Net, you may find resources whose names you can see but that you can't actually look at; that just means that the permissions don't let you look inside them.

Many of the computers you travel to on the Net are UNIX systems. For more information about UNIX permissions and the commands that display and change them, see our book *UNIX For Dummies,* 2nd Edition (IDG Books Worldwide, 1995).

If you have information on a networked system, you probably want to protect it in the same way. Although you can screen out ordinary users, remember that system administrators and sometimes clever intruders can override permissions. If you have something of an extremely personal nature that you feel compelled to leave on the Net, it's worth learning how to encrypt it so that no one can decode it without the encryption key you used. Learn all about privacy and encryption from one of our all-time favorite books, *Internet Secrets* (IDG Books Worldwide, 1995.)

How to Get Off

After you've gotten yourself on the Internet, you're inevitably placed in the position of having to get off. There are more and less graceful ways of getting off (and, depending on how far you've gone, potentially layers of systems to exit from).

If you use a modem to dial in, you can always hang up the phone from your terminal program. A cleaner, more polite way to leave, however, means saying good-bye to everyone you've said hello to. The problem is that not all computers say good-bye in the same language. The following list shows some commonly used exit sequences:

- ✔ Type **exit**
- ✔ Press Ctrl-D (popular on always excessively terse UNIX systems)
- ✔ Type **logout**
- ✔ Type **bye**

If none of these works, try typing **help** to see whether the system has any clues for you. If you can't get help, use your terminal program to hang up the phone and don't feel guilty about it.

If you use the telnet command, which lets you log in to other computers on the Internet, you may have signed on to other systems in addition to the one you originally dialed in to. UNIX telnet programs recognize the escape sequence Ctrl-] (press the Ctrl key and then the right square bracket key while keeping the Ctrl key pressed). Remember that you have to exit from all the systems you have signed on to. You aren't really out until you've exited from your account on your own Internet service provider. You may at that point begin to see random characters generated across your screen while your modem listens to an empty line. Or, more likely, the modem will hang up by itself with a satisfying click. Whew!

Some Other Ways to Connect to the Net

Before we leave the topic of connecting to the Net, let's take a last look at some other, less well-known, ways to hook up.

B-b-b-bulletin boards. . . .

Electronic bulletin-board systems, abbreviated BBS, or BBSs for plural, provide on-line services generally on a smaller scale and often with a particular focus. We say "generally" because Usenet, a bulletin board that's part of the Internet's offerings, could in no manner be considered small or of limited focus. (Chapter 9 tells you all about Usenet.) Anyway, bulletin-board systems are often local, often very cheap, and sometimes even free to the caller. They might provide e-mail, chatting (on-line conversations with other users), forums about special interests, games, ads, and lots, lots more. We've found bulletin-board users to be very friendly and welcoming to newcomers. The downside is that, because they may not have much funding, they can be flaky at times and you don't have much recourse in tracking down problems.

Local bulletin boards offer people a new way to meet. After you've established a pal on the board, you don't have to leave him there. Many bulletin-board regulars find fun and interesting things to do together that have nothing to do with computers.

Mail call

Several commercial systems are available that do just electronic mail, including AT&T Easylink Mail, SprintMail, and MCI Mail. There's a mystical connection between long-distance telephony and e-mail, apparently. MCI started MCI Mail itself, but the other two inherited their mail systems when they bought other computer networking businesses. They're all low-profile, but they're quite large — Easylink is reputedly bigger than America Online.

 MCI Mail is unique in that it provides 800 access all over the U.S. with no hourly on-line charges. If you live in an area in which no other providers are a local call away or if you travel frequently, MCI Mail's toll-free access makes it quite attractive. They're also unusual in that you pay only an annual fee and a per-message charge for outgoing mail. Incoming mail is free. It's just e-mail — none of the Internet's other services — but it's much better than nothing.

Wireless

Cabling is often a problem for mobile computing. People who carry their laptops with them want to connect from wherever they are, and it's not always easy to dial in. Progress is being made toward wireless Internet connection; it's already available from some providers.

WinSock? Like at an airport?

No, WinSock is short for *Win*dows *Sock*ets. It's like this: Back in the dark ages of PC networking, five years ago, several different software vendors wrote PC Internet packages. In each case, the vendor documented the functions that its package provided so that other people could write Internet applications of their own that worked with the vendor's package.

Unfortunately, each vendor's functions were slightly different in the details, even though functionally they all did the same things, so that applications which worked with one didn't work with another. Some vendors boasted that they had compatibility libraries for four or five other vendors so that programs which expect to use the other vendors' libraries will work. (It's similar to the situation with electrical appliances in Europe: All the power is the same, but all the plugs are different. If you bring an English sewing machine to France, for example, you can't use it unless you can find an adapter plug.)

In 1991, all the network vendors were gearing up to produce Windows Internet packages. One day a bunch of them got together at a trade show and thrashed out a common, standard set of functions for Windows Internet applications. Every Internet software vendor, even Microsoft, quickly agreed to support this so-called Windows Sockets standard, or WinSock. (It's called Sockets because its design is based on a UNIX package by that name with which all the vendors were familiar.)

In practice, therefore, any Windows Internet application you find that uses WinSock (whether it's commercial, shareware, or free) should work with any Windows Internet package. In the annals of software development, this degree of compatibility is virtually unprecedented, so let's hope that it's a harbinger of things to come.

Some phone numbers

Here are the voice phone numbers for some of the national providers we've listed in this chapter. Chapter 20 has a much larger list of regional and local Internet providers.

America Online	(800) 827-6364
Ardis	(800) 494-1728
CompuServe	(800) 380-9535
Delphi Internet	(800) 544-4005
IBM Internet	(800) 888-4103
MCI Mail	(800) 444-6245
Microsoft Network	(800) 386-5550
Netcom	(800) 501-8649
Prodigy	(800) 776-3449
Skytel	(800) 395-5840

Fire at the wall

Lots of PCs in big companies are loaded up with Internet software and have network connections with a hookup to the Internet, so if you're so blessed, you can run programs on your computer and hook right up to the Net. Right? Not quite.

If you're in a large organization that has (not altogether unreasonable) concerns about confidential company secrets leaking out by way of the Internet, a *firewall* system placed between the company network and the outside world may limit outside access to the internal network.

The firewall is connected to both the internal network and the Internet, so any traffic between the two has to go through the firewall. Special programming on the firewall limits which kind of connections can be made between the inside and outside and who can make them.

In practice, you can use any Internet service that is available within the company, but for outside services you're limited by what can pass through the firewall system. Most of the standard outside services — such as logging in to remote computers, copying files from one computer to another, and electronic mail — should be available, although the procedures may be somewhat more complicated than what's described in this book, involving something called a *proxy server*.

Often, you have to log in to the firewall system first and from there get to the outside. It's usually impossible for anyone outside the company to get access to systems or services on the inside network (that's what the firewall is for). Except for the most paranoid of organizations, electronic mail flows unimpeded in both directions.

Keep in mind that you probably have to get authorization to use the firewall system before you can use *any* outside service other than mail.

Chapter 3
The Net, Your Kids, and You

Stop Making Sense

We're all trying to make sense of the Internet and what it means for us and our families. Nobody has the ultimate answer, but we can talk about some of the major issues being raised, the benefits we see, and the potential problems. The Net has dramatic implications in the education, entertainment, and socialization of our children. The more we know and are actively involved, the better choices we can make.

What's in it for us?

We're just beginning to discover the myriad ways in which the Internet can be exciting in the context of our families' lives. Here are some of the ways in which we think that the Internet enhances our lives:

- ✔ It provides us with personal contact with new people and cultures.
- ✔ It helps us develop and improve our reading, writing, research, and language skills.
- ✔ It provides support for families with special needs.
- ✔ It is an exciting new outlet for artistic expression.

Not everything new is wonderful, and not everything wonderful is new. In talking about children, we need to make distinctions: Are these preschoolers or college kids? What makes sense for one group in this case usually doesn't map to another, so let's consider how the Internet works for different age groups.

The Internet for young children

We have to say up front that we are strong advocates of allowing children to be children, and we believe that children are better teachers than computers are. Neither John nor Carol owns a television set, and none of our kids watch TV. Now that you know our predisposition, maybe you can guess what we're going to say next: We are not in favor of sticking a young child in front of a screen. How young is young? We feel that younger than age 7 is young. Many educators feel that unstructured computer time under age 11 is inappropriate. We recommend that children get as much human attention as possible and believe that computers make lousy babysitters. At that age, children benefit more from playing with trees, balls, clay, crayons, paint, mud, monkey bars, bicycles, and other kids.

Frankly, even if you do want to let your small kids use the Internet, there's not much out there for the prereading set anyway.

The Internet for K–12

K–12 is the label that's given to all the education that happens in the United States between preschool (nursery school or day care) and college. It's a broad category. We use it here because many mailing lists and newsgroups use the K–12 designation and it seems to be common ground for many people. We think that Internet access is more appropriate for somewhat older children (fourth or fifth grade and older), but your mileage may vary.

The Internet is an incredible way to expand the walls of a school. The Net can connect you to other schools and to libraries, research, museums, and other people. You can visit the Louvre and the Sistine Chapel; practice your French or Spanish or Portuguese or Russian or Japanese; and hear new music and make new friends.

School projects such as the Global Schoolhouse connect kids around the world by working collaboratively on all kinds of projects. You can send an e-mail message to the Global Schoolhouse at andresyv@cerf.net or check out the foundation's Web site at http://gsn.org. (We explain these funny-looking locations in Chapter 4, so you can come back here later and follow up on them.) You can subscribe to a mailing list (Chapter 8 has all the details) by sending to lists@gsn.org an e-mail message that contains in the body of the text this single line:

```
subscribe global-watch Your Real Name
```

College and the Net

The Internet has had a home in universities for a long time, but what's happening with the World Wide Web is new for everyone. Much of the inspiration and perspiration of the volunteers who are making information available to everyone is coming from universities, both students and faculty, who see the incredible potential for learning.

Many campuses provide free access to the Internet for their students and staff. Campuses that allow you to register early sometimes give you that access when you register, even months in advance. If you're going to go anyway, you can get a jump on your Internet education before you even get to campus.

The Internet (more specifically, e-mail) is rapidly becoming a popular way for parents and college kids to stay in touch. It's much cheaper than phoning home and easier than coordinating schedules. Forwarding mail to other family members allows for broader communication. We noticed one more surprising benefit: In our experience, families tend to fight less when they're communicating by e-mail. Somehow, when folks have time to think about what they're going to say before they say it, it comes out better.

Checking out colleges on the Net

Most colleges and universities have or are rapidly creating sites on the Web. For starters, check out this location:

```
http://www.mit.edu:8001/people/
    cdemello/univ.html
```

This site links to more than 600 university sites around the world. If you don't know what we mean by "checking out a site on the Web," don't panic: We tell you all about it in Chapter 4. We just want you to know about some of the stuff that's out there.

After you're a little more adept at using the Net, you can research classes and professors to get a better idea of what appeals to you.

Finding a job by using the Net

Not just for students, the Net is an incredible tool for finding a job. It's especially good for students because it provides a powerful, economical way to conduct a real job *search*. You can publish your résumé on-line for prospective employers. You can check out the Monsterboard, an amazing compilation of job-related information that enables you to search by discipline (the area of study — all searches need the other kind) or geography or a host of other criteria. You can find the Monsterboard at `http://www.monster.com/`. And you can research companies to find ones you might like to work for. John got his second job (not the one right out of school — the one after that) and his first book contract through contacts he made on Usenet, which we discuss in Chapter 9.

When the Net *is* college

It's no exaggeration to say that many people are learning more on the Net than they ever did in school. There are many factors to consider, but the Net requires motivation, and motivated learning is much more fun. The Net provides equal opportunity beyond the imagination of those locked in physical settings. The Net is open to everyone of any color, height, belief, and description. People previously locked out of educational opportunities by physical handicap, economic need, or geography find the Net an empowering, life-altering experience.

Beyond the informal education that's already available, organizations are actively working to establish formal on-line colleges. Virtual Online University (VOU) just completed its first full semester. It's not yet accredited, but all colleges and universities begin that way. For more information, you can send an e-mail message to `billp@showme.missouri.edu`.

Of Paramount Concern

Perhaps highest on the list of parents' concerns about Internet access for children is the question of access to inappropriate material. We say "perhaps" the highest for two reasons:

- ✔ Parents who have taken the time to learn about access issues understand that the threat is not so great as some would have us believe and that, with reasonable attention, this concern can become a nonissue.

- ✔ Parents who have thought about the issues on a larger scale are more concerned that reactionary sentiment and hyperbole pose a real threat to our freedom of expression and that, ultimately, it is a much greater danger to our children.

But *Time* magazine said. . . .

If you're part of mainstream America, you probably saw or heard about, in the summer of 1995, *Time* magazine's sensationalist "Cyberporn" cover story. You might not have seen its retraction in tiny print, however.

If you missed the details, here's the gist of it: A Carnegie-Mellon student-turned-entrepreneur took a look at on-line pornography. He wrote a lurid book about marketing pornography and sold software to dial-up computer bulletion-board systems to help them with their pornographic needs. He then "gathered data" about the widespread proliferation of pornography on these bulletin boards but, for some reason, made the completely unsupportable leap to claim that what's available on the Internet is the same as what's on local, membership-only, pay-to-use bulletin boards.

It was as though he claimed that because glossy magazines found in certain kinds of stores are full of naughty pictures, *Reader's Digest* (which is also a magazine, after all) is full of naughty pictures. Although the student's report had not been reviewed by anyone familiar with the area of study (a standard prerequisite for all academic publications), the *Georgetown Law Review* decided to publish it, and *Time* picked it up as a "scoop."

The real problem is the gross misrepresentation of facts. The Internet is not replete with pornography. Pornography is not easily available to children on the Net. (It's in certain easily identifiable areas, and to get access to most of it, you have to sign up and pay with a credit card.) With guidance, parents can go a long way toward ensuring healthy, constructive Internet experiences for their children.

Some laws that have been proposed would outlaw "indecent" content on the Net, but they miss the point (not to mention that they're probably unconstitutional). The focus should be on how this manipulation of fraudulent data is being used to push for regulation and censorship of a raw communications medium. Ask yourself who stands to gain the most by controlling the content of the Internet. Ask yourself whether you believe that someone has the right to read your personal mail or listen to your personal phone calls. If you think that your privacy is something to be cherished, you'll understand that the answers to protecting our children lie not in having Big Brother regulate the content of the Internet but rather in designing ways to guide our children's access and choices.

Many people are working hard to solve these problems, and most believe that we're well on our way to providing Internet access with parental guidelines. We talk about some of the forms this guidance can take and trust that you'll find a solution that works for your family.

Whew! We'll get down off our soapbox now!

Parental guidance required

Parents, educators, and free-speech advocates alike agree that there is no substitute for parental guidance when it comes to the subject of Internet access. Just as we as parents want our children to read good books and see quality films, we also want them to find the *good* stuff on the Net. If you take the time to learn with your children, you have the opportunity to share the experience and to impart critical values and a sense of discrimination that your children need in all areas of their lives.

Remember that the good stuff on the Net far outweighs the bad. Sexually explicit material does exist, but it's a minuscule percentage of all that's out there (it represents a much smaller percentage of what's on the Net than the material you find in an average bookstore), and *it's not easily available.* You have to work to get at it, and, more and more frequently, you have to *pay* to get to most of it.

Today, software aids are being developed almost daily to help parents and educators tap the invaluable resources of the Net without opening Pandora's box. Remember that every child is different and that what may be appropriate for your children may not be appropriate for someone else's. You have to find what's right for you.

Rating the ratings

Several schemes have been proposed that involve the rating of Internet content. But who will rate the material, and whose ratings can you trust? Is the author of a Web page or other on-line material the right person to assign the ratings? Probably not. Internet software designers are adding provisions for third-party ratings so that, if you want, you can select or exclude material by the ratings, although the guidelines the raters use may not be the ones you would choose.

Other software under development will let parents limit access by their own criteria. A parent who feels strongly about warthogs and asparagus, for example, could block all material about those subjects. Or, more realistically, they could block heavy fictionalized violence and still permit access to medical information about sexually transmitted diseases.

Consumer's choice

Because parents are paying for on-line services, services that want to remain competitive are vying for parental dollars by providing features to help families control Internet access:

- ✔ **America Online:** Enables you to block access to chat rooms that may not be appropriate for children and to restrict access to discussion groups and newsgroups based on keywords you choose. Parental blocking is available at no extra cost.

- ✔ **CompuServe:** Has announced plans for providing "child-safe" on-line services to begin in early 1996. Check with CompuServe to see whether those services are available.

- ✔ **Prodigy:** Restricts everyone from posting material inappropriate for children in public forums or chat rooms. It restricts access to the Internet by requiring parental consent in the form of the parent's credit card. Prodigy logs which sites children visit and provides the report to the parent.

- ✔ **Microsoft Network:** Provides minimal blocking. If you attempt to download from the Net any material classified for people 18 years or older, you are asked to fill in a form and return it before you can download the material.

Software sentries

More and more products are appearing on the market to help parents restrict access or monitor usage by some sort of activity report. If you choose to use one of these systems, remember that they are not a substitute for your direct involvement with your child's Internet experience; they all filter based on keywords and fixed lists of systems that are believed (by the programs' authors) to have objectionable material. Here are a few of these programs we're aware of.

Cybersitter, a Windows-based Internet filtering program, blocks WWW sites and newsgroups and filters e-mail. Cybersitter also generates a report of site visits:

> Solid Oak Software, Inc.
> P.O. Box 6826
> Santa Barbara, CA 93160
> (800) 388-2761
> **E-mail:** info@solidoak.com
> **URL:** http://www.solidoak.com

Net Nanny is a PC-based product that monitors all PC activity, both on-line and off the Net in real-time. The parent- (or employer- or teacher-) defined dictionary enables you to determine what's not appropriate in your home. Net Nanny creates a log of children's activities:

> Trove Investment Corporation
> 525 Seymour St., Main Floor
> Vancouver, B.C., Canada, V6B 3H7
> **E-mail:** netnanny@netnanny.com
> **URL:** http://giant.mindlink.net/netnanny/

SurfWatch, available for both the PC and the Macintosh, screens for newsgroups likely to contain sexually explicit material and keeps a computer from accessing specified WWW, FTP, Gopher, and chat sites:

SurfWatch Software
105 Fremont Avenue, Suite F
Los Altos, CA 94022
(415) 948-9500
E-mail: press@surfwatch.com

Help for Parents of Kids with Problems

One of the most profound and heartening human experiences available on the Net has to do with the help that total strangers freely offer one another. The incredible bonds that form from people sharing their experiences, struggles, strengths, and hopes redefine what it means to reach out and touch someone. We encourage everyone who has a concern to look for people who share that concern. Our experience of participating in mailing lists and newsgroups related to our own problems compels us to enthusiastically encourage you to check things out on-line. You can do so with complete anonymity. You can watch and learn for a long time, or you can jump into the fray and ask for help.

We caution you that everyone who gives advice is not a medical expert. You have to involve your own practitioners in your process. Many people have found enormous help, however, from people who have gone down similar paths before them. For many of us, it has made all the difference in the world.

We list in this chapter a few of the available on-line mailing lists and discussion groups. There's almost certainly a mailing list or group specific to your needs regardless of whether we list it here, and new groups are added every day. If you're using a commercial provider such as America Online, Prodigy, MSN, or CompuServe, your provider has special forums that may interest you as well.

Later in this book (in Chapters 8 and 9), we describe how to use e-mail mailing lists and Usenet newsgroups. If you find something of interest in the rest of this chapter, you'll have a reason to learn how to do it.

Notice that some lists are *talk* lists, which feature free-flow discussion; some lists have very focused discussions, and some lists are almost purely academic. It's not always obvious from the name. If it looks interesting, subscribe and see what sort of discussion is going on there. It's easy enough to unsubscribe if you don't like it. Table 3-1 lists some interesting lists on the Net.

Table 3-1   Self-Help Mailing Lists on the Internet

Resource Name	Description	To Contact
add-parents	Support and information for parents of children with attention deficit or hyperactivity disorder	Send e-mail to `add-parents-request@mv.mv.com`
our-kids	Support for parents and others regarding the care, diagnosis, and therapy for young children with developmental delays	Send the e-mail message *subscribe our-kids* to `majordomo@t bag.osc.edu`
behavior	Support for behavioral and emotional disorders in children	Send the message *subscribe behavior* to `listserv@astuvm. inre.asu.edu`
deafkids	Support for deaf children	Send the message *subscribe deafkids* to `listserv@sjuvm. stjohns.edu`
cshcn-l	Support for children with special health-care needs	Send the message *subscribe cshcn-l* to `listserv@nervm. nerdc.ufl.edu`
dadvocat	Support for dads of children with disabilities	Send the message *subscribe dadvocat* to `listserv@ukcc. uky.edu`
ddline	Children's disability list	Send the message *subscribe ddline* to `listserv@uicvm. uic.edu`
ds-c-imp	Overview of childhood-impairment issues	Send the message *subscribe ds-c-imp* to `listserv@list. nih.gov`
ds-c-sb1	Support for people with spina bifida	Send the message *subscribe ds-c-sb1* to `listserv@list. nih.gov`
ds-c-00	Discussion of major childhood-measures issues	Send the message *subscribe ds-c-00* to `listserv@list. nih.gov`

The Internet in Schools

Schools are actively debating Internet access for their students. Teachers and parents go round and round, and ignorance seems to prevail. Find out as much as you can and get involved. The more you know, the more you can advocate for appropriate access.

A wonderful book called *The Internet for Teachers,* by Bard Williams (published by IDG Books Worldwide, 1995) can help you understand all that can be gained from the Internet and can arm you with the information you'll need to face hordes of cynics, including school administrators, teachers, and other parents. The book focuses on the Net from an educator's perspective, including why the Net is important, how to use it, and where to find education-specific resources. Although it's aimed at teachers, it's a great find for parents.

Contractually speaking

Many kids are smart. Smart kids can find ways around rules, and smart kids can find ways around software systems designed to "protect" kids. Many institutions rely successfully on students' signed contracts that explicitly detail what is appropriate and what is inappropriate system use. Students who violate one of these contracts lose their Internet or computer privileges.

We believe that this approach is a good one. In our experience, kids are quicker and more highly motivated and have more time to spend breaking in to and out of systems than most adults we know, and this method encourages them to do something more productive than electronic lock-picking.

Industrial-strength cyberprotection

It's not just schools that are trying to restrict access to the Internet. Some corporations, fearful of their employees wasting time on personal interests, are turning to software products that limit users to what the employer deems appropriate. Our personal experience is that the most highly creative and productive environments were the least restrictive ones, but you'll have to verify that for yourself.

WebTrack, an institutional software product, logs Internet access and denies access to certain categories of sites (it's available free of charge to K–12 schools):

Webster Networks Strategies
1100 5th Avenue South, Suite 308
Naples, FL 33940
(800) WNS-0066 or (813) 261-5503
E-mail: info@webster.com
URL: http://www.webster.com/

Mailing Lists for Parents and Kids

Chapter 8 tells you how to subscribe to mailing lists. In the remainder of this chapter, we provide just the list name and its description. Many more are available where these come from, so if none of them strikes your fancy, don't despair.

kidmedia

This mailing list is a professional-level discussion group for people interested in children's media (television, radio, print, and data). To subscribe, send mail to `kidmedia-request@airwaves.chi.il.us` for individual articles or to `kidmedia-d-request@airwaves.chi.il.us` for daily digests. On the subject line, enter **SUBSCRIBE**, **UNSUBSCRIBE,** or **HELP** (to receive the charter and info file).

kidsphere

The `kidsphere` list was established in 1989 to stimulate the development of an international computer network for use by children and their teachers. Send subscription requests to `kidsphere-request@vms.cis.pitt.edu.`

kids

On this list, children post messages to other children. Send subscription requests to `kids-request@vms.cis.pitt.edu.`

dinosaur

For subscription requests to this low-volume list about dinosaurs, send a message to `listproc@lepomis.psych.upenn.edu` in the following format:

```
SUBSCRIBE DINOSAUR <yourname>
```

pen-pals

This list provides a forum in which children correspond electronically with each other. The list is not moderated, but it is monitored for content. Send subscription requests to `pen-pals-request@mainstream.com.`

y-rights

This group, open to everyone, discusses the rights of kids and teens. Send an e-mail message to LISTSERV@SJUVM.BITNET. In the text of the message, include one of these lines:

- ✔ **To subscribe to the list:** SUB Y-RIGHTS *firstname lastname* (substitute your own first and last name)
- ✔ **To receive the daily digest of the list:** SET Y-RIGHTS DIGEST *firstname lastname*
- ✔ **To receive the list of previous discussions:** GET Y-RIGHTS FILELIST *firstname lastname*

Kid cafés

Kid cafés are mailing lists that exist for kids ages 10 to 15 to have conversations with other kids — kids in general and kids in specific. Kids can find "keypals" with similar interests and exchange messages with them.

Several different kid cafés are available, depending on whether a child is joining as an individual or as part of a school class. The cafés in the following list are all LISTSERV lists managed at LISTSERV@VM1.NODAK.EDU (see Chapter 8 for details about how to subscribe):

KIDCAFE-INDIVIDUAL   Individual participants looking for keypals

KIDCAFE-SCHOOL   Classroom groups looking for keypals

KIDCAFE-TOPICS   Open discussion of any appropriate topic

KIDCAFE-QUERY   Questions asked of other kid café participants

Another mailing list

Table 3-2 shows you some other kid-oriented lists you and your family might enjoy.

Table 3-2	**Mailing Lists for and about Kids**	
Resource Name	*Description*	*To Contact*
kidlit-l	A list about children's and youth literature	Send the message *subscribe kidlit-l* to `listserv@bingvmb. cc.binghamton.edu`
kids-act	"What can I do now?"	Send the message *subscribe kids-act* to `listserv@vm1. nodak.edu`
kidzmail	Kids exploring issues and interests electronically	Send the message *subscribe kidzmail* to `listserv@asuvm. inre.asu.edu`
childlit	Children's literature: criticism and theory	Send the message *subscribe childlit* to `listserv@rutvm1. rutgers.edu`
childri-l	Discussion of U.N. convention on the rights of children	Send the message *subscribe childri-l* to `listserv@nic. surfnet.nl`
ecenet-l	Early-childhood education and young children (0–8 years old)	Send the message *subscribe ecenet-l* to `listserv@vmd. cso.uiuc.edu`
eceol-l	Early-childhood education	Send the message *subscribe eceol-l* to `listserv@maine. maine.edu`
father-l	Importance of fathers in children's lives	Send the message *subscribe father-l* to `listserv@vm1. spcs.umn.edu`

Newsgroups for Parents and Kids

Usenet newsgroups provide a way for Internet users around the world to hold conversations, and it's a great way for kids to converse too. Usenet also has a number of newsgroups for parents and teachers. We describe how to read newsgroups in Chapter 9. Table 3-3 shows some newsgroups that might be of interest to you and your family.

Table 3-3	Usenet Newsgroups for and about Kids
Newsgroup	*Topic*
misc.kids	Children and their behavior and activities
misc.kids.computer	The use of computers by children
misc.kids.health	Children's health
misc.kids.pregnancy	The first nine months
misc.kids.vacation	The joys and perils of kids on vacation
rec.games.chess	Chess and computer chess
rec.games.corewar	The Core War computer challenge
rec.games.design	Game-design and related issues
rec.roller-coaster	Roller coasters and other amusement park rides
rec.railroad	For fans of real trains
rec.scouting	Youth scouting organizations worldwide
soc.college	College, college activities, and campus life
alt.parents-teens	Parent-teenager relationships

Some Internet providers make available an entire set of K–12 groups, intended for teachers and schoolchildren in elementary and high schools. The first part of the names of these newsgroups is k12.

Web Sites for Kids

OK, we admit it: Web sites can be the coolest thing since sliced bread. Here are some sites from around the world especially for kids. To get to these sites, you have to know how to use a browser, such as Netscape, Mosaic, or Lynx (we tell you how in Chapter 4).

A word of warning: When you're looking for fun, we tend to think that color and graphics make all the difference. If you spend a great deal of time on the Web, you probably won't be satisfied for long with a text-only interface: To get the best from the Web, you need a color monitor and a SLIP/PPP connection. If those items aren't available to you, by all means check stuff out anyway, but you might have more fun in the text-based world of mailing lists and newsgroups, where content is more important than form.

Kids' Space

A site for children to enhance basic computer skills through their real participation and use of the Internet:

http://plaza.interport.net/kids_space/

KidPub WWW Publishing

A Web page full of stories written by and for kids. Get your story published here. Become (slightly) famous!

http://www.en-garde.com/kidpub/

The Canadian Kid's page

The page about and for kids in Canada and their parents:

http://www.onramp.ca/~lowens/107kids.htm

The UK Children's page

Emma (7) and Alice (9) Bowen and their parents invite you to this page, full of their stories, poems, pictures, and sounds and lots of links to other pages on both sides of the Atlantic:

http://www.comlab.ox.ac.uk/oucl/users/jonathan.bowen/
children.html

The Italy Children's page

A page for children in Padua, Italy (in English):

http://www.pd.astro.it/forms/dearlife.shtml

The East Palo Alto, Plugged In group

Plugged In is a nonprofit group that tries to bring the high-tech resources of the Silicon Valley to the children in and around the city of East Palo Alto, an impoverished corner of Silicon Valley. This page both describes Plugged In and showcases some of the kids' projects.

http://www.pluggedin.org/

Premiers pas sur Internet

A kids' page in France, in French, for French-speaking kids everywhere:

http://www.cnam.fr/momes/

The Wangaratta Primary School page

The home page for a primary school northeast of Melbourne, Australia. The school has been there since 1851, but the Web page dates only from July 1995. Find out what a kookaburra sounds like. (It's not much to look at, but its cry is totally radical.)

http://www.ozemail.com.au/~ctech/wps.htm

The KidsWeb from the GATE students

Teachers and kids in a Gifted And Talented Education program in Virginia:

http://wwwp.exis.net/~gatelab/kidspage.htm

Part II
Using Your Internet Account

The 5th Wave   By Rich Tennant

In this part . . .

Rumors, gossip, bad jokes, artistic pictures — the Internet has it all. In this section, we look at one of the oldest Net services, e-mail, and one of the newest, the World Wide Web. They're the two most important and most useful parts of the Net, and here's where you get going on them quickly.

Chapter 4

Netscape, Mosaic, and the Wild, Wonderful, Wacky World Wide Web

Doubtless you've heard a great deal about Netscape, the "killer application" for the Internet. Well, here it is. We begin by briefly enumerating the Netscape features that have rocketed it to the top of the Internet hit parade:

- ✔ It combines text, pictures, graphics, sounds, and animations in lots of attractive ways.

- ✔ It runs reasonably well even on inexpensive dial-up connections.

- ✔ The latest version (2.0) handles many new Internet services in addition to the Web.

- ✔ It has an extremely cool, shooting-comets animated icon (a major improvement over a heavy-breathing letter *N* in early versions).

- ✔ Its authors give it away for free.

We'll refrain from suggesting which of those important features is the *most* important.

You can use Netscape only if you have a SLIP/PPP Net connection. Fortunately, many other programs do roughly the same thing as Netscape, including one called Lynx, which works just fine over a text-only, dial-up connection. We'll come back to Lynx at the end of this chapter.

Hyper-what?

Netscape is a *World Wide Web browser.* The World Wide Web (WWW, W3, or, from now on, the Web) is a bunch of "pages" of information. Each page can be a combination of text, pictures, and other stuff. (We're vague about the other stuff because they're adding new kinds of other stuff every day.) What makes Web pages interesting is that they contain *hyperlinks,* usually just called *links* because the Net already has plenty of hype. Each link refers to another Web page, and when you click on a link, your browser fetches the page the link connects to. That page will have more links that take you to yet other places. This system of interlinked documents is known as *hypertext.*

Hypertext is the buzzword that makes the Web go. It's one of those simple ideas that turns out to have a much bigger effect than you would think.

What's the Big Deal?

If you've ever done research in an area you know little about, you found yourself in a library, staring at the card catalog. You begin with one bit of information, such as a subject or a name. You look up one subject and begin reading the cards. All kinds of new ideas flash into your mind about ways you can continue your search with other subjects or other names. Even if you write down all the ideas, you inevitably have to pick one of them to follow and then leave your current drawer and find the next. Then you begin again, and again your search may send you in an entirely different direction.

As you follow more and more leads, you may have to back up, look at choices you made earlier, and see what trying a different tack would bring. If you take careful notes, this process may be relatively easy, but chances are that you have to retrace many of your steps.

Hypertext organizes data to help this kind of information retrieval. It keeps one finger in one drawer and another finger in another drawer and so on to help you to go down one path and then go back to try a different one. Hypertext can have a hundred or more fingers in drawers all over the *planet.* (You might think of it as an extremely large but friendly alien centipede made of information.)

In traditional libraries (both the kinds with books and the kinds in computers), information is organized in a relatively arbitrary hierarchy, in the order in which it's found or in alphabetical order. These orders reflect nothing about the relationships among different pieces of information. In the world of hypertext, information is organized in relationship to other information. In fact, the relationships between different pieces of information are often much more valuable than the pieces themselves.

Hypertext also allows the same set of information to be arranged in multiple ways at the same time. In a conventional library, a book can be on only one shelf at a time; a book about mental health, for example, is shelved under medicine or psychology, but it can't be in both places at one time. Hypertext is not so limited, and it's no problem to have links from both medical topics and psychological topics to the same document.

Suppose that you are interested in what influenced a particular historical person. You can begin by looking at the basic biographical information: where and when she was born, the names of her parents, her religion, and other basic stuff like that. Then you can expand on each fact by learning what else was happening at that time in her part of the world, what was happening in other parts of the world, and what influence her religion may have had on her. You draw a picture by pulling together all these aspects and understanding their connections — a picture that's hard to draw from just lists of names and dates.

A hypertext system creates the connections between pieces of information that enable you to find related information easily. As you draw the connections between the pieces of information, you can begin to envision the web created by the links between the pieces. What's so remarkable about the Web is that it connects pieces of information from all around the world, on different machines, in different databases, all pretty much seamlessly (a feat you'd be hard-pressed to match with a card catalog).

Browsing Away

Writing Web browsers is fun for programmers, so there are quite a few different browsing programs available. We discuss two of the most popular: Netscape, which is what everyone who has something better than a plain text dial-up connection uses, and Lynx, for the dial-up crowd.

If you have another window-oriented browser, such as any of the many versions of Mosaic, nearly everything we say about Netscape also applies. (It's no coincidence because Netscape was written by many of the same people who originally wrote Mosaic.) Internet Explorer, the Windows 95 Web browser from Microsoft, is also similar to Netscape, as are WebSurfer and the Web browsers built-in to America Online and Prodigy.

Hypertext: A reminiscence

John writes:

The term and concept of hypertext were invented around 1969 by Ted Nelson, a famous computer visionary who has been thinking about the relationship between computers and literature for at least 25 years now — starting back when most people would have considered it stupid to think that such a relationship could exist. Twenty years ago, he claimed that people would have computers in their pockets with leatherette cases and racing stripes. (I haven't seen any racing stripes yet, but otherwise he was dead on.)

Back in 1970, Ted told me that we all would have little computers with inexpensive screens on our desks with super whizzo graphical hypertext systems. "Naah," I said. "For hypertext, you'll want a mainframe with gobs of memory and a high-resolution screen." We were both right, of course, because what we have on our desks in the 1990s are little computers that are faster than 1970s mainframes and that have more memory and better screens.

Various hypertext projects have come and gone over the years, including one at Brown University (of which Ted was a part) and one at the Stanford Research Institute (which was arguably the most influential project in computing history because it invented screen windows and mice).

Ted's own hypertext system, Project Xanadu, has been in the works for about 15 years, under a variety of financing and management setups, but with many of the same people slogging along and making it work. The project addresses many issues that other systems don't. In particular, Ted figured out how to pay authors for their work in a hypertext system, even when one document has pieces linked from others and the ensuing document consists almost entirely of a compendium of pieces of other documents. For a decade, I've been hearing every year that Xanadu, and now a smaller Xanadu Light, which takes advantage of a great deal of existing software, will hit the streets the next year. This year I hope that they're right.

Margy adds:

Now that the World Wide Web has brought a limited version of hypertext to the masses, Ted is now hoping to build a Xanadu-like system on the Web. Stay tuned for developments!

Getting Netscape Installed

With luck, Netscape is already installed on your computer. Without luck, it isn't, but fortunately it's not difficult to install.

Even if you already have a copy of Netscape, new versions come out every couple of months, and it's worth knowing how to upgrade because now and then the new versions are better than the old ones. The steps are relatively simple:

1. **Get a copy of the Netscape installation package on your computer.**

2. **Unpack the installation package.**

3. **Install the software.**

Naturally, because computers are involved, each of these steps is a little more difficult than necessary.

Getting the package

Your provider may have given you a copy of Netscape on a disk. (This gift is of dubious legality, but many of them do so anyway.) If not, you can download it from the Net. Because Netscape is so popular, you can find it in several different places, many of which are listed in Table 4-1. These servers all provide the files via the FTP system, which means that you need an FTP program in order to retrieve the files. Chapter 10 discusses the details of FTP.

Table 4-1	Netscape Distribution Servers	
Host	*Directory*	*Where*
ftp.netscape.com	/netscape/	U.S.
ftp2.netscape.com	/netscape/	U.S.
ftp3.netscape.com	/netscape/	U.S.
ftp4.netscape.com	/netscape/	U.S.
ftp5.netscape.com	/netscape/	U.S.
ftp6.netscape.com	/netscape/	U.S.
ftp7.netscape.com	/netscape/	U.S.
ftp8.netscape.com	/netscape/	U.S.
ftp.cs.umn.edu	/packages/X11/contrib/netscape/	U.S.
server.berkeley.edu	/pub/netscape/	U.S.
ftp.pu-toyama.ac.jp	/pub/net/WWW/netscape	Japan
ftp.eos.hokudai.ac.jp	/pub/WWW/netscape	Japan
ftp.leo.chubu.ac.jp	/pub/WWW/netscape	Japan

Now that you've flipped through Chapter 10 and know how to use FTP, connect to the FTP server that's closest to you (at least in the same country you are). Change to the directory on the server where Netscape lives. You should see three subdirectories: windows, unix, and mac. Change to the appropriate subdirectory for your kind of computer and get the Netscape distribution file for your system. For Windows users, the distribution is a file with a name such as N16E200.EXE or N32E200.EXE. (The last half of the filename changes whenever they update Netscape). Get the N16 file if you're running Windows 3.1, or the N32 file if you're running Windows 95 or NT.

If you already have another browser, such as Mosaic, Websurfer, or an older version of Netscape, you can use your existing browser to get the new version of Netscape and avoid the need to fight with an FTP program. Tell your browser to go to the following address and then follow the instructions:

```
http://home.netscape.com/comprod/mirror/index.html
```

We're home — let's unpack and install

After you have the Netscape distribution file, you have to unpack it before you can install it (these instructions are for Windows):

1. **Create a directory called \NSINST.**

   This directory is just temporary for installing the program — it's not where Netscape will live. From the Windows File Manager, choose File➪Create Directory. From Windows 95, use My Computer or Explorer and choose File➪New.

2. **Put the Netscape distribution file in that directory.**

   The file's name begins with N16 or N32. Just drag it there in File Manager, My Computer, or Explorer.

3. **The distribution file contains a program — run it.**

   The program extracts a bunch of files from the distribution file. (It's called a *self-extracting archive* in the lingo.)

   There are a couple of ways to run the program, but the simplest is just to double-click the filename in File Manager, My Computer, or Explorer. You now have several dozen files in your \NSINST directory, including a file called SETUP.EXE.

4. **Run the setup program to install Netscape.**

   That's the SETUP.EXE file. Double-click its filename to run it. The setup program then installs Netscape for you. It asks a bunch of questions, but the default answers for all of them are OK. It installs Netscape in the \NETSCAPE directory, unless you tell it otherwise.

5. **Try out Netscape.**

   Click the attractive, new icon that Netscape installed. It shows you a bunch of legal boilerplate stuff describing the license conditions for Netscape. If you can stand the conditions (most people can), click to indicate your acceptance. Netscape then starts up.

6. **When you're happy with the installed Netscape, delete the \NSINST directory.**

   You don't need the installation files anymore, and they take up a great deal of disk space.

 If you're upgrading from an older version of Netscape to a newer one, you can install the new version and it replaces the old one. When the installation program asks whether to replace NETSCAPE.INI, say No to keep your existing Netscape settings.

If you have installed the excellent shareware WinZIP program, you can use it to automate the entire installation process. As soon as you've retrieved the N16 or N32 file, open it in WinZIP. (Even though it ends with .EXE, it's really a ZIP file.) Then click on Install. WinZIP creates a temporary directory, extracts the files, and runs Setup. Later, when you return to WinZIP, it gets rid of the junk. See Chapter 10 for more information about WinZIP.

Surf, Ho!

Whew! Now that you have Netscape installed, let's take it out for a spin. (Too darned many metaphors — are we driving or surfing here?)

The page that's displayed when you start Netscape depends on how it's set up; many providers arrange to have it display their home page.

At the top of the screen are a bunch of buttons and the Location line, which contains the *Uniform Resource Locator,* or *URL,* for the current page. URLs are an important part of Web lore because they're the secret codes that name all the pages in the Web. See the sidebar "Duke of URL," later in this chapter, for details.

Getting around

The primary skill you need (if we can describe something as basic as a single mouse-click as a skill) is to learn how to move from page to page on the Web.

It's easy: You just click any link that looks interesting. Underlined blue text and blue-bordered pictures are links. If you're not sure whether something is a link, click it anyway because, if it's not, it won't hurt anything. (Clicking outside a link selects the text you click on, as in every other Windows program.)

Backward, ho!

Web browsers remember the last few pages you visited, so if you click on a link and decide that you're not so crazy about the new page, you can easily go back to the preceding one. To go back, click on the Back button (its icon is an arrow pointing to the left) or press Alt-←.

All over the map

Some picture links are *image maps,* like the big picture in the middle of Figure 4-1. With a regular link it doesn't matter where you click, but in an image map it does. The image map here is typical and has a bunch of obvious places you click for various kinds of information. (All the 1990 census data except private individual info is on-line on the Net, by the way.) Some image maps are actual maps — for example, a map of the U.S. at the weather bureau that shows you the forecast at the place you click (look for it at the URL http://ww.nnic.noaa.gov/.)

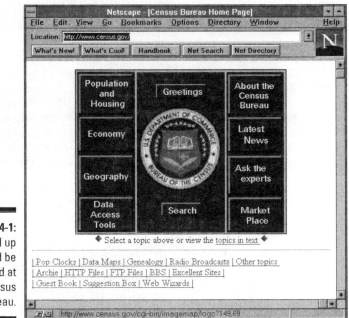

Figure 4-1:
Stand up and be counted at the Census Bureau.

As you move the mouse cursor around the Netscape page, whenever you're pointing at a link, the place you linked to appears in small type at the bottom of the screen. If the link is an image map, the link is followed by a question mark and two numbers that are the X and Y positions in the map where you are. The numbers don't matter to you (it's up to the Web server to make sense of them), but if you see a pair of numbers counting up and down when you move the mouse, you know that you're in an image map.

Going around

These days everyone and his dog has a home page. (See `http://users.aimnet.com/~carver/cindy.html` or `http://www.sdsmt.edu/other/dogs/groups/working/samoyed/pictures/joey.html`, for example.) Lots of times in a mail message, you get a URL (the name of a Web page; for details, see the sidebar "Duke of URL," later in this chapter).

Here's the official way to go to a page whose URL you have:

1. **Choose File▷Open Location (or press Ctrl+L).**

2. **Type the URL in the window that pops up.**

   The URL is something like `http://dummies.com/`.

3. **Press Enter.**

You can save a valuable keystroke (one keystroke may not seem like much, but after an entire day you might have saved as much as, oh, two dozen keystrokes — never mind) by clicking on the Location window at the top of the Netscape window. Type the URL directly in that window, and then press Enter.

Ninety-nine percent of URLs begin with `http://`, so Netscape lets you leave that part out. For example, you could have typed just `dummies.com` here. This featurette is Netscape-only — you have to type the whole thing for other browsers.

If you receive URLs in electronic mail, Usenet news, or anywhere else on your Windows PC, you can use the standard Windows cut-and-paste techniques and avoid retyping:

1. **Highlight the URL in whatever program is showing it.**

2. **Press Ctrl+C to copy it to the Windows Clipboard.**

3. **Click on the URL window in Netscape.**

4. **Press Ctrl+V to paste in the URL, and then press Enter.**

Duke of URL

Part of the plan of the World Wide Web is to link together all the information in the known universe, starting with all the stuff on the Internet and heading up from there. (This may be a slight exaggeration, but we don't think so.)

One of the keys to global domination is to give everything (at least everything that could be a Web resource) a name and, in particular, a consistent name so that no matter what kind of thing a hypertext link refers to, a Web browser can find it and know what to do with it.

Look at this typical URL:

`http://dummies.com/dummies.htm`

The first thing in a URL, the word before the colon, is the *scheme,* which describes the way a browser can get to the resource. Ten schemes are defined, but by far the most common is `http`, the HyperText Transfer Protocol that is the Web's native transfer technique. (Don't confuse `http`, which is the way pages are sent over the Net, with HTML, which is the way the pages are coded internally. We get to that in Chapter 5.)

The details of the rest of the URL depend on the scheme, but most schemes use a consistent syntax. Following the colon are two slashes (always forward slashes, never reverse slashes, not even on DOS machines) and the name of the host computer on which the resource lives; in this case, `dummies.com`. Then there's another slash and a *path,* which gives the name of the resource on that host (in this case, a file named `dummies.htm`).

Web URLs allow a few other optional parts. They can include a *port number,* which, roughly speaking, says which of several programs running on that host should handle the request. The port number goes after a colon after the host name, like this:

`http://dummies.com:80/dummies.htm`

The standard `http` port number is 80, so if that's the port you want (it usually is), you can leave it out. Finally, a Web URL can have a *search part* at the end, following a question mark, like this:

`http://dummies.com:80/`
`   dummies.htm?plugh`

Not all pages can have search parts, but for those that do, it tells the host, uh, what to search for. (You rarely type a search part yourself, but they're often constructed for you from fill-in fields in Web pages.)

Two other useful URL schemes are `mailto` and `file`. A `mailto` URL looks like this:

`mailto:ninternet@dummies.com`

That is, it's an e-mail address. When you choose a `mailto` URL in Netscape, it pops up a window in which you can enter an e-mail message to the address in the URL. It's most commonly used for sending comments to the owner of a page.

The `file` URL specifies a file on your computer. It looks like this:

`file:///C|/WWW/INDEX.HTM`

On a DOS computer, that means a Web page stored in the file C:\WWW\INDEX.HTM. The colon turns into a vertical bar (because colons in URLs mean something else), and the reverse slashes turn into forward slashes. File URLs are useful mostly for looking at GIF and JPG graphics files and for looking at a Web page you just wrote and stuck in a file on your disk.

There are a bunch of other URL types, but this is plenty for now.

Netscape's dirty little secret

One major thing keeps Netscape from being the perfect Internet program. It can be slow. Really, really slow. Readers of a certain age may remember an old Bob and Ray radio skit about the STOA. That's the Slow. . .Talkers. . .Of. . .America. The head of the S. . .T. . .O. . .A (played by Bob) put long. . .pauses. . .between. . .his. . .words, so long that you just wanted him to hurry up and finish his sentences. Netscape can feel like that.

There are two separate slowness problems. One is that fancy multimedia screens require a great deal of data, which means that they take a long time to transfer over any except the fastest networks. The other is that Netscape is, to use a technical computer term, kind of a pig. (It's not as piggish as some other Net browsers, but it's still pretty bad.) The standard rule of thumb says that you need a 486/33MHz computer with 8 megabytes of RAM to get reasonable performance, and we can report from experience that if you run Netscape on a computer of that size, it still spends an awful lot of time swapping pieces of itself back and forth from the disk. If you have a Pentium and 32 megabytes of RAM, it's fast.

You can do a few things to speed up Netscape, which we address in Chapter 5. (This is a ploy to keep you reading.)

Enough, already

Sooner or later even the most dedicated Web surfer has to stop to eat or attend to other bodily needs. You leave Netscape in the same way you leave any other Windows program: by choosing File⇨Exit or pressing Alt+F4. For some reason, after the Netscape window vanishes, Netscape does something else for 10 or 15 seconds before giving your computer back to you (a digital power trip, no doubt), so if your computer seems to hang after you tell Netscape to exit, wait a few seconds before you give up on it.

Hey, What about Us Shell Users?

Oh, whoops, right. For those of you still living a mouse-free existence, you can still do some serious Web surfing. Indeed, considering how slow it can be to load up all the pictures in Netscape, picture-free Lynx can be a welcome change.

Because Lynx is a text-only browser, there are some things it can't do. Within those limitations, though, it's a good program.

Life with Lynx

All UNIX shell providers should have Lynx available because it's free. To start it, you type **lynx** at the UNIX shell prompt. It starts up and displays a home page on the screen, as shown in Figure 4-2.

Because most text screens can't do underlining, the links are shown in reverse video. Bracketed text or the word [IMAGE] appears where a picture would be displayed. One link on the screen is *current* and is highlighted in a different color. (On our screen, it's yellow rather than white text, which doesn't show up on a black-and-white page. Use your imagination.) Lynx thoughtfully puts some help information on the bottom two lines, which makes it much easier to use.

Figure 4-2:
Lynx says
"Hi."

Wandering around

Nearly all Lynx commands are single keystrokes.

The up and down arrows move from link to link on the current page. If the page is more than one screenful, the page scrolls as necessary. To move to the next screen of the current page, press the spacebar or press + and – to move forward and backward a screen at a time.

You use the up and down arrows to move from link to link, even when the links are next to each other on a line. For example, you might have a few lines on the screen like this:

```
Famous philosophers:

[Moe] [Larry] [Curly] [Socrates]
```

If the highlight is on Larry, you press the cursor Up key to go to Moe and press the cursor Down key to go to Curly. The left and right arrows mean something else, which we address next.

After you have a link you like, press the right-arrow key or Enter to follow that link. After Lynx fetches the new page, you can press the arrow keys to move around the new page. Pressing the left-arrow key takes you back to the preceding page. You can press the left arrow several times to go back several pages.

There are a few things Lynx just can't do, most notably image maps. It tells you that there's an image, but because you can't see the image and you can't use a mouse, there's no way to click on it. Fortunately, any sensible Web page that has an image map offers some other way to get to the places the image map would otherwise take you. There's either a set of text links under the image or, in some cases, a link that says something like "Click here for a text-only version of this page." Lynx gives you a nice, clean, image-free page from which to work.

To go to a specific URL, press **g** for *go-to*, and then type the URL on the line that Lynx provides, followed by pressing Enter.

Leaving Lynx

When you're finished with Lynx, press **q** to exit. Lynx asks whether you're sure that you want to quit; press **y**.

Is that all there is?

Of course not. Lynx is bristling with features, just like any other modern computer program. Just about every possible keystroke means something to Lynx. We discuss a bunch of them in Chapter 5. But the arrow keys and g and q are all you really need in order to get going.

If All Else Fails. . . .

If you don't even have access to Lynx on your system, a few systems offer public access to it. If you have access to telnet, these systems let you Lynx around:

- ✔ `lynx.cc.ukans.edu` (Kansas, log in as *www*)
- ✔ `sunsite.unc.edu` (North Carolina, log in as *lynx*)

- gopher.msu.edu (Mississippi, log in as *web*)
- sailor.lib.md.us (Maryland, log in as *guest*)
- gopher.msu.edu (Michigan, log in as *web*)

They're not as good as running Lynx on your own provider's system (they're slower, and some options don't work), but they're better than nothing.

The 5th Wave   By Rich Tennant

"QUICK KIDS! YOUR MOTHER'S FLAMING SOMEONE ON THE INTERNET!"

Chapter 5
Stupid Netscape Tricks

. . . .

In This Chapter

▶ Making Netscape sing and dance

▶ Making Lynx hum and shuffle

▶ Making your own Web pages

▶ Beyond Netscape

. . . .

As Netscape has evolved from an unknown newcomer in the Web biz to the big gorilla on the block, it has gained a few new features. Lots and lots of features. Lots and lots and lots of features. Netscape 1.2 already had about as many features as any single human could comprehend, but just in case someone somewhere understood the whole thing, version 2.0 added another truckload of them, so now it's beyond anyone's comprehension.

In this chapter we look at some of the more useful and understandable of Netscape's many skills. Because Lynx can do many of the same things that Netscape can (less flashily, but quite effectively), we cover the Lynx equivalents too.

Speeding Up Netscape

The first order of business is to make Netscape a little faster. There are a handful of tricks you can use.

When Netscape starts up, by default it loads the large and attractive Netscape home page. After one or two times, beautiful though the home page is, you'll probably find that you can do without it. Choose Options⇨General and click the Appearance tab. Under Window Styles, you'll see Start With. Either choose Blank Page to avoid any automatic start-up or enter the name of a page you would rather see (your provider's status page, for example). Then click OK.

Also on the Options menu, uncheck Auto Load Images. (That is, choose Options from the menu and look to see whether a check mark appears to the left of the Auto Load Images command. If it does, choose the command @ to remove the check mark. If there's no check mark, *don't* choose the command, but press Esc instead.)

Turning off Auto Load Images tells Netscape to load the text part of Web pages, which is small, but to hold off on the larger images. It displays a funny cracked-tablet icon where the images go. Windows users click the image with the *right* mouse button and choose Load this Image to fetch a particular image. Mac users double-click.

When Netscape retrieves a page you've asked to see, it stores the page on disk. If you ask for the same page again five minutes later, Netscape doesn't have to retrieve the page again. The space Netscape uses to store pages is called its *cache* (pronounced "cash" because it's French). The more space you tell Netscape to use for its cache, the faster pages appear the second time you look at them. Choose Options⇨Network and click the Cache tab to find out the maximum size of the cache: We like to set Disk Cache to at least 1024 KB (1 MB). The default of 5MB is about right unless you have a really tiny disk.

Because Netscape caches pages and images retrieved from the Web, even if you tell it not to load images, you get a fair number of them anyway because they already would have been loaded and are still in the cache.

Another way to speed things up is to choose Options⇨Network and click the Connections tab. By default Netscape can have as many as four simultaneous retrievals going, with the limit specified here. We find that if you drop this number to two, things seem snappier.

Form and Function

Back in the Dark Ages of the Web (in 1993), Web pages were just pages to look at. But that wasn't anywhere near enough fun nor complicated enough, so Web forms were invented. A *form* is sort of like a paper form, with fields you can fill out and then send in. Figure 5-1 shows a typical form.

The top two lines in the form are fill-in text boxes in which you type, in this case, your name and e-mail address. Under that is a set of *check boxes*, in which you check whichever ones apply (all of them, we hope). Under that is a set of *radio buttons*, which are like check boxes except that you can choose only one of them. Under that is a *list box*, in which you can choose one of the

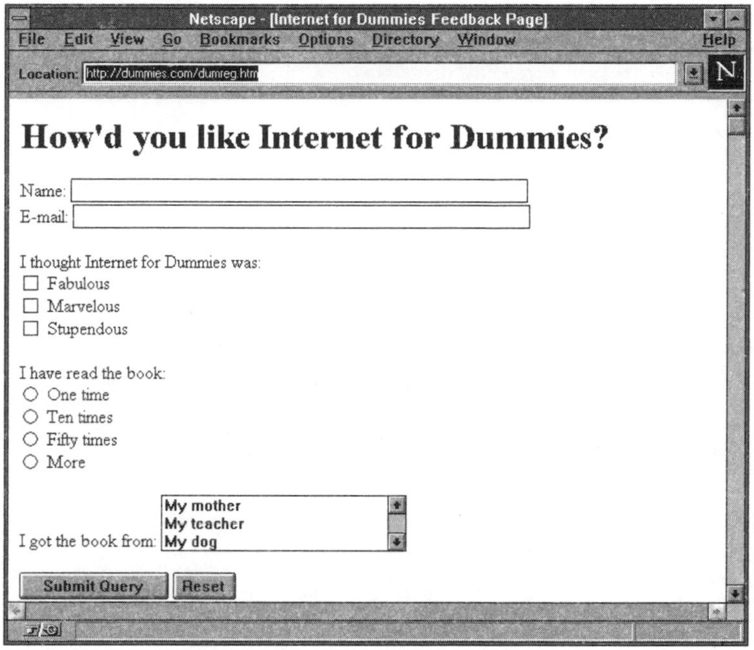

Figure 5-1:
Form-ally
speaking.

possibilities in the box. In most cases, there are more entries than fit in the box, so you scroll them up and down. Usually you can choose only one entry, but some list boxes let you choose more.

At the bottom of the form are two buttons. The one on the left sends the filled-out form back to the Web server for processing, and the one on the right clears the form fields back to their initial state and sends nothing.

After the data is sent from the form back to the Web server, it's entirely up to the server how to interpret it.

Lynx handles forms just like Netscape does (one of Lynx's best features), as shown in Figure 5-2. You move from field to field on a Lynx by pressing the up- and down-arrow keys, the same as always. To submit a form, move to the Submit button and press Enter.

Some Web pages have *search items*, which are simplified one-line forms that let you type some text, invariably interpreted as keywords to search for. Depending on the browser, a Submit button may be displayed to the right of the text area or you may just press Enter to send the search words to the server.

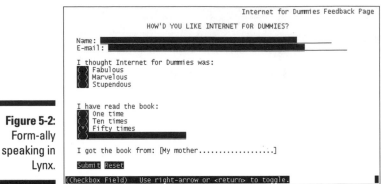

```
                                        Internet for Dummies Feedback Page
                            HOW'D YOU LIKE INTERNET FOR DUMMIES?
          Name: ████████████████████████████████████████████
          E-mail: ███████████████████████████████████████

          I thought Internet for Dummies was:
          █  Fabulous
          █  Marvelous
          █  Stupendous

          I have read the book:
          █  One time
          █  Ten times
          █* Fifty times
          ████████████████████████████████████████████
          I got the book from: [My mother..................]

          Submit Reset
          (Checkbox Field)   Use right-arrow or <return> to toggle.        █
```

Figure 5-2:
Form-ally
speaking in
Lynx.

Whenever a page has only one field to enter, you can press Enter to continue. If more than one field exists, you need the Submit button.

It's a Save

Frequently you see something on a Web page that's worth saving for later. Sometimes it's a Web page full of interesting information, or a picture, or some other kind of file.

Fortunately, saving stuff from Netscape is easy: Hold down the Shift key while you click the link to the item you want. Netscape displays the standard Windows file-selection dialog box, in which you can specify the name to save the incoming file.

Saving Lynx pages

Saving files in Lynx is a little more complicated but still not too difficult. How you do it depends on whether you want to save a page that Lynx knows how to display or to do something else.

Whenever Lynx saves something to disk, it saves it to your *provider's* disk. If you want it on your own PC, you have to download it yourself. See Chapter 15, the section "Uploading and Downloading."

To save a page that Lynx can display in a file, first move to the page so that it's displayed on your screen. Then press **d** for download. Lynx prompts you with the various ways it knows to save the page; usually the only option is to save to disk, which lets you specify on your provider's system a filename in which to save it. Alternatively, you can press **p** for print, which gives you three options:

- ✔ Save to disk, just like **d**.
- ✔ Mail to yourself, frequently the most convenient option.
- ✔ Print to screen. Turn on "screen capture" in the terminal program in your PC, which saves the contents of the page as it goes by on the screen.

Saving anything else in Lynx

This is the easiest part. If you choose a link that goes to an image, program, or other sort of document that Lynx can't handle, it stops and tells you that it can't display this link. You press **d** to download it to a local file, for which you specify the name, or **c** to cancel and forget that link.

Doing Doing Two Two Things Things at at Once Once

Netscape is what's known in the trade as a *multithreaded* program. What this means in practice is that you can have it do several things at a time.

Most usefully, if you ask Netscape to begin downloading a big file, it displays a small window in the corner of your screen with a "thermometer" showing the download progress. Some people consider watching the thermometer grow enough entertainment (we do when we're tired enough), but you can click back to the main Netscape screen and continue surfing. You can also have several Web browser windows open at a time by choosing <u>W</u>indow⇨New Netscape <u>B</u>rowser to create a new window. We find this the most useful way to look at two related pages side by side (or overlapping) on the screen.

Doing two or three things at a time in Netscape when you have a dial-up Net connection is not unlike squeezing blood from a turnip — there's only so much blood to be squeezed. In this case the blood is the amount of data it can pump through your modem. A single download task can keep your modem close to 100 percent busy, and anything else you do shares the modem with the download. When you do two things at a time, therefore, each one happens more slowly than it would by itself.

If one task is a big download and the other is a Web browser, it usually works OK because you spend a fair amount of time looking at what the Web browser is displaying; the download can then run while you think. On the other hand, although Netscape lets you start two download tasks at a time (or a dozen if you're so inclined), there's no point in doing more than one at a time because it's no faster to do them in parallel than one after another, and it can get confusing.

Lynx users are in a somewhat different situation because Lynx displays only one window at a time. In theory you can run two copies of Lynx and switch back and forth, but in practice it's not worth the trouble. Because Lynx is running on your provider's system, it can take advantage of your provider's high-speed Net connection, and even large files load pretty quickly.

Hot off the List

All Web browsers have *bookmarks*, sometimes called a *hot list*. Whatever you call them, they're a list of Web pages you like to visit, so you don't have to type the URLs every time you want to go to one of them.

There are two general ways to handle bookmarks. One is to think of them as a menu so that you can choose individual bookmarks from the menu bar of your browser. The other is to think of them as a custom-built page of links so that you go to that page and then choose the link you want. Lynx takes the latter, custom Web page approach. Netscape, a prime example of the Great Expanding Blob approach to software design, does both.

Marking Netscape

Netscape bookmarks lurk under the <u>B</u>ookmarks menu. To add a bookmark for the currently displayed Web page, choose <u>B</u>ookmarks⇨<u>A</u>dd Bookmark or press Ctrl+A. The bookmarks themselves appear as entries on the Bookmarks menu. To go to one of the pages in your bookmark list, just choose its entry in the Bookmarks menu.

If you're like most users, your bookmark menu will get bigger and bigger and crawl down your screen and eventually end up flopping down on the floor, which is both unattractive and unsanitary. Fortunately, you can smoosh (technical term) your menu into a more tractable form. Choose <u>B</u>ookmarks⇨<u>G</u>o to Bookmarks, or press Ctrl+B to display your bookmarks page, as shown in Figure 5-3.

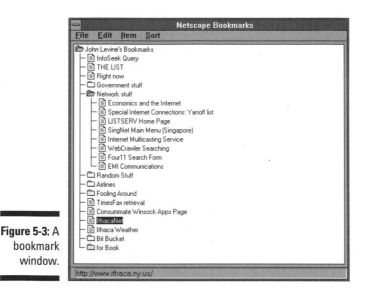

Figure 5-3: A bookmark window.

Because all these bookmarks are "live," you can go to any of them by clicking them. (You can leave this window open while you move around the Web in your main browser window.) You can also add separator lines and submenus to organize your bookmarks and make the individual menus less unwieldy. In the bookmark window, choose Item⇨Insert Separator to add a separator line and Item⇨Insert Header to add a new submenu header. (It asks you to type the name of the submenu before it creates the header.) You can then drag the bookmarks, separators, and headers up and down to where you want them in the bookmark window. Drag an item to a header to put it in that header's submenu, and double-click a header to display or hide that submenu. Any changes you make in the bookmark window are immediately reflected in the Bookmarks menu, so it's pretty easy to fiddle with the bookmarks until you get something you like.

When you're done fooling with your bookmarks, choose File⇨Close to close the window.

Marking Lynx

The Lynx bookmark scheme is a complete anticlimax compared to Netscape. It's controlled by two (count 'em — two) letters.

To add the current page to your bookmark list, press **a**. Lynx gives you the choice of adding a link to the page on the screen (**d** for document) or copying the highlighted link (**c** for current).

To look at (view) your current bookmark list, press **v**. When you're looking at your bookmark list, you move through it and choose links in the same way as you do on any other Web page. You can remove links from the bookmark page by pressing **r**. (Oh, wait — that makes five letters. We lied.)

If you're using Lynx on your own UNIX account, your bookmarks are saved in a file between Lynx sessions. On the other hand, if you're using telnet to connect to a Lynx system somewhere else, the bookmarks exist only through a single Lynx session, and they're discarded when you quit.

The Dead-Tree Thing

For about the first year that there were Web browsers, they all had print commands that didn't work. People finally figured out how to print Web pages, and now they all can do it.

To print a page from Netscape, just click the Print button or choose File⇨Print. Reformatting the page to print it can take a while, so patience is a virtue. Fortunately, Netscape displays a progress window to keep you apprised of how it's doing.

Printing in Lynx is easy in principle: You press **p**. But if you're dialed in to your provider, printing on your provider's computer doesn't do you much good, so Lynx gives you some options, the most useful of which are save to disk (so that you can download it and print it locally) or e-mail it to yourself (so that you can download it and print it locally). Are you detecting a pattern here?

Becoming Famous on the Web

After a while, every Web user thinks about putting up her own personal Web pages. It's not difficult to create a Web page, although it's difficult to create a *good* Web page. Most providers have some arrangement to let you install your pages on their server so that if your login is *elvis*, your home page is something like http://www.dummies.net/~elvis. Sometimes this is part of the basic package, and sometimes it costs extra. If your pages become wildly popular, the provider invariably will charge extra for the extra load it causes on the system.

The details of creating Web pages are beyond the scope of this book, but, generally speaking, here's what you have to do.

✔ Create the pages as files on your disk by using a text editor (if you're really hard-core) or a specialized HTML editor (if you're more normal).

✔ Test them with Netscape and other browsers to make sure that they work the way you want them to.

✔ Upload them to your provider's computer and put them in the appropriate place (wherever the provider says).

✔ Update the pages often enough to keep them interesting.

Web pages are stored as text files containing a mixture of text and HTML commands, like this:

```
<HTML>
<HEAD>
<TITLE>Margy Levine Young's Home Page</TITLE>
</HEAD>
<BODY>
<H1>Who Cares Who Margy Levine Young Is?</H1>
Why do you care who I am? Because I've co-written a bunch
     of the "...For Dummies" <A
     HREF="books.htm">books</A> for IDG Books World-
     wide, that's why. One of my co-authors is none
     other than the internationally famous John
     Levine (alias my brother)!
<P>
```

For more info about writing Web pages, see our book *Internet SECRETS* as well as *HTML For Dummies,* by Ed Tittel and Steve James, and *Creating Cool Web Pages with HTML* by Dave Taylor (all published by IDG Books Worldwide).

Beyond Netscape

Netscape is the best-known Web browser, but there are lots more, many of which are in some ways better than Netscape. Here are a few to look at:

Mosaic: The original Web browser from the University of Illinois. The original student authors of Mosaic were all tempted away to work for commercial Web companies, but a new generation of students has been working away and has made it quite a nice program. We find it much less buggy than Netscape:

```
http://www.ncsa.uiuc.edu/
```

Internet Explorer: Microsoft's entry into the Web browser sweepstakes. It's fast and full of features. Works only on Windows 95 (surprise). You can download it from MSN if you have an account, or it comes as part of Microsoft PLUS!. Or find it at:

```
http://www.windows.microsoft.com/windows/ie/ie.htm
```

Netshark: A browser from Intercon, a commercial Net software vendor. The 1.03 version we tried was extremely buggy, but when they fix it, it'll be a nice program.

```
http://netshark.inter.net/
```

Spry Mosaic: The version of Mosaic that's in *Internet in a Box* and now distributed by CompuServe. If you have a CompuServe account, you can download a copy of this for free as part of its Internet setup. Other users can get a somewhat outdated demo version.

Yet more Netscape tricks

We've barely scratched the surface of what Netscape can do, particularly as they finish Netscape 2.0 (which, as we write, has been released in only a very incomplete beta test version.)

✔ Secure transactions (already present in Netscape 1.1): Because the contents of forms and other messages you send to WWW servers are encrypted, you can send credit-card numbers and other sensitive data in a way that's difficult to spy on. After students in California found some embarassing security holes in 1.2, Netscape sensibly offered cash prizes to people who report bugs in 2.0 so that it can find and fix any remaining errors.

✔ Multiple viewers: Netscape 1.2 knows how to display about five kinds of data, and Netscape 2.0 adds many more. In either version, if Netscape finds a page containing data of a type it doesn't know about, it offers you the option of configuring a viewer and telling it which program on your system it should run to handle that data. For a good example, look at `http://www.realaudio.com`, to download a "viewer" (actually a player) to play real-time audio as it arrives over the Net. Way cool.

✔ Java: The coolest thing yet, this programming language lets Netscape 2.0 automatically download and run *applets,* which are little programs that can make Web pages "live" and interact with you. We expect that Java will start working in versions of Netscape in early 1996.

Chapter 6
Mailing Hither, Mailing Thither

● ●

● ●

*E*lectronic mail is without a doubt the most popular Internet service. Every system on the Net supports some sort of mail service, which means that, no matter what kind of computer you're using, if it's on the Internet, you can send and receive mail.

Because mail, much more than any other Internet service, is connected to many non-Internet systems, you can exchange mail with lots of people who are not on the Internet in addition to all the people who *are* on it (see Chapter 17 for help in finding e-mail addresses).

What's My Address?

Everyone with e-mail access to the Net has an *e-mail address,* which is the cyberspace equivalent of a postal address or a phone number. When you send an e-mail message, you enter the address or addresses of the recipients so that the computer knows who to send it to.

Before you do much mailing, you have to figure out your electronic-mail address so that you can give it to people who want to get in touch with you. And you have to figure out some of their addresses so that you can write to them. (If you have no friends or plan to send only anonymous hate mail, you can skip this section.)

Internet mail addresses have two parts, separated by an @ (the *at* sign). The part before the @ is the *mailbox,* which is (roughly speaking) your personal name, and the part after that is the *domain,* usually the name of your Internet provider, such as aol.com or tiac.net.

The mailbox is usually your *username,* the name your provider assigns to your account. If you're lucky, you get to choose it; in other cases, providers have standardized the naming conventions and you get what you get. Some usernames include first names, last names, initials, first name and last initial, first initial and last name, or anything else, including completely *made-up* names. Over the years, for example, John has had usernames such as john, johnl, jrl, jlevine, jlevine3 (must have been at least three jlevines there), and even q0246; Carol has been carol, carolb, cbaroudi, and carol377 (the provider threw in a random number); and Margy tries to stick with margy but has ended up with margyl or 73727,2305 on occasion. A few systems still assign names such as usd31516. Ugh.

Back when many fewer e-mail users were around and most users of any particular system knew each other directly, it wasn't all that difficult to figure out who had what username. These days, because it's becoming much more of a problem, many organizations are creating consistent mailbox names for all users, most often by using the user's first and last names with a dot between them. In this type of scheme, your mailbox name may be something like elvis.presley@bluesuede.org, even though your username is something else. (If your name isn't Elvis Presley, adjust this example suitably. On the other hand, if your name *is* Elvis Presley, please contact us immediately. We know some people who are looking for you.)

Having several names for the same mailbox is no problem, so the new, longer, consistent usernames are invariably created in addition to — rather than instead of — the traditional short nicknames.

The domain for providers in the United States usually ends with three letters (called the *zone*) that give you a clue to what kind of place it is. *Commercial* organizations end with .com, which includes both providers such as America Online (AOL) and CompuServe and many companies that aren't public providers but that are commercial entities, such as amrcomp.com (American Airlines), cabotcheese.com (the Cabot Creamery in Vermont, which makes really good Cheddar cheese), and iecc.com (the Invincible Electric Calculator Company). Educational institutions end with .edu, networking organizations end with .net, U.S. government sites end with .gov, military sites end with .mil, and organizations that don't fall into any of those categories end with .org. Outside the U.S., domains usually end with a country code such as fr for France or zm for Zambia. New domains were being registered at a ferocious rate until September 1995, when the main domain registry began charging for registrations.

Domain names are traditionally represented in uppercase (BLUESUEDE.ORG) and mailbox names in lowercase or mixed case (Elvis). But case never matters in domains and rarely matters in mailbox names. To make it easy on your eyes, therefore, most of the domain and mailbox names in this book are shown in lowercase. If you're sending a message to another user in your domain (same machine or group of machines), you can leave out the domain part when you type the address. For example, if you and a friend both use AOL, you can leave out the @aol.com part of the address when you're writing to each other.

If you don't know what your e-mail address is, a good approach is to send yourself a message and use your login name as the mailbox name. Then examine the return address on the message. Or you can send a message to Internet For Dummies Mail Central at ninternet@dummies.com, and a friendly robot will send back a message with your address. (While you're at it, tell us whether you like this book because we authors see that mail too.) Chapter 17 has more suggestions for finding e-mail addresses.

Far too many mail programs

One of the nice things about the Internet is that you can connect hundreds of different kinds of computers to it. But one of the less nice things is that on those hundreds of different kinds of computers you have hundreds of different kinds of programs to do the same thing.

For you mail users, here's a cheat sheet:

If you use a Windows PC or Mac with a SLIP/PPP connection, you most likely use Eudora, described later in this chapter, to send and receive e-mail. Eudora works pretty well, and one version is free. Some people use Netscape, which isn't a great mail program, but everyone has it and it's free.

If you use a commercial shell provider or a UNIX workstation, you almost certainly can use Pine (also described later in this chapter).

If you use a commercial provider such as AOL or CompuServe, you use the mail program your provider provides. If you use MSN, you use Microsoft Exchange, which comes with Windows 95. Part IV discusses those systems, but we recommend that you read this chapter before you jump to the chapter that discusses your specific provider.

If you're connected some other way, you probably have a different mail program. For example, you may be using a PC in your company's network which runs cc:Mail or Microsoft Mail and has a mail-only link to the outside world. We don't describe cc:Mail here (although there's the *cc:Mail for Dummies Quick Reference,* by Victor Robert Garza, published by IDG Books Worldwide.)

Regardless of what kind of mail you're using, the basics of reading, sending, addressing, and filing mail work pretty much the same way, so it's worth looking through this chapter even if you're not using any of the mail programs we describe here.

My Mail Is Where?

You have your e-mail address. Cool. Next we're going to tell you how to send and receive mail — and what you can do with it. But first, there's the tiny detail of where your mail is stored. When your mail arrives, unless you are one of the lucky (or rich) few whose computers have a permanent Internet connection, the mail doesn't get delivered to your computer automatically. Mail gets delivered instead to a *mail server,* which is sort of like your local post office. In order for you to actually get your mail, you have to go and get it. Well, actually your *mail* program has to go and get it. And in order for you to send mail, your *mail* program has to take it to the post office.

If you're using a shell account or a commercial on-line service, the mail server is actually the same computer you connect to when you're dialed in (this is an oversimplification, but it's close enough) so that when you run your provider's mail program, the mail is right there for you to read, and it can drop outgoing mail directly in the virtual mail chute.

If you're using a SLIP/PPP account, when your mail program picks up the mail, it sucks your mail from your provider to your PC or Mac at top speed. After you have your mail on your local computer, you can disconnect, a good idea if your provider charges by the hour. Then you can read and respond to your mail while the meter isn't running — that is, while you're "off-line." After you're ready to send your responses or new messages, you can reconnect and transmit your outgoing mail, again at top network speed.

Mailers, Mailers, Everywhere

So now you know what your address is, or else you've decided that you don't care. Either way, it's time for some hand-to-hand combat with your e-mail system.

The bad news is that there are countless mailer programs — programs that read and write electronic mail messages. At least there are so many that none of us felt up to the task of counting them. You've got your freeware, you've got your shareware and your commercial stuff, and stuff probably came with your computer. They all do more or less the same thing because they're all mail programs, after all. If you use a commercial service such as AOL, they, of course, use their own mailer. When you're actually ready to send mail, turn to your provider-specific chapter in Part IV for details. Meanwhile, we recommend that you keep reading so that you get a broader picture of e-mail do's and don'ts.

After you understand what a mailer's supposed to do, it's much easier to figure out how to make a specific mailer do what you want it to, so we picked the three most popular mailers to show you the ropes. For SLIP/PPP users, we picked Netscape and Eudora. For shell account users, we picked Pine.

✓ **Eudora:** A popular mailer that runs under Microsoft Windows and on Macintoshes. Eudora up- and downloads mail to your mail server too. Eudora is popular for two reasons: It's easy to use, and it's really cheap. You can get a freeware version for free, and an enhanced commercial version costs only about $65. The examples here are made by using the commercial version, but the freeware looks nearly the same, minus a few bells and whistles.

✓ **Netscape:** Yes, the same Netscape you met in Chapter 4 while surfing the World Wide Web. The newest versions (2.x) of Netscape make it an adequate if not superb mail program as well as a Web browser. It runs on your own computer and up- and downloads mail to your mail server. We strongly prefer Eudora, but because some people are stuck with Netscape, we mention it here.

✓ **Pine:** A rather nice mail program with a full-screen terminal interface. Pine stands for "*Pine is not E*lm" (at the time Pine was written, another mail program called Elm was the standard) and can also be used to read Usenet news, but we talk more about that in Chapter 9. It's generally available from most shell providers because it's (No, wait! You guessed!) free. If you're using a shell system, Pine runs on your provider's computer, and you type commands at it by using a terminal program on your computer.

Do You Have a Mail Program Installed?

If you're using a Windows or Mac computer with SLIP/PPP, there's probably a mail program in the software package installed on your computer. If not, you can always use Netscape, which we discussed in close anatomical detail in Chapter 4.

If you want to give Eudora a try and she's not already installed on your computer, you can find out the grisly details, along with lots more details about day-to-day use of Eudora, in Chapter 10 of *MORE Internet For Dummies*.

Sending Mail Is Easy

Sending mail is easy enough that we show you a few examples rather than waste time explaining the theory.

Mail with Eudora

This section tells you how to run Eudora and send some mail:

1. **From your PC or Mac, start Eudora.**

   From Windows, start Eudora by clicking her Program Manager icon, which looks like an envelope. In Windows 95, her icon is on the desktop or in a folder. Mac users click Eudora's icon. You should see an introductory "splash" window that goes away after a few seconds and then a window is displayed. Exactly what's in the window varies depending on what you were looking at the last time you ran Eudora.

2. **To send a message, you choose Message⇨New message from the menu (or if you're lazy and can remember shortcut keys, it's Ctrl+N).**

   Eudora pops up a new message window.

3. **Type the recipient's address (**ninternet@dummies.com**, for example).**

4. **Press Tab to skip to the Subject field (it already knows who you are — you don't have to tell it that), and type a subject.**

5. **Press Tab a few more times to skip the Cc: and Bcc: fields (or type the addresses of people who should get carbon copies and blind carbon copies of the message).**

   The term "carbon copy" should be familiar to those of us who were born before 1960 and remember the antiquated practice of putting sheets of carbon-coated paper between sheets of regular paper to make extra copies when using a typewriter. (Please don't ask us what a typewriter is.) In electronic-mail systems, a carbon copy is simply a copy of the message you send. All recipients, in both the To: and Cc: fields, see who's getting a copy of this message. *Blind carbon copies* are copies sent to people without their names appearing on the message. *You* can figure out why you might want to send a copy to someone but not want everyone else to know that you had.

6. **Press Tab to move to the large area and then type your message.**

7. **To send the message, you click the button in the upper right corner of the message window, which, depending on how Eudora is set up, is marked Send or Queue.**

   If the button is marked Send, as soon as you click it Eudora tries to send the message and puts up a little status window that contains incomprehensible status messages. If, on the other hand, it's marked Queue, your message is stashed in your "outbox" for sending later.

The usual reason to have a Queue button is that you have a dial-up SLIP/PPP connection so that your computer isn't connected to the Net all the time. After you've queued a few messages, you can send them all at one time.

8. **If your computer isn't already connected, dial up and get your computer connected to your provider.**

Then switch back to Eudora and from the menu choose File⇨Send Queued Messages (Ctrl+T for the lazy) to transmit all the messages you've queued up.

Even if you leave your computer connected while you write your mail, it's not a bad idea to set Eudora to queue the mail and not send it until you tell it to. (Choose Special⇨Settings from the Eudora menu, go to the Sending Mail category, and be sure that Immediate Send isn't checked.) That way, you have a few minutes after you write each message to ponder whether it's really a message you want to send. Even though we've been using e-mail for almost 20 years, we still throw away many of the messages we write before we send them.

After you have sent a piece of e-mail, there's no way to cancel it!

The same idea, using Netscape

The steps for sending mail from Netscape are almost identical to those for sending mail from Eudora (you're doing the same thing, after all):

1. **Start Netscape.**

2. **Choose Window⇨Netscape Mail.**

   This step opens the Netscape mail window. The first time you give the command, Netscape asks you for the password for your mailbox, which is usually the same as the password for your Internet account.

   Netscape may try to retrieve any waiting mail; click Cancel or the red stop sign if you don't want it to bother. You see the Netscape Mail window.

3. **Click the New Mail button on the icon bar.**

   Yet another window opens, with a blank message template.

4. **Fill in the recipient's address (or addresses), indicate the subject, and type the message.**

5. **Click Send to send the message.**

TIP

Getting ANSI

If, when you're trying to run Pine on your UNIX shell account, you get a strange message that looks something like this:

```
Your terminal, of type "ansi,"
is lacking functions needed to
run pine.
```

you have to utter a magic spell before continuing. Type this line:

```
setenv TERM vt100
```

or if your provider's system doesn't grok that:

```
TERM=vt100 ; export TERM
```

Be sure to capitalize the commands exactly as you see here. Now try again. (You're giving it some hints about which kind of terminal your computer is pretending to be. Trust us — the details aren't worth knowing.)

From a UNIX shell account

We presume that your shell provider has Pine all installed and ready to go (if not, call up and complain; there's no excuse not to have it available):

1. **Run Pine by typing** pine.

   You see Pine's main menu, shown in Figure 6-1.

2. **Press** c **to compose a new message.**

   Pine displays a nice, blank message, all ready for you to fill in.

3. **On the To line, type the address you want to send mail to and press Enter (or Return — same thing).**

   Pine displays a screen like the one shown in Figure 6-2. At the bottom of the screen are a bunch of options preceded by a funny-looking caret sign and a letter. The caret sign indicates the Ctrl key on your keyboard. To choose an option, press the Ctrl key and the letter of the option that interests you (such as Ctrl+G for ^G to get help).

4. **On the Cc: line you can enter addresses of other people to whom you want to send a copy of this message.**

5. **Press Enter to get to the line labeled** Attchmnt:

   Whether the programmers can't spell or the lazy typists have struck or they abbreviate things so that people won't know that they can't spell, no one really knows. But this line is for *attachments* — files you want to send along with your message. You can enter the name of a file, even a file that contains stuff that isn't text, and Pine will send it along with your message.

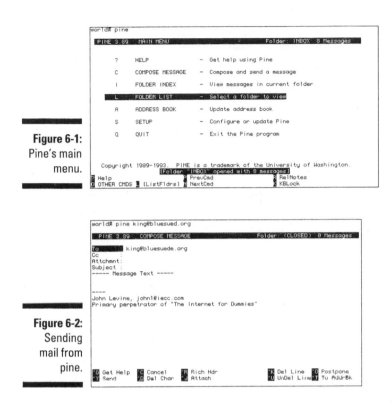

Figure 6-1:
Pine's main
menu.

Figure 6-2:
Sending
mail from
pine.

6. **Press Enter to get to the subject of your message, and then enter something descriptive about the content of your message.**

Subject lines that say something like "A message from Harley" are somewhat less useful than something like this:

```
Subject: Hound dogs
```

7. **Press Enter to get to the part we've all been waiting for and enter your message.**

It can say anything you want, and it can be as long as you want. Here's a short example:

```
When you said that I ain't nothing but a hound dog, did
you mean a greyhound, a basset hound, or some other kind
of hound?

Signed, A Curious Admirer
```

To enter the message text, Pine automatically runs the simple text editor pico, which, with any luck, you already know how to use. If you don't know how to run pico but you know how to run another UNIX editor, ask your

Internet service provide to help you set up Pine to use the editor you do know how to run. (Some providers ask you when they configure your account.) You have to be able to stumble through some type of editor, so if you don't know any, starting with pico is as good a place as any. For more editor details, see *UNIX For Dummies,* 2nd Edition, by John Levine and Margaret Levine Young (published by IDG Books Worldwide, 1995).

Type the message. If you don't know how to use any editor features, you can use pico perfectly well without using any. Just type your message. Press the arrow keys on the keyboard to move around if you need to make changes.

8. When you're finished, press Ctrl-X to save the message and return to Pine.

Pine responds with this message:

```
Send message? [y] :
```

9. Press y or Enter to send your message.

The Pine program responds with a cheery [Sending mail.....] message, and you're all set.

Pine lets you do all kinds of other nifty things; gobs of information about it is available in our fat book *Internet SECRETS* (IDG Books Worldwide, 1995), and you must be getting tired of our plugs for our other books. (We'll try to stop now.)

Mail Call!

If you begin sending e-mail (and in most cases, even if you don't), you begin receiving it. The arrival of e-mail is always exciting, even when you get 100 messages a day.

Using Eudora

One seriously cool feature of Eudora is that you can do much of what you do with mail while you're not connected to your account and paying by the minute. On the other hand, when you really do want to check your mail, you have to be connected. Eudora allegedly can figure out that you're not connected and dial in for you, but in our experience this "feature" doesn't always work.

If you don't have a full-time Net connection, follow these steps to get your mail:

1. Make your Net connection, if you're not already connected.

2. Start up Eudora.

3. **If she doesn't retrieve mail automatically, choose File➪Check Mail (or press Ctrl+M) to retrieve your mail.**

   If you have a full-time Net connection, Eudora probably is set up to retrieve your mail automatically, in which case you only have to start Eudora and she'll get your mail. (In addition, if you leave Eudora running, even hidden at the bottom of your screen as an icon, she'll automatically check for new mail every once in a while.)

   If you have mail on the Mac, Eudora blows a horn and shows you a cute picture of a rooster with a letter in his beak. If you don't have any mail, you don't get any sound effects, but you do get a nice picture of a snake. Windows users don't get the animals. If you have a sound card, however, she sings a little song to announce new mail.

   The mail appears in your inbox, a window that Eudora labels In, one line per message.

4. **To see a message, double-click the line or click the line and press Enter.**

   To stop looking at a message, double-click the box in the upper left corner of the message window (the standard way to get rid of a window) or press Ctrl+W.

Buttons at the top of the In window or at the top of your screen (depending on your version of Eudora) let you dispose of your mail. From Windows, if the message isn't already on your screen, first click (once) the message you want, which should highlight it. Then click the trashcan button to discard the message or the printer icon to print it. Using the Macintosh version of Eudora, choose a message by clicking it. Press Delete to delete it, or choose Print from the File menu to print it.

There's much more you can do to messages, which we discuss in Chapter 7, but that's enough for now.

When you're finished with your mail, you leave Eudora in the same way as you leave any other Mac or Windows program. Before you go, you'll sometimes want to empty your Trash mailbox, which is where deleted messages are deposited. You do that by choosing Special➪Empty Trash from the menu.

Using Netscape

Reading mail with Netscape is similar to reading it with Eudora:

1. **Start Netscape.**

2. **Choose Window➪Netscape Mail.**

   This step opens the Netscape mail window. It may try to retrieve any waiting mail immediately; if it doesn't, click the Get Mail button. Incoming mail is filed in your INBOX folder.

3. **Click the Inbox icon in the left column of the screen to see the messages in your inbox.**

   The upper right part of your screen shows the subject lines for incoming mail.

4. **Click each message to read it, or click Next or Previous to read messages in order.**

After you have a message on the screen, you can click the Print, Delete, and other buttons to dispose of messages. We discuss the other functions in Chapter 7.

Using Pine

When you log in to your shell account, you usually get a little message that says "You have new mail" if you do or "You have mail" if stuff you've already seen is hanging around. Depending on some obscure parameter, your mail gets checked periodically, and when you have new mail, you get the "You have new mail" message again. If the interval at which your mail is being checked isn't small enough to satisfy your curiosity about whether you *really* have new mail, however, you can ask your provider to change the parameter or you can run Pine whenever you feel the urge.

If you've been using a PC with Windows or a Macintosh and have never experienced the utter thrill of computing without being able to point and click, you might — right this minute — be on the brink of a profound moment that will make you thank the stars for all you have now and have taken for granted. Hide your mouse. It's of no use to you now. It will only frustrate you even more if you try to use it. All the navigation you'll be doing requires you to use letters or arrow keys.

Here are the steps to follow:

1. **Type the** pine **command.**

   Pine's main menu lets you choose from a variety of activities, but if you have mail, the choice L Folder list is highlighted (refer to Figure 6-1).

2. **Press Enter to see the list of folders you can choose from.**

   When you're just starting out, you don't have much to choose from, but that can change. Right now you're interested in the one labeled INBOX. INBOX should be highlighted. Press Enter to see your mail.

   Pine displays a list of messages, like the one shown by Pine in Figure 6-3.

Figure 6-3:
Pine lists
newly
arrived
messages.

```
N 1  Aug 15 David_Baroudi@toge    (1,625) Re: what Josh might want...
N 2  Aug 17 jake nose             (948)
N 3  Aug 16 P.ALTMAN              (982) Re: Bonjour
N 4  Aug 16 P.ALTMAN              (1,343) Bonjour
N 5  Jun 22 Hockey12@aol.com      (2,658) e-mail headers
N 6  Jun 21 Yuki Kaneshige        (1,037) Help!
N 7  Jun 21 Kenyon, Joe           (2,452) Antarctica
N 8  Jun 21 Jimtex1@aol.com       (879) address request
N 9  Jun 17 Claudio Colajacomo    (1,641) SLIP info
N 10 Jun  8 rbernste@btg.com      (2,562) Re: ARE YOU REALLY OUT THERE????????
```

3. **The message that's highlighted is the current message. To choose a different one, press the arrow keys or press** P **for the previous message or** N **for the next message.**

   When you've chosen the message you want to read, press Enter.

   Pine displays your message.

   After you've read a message, you have several choices about what to do with it. We talk about the details of deleting, forwarding, and filing messages in Chapter 7.

4. **To read your next message, press** N**; to read the preceding message, press** P**; to return to the index of messages in the folder you are reading (in our case, INBOX), press** I**.**

5. **When you're finished reading mail, press** Q **to quit.**

   Pine asks you whether you really want to do that. (What — leave this program? But it's so wonderful!) Reassure it by pressing **Y**.

A Few Words from the Etiquette Ladies

Sadly, the Great Ladies of Etiquette, such as Emily Post and Amy Vanderbilt, died before the invention of e-mail. But here is what they might have suggested about what to say and, more important, what *not* to say in electronic mail.

E-mail is a funny hybrid, something between a phone call (or voice mail) and a letter. On one hand, it's quick and usually informal; on the other hand, it's written rather than spoken, so you don't see a person's facial expressions or hear her tone of voice.

A few words of advice:

✔ When you send a message, watch your tone of voice.

✔ Don't use all capital letters — it looks like you're SHOUTING.

✔ If someone sends you an incredibly obnoxious and offensive message, as likely as not it's a mistake or a joke gone awry. In particular, be on the lookout for failed sarcasm.

Flame Off!

Pointless and excessive outrage in electronic mail is so common that it has a name of its own: *flaming*. Don't flame. It makes you look like a jerk.

When you get a message so offensive that you just *have* to reply, stick it back in your electronic inbox for a while and wait until after lunch. Then, don't flame back. The sender probably didn't realize how the message would look. In about 20 years of using electronic mail, we can testify that we have never, never, regretted *not* sending an angry message. (But we *have* regretted sending a few. Ouch.)

When you're sending mail, keep in mind that someone reading it will have no idea of what you *intended* to say — just what you *did* say. Subtle sarcasm and irony are almost impossible to use in e-mail and usually come across as annoying or dumb instead. (If you're an extremely superb writer, you can disregard this advice, but don't say that we didn't warn you.)

Sometimes it helps to put in a : -) (called a *smiley*), which means "this is a joke." (Try leaning way over to the left if you don't see why it's a smile.) In some communities, notably CompuServe, ⟨g⟩ or ⟨grin⟩ serves the same purpose. Here's a typical example:

```
People who don't believe that we are all part of a warm,
caring community who love and support each other are no bet-
ter than rabid dogs and should be hunted down and shot. :-)
```

Smileys sometimes help, but if a joke needs a smiley, maybe it wasn't worth making. It may sound as though all your e-mail is supposed to be humorless. It's not that bad, but until you have the hang of it, limit the humor. You'll be glad you did.

Hey, Mr. Postmaster

Every Internet host that can send or receive mail has a special mail address called postmaster that's guaranteed to get a message to the person responsible for that host. If you send mail to someone and get back strange failure messages, you might try sending a message to the postmaster. If king@bluesuede.org returns an error from bluesuede.org, for example, you might try a polite question to postmaster@bluesuede.org. The postmaster is usually an overworked volunteer system administrator, so it's considered poor form to ask a postmaster for favors much greater than "Does so-and-so have a mailbox on this system?"

BTW, what does IMHO mean? RTFM!

E-mail users are often lazy typists, and many abbreviations are common. Here are some of the most widely used:

Abbreviation	What It Means
BTW	By The Way
IMHO	In My Humble Opinion
RSN	Real Soon Now (vaporware)
RTFM	Read The Manual — you could and should have looked it up yourself
TIA	Thanks In Advance
TLA	Three-Letter Acronym

Another possibility to keep in the back of your mind is that it's technically not difficult to forge e-mail return addresses, so if you get a totally off-the-wall message from someone that seems out of character for that person, somebody else may have forged it as a prank. (No, we won't tell you how to forge e-mail. How dumb do you think we are?)

How Private Is E-Mail?

Relatively, but not totally. Any recipient of your mail might forward it to other people. Some mail addresses are really mailing lists that redistribute messages to many other people. In one famous case, a mistaken mail address sent a message to tens of thousands of readers. It began, "Darling, at last we have a way to send messages that is completely private."

The usual rule of thumb is not to send anything you wouldn't want to see posted next to the water cooler or perhaps scribbled next to a pay phone. The latest e-mail systems are beginning to include encryption features that make the privacy situation somewhat better so that anyone who doesn't know the keyword used to scramble a message can't decode it.

The most common tools for encrypted mail are known as *PEM* (privacy-enhanced mail) and *PGP* (pretty good privacy.) PGP is one of the most widely used encryption programs, both in the U.S. and abroad. Many experts think that it is so strong that even the National Security Agency can't crack it. We don't know, but if the NSA wants to read your mail, you have more complicated problems than we can help you solve.

PGP is available free of charge on the Net. For more information about privacy and security issues, including how to get started with PGP, see our book *Internet SECRETS* (IDG Books Worldwide, 1995) — whoops, we did it again.

Table 6-1 shows how to address e-mail to people who use a type of on-line account that's different from your own. Find the *column* that corresponds to the on-line server you use. Then find the *row* for the type of service your friend has.

Table 6-1		How to Address E-Mail Messages to On-Line Services				
If you have this type of account:	You can send e-mail to this type of account	(using this sample user ID):				
		Internet	*AOL*	*CompuServe*	*Prodigy*	*MSN*
	Internet	santa@northpole.com	SteveCase	77777,7777	A1B2C3	BillGates
	AOL	santa@northpole.com	SteveCase@aol.com	77777.7777@compuserve.com	A1B2C3@prodigy.com	BillGates@msn.com
	CompuServe	santa@northpole.com	SteveCase	77777.7777@compuserve.com	A1B2C3@prodigy.com	BillGates@msn.com
	Prodigy	INTERNET: santa@ northpole.com	INTERNET:SteveCase@ aol.com	77777,7777	INTERNET:A1B2C3@ prodigy.com	INTERNET:BillGates@msn.com
	MSN	santa@northpole.com	SteveCase@aol.com	77777.7777@compuserve.com	A1B2C3	BillGates@msn.com
		santa@northpole.com	SteveCase@aol.com	77777.7777@compuserve.com	A1B2C3@prodigy.com	BillGates

Chapter 7

Putting Your Mail in Its Place

- -

In This Chapter

▶ Deleting mail

▶ Responding to mail

▶ Forwarding and filing mail

▶ Spotting and avoiding chain letters

▶ Sending and receiving exotic mail and mail attachments

▶ Exchanging mail with robots and fax machines

- -

*O*K, now you know how to send and receive mail. It's time for some tips and tricks to make you into a real mail aficionado. After you've seen a message, you can do a bunch of different things with it (much the same as with paper mail). Here are your usual choices:

✔ Throw it away

✔ Reply to it

✔ Forward it to other people

✔ File it

Unlike with paper mail, you can do any or all of these things to each message. If you don't tell your mailer what to do to a message, the message either stays in your mailbox for later perusal or sometimes, when you're using Pine, for example, the message gets saved to a read-messages folder.

If your mailer automatically saves messages in a read-messages folder, be sure to go through the folder every week or so or else it will become enormous and unmanageable.

Handling Mail with Eudora, Netscape, and Pine

When you first begin to get e-mail, it's so exciting that it's difficult to imagine just throwing it away. But eventually you *have* to learn how to do this or else you'll run out of room. Start early. Delete often.

The physical act of throwing away mail is easy enough that you've probably figured out how to do it already. Using the Windows version of Eudora, you click a message and then click the trash can or press Ctrl+D. In the Macintosh version of Eudora, you can click the message and press Delete. If the message is open, press ⌘-D or choose Delete from the Message menu. In Netscape, select the message and click the Delete button on the toolbar or press the Del key. From Pine, press **D** for Delete.

Often you can delete mail without even reading it. If you subscribe to mailing lists, certain topics might not interest you. After you see the subject line, you might want to delete it without reading it. If you're the kind of person who reads everything sent to you by Ed McMahon, you might have problems with junk e-mail too. Consider getting professional help.

Back to you, Sam: Replying to mail

There are a couple of things you should know about replying to mail. It's easy enough to do: In Eudora, choose Message⇨Reply or click the icon that looks like a U-turn sign; in Netscape, click the Reply icon on the toolbar or choose Message⇨Reply from the menu or press Ctrl+R; in Pine, press **R**.

Pay attention to two things in particular:

✔ Where does the reply go? Look carefully at the To: line your mailer program has filled out for you. Is that who you thought you were addressing? If the reply is to a mailing list, did you really intend to post to that list, or is your message of a more personal nature and might be better addressed to the individual who sent the message? Did you mean to reply to a group? Are all the addresses you think you're replying to included in the To: list? If the To: list isn't right, you can move the cursor to it and edit it as necessary.

✔ Do you want to include the content of the message you're replying to? By default Eudora begins your reply message with the content of the message you're replying to. Netscape does not. Pine asks you whether to include it. We suggest that you begin by including it and then edit the text to just the relevant material. If you don't give some context to people who get a great deal of e-mail, your reply will make no sense. So if you're answering a question, include the question in the response. You don't have to include the entire text, but give your reader a break. She might have read 50 messages since she sent you mail and might not have a clue what you're talking about unless you remind her.

When you reply to a message, your mailer fills in the Subject field with the letters *Re:* (short for regarding) and the Subject field of the message you're replying to.

Hot potatoes: Forwarding mail

You can forward e-mail along to someone else. It's easy. It's cheap. Forwarding is one of the nicest things about electronic mail and at the same time one of the worst. It's good because you can easily pass along messages to people who need to know about them. It's bad because you (not you personally but, um, people around you — that's it) can just as easily send out floods of messages to recipients who would just as soon not hear yet another press release from the local Ministry of Truth. So you have to think a little about whether you will enhance someone's quality of life by forwarding a message to him. (If you don't care about quality of life, pick some other criterion.)

What's usually called *forwarding* a message involves wrapping the message in a new message of your own, sort of like sticking Post-It notes all over a copy of it and mailing the copy and Post-Its to someone else.

Forward with Eudora

To forward a message with Eudora:

1. **Choose Message⇨Forward from the menu or click the icon of the road sign with the arrow pointing up.**

   Eudora opens a new window with the cursor in the To: field.

2. **Fill in the** To:, Cc:, **and** Bcc: **fields.**

   Tell Eudora to whom you want to forward this message. Notice that she filled in the Subject field with the Subject field of the message you're forwarding.

Eudora provides the forwarded text in the message part of the window. Each line is preceded by the greater-than sign (>). You then get to edit the message and add your own comments. See the following sidebar, "Fast forward," for tips about pruning forwarded mail.

3. **Click Send or Queue.**

Fast forward

When you're forwarding mail, it's generally a good idea to get rid of uninteresting parts. All the glop in the message header is frequently included automatically in the forwarded message, and almost none of it is comprehensible, much less interesting, so get rid of it.

The tricky part is editing down the text. If the message is short, a screenful or so, you probably should leave it alone:

```
>Is there a lot of demand for
 >fruit pizza?

>In answer to your question, I
 >checked with our research
 >department and found that the
 >favorite pizza toppings in
 >the 18-34 age group are
 >pepperoni, sausage, ham,
 >pineapple, olives, peppers,
 >mushrooms, hamburger, and
 >broccoli. I specifically
 >asked about prunes and they
 >said that there was no
 >statistically significant
 >response about them.
```

If it's really long and only part of it is relevant, you should, as a courtesy to the reader, cut it down to the interesting part. We can tell you from experience that people pay much more attention to a concise, one-line e-mail message than they do to 12 pages of quoted stuff followed by a two-line question.

Sometimes it makes sense to edit material even more, particularly to emphasize one specific part. When you do so, of course, be sure not to edit to the point where you put words in the original author's mouth or garble the sense of the message, as in the following reply:

```
>In answer to your question, I
 >checked with our research
 >department and found that the
 >favorite pizza toppings ...
 >and they said that there was
 >no statistically significant
 >response about them.
```

That's an excellent way to make new enemies. Sometimes it makes sense to paraphrase a little — in that case, put the paraphrased part in square brackets, like this:

```
>[When asked about prunes on
 >pizza, research] said that
 >there was no statistically
 >significant response about
 >them.
```

People disagree about whether paraphrasing to shorten quotes is a good idea. On one hand, if you do it well, it saves everyone time. On the other hand, if you do it badly and someone takes offense, you're in for a week of accusations and apologies that will wipe out whatever time you may have saved. The decision is up to you.

Not-so-straightforward: Redirecting mail with Eudora

Sometimes the mail you get might really have been intended for someone else. You probably will want to pass it along as is, without sticking the greater-than character at the beginning of every line, and you should leave the sender and reply-to information intact so that if the new recipient of the mail wants to respond, the response goes to the originator of the mail, not to you just because you passed it on. Eudora calls this process *redirecting;* you can redirect mail by choosing Message⇨Redirect from the menu or clicking the right-turn arrow icon. Eudora sticks in a polite by-way-of notice to let the new reader know how the message found her.

Other mailers call this feature *remailing* or *bouncing,* and it's the electronic version of scribbling another address on the outside of an envelope and dropping it back in the mailbox. Unlike reading paper mail, you can read e-mail without having to tear open the envelope (but these analogies are never perfect).

Forward with Netscape

Forwarding with Netscape is almost exactly the same as with Eudora. When a message is on-screen, click the Forward button and Netscape opens a new window for your message. The main difference is that, because Netscape treats the old message as an attached file, you can't edit it, although you can add comments of your own to send along with it.

Forward with Pine

To forward a message from Pine:

1. **Press** F **for Forward.**

   Pine begins a new message, allowing space for your message, followed by a broken line labeled Forwarded Message with the text of the forwarded message at the bottom. Notice that Pine uses the subject of the forwarded message as the subject of this message with (fwd) at the end to alert the reader that this message has been forwarded.

2. **Enter in the** To: **and** Cc: **fields the address where you want the message forwarded.**

3. **Enter any commentary you want in the message field. Notice that you can edit the forwarded message just as you can edit your own message.**

   See the preceding sidebar, "Fast forward," for tips about pruning the forwarded message.

4. **Press Ctrl-X to send.**

Cold potatoes: Saving mail

Saving e-mail for later reference is similar to putting potatoes in the fridge for later (don't knock it if you haven't tried it — day-old boiled potatoes are yummy with enough butter or sour cream). Lots of your e-mail is worth saving, just like lots of your paper mail is worth saving. (Lots of it *isn't,* of course, but we already covered that subject.)

You can save e-mail in a few different ways:

  ✔ Save it in a folder full of messages.

  ✔ Save it in a regular file.

  ✔ Print it and put it in a file cabinet with paper mail.

The easiest method usually is to stick messages in a folder (a folder is usually no more than a file full of messages with some sort of separator between each message). Many mail programs have by default a bad habit of saving all your incoming messages in a file named something like read-messages or mbox, except for the messages you delete. This plan might have made sense back in the Paleozoic era, when on a really busy day you might have gotten five messages. Now it makes about as much sense as handling your paper mail by stuffing it all in your desk drawer. If you let your mailer save messages in this manner, your read-messages file will grow like the giant blob in that old sci-fi movie until it devours all storage in sight. This method is generally not considered Effective Disk Space Management, so don't let it happen to you.

To avoid death by blob, file or discard things yourself. First you have to make sure that your mailer doesn't stash messages without telling you. Disabling the automatic-filing feature is usually possible by twiddling a configuration parameter somewhere. Ask for your Internet provider's help. If you're desperate, you might try reading the manual, although too many manuals these days merely assert that the program is user-friendly and therefore intuitively obvious.

Two general approaches are used in filing mail: by sender and by topic. Whether you use one or the other or both is mostly a matter of taste. Some mail programs (such as Pine) help you file stuff by the sender's name, so if your friend Fred has the username fred@something.or.other, when you press S to save a message from him, Pine asks whether you want to put it in a folder called fred. Of course, if some crazed system administrator has given him the username z921h8t@something.or.other, the automatic naming can leave something to be desired, so make up names of your own.

For filing by topic, it's entirely up to you to come up with the folder names. The most difficult part is coming up with memorable names. If you're not careful, you end up with four folders with slightly different names, each with a quarter of the messages about a particular topic. Try to come up with names that are obvious, and don't abbreviate. If the topic is accounting, call the folder `accounting` because if you abbreviate you'll never remember whether it's called `acctng`, `acct`, `acntng`, or any of a dozen other short abbreviations.

Filing with Eudora

Eudora makes filing mail a little easier in two ways. First, she shows you all the folder names you've already created so that you're less likely to create another folder for the same topic with a similar name. Second, she enables you to create hierarchies of folders so that under the heading Jazz, for example, you might have folders called CD Recommendations and Women in Jazz. Third, the commercial (not freeware) version of Eudora can file messages for you automatically: You can create *filters* that tell Eudora, for example, "Any message that comes from the `POULTRY-L` mailing list should be automatically filed in the Chickens folder."

Filing with Netscape

To save a message by using Netscape's mailer, select the message and choose <u>M</u>essage⇨<u>M</u>ove from the menu. Then choose the folder name from the list that appears. To make a new folder, choose <u>F</u>ile⇨<u>N</u>ew Folder from the menu.

Filing with Pine

To save a message in a folder, press **s** when you are looking at the message or when it's highlighted in your list of messages. To create a new folder, tell Pine to save a message to a folder that doesn't exist (yet). Pine asks whether you want to create it — press **y** to do so.

Sending and receiving exotic mail and mail attachments

Sooner or later, just plain, old, everyday e-mail is not going to be good enough for you. Someone's gonna send you a picture you just have to see, or you're gonna want to send something cool to your new best friend in Paris. When we talk about sending stuff other than text through the mail, we're talking about using special file formats and systems that can read them. Sometimes the entire message is in a special format (such as MIME, which we talk about in a couple of sentences), and sometimes people *attach* things to their mail. Attachments come in many flavors; for a complete discussion of file formats and how to read them, see Chapter 18. Meanwhile, we'll tell you about MIME, a convention for including stuff other than plain text in e-mail messages. MIME stands for stands for *m*ultipurpose *i*nternet *m*ail *e*xtensions. Whoopee.

Sound! Pictures! Action!

MIME supports a long list of the kinds of stuff, ranging from slightly formatted text using characters (such as `*emphasis*` for *emphasis*) up through color pictures, full-motion video, and high-fidelity sound. The group that designed

Chain letters: Arrrrrgggghhh!

One of the most obnoxious things you can do with e-mail is to pass around chain letters. Because all mail programs have forwarding commands, with only a few keystrokes you can take a chain letter and send it along to hundreds of other people. Don't do it. Chain letters are cute for about two seconds, and then they're just annoying.

A few chain letters just keep coming around and around, despite our best efforts to stamp them out. Learn to recognize them now and avoid embarrassment later. Here are some of the hangers-on:

The Good Times virus hoax: Somewhere around December 1994, a nasty chain letter appeared on America Online (AOL) disguised as a warning that a horrible computer virus capable of erasing your hard disk was being spread by e-mail. The virus allegedly arrived in e-mail bearing the words "Good Times." The chain letter, not the virus, spread rapidly throughout the Internet and major corporations and on bulletin boards and Usenet groups. Well-intentioned individuals quickly sent it to everyone they knew. Computer viruses are spread though infected programs that, after they are run, can have malicious affects. E-mail is essentially text — not a program — that in and of itself cannot cause damage to your disk.

Dying boy wants greeting cards: (Sometimes it's business cards.) Not anymore, he doesn't. Several years ago, an English boy named Craig Shergold was hospitalized with what was thought to be an inoperable brain tumor. Craig wanted to set the world record for most greeting cards. Word got out, and Craig received millions and millions of cards and eventually got into the *Guinness Book of World Records.* When it turned out that maybe the tumor wasn't inoperable, U.S. TV billionaire John Kluge paid for Craig to fly to the United States for an operation, which was successful. So Craig is OK now and definitely doesn't want any more cards. (You can read all about this story on page 24 of the July 29, 1990, edition of the *New York Times.*) Guinness is so sick and tired of the whole business that it closed the category — no more records for the most cards are accepted. If you want to help dying children, give the two dollars that a card and stamp would have cost to a children's welfare organization, such as UNICEF.

The modem-tax rumor: In 1987 the Federal Communications Commission (FCC) briefly floated a proposal for a technical change to the rules governing the way on-line services, such as CompuServe and AOL, are billed for their phone connections. Implementing the proposal would have had the effect of raising the prices these services charge. Customers of on-line services made their opposition clear immediately and loudly, members of Congress made concerned inquiries, and the proposal was dropped — permanently. Undated alarmist notices about the proposal unfortunately have circulated around bulletin boards ever since. If you see yet another modem-tax scare, demand the FCC's current docket number because the FCC — as a government bureaucracy — can't blow its nose without making announcements, accepting comments, and so on. So no docket means no action, which means that it's the same old rumor you should ignore.

Make big bucks with a chain letter: These letters usually have the subject MAKE.MONEY.FAST, are signed by "Dave Rhodes," contain lots of testimonials from people who are now rolling in dough, and tell you to send $5 or so to the name at the top of the list, put your name at the bottom, and send the message to a zillion other suckers. Some even say "This isn't a chain letter" (you're supposedly helping to compile a mailing list or something — your 100 percent guaranteed tip-off that it's a chain letter). Don't even think about it. These chain letters are extremely illegal, and, besides, they don't even work. (Why send any money? Why not just add your name and send it on?) Think of them as gullibility viruses. Just ignore them, or perhaps send a polite note to the sender's postmaster to encourage her to tell users not to send any more chain letters.

The "two-fifty" cookie recipe: According to this one, someone was eating chocolate-chip cookies somewhere (Mrs. Fields and Neiman-Marcus are frequently cited) and asked whether she (it was always a she) could have the recipe. "Sure," came the answer, "that'll be two-fifty, charged to your credit card." "OK." When the credit-card statement came, it turned out to be 250 *dollars,* not two dollars and fifty cents. So in retribution the message concludes with the putative Mrs. Fields or Neiman-Marcus recipe, sent to you for free. The story is pure hooey: Mrs. Fields' recipes are in her cookbook; and Neiman's doesn't give theirs out. The recipe, which varies somewhat from one version to the next, makes perfectly OK cookies, but we don't think that it's any better than the one on the back of the bag of chips. This same story, by the way, circulated hand-to-hand in the 1940s and 1950s, except that the recipe was for a red-velvet cake served at the restaurant at one of the big New York department stores. It wasn't true then either.

MIME had enough sense to realize that not everyone has a computer that can handle all the fancy high-end stuff, so a single MIME message can contain alternative forms of the same thing, such as beautifully formatted, typeset text for people with fancy video screens and plain text for people on simple terminals. Because MIME also handles nested messages, a single MIME message might contain a document and a couple of illustrations that go with it.

MIME is supposed to be a *four-wheel-drive mail system,* which means that MIME messages can be delivered over all sorts of hostile and unhelpful mail links. They do this by disguising the MIME contents as plain old text. (At least it looks like text to the computer. To us it looks more like `QW&IIdfhfFX97/$@.`) You can recognize a MIME message by looking for special mail headers that look something like this:

```
MIME-version: 1.0
Content-type: TEXT/PLAIN; CHARSET=US-ASCII
Content-transfer-encoding: 7BIT
```

The first line says that the message is using Version 1.0 of the MIME standard (the only version defined so far). The second line says that this particular message contains plain, old text. The third line says that the text is represented in the message as — get this — text. (Computers are so dim that even this isn't obvious to them.) Different kinds of messages use different Content-type headers. At this point, they all use the same Content-transfer-encoding.

- ✔ If you're using a mail program that is *MIME-compliant*, as the jargon goes, you know that you have a MIME message because, as you're reading your mail, a window pops up all of a sudden with a picture or formatted text or perhaps your computer begins singing the message to you (and you thought that singing telegrams were a thing of the past). Eudora and Pine are MIME-compliant. America Online can send and receive MIME mail, but the other commercial on-line services are still working on it as of the end of 1995.

- ✔ If your mail program doesn't know about MIME and you get a MIME-ized message, it shows up as a large message in your mailbox. If it contains text, about half the kinds of tarted-up text are readable as is, give or take some ugly punctuation. The sound and pictures, on the other hand, are totally hopeless because they are just binary digitized versions of the images and not any sort of text approximation.

- ✔ If you get a picture or sound MIME message and your mailer doesn't automatically handle it, clunky but usable methods may exist for saving the message to a file and extracting the contents with separate programs. Consult your Internet service provider's help desk.

Getting attached

To send things such as pictures, programs, and movies (*yes*, movies) by using electronic mail, you often send or receive them as attachments. The e-mail comes, sort of like a cover letter with a package. You have to unwrap the attachment separately. You may or may not have the software you need in order to read the package you receive, but Chapter 18 tells you how to tell what you're looking at and what your likely next step is toward making it comprehensible.

Eudora attachments

To send attachments with Eudora, choose Message⇨Attach Document menu, or click the Attach icon (a disk in front of a folder) or press Ctrl+H. Eudora helps you choose the document you want to attach. The word "document" is used loosely here — Eudora means any old file you choose to attach.

If you drag a file from the Windows File Manager to Eudora, she attaches it to the message you're writing. If you're not writing a message, she starts one for you.

When Eudora receives mail with attachments, she automatically saves them to your disk and tells you where they are and what they're called.

Netscape attachments

In Netscape you click the Attach button to send an attachment. Unlike most other mail programs, Netscape lets you attach any file or document you can describe with a *URL* (*Uniform Resource Locator,* the naming scheme used on the Web; see Chapter 4). It gives you your choice of attaching a document, by default the last message or page you were looking at, or attaching a file — click Document or File. If you attach a file, you can click the Browse button to choose the file to attach. When you've decided what to attach, click OK to attach the file to the outgoing message.

For incoming mail, Netscape displays any attachments that it knows how to display itself (Web pages, GIF, and JPG image files). For other kinds of attachments, Netscape displays a little description of the file, which you can click. At this point Netscape runs an appropriate display program, if it knows of one, or asks you whether to save the attachment to a file or to configure a display program in order to display the attachment.

Pine attachments

To attach stuff with Pine, enter the filenames of what you want to attach, separated by commas. When you press Enter after you've entered your attachments, Pine goes and gets the file. If Pine can't find the file, it enters the file in your list of attachments anyway but tells you that it can't find it, so pay careful attention.

When Pine reads a message with attachments, it tells you which attachments you have and displays them if they're in a format that it comprehends. Generally what happens is that you save them with a filename of your choosing and then read them with other software. (Chapter 18 has info about just what kind of file you might have received.)

Hey, Mr. Robot

Not every mail address has an actual person behind it. Some are mailing lists (which we talk about in Chapter 8), and some are *robots*. Mail robots have become popular as a way to query databases and retrieve files because it's much easier to set up a connection for electronic mail than it is to set up one that handles the more standard file transfer. You send a message to the robot (usually referred to as a *mail server*), it takes some action based on the contents of your message, and it sends back a response. If you send a message to `ninternet@dummies.com`, for example, you get back a response telling you your e-mail address.

The most common use for mail servers is to put yourself on and off mailing lists, which we explore in gruesome detail in Chapter 8. They're also used to retrieve files from FTP file archive sites (see Chapter 10 for details). Companies use them to send back canned responses to requests for information sent to info@whatever.com.

Your Own, Personal Mail Manager

After you begin sending e-mail, you probably will begin to receive quite a bit of it, particularly if you put yourself on some mailing lists (see Chapter 8). Your incoming mail soon becomes a trickle, then a stream, then a torrent, and pretty soon you can't walk past your keyboard without getting soaking wet, metaphorically speaking.

Fortunately, most mail systems provide ways for you to manage the flow and avoid ruining your clothes (enough of this metaphor already). If most of your messages come from mailing lists, you should check to see whether the lists are available instead as *Usenet* newsgroups (see Chapter 9). Usenet newsreading programs generally enable you to look through the messages and find the interesting ones much quicker than your mail program does and to sort the messages automatically so that you can quickly read or ignore an entire *thread* (conversation) of messages about a particular topic. Your system manager can usually arrange to make particularly chatty mailing lists look like Usenet newsgroups. At our site, we handle about 40 mailing lists that way.

On Macs and PCs, Eudora users can create *filters* that can automatically check incoming messages against a list of senders and subjects and file them in appropriate folders. Other mail programs have similar filtering features.

All this automatic-sorting nonsense may seem like overkill, and if you get only five or ten messages a day, it is. But after the mail really gets flowing, you find that dealing with your mail is taking much more of your time than it used to. So keep those automated tools in mind — if not for now, then for later. *Internet SECRETS* (IDG Books Worldwide, 1995, and aren't you getting tired of us plugging our other books?) includes ways to filter your mail and even tells you how to create your own automatic mail responder.

Chapter 8

Mail, Mail, the Gang's All Here

. . . .

In This Chapter

▶ Mailing lists

▶ Getting more or less junk mail

▶ A few interesting mailing lists

▶ Mail servers

. . . .

Are You Sure That This Isn't Junk Mail?

Now that you know all about how to send and receive mail, only one thing stands between you and a rich, fulfilling, mail-blessed life: You don't know many people with whom you can exchange mail. Fortunately, you can get yourself on lots of mailing lists, which ensures that you arrive every morning to a mailbox with 400 new messages. (Maybe you should start out with one or two lists.)

The point of a mailing list is simple. The list has its own special e-mail address, and anything that someone sends to that address is sent to all the people on the list. Because they in turn often respond to the messages, the result is a running conversation.

Different lists have different styles. Some are relatively formal, hewing closely to the official topic of the list. Others tend to go flying off into outer space topicwise. You have to read them for a while to be able to tell which list works which way.

Usenet newsgroups are another way to have running e-mail-like conversations, and the distinction between the two is blurry. (Because some topics are available both as mailing lists and on Usenet, people with and without access to news can participate.) Chapter 9 discusses Usenet.

Getting on and off Mailing Lists

The way you get on or off a mailing list is simple: You send a mail message. Two general schools of mailing-list management exist: the *manual* and the *automatic*. Manual management is the more traditional way: Your message is read by a human being who updates the files to put people on or take them off the list. The advantage of manual management is that you get personal service; the disadvantage is that the list maintainer may not get around to servicing you for quite a while if more pressing business (such as her real job) intervenes.

These days it's more common to have lists maintained automatically, which saves human attention for times when things are fouled up. The most widely used automatic mailing managers are families of programs known as LISTSERV, Majordomo, and Listproc, which get their own sections later in this chapter.

For the manual lists, there is a widely observed convention regarding list and maintainer addresses. Suppose that you want to join a list for fans of James Buchanan (the 15th President of the United States, the only one who never married, in case you slept through that part of history class), and the list's name is buchanan-lovers@dummies.com. The manager's address is almost certainly buchanan-lovers-request@dummies.com. In other words, just add -request to the list's address to get the manager's address. Because the list is maintained by hand, your request to be added or dropped doesn't have to take any particular form, as long as it's polite. Please add me to the buchanan-lovers list does quite well. When you decide that you have had all the Buchanan you can stand, another message saying Please remove me from the buchanan-lovers list does equally well.

Messages to -request addresses are read and handled by human beings who sometimes eat, sleep, and work regular jobs as well as maintain mailing lists. Therefore, they don't necessarily read your request the moment it arrives. It can take a day or so to be added to or removed from a list, and after you ask to be removed you usually get a few more messages before they remove you. If it takes longer than you want, be patient. And *don't* send cranky follow-ups — they just cheese off the list maintainer.

LISTSERV, the studly computer's mail manager

The BITNET network (a network of large computers, now mostly merged into the Internet) was set up so that the only thing it could do was ship files and messages from one system to another. As a result, BITNET users quickly developed lots and lots of mailing lists because no other convenient way — such as Usenet news — was available to stay in touch.

How to avoid looking like an idiot

Here's a handy tip: After you subscribe to a list, don't send anything to it until you've been reading it for a week. Trust us — it has been getting along without your insights since it began, and it can get along without them for one more week.

This method gives you a chance to learn the sorts of topics that people really discuss, the tone of the list, and so on. It also gives you a fair idea about which topics people are tired of. The classic newcomer gaffe is to subscribe to a list and immediately send a message asking a dumb question that isn't really germane to the topic and that was beaten to death three days earlier. Bide your time, and don't let this happen to you.

The number-two newcomer gaffe is to send a message directly to the list asking to subscribe or unsubscribe. This type of message should go to a request or LISTSERV, Majordomo, or Listproc address, where the list maintainer (human or robotic) can handle it, *not* to the list itself, where all the other subscribers can see that you screwed up.

To summarize: The first message you send, to join a list, should go to a `something-request` or `LISTSERV` or `majordomo` or `listproc` address, *not* to the list itself. After you've joined the list, *then* you can send messages to the list.

Because maintaining all those mailing lists was (and still is) a great deal of work, in order to manage the mailing lists the BITNET crowd came up with a program called *LISTSERV,* which originally ran on great big IBM mainframe computers. (The IBM mainframe types have an inordinate fondness for eight-letter uppercase names EVEN THOUGH TO MOST OF US IT SEEMS LIKE SHOUTING.) Originally, only users on machines directly connected to BITNET could use LISTSERV, but current versions have been improved so that anyone with an Internet address can use them. Indeed, LISTSERV has grown to the point where it is an all-singing, all-dancing mailing-list program with about 15 zillion features and options, almost none of which you care about.

LISTSERV is a little klunky to use, but it has the great advantage of being able to easily handle enormous mailing lists that contain thousands of members, something that makes the regular Internet mail programs choke. (LISTSERV can send mail to 1,000 addresses in about five minutes, for example, whereas that would take the regular Internet `sendmail` program more than an hour.)

You put yourself on and off a LISTSERV mailing list by sending mail to `LISTSERV@some.machine.or.other`, where `some.machine.or.other` is the name of the particular machine on which the mailing list lives. Because LISTSERV list managers are computer programs, they're pretty simpleminded, so you have to speak to them clearly and distinctly.

Urrp! Computers digest messages!

Some mailing lists are *digested*. No, they're not dripping with digital gastric juices — they're digested more in the sense of *Reader's Digest*. All the messages over a particular period (usually a day or two) are gathered into one big message with a table of contents added at the front. Many people find this method more convenient than getting messages separately because you can easily look at all the messages on the topic at one time.

Some mail and newsreading programs give you the option of dividing digests back into the individual messages so that you can see them one at a time yet still grouped together. This option is sometimes known as *undigestifying*, or *exploding*, a digest. (First it's digested, and then it explodes, sort of like a burrito.) Check the specifics of your particular mail program to see whether it has an option for digest-exploding.

Suppose that you want to join a list called SNUFLE-L (LISTSERV mailing lists usually end with -L), which lives at bluesuede.org. To join, send to LISTSERV@bluesuede.org a message that contains this line:

```
SUB SNUFLE-L Roger Sherman
```

You don't have to add a subject line or anything else to this message. SUB is short for subscribe, SNUFLE-L is the name of the list, and anything after that is supposed to be your real name. (You can put whatever you want there, but keep in mind that it will show up in the return address of anything you send to the list.) Shortly afterward, you should get two messages back:

✔ A chatty, machine-generated welcoming message, telling you that you've joined the list, along with a description of some commands you can use to fiddle with your mailing-list membership. Sometimes this message includes a request to confirm that you got this message. Follow the instructions by replying to this message with the single word *OK* in the body of the message. This helps lists ensure that they aren't mailing into the void. If you don't provide this confirmation, you don't get on the list.

✔ An incredibly boring message, telling you that the IBM mainframe ran a program to handle your request and reporting the exact number of milliseconds of computer time and number of disk operations the request took. Whoopee. (It's sobering to think that somewhere there are people who find these messages interesting.)

Keep the chatty, informative message that tells you about all the commands you can use when you're dealing with the list. For one thing, it tells you how to get *off* the mailing list if it's not to your liking. We have a folder called Mailing Lists in our mail program, in which we store the welcome messages from all the mailing lists we join.

After you've subscribed, to send a message to this list, mail to the list name at the same machine — in this case, SNUFLE-L@bluesuede.org. Be sure to provide a descriptive Subject: for the multitudes who will benefit from your pearls of wisdom. Within a matter of minutes, people from all over the world will read your message.

To get off a list, you again write to LISTSERV@some.machine.or.other, this time sending

```
SIGNOFF SNUFLE-L
```

or whatever the list's name is. You don't have to give your name again because after you're off the list LISTSERV has no more interest in you and completely forgets that you ever existed.

Some lists are more difficult to get on and off than others. Usually you ask to get on a list, and you're on the list. In some cases, however, the list isn't open to all comers, and the human list owner screens requests to join the list, in which case you may get some messages from the list owner to discuss your request to join.

To contact the actual human being who runs a particular list, the mail address is OWNER- followed by the list name (OWNER-SNUFLE-L, for example). The owner can do all sorts of things to lists that mere mortals can't do. In particular, the owner can fix screwed-up names on the list or add a name that, for some reason, the automatic method doesn't handle. You have to appeal for manual intervention if your mail system doesn't put your correct network mail address on the From: line of your messages, as sometimes happens when your local mail system isn't set up quite right.

Stupid LISTSERV tricks

The people who maintain the LISTSERV program have added so many bells and whistles to it that it would take an entire book to describe them all and, frankly, they're not that interesting. But here are some stupid LISTSERV tricks. For each of them, you send a message to LISTSERV@some.machine.or.other to talk to the LISTSERV program. You can send several commands in the same message if you want to do two or three tricks at one time.

✔ **Temporarily stop mail:** Sometimes you're going to be away for a week or two and you don't want to get a bunch of mailing-list mail in the meantime. But because you're planning to come back, you don't want to take yourself off all the lists, either. To stop mail temporarily from the SNUFLE-L mailing list, send

```
SET SNUFLE-L NOMAIL
```

and it will stop sending you messages. To turn the mail back on, send this message:

```
SET SNUFLE-L MAIL
```

✔ **Get messages as a digest:** If you're getting a large number of messages from a list and would rather get them all at one time as a daily digest, send this message:

```
SET SNUFLE-L DIGEST
```

Not all lists can be digested (again, think of burritos), but the indigestible ones let you know and don't take offense.

✔ **Find out who's on a list:** To find out who subscribes to a list, send this message:

```
REVIEW SNUFLE-L
```

Some lists can be reviewed only by people on the list, and others not at all. Some lists are enormous, so be prepared to get back an enormous message listing thousands of subscribers.

✔ **Get or not get your own mail:** When you send mail to a LISTSERV list of which you're a member, it usually sends you a copy of your own message to confirm that it got there OK. Some people find this process needlessly redundant. ("Your message has been sent. You'll be receiving it shortly." Huh?) To avoid getting copies of your own messages, send this message:

```
SET SNUFLE-L NOACK
```

To resume getting copies of your own messages, send this one:

```
SET SNUFLE-L ACK
```

✔ **Get files:** Most LISTSERV servers have a library of files available, usually documents contributed by the mailing-list members. To find out files which are available, send:

```
INDEX
```

✔ To have LISTSERV send you a particular file by e-mail, send this message:

```
GET fname
```

where *fname* is the name of a file from the INDEX command. On IBM systems, files have two-part names separated by a space (for example, GET SNUFLE-L MEMO).

✔ **Find out which lists are available:** To find out which LISTSERV mailing lists are available on a particular host, send this message:

```
LIST
```

Note: Keep in mind that just because a list exists doesn't necessarily mean that you can subscribe to it. But it doesn't hurt to try.

✔ **Get LISTSERV to do other things:** Lots of other commands lurk in LISTSERV, most of which apply only to people on IBM mainframes. If you're one of these people or if you're just nosy, send a message containing this line:

```
HELP
```

and you'll receive a helpful response that lists other commands.

An excellent choice, sir

The other widely used mailing-list manager is Brent Chapman's *Majordomo*. It started out as a LISTSERV wannabe for workstations but has evolved into a system that works quite well. Because of its wannabe origins, Majordomo commands are almost but (pretend to be surprised now) not quite the same as their LISTSERV equivalents.

The mailing address for Majordomo commands, as you might expect, is majordomo@some.machine.or.other. Majordomo lists tend to have long and expressive names. One of our favorites is called explosive-cargo, a very funny weekly column written by a guy in Boston who in real life is a computer technical writer. To subscribe, because the list is maintained on host world.std.com, send the following message to Majordomo@world.std.com:

```
subscribe explosive-cargo
```

Note: Unlike with LISTSERV, you *don't* put your real name in the subscribe command.

To unsubscribe:

```
unsubscribe explosive-cargo
```

After you have subscribed, you can send a message to everyone on the mailing list by addressing it to listname@some.machine.or.other. (You can't post messages to explosive-cargo because it's a list only for announcements; that is, only the guy in Boston who runs it is allowed to post messages.)

Stupid Majordomo tricks

Not to be outdone by LISTSERV, Majordomo has its own set of not particularly useful commands (as with LISTSERV, you can send as many of these as you want in a single message):

✔ To find out which lists at a Majordomo system you're subscribed to:

```
which
```

✔ To find all the lists managed by a Majordomo system:

```
lists
```

✔ Majordomo also can keep files related to its lists. To find the names of the files for a particular list:

```
index name-of-list
```

✔ To tell Majordomo to send you one of the files by e-mail:

```
get name-of-list name-of-file
```

✔ To find out the rest of the goofy things Majordomo can do:

```
help
```

✔ If you need to contact the human manager of a Majordomo system because you can't get off a list you want to leave or otherwise have an insoluble problem, send a polite message to `owner majordomo@ hostname`. Remember that because humans eat, sleep, and have real jobs, it may take a day or two to get an answer.

Listproc: Third-place list manager

Listproc is not as widely used as LISTSERV and Majordomo, but it is increasing in popularity because it is easier to install than LISTSERV, cheaper, and almost as powerful.

To subscribe to a Listproc mailing list, you send the message

```
subscribe listname yourname
```

to `listproc@some-computer`. To subscribe to the (hypothetical) `chickens` mailing list on `dummies.com`, for example, you send the message

```
subscribe chickens George Washington
```

to listproc@dummies.com (assuming that you were named after the same person that the first President of the United States was).

To get off the mailing list, send the message

```
signoff listname
```

to the same address. You don't have to provide your name — the Listproc program should already know it!

After you have subscribed to the list, you can send messages to everyone on the list by addressing e-mail to listname@some-computer; for example, chickens@dummies.com (don't try it — there's no such mailing list!).

To find out other things Listproc can do, send the message *help* to listproc@whatever, where *whatever* is the name of the computer on which the Listproc mailing list lives.

Sending messages to mailing lists

OK, you're signed up on a mailing list. Now what? First, as we said a few pages back, wait a week or so to see what sort of messages arrive from the list — that way, you can get an idea of what you should or should not send to it. When you think that you've seen enough to avoid embarrassing yourself, try sending something in. That's easy — you mail a message to the mailing list. The list's address is the same as the name of the list: buchanan-lovers@dummies.com or snufle-l@bluesuede.org or whatever. Keep in mind that hundreds or thousands of people will be reading your pearls of wisdom, so try at least to spell things correctly. (You may have thought that this was obvious, but you would be sadly mistaken.) On popular lists, you may begin to get back responses within a few minutes of sending a message.

WARNING!

LISTSERV, Listproc, and Majordomo: They could have made it the same, but n-o-o-o-o

Because LISTSERV, Listproc, and Majordomo work sort of in the same way, even experienced mailing-list mavens get their commands confused. Here are the important differences:

✔ The address for LISTSERV is LISTSERV @hostname, the address for Majordomo is majordomo@hostname, and the

address for Listproc is listproc @hostname.

✔ To subscribe to a LISTSERV or Listproc list, send subscribe followed by the list name followed by your real name. To subscribe to a Majordomo list, just send subscribe and the list name.

Some lists encourage new subscribers to send in a message introducing themselves and saying briefly what their interests are. Others don't. So don't send anything until you have something to say.

After you watch the flow of messages on a list for a while, all this becomes obvious.

Some mailing lists have rules about who is allowed to send messages, meaning that just because you're on the list doesn't automatically mean that any messages you send will appear on the list. Some lists are *moderated:* Any message you send in gets sent to a human *moderator,* who decides what goes to the list and what doesn't. This may sound sort of fascist, but in practice the arrangement makes a list about 50 times more interesting than it would be otherwise because a good moderator can filter out the boring and irrelevant messages and keep the list on track. Indeed, the people who complain the loudest about moderator censorship are usually the ones whose messages most deserve to be filtered out.

Another rule that sometimes causes trouble is that many lists allow messages to be sent only from people whose addresses appear on the list. This rule becomes a pain if your mailing address changes. Suppose that you get a well-organized new mail administrator and that your official e-mail address changes from `jj@shamu.pol.bluesuede.org` to `John.Jay@bluesuede.org`, although your old address still works. You may find that some lists begin *bouncing* your messages (sending them back to you rather than to the list) because they don't understand that `John.Jay@bluesuede.org`, the name under which you now send messages, is the same as `jj@shamu.pol.bluesuede.org`, the name under which you originally subscribed to the list. Worse, LISTSERV doesn't let you take yourself off the list, for the same reason. To resolve this mess, you have to write to the human list owners of any lists in which this problem occurs and ask them to fix the problem by hand.

Boing!

Computer accounts are created and deleted often enough and mail addresses change often enough that, at any given moment, a large list always contains some addresses that are no longer valid. So if you send a message to the list, your message is forwarded to these invalid addresses, and a return message reporting the bad addresses is generated for each of them. Normally, mailing-list managers (both human and computer) try to deflect the error messages so that they go to the list owner, who can do something about them, rather than to you. But as often as not a persistently dumb mail system sends one of these failure messages directly to you. Just ignore it because there isn't anything you can do about it.

TIP

Mailing lists versus Usenet news

Many mailing lists are "gatewayed" to Usenet newsgroups (see Chapter 9), which means that all the messages you would receive if you subscribed to the mailing list appear as items in the newsgroup, and vice versa. Most gateways are two-way: Anything you mail to the list also shows up in the newsgroup, and anything you post as a news item also goes to the list. A few are one-way, usually because of sloppy gateway management, and many of them are moderated, which means that you have to mail any items to the human moderator, who filters out inappropriate messages.

Whether you get a particular list as mail or news is largely a matter of personal taste. The advantages of receiving lists as mail are that mail items tend to arrive faster than news items do (usually

by only a few hours); mail items stick around until you explicitly delete them whereas news is deleted automatically after a few days; and s ome mail programs are more flexible than the newsreading programs. The advantages of receiving lists as news are that items are collected in a newsgroup rather than mixed in with your mail; items are automatically deleted unless you save them, avoiding mailbox bloat if you don't read and clean up your mail every day; and news programs usually do a better job than mail programs of collecting threads of related messages so that you can read them in order.

If you don't care which way you get your stuff, get it as news because the load on both your local computer and the network in general is considerably lower that way.

The Fine Points of Replying to Mailing-List Messages

Often you receive an interesting message from a list and want to respond to it. But when you send your answer, does it go *just* to the person who sent the original message, or does it go to the *entire list?* It depends, mostly on how the list owner set up the software that handles the list. About half the list owners set it up so that replies go automatically just to the person who sent the original message, on the theory that your response is likely to be of interest only to the original author. The other half set it up so that replies go to the entire list, on the theory that the list is a running public discussion. In messages coming from the list, the mailing-list software automatically sets the Reply-To: header line to the address where replies should be sent.

Fortunately, you're in charge. When you start to create a reply, your mail program should show you the address it's replying to. If you don't like the address it's using, change it. Check the To: and Cc: fields to make sure that you're sending your message where you want.

While you're fixing the recipient's address, you may also want to fix the `Subject:` line. After a few rounds of replies to replies to replies, the topic of discussion often wanders away from the original topic, and it's nice to change the subject to better describe what's really under discussion.

Some Interesting Lists

A large number of lists reside on the Internet — so many, in fact, that entire *books* have been written that just enumerate all the *lists.* To get you started, here are a bunch of lists we find interesting in addition to short descriptions of what they are. Each is accompanied by at least one of the following codes, describing what kind of list it is:

- ✔ **Internet:** Internet-type list. To get on or off or to contact the human who maintains the list, write to `whatever-request@sitename`. In the text of your e-mail, state what you want. A human being handles these requests.

- ✔ **LISTSERV:** BITNET LISTSERV-type list. To get on or off, send e-mail to `listserv@sitename`. In the body of the e-mail, use the LISTSERV commands detailed earlier in this chapter. For example:

```
sub LISTNAME Your Name
signoff LISTNAME
```

  To contact the relevant human, send mail to `owner-whatever@sitename`.

- ✔ **Majordomo:** A Majordomo list. To get on or off, send a "subscribe" or "unsubscribe" message to `Majordomo@sitename` asking to subscribe to the list name we give. For example:

```
sub listname
unsubscribe listname
```

- ✔ **Moderated:** Moderated list. Messages are filtered by the human list owner (moderator).

- ✔ **News:** List is also available as Usenet news, which is usually the better way to receive it (see the preceding sidebar, "Mailing lists versus Usenet news." Nearly all BITNET lists are also available as a special kind of newsgroup, but this list marks only lists available as regular news.

- ✔ **Digest:** Messages normally arrive as a digest rather than one at a time.

(None of the mailing lists is a Listproc list, so there's no code for it.)

Telecom Digest
telecom-request@eecs.nwu.edu
Internet, Moderated, News, Digest

Discussions of telephones ranging from the technical to the totally silly, such as what the official telephone song should be. This heavily moderated, high-volume list has the only full-time moderator on the Net, supported by grants from Microsoft, the International Telecommunications Union in Switzerland, and the occasional generous reader.

Risks Digest
Majordomo@csl.sri.com
Majordomo (list name risks) Moderated, News, Digest

This forum discusses risks to the public in computers and related systems. It covers the risks of modern technology, particularly of computer technology (lots of great war stories).

Weather Talk
LISTSERV@vmd.cso.uiuc.edu
LISTSERV (list names below) Moderated

Weather Talk talks about relatively technical weather discussions. If you join WX-TALK, that's the discussion list. Several announcement-only lists send out National Weather Service forecasts and reports. WX-NATNL contains nationwide forecasts delivered twice daily, which is probably more weather than you want in your mailbox unless you have some way to sort it out and discard it automatically after a day or two. Other Weather Service bulletins are shown in this list:

- ✔ **WX-SWO:** For severe-weather warnings in nearly incomprehensible weather shorthand
- ✔ **WX-WATCH:** For tornado and thunderstorm watches, also in shorthand
- ✔ **WX-WSTAT:** For other weather watches in shorthand
- ✔ **WX-TROPL:** For daily (or more frequently during the height of the season) tropical storm and hurricane outlooks
- ✔ **WX-PCPN:** For heavy rain and snow reports
- ✔ **WX-SUM:** For the national weather summary
- ✔ **WX-STLT:** For satellite observations
- ✔ **WX-LSR:** For local storm reports
- ✔ **WX-MISC:** For other weather bureau reports

Subscribe to them all, and your mailbox will fill so fast that your head will swim.

Privacy Forum Digest
LISTSERV@vortex.com
LISTSERV (list name PRIVACY), Moderated

This running discussion of privacy in the computer age has lots of creepy reports about people and organizations you would never expect were snooping on you (ambulance drivers, for example).

Tourism Discussions
LISTSERV@trearn.bitnet
LISTSERV (list name TRAVEL-L)

The TRAVEL-L list covers travel and tourism, airlines, guidebooks, places to stay — you name it. Because participants come from all over the world (the system host is in France), you get lots of tips you would never get locally.

Computer Professionals for Social Responsibility
LISTSERV@gwuvm.bitnet
LISTSERV (list name CPSR)

CPSR is an organization of computer people interested in the social effects of computing. This list contains mostly reports about CPSR activities.

The Jazz Lover's List
LISTSERV@vm.temple.edu
LISTSERV (list name JAZZ-L)

This friendly, laid-back ongoing discussion makes no claim to staying "on-topic" but instead to creating a salon-type atmosphere in which "like-minded intelligent people from diverse backgrounds" can make real connections.

Tall Ships
LISTSERV@vccscent.bitnet
LISTSERV (list name TALLSHIP)

The discussion in this list is all about sailing and operating traditional sailing vessels.

Liberal Judaism
liberal-judaism@shamash.nysernet.org
Internet, Moderated, Digest

Nonjudgmental discussions of liberal Judaism (Reform, Reconstructionist, conservative, secular humanist, and so on), issues, practices, opinions, and beliefs take place here. Include your real name in your request.

Offroad Enthusiasts
offroad-request@ai.gtri.gatech.edu
Internet, Digest

The Offroad list is partly about off-road driving and mostly about four-wheel-drive vehicles. It's full of fun-lovers. Be sure to include a signature or some other copy of your mailing address.

Subscribing to BITNET lists

Several lists have BITNET addresses, such as LISTSERV@gwuvm.bitnet. It turns out that these aren't valid Internet addresses, although most Internet systems know how to send mail to them anyway.

If your system doesn't grok BITNET addresses, fool it this way:

LISTSERV%gwuvm.bitnet@cunyvm.cuny.edu

That is, change the original at-sign (@) to a percent (%) and add @cunyvm.cuny.edu at the end. This line tells your system to forward your message to a system (CUNYVM at the City University of New York) that is well-connected to BITNET and sends it on for you.

Finding Other Mailing Lists

Thousands of mailing lists exist. It's difficult to keep score. We included a disk full of mailing lists in our book *Internet Secrets* (IDG Books Worldwide, 1995). (The disk can be read by DOS, Windows, and any Macintosh that can read a PC disk — most can these days.)

The Usenet group news.lists also has an extensive monthly list of mailing lists. If you get Usenet news, you can probably find this list there (see Chapter 9). Or you can get it by mail by sending the following cryptic message to mail-server@rtfm.mit.edu:

```
send USENET/news.lists/P_A_M_L,_P_1_17
send USENET/news.lists/P_A_M_L,_P_2_17
```

(That last weird part stands for *p*ublicly *a*ccessible *m*ailing *l*ists, Part 1 of 17, and so on. If you like what you see, you can get the rest of the parts in the same way.) FTP users can FTP the list from rtfm.mit.edu, where it's in the directory pub/USENET/news.lists under the same names, or read it in Usenet, where it's posted monthly to the newsgroup news.lists. The lists are growing fast, so by the time you read this, there may be more than 17 parts. (See Chapter 10 to learn how to get the list by using FTP.)

Part III
The Rest of the Net

The 5th Wave   **By Rich Tennant**

"Awww jeez- I was afraid of this. Some poor kid, bored with the usual chat lines, starts looking for bigger kicks, pretty soon they're surfin' the seedy back alleys of cyberspace, and before you know it they're into a file they can't 'undo'. I guess that's why they call it the Web. Somebody open a window!"

In this part . . .

There's much more to see and do on the Net. In this section, we look at many of the other services the Net has to offer, including Gopher and FTP.

Chapter 9

All the News That Fits and Considerably More

Whose News Do You Use?

There's news, and then there's *Usenet news*. For more than 15 years a gigantic, ever-growing, all-encompassing bulletin board has been insinuating itself into computers and wrapping itself around the globe. *Usenet* (also referred to as *Net news,* the name of the system that manages and transports its messages) consists of *articles* created by and posted by ordinary people, or *users*. Articles bear a striking similarity to e-mail messages, and often programs that read news read e-mail too. *Newsgroups*, the name given to the interest groups that comprise Usenet, are not all that different from mailing lists except that the articles aren't distributed to everyone who's interested. Instead, they're posted where those who are interested can read them.

You'll find news you won't find on TV, on the radio, or in a newspaper or magazine. And Usenet news isn't limited to what commercial sponsors know will sell.

Big bags o' news

Mailing lists are an OK way to send messages to a small number of people, but they're a lousy way to send messages to a large number of people. For one thing, just maintaining a big list with thousands of people is a great deal of work for a list manager, even if you automate most of it with something like LISTSERV, which was discussed in Chapter 8. (On a large list, every day a few of the addresses go bad as people move around and system managers reconfigure addresses.) For another thing, just shipping the contents of messages to thousands and thousands of addresses puts a huge load on the system that sends them out.

Usenet solves that problem while creating a host of others. The principle is simple: Every Usenet site ships a copy of all articles it has received to all its neighbors several times a day. (To avoid wasted effort, each article contains a list of sites it has already been sent to.) It's sort of a global game of Whisper Down the Lane, although computers don't scramble the messages at each stage the way people do. Different connections run at different speeds, but for the most part news articles slosh around to all except the most remote parts of Usenet within a day or two. If your host is directly on the Internet rather than connected over the phone, most news arrives within a few hours.

Depending on your Internet provider or commercial on-line account (you were waiting for us to say that, weren't you?), the way you access Usenet newsgroups, and to some extent what news is available to you, varies. If you use a commercial on-line provider, check the chapter for your provider in Part IV for the details of how to read news.

Being a newsgroupie

Every day more than 50,000 articles appear at a typical, well-connected news machine. To make it possible to sort through this mass of stuff, all items are assigned to *newsgroups*, which are topic headings. More than 10,000 newsgroups exist, ranging from the staid and technical (computer data communications, for example) to the totally goofy (urban legends, such as the one about the poodle in the microwave). You have to choose a small number of groups to read and ignore the rest because more news arrives every day than even the late Evelyn Wood could read.

You can easily *subscribe* and *unsubscribe* to any group received by your machine. The details vary depending on your newsreader, but it's much easier than subscribing and unsubscribing from mailing lists. Many people begin reading a group by looking at a few articles and then stop reading it if it looks boring. Depending on how much time you plan to spend reading news, you may add several groups when you're less busy and then drop all except the ones directly related to work when the crunch hits. We suppose theoretically that you could stop reading news altogether, just like you could stop drinking coffee altogether — way too painful to contemplate.

Where did Usenet come from?

North Carolina, originally. In 1980 two students came up with the first version to run on a couple of UNIX machines. Their original version, now known as *A* news, seemed pretty cool because it could transfer as many as a dozen articles a day from one machine to another by using a networking scheme called *UUCP* (*U*NIX-to-*U*NIX *copy*), which is a clunky but reliable dial-up communications program that comes with all UNIX systems. Within a few years Usenet had spread to several other universities and several software companies in a completely rewritten version called *B* news, then transferring as many as a thousand messages a day. Usenet was established enough to be featured in an article in the October 1983 issue of *Byte* magazine, which boasted that more than 500 news sites were in existence. (John can't resist pointing out that his site was called `ima` — you can find it near the upper right corner of the network map on page 224 of the issue.)

Throughout the ensuing decade Usenet has spread like a disease. Now more than 30,000 sites send out news, and probably at least that many more sites just read it. Most of the original dial-up links have been replaced by permanently connected Internet network links using a communications scheme called *NNTP*, for *N*et *n*ews *transfer protocol*. (And you thought that all acronyms were obscure.) A great deal of news is still sent over the telephone by way of UUCP, but an increasing amount of it is sent by way of exotic means, including satellite (using a spare channel that belongs to a national beeper company), CD-ROM, and even magnetic tapes (the tapes are sent to such countries as Malaysia, where long modem phone calls are impractical, and also to such places as the FBI, where internal computer users are prohibited from connecting to outside networks).

The volume of news has increased from a few hundred articles per day in 1983 to upward of 50,000 articles (more than 200MB of text) per day now. And Usenet is still growing.

Some sites still use B news, even though its own authors officially pronounced it dead more than five years ago. Current news systems include *C news,* which is a faster, more maintainable, complete rewrite of B news, and INN, a new version designed to work well in Internet networked environments. Fortunately, because they all function in pretty much the same way, you don't have to worry about which version you're using.

The newsgroup thicket

Newsgroups have multipart names separated by dots, as in `comp.dcom.fax` (a group devoted to fax machines and fax modems). Some providers hide the real names from you in an attempt to be user-friendly. Sometimes they also hide certain groups from you, but if you know the name of the group you're looking for, you usually can get to it.

The plan is that newsgroups are arranged in *hierarchies.* The first part of the name describes the general kind of newsgroup. When a bunch of newsgroups are related, their names are related too. For example, all the newsgroups having to do with data communications are filed as `comp.dcom.something`. Here are the top-level names of the seven *official* Usenet hierarchies distributed to nearly every news site:

- ✔ **comp:** Topics having something to do with computers (lots of fairly meaty discussions)

- ✔ **sci:** Topics having something to do with one of the sciences (also fairly meaty)

- ✔ **rec:** Recreational newsgroups (sports, hobbies, the arts, and other fun endeavors)

- ✔ **soc:** Social newsgroups (both social interests and plain socializing)

- ✔ **news:** Topics having to do with Net news itself (a few groups with introductory material and the occasional important announcement should be read by everyone — otherwise, not very interesting unless you're a news *weenie*)

- ✔ **misc:** Miscellaneous topics that don't fit anywhere else (the ultimate miscellaneous newsgroup is called `misc.misc`)

- ✔ **talk:** Long arguments, frequently political (widely considered to be totally uninteresting except to the participants)

Note: Lots of less widely distributed, or less widely sanctioned, sets of newsgroups are mentioned later in this chapter, primarily the `alt` (*alt*ernative) hierarchy.

Regional groups

All the mainstream groups are, in theory at least, of interest to people regardless of where they live. But many topics are specific to a particular place. Suppose that you live near Boston and you want recommendations of restaurants where you can take small children and not be snarled at. (This topic really came up.) Although some newsgroups in the `rec` hierarchy discuss food, because most readers are likely to be nowhere near Boston, you're likely to get more snappy comments than useful restaurant tips (someone in Texas, for example, may note that if you don't mind driving to Dallas for dinner, you can find one there).

Fortunately, local and regional groups exist for local and regional discussions. An `ne` hierarchy for topics of interest to New England includes such groups as `ne.food`, which is just the place to ask about kiddie restaurants. (The answers, by the way, turned out to be practically any ethnic restaurant and one yuppie place in the suburbs that made a big deal about having an annex featuring hot dogs and babysitters so that Mom and Dad can eat their fancy meal in elegant silence.) State and regional hierarchies exist for most places that have enough Usenet sites to make it worthwhile: ny for New York, ba for the San Francisco Bay Area, and so on.

Universities and other organizations large enough to have a great deal of Net news users often have hierarchies of their own, such as mit for MIT. Many companies have their own local sets of newsgroups for announcements and discussions about company matters. At a software company where one of us used to work, for example, every time someone logged in a change to one of our programs, the description of the change was sent out as a local news item so that everyone else could keep up with what was changing. Naturally, local company groups are sent around only within the company. Ask around to find out what organization or regional newsgroups your system gets, because it's basically up to your system manager to decide what to get.

Enough Already — Let's Read Some News

There are lots and lots of news programs available, for every kind of computer that's attached to the Net. In our examples, we use Free Agent, a widely used Windows news reader because:

- ✔ It's easy to install.
- ✔ It works well.
- ✔ It's free.

Free Agent is the junior version of an inexpensive commercial program called Agent, which does all the same things as Free Agent and more (such as reading e-mail).

Netscape, the famous Web browser we met in Chapters 4 and 5 also can be used as a newsreader. The Netscape newsreader looks a great deal like Free Agent (probably not a coincidence because Free Agent is so good). In Netscape, choose <u>W</u>indow⇨Netscape News to open a news window.

Hey — not everyone uses Windows

Oh, right. For shell provider users, several newsreaders are available. See Chapter 15 for details.

Mac users also have a variety of news-readers, including the classic Nuntius, News-Watcher, and, of course, Netscape.

No matter which newsreader you use, you do the same basic steps (it's all the same news, after all), so the examples here still point the way.

Getting Installed

Free Agent is a blessedly simple program to install. You retrieve it, unpack the files, and run it:

1. **Use FTP to connect to** `ftp.forteinc.com`, **change to directory** `pub/forte/free_agent`, **and download the file fagent10.zip.**

   See Chapter 10 for more details about downloading. If you already have a Web browser available, you can tell it to retrieve the ZIP file at `ftp://ftp.forteinc.com/pub/forte/free_agent/`. (The latest version of the program file is `fagent10.zip`.)

2. **Create on your disk a directory called C:\AGENT.**

   This directory is where the Free Agent software and files will be stored. You can put the Free Agent program anywhere you want as long as it has a directory of its own.

3. **Unzip the downloaded file into the new directory.**

   If you have WinZip (which we describe in Chapter 10), double-click FAGENT10.ZIP in File Manager (or My Computer or Explorer, if you have Windows 95), and then use WinZIP to extract the files into the new directory. If you have the older DOS PKUNZIP, move FAGENT10.ZIP into the new directory, and run PKUNZIP FAGENT10.

4. **Make an icon for Free Agent.**

   In Windows 3.1 the easiest way to do that is to drag the file AGENT.EXE from the File Manager into the Program Manager window where you want it. In Windows 95, choose the filename in My Computer or Explorer, hold down the *right* mouse button, and drag the filename to the desktop or into a folder. An icon appears.

5. Run Free Agent to complete the setup process.

First it displays a terms-and-conditions window. Assuming that you accept the terms, click OK.

6. Enter the info that Free Agent needs to start reading news.

It asks for the name of your NNTP server (the computer at your provider where the news is stored) and the SMTP server (the computer that handles outgoing mail). These names usually are the same; your Internet provider should have given the name (or names) to you. If not, ask for them.

Free Agent also wants your e-mail address and full name so that it can put them in the headers of mail you send while reading news (responses to articles, mostly). Finally, you can set the time zone your computer is in. Then click OK.

If you already have another news program installed, click the bar Use Information from Another Program so that Free Agent can copy the configuration you already have. It even picks up the names of newsgroups to which you've subscribed and which articles you've already seen.

7. Free Agent suggests going on-line and getting the available newsgroups.

Do so. It takes awhile because most providers carry more than 10,000 groups, but you have to do it only once. (It skips this step if it copied subscription info from another program.)

Finally, Some Actual Newsreading

After you've done all the setting up, reading news is relatively easy.

The basic Free Agent screen, shown in Figure 9-1, has three windows. In the upper left corner is a list of newsgroups. In the upper right corner is a list of available articles in a newsgroup. And at the bottom is an article in that group.

Free Agent has a wonderful little row of icons in its toolbar, but it's not easy to guess what they might do. Luckily, you don't have to guess. Position the mouse pointer over an icon for a few seconds *without clicking,* and the name of the icon appears. For example, the leftmost icon (the lightning bolt) turns out to be called Get New Headers in Subscribed Groups. (In this case, a picture is worth six words.)

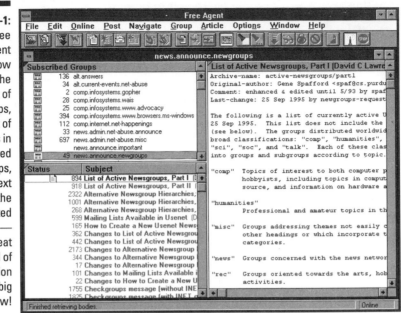

Figure 9-1:
The Free
Agent
window
shows the
list of
newsgroups,
the list of
articles in
selected
newsgroups,
and the text
of the
selected
article —
a great
deal of
information
in one big
window!

First, subscribe

You begin by subscribing to some likely groups, by scrolling through the list of groups. You can zoom it to full screen by clicking in the group list and then pressing **Z**. (Press **Z** again to unzoom.) To subscribe to a group, click that group and then choose Group⇨Subscribe or press Ctrl+S. If you're not sure what to subscribe to, start with news.announce.newusers.

Even though the list is in alphabetical order, finding group names can be difficult. You can use the usual Windows text search (choose Edit⇨Find, press Ctrl+F, or click the flashlight icon) to search for group names.

Second, headers

After you've subscribed to a group or two, you can retrieve some article headers. Click the Get New Headers in Subscribed Groups icon (the leftmost icon on the toolbar, the lightning bolt over three little folders) to retrieve the headers (titles and authors) of articles in the groups in which you're interested.

Third, actual articles

After you've retrieved the headers, whenever you click a newsgroup name the available articles in that group are displayed in the right window. Double-click an article, and it fetches the contents and you can read it. (Wow! At last!)

Articles are grouped into *threads*, or related articles on (theoretically) the same topic. When you're looking at an article in a thread, press **N** to highlight the header for the next article in the thread, or the next thread if that's the last article in this thread, or Ctrl+N to go to the next article in the thread and retrieve it automatically.

Now you can click on groups and articles to find and read the articles in which you're interested.

Off-line reading

Free Agent is set up so that you can read articles off-line (see the following sidebar, "Saving dough: Reading news off-line," for reasons why you would want to do that). The second icon from the right on the toolbar, the one that looks like a radio antenna, is the Go Online/Offline button. It shows whether Free Agent is on-line (connected to the news server) or off-line.

Saving dough: Reading news off-line

If you discover that you're a news junkie (or maybe you already knew it) *and* you're paying an arm and a leg for Net access through a commercial provider, you're a good candidate for an off-line newsreader such as Free Agent. The idea is that you suck down news from your provider at top speed and then hang up and read at your leisure without the meter running.

When you first fire up Free Agent, you can tell it to download a list of the titles of all the new articles in the groups to which you subscribe. Then you can disconnect. Now you can, without hurrying, look at the titles and choose the articles that look interesting. You reconnect, download the contents of those articles, and hang up again. Now you can read the articles, again without having to hurry.

This process sounds like a pain in the neck, but a good news program can make it easy.

Commercial providers vary in whether they support off-line reading. Check your provider's chapter in Part IV for the best strategy for you.

To avoid having to connect and disconnect to your provider manually, set your Internet software to "Dial on Demand" (so that it connects to your provider when Free Agent goes on-line), and set the disconnect time-out to one minute (so that it disconnects a minute after Free Agent goes off-line).

To get the new available articles, connect to your provider, start Free Agent, and click the Get New Headers in Subscribed Groups icon (the leftmost icon on the toolbar). It retrieves all the headers at top speed. Then click the Go Online/ Offline icon (the antenna) to tell Free Agent to go off-line. Your Internet software should hang up soon after.

Next look at the headers as just discussed, but rather than double-click the interesting articles, press **M** to mark them for later retrieval. It marks them with a little downward-pointing arrow, to say that they'll be downloaded.

When you've marked all the articles you want, click the Get Marked Article Bodies icon, the third icon from the left — it's a download arrow with a lightning bolt. Free Agent connects to your provider and downloads just the articles you asked for. As each article is loaded, its download arrow changes to a little sheet of paper to show that the article is present. Then click the Go Online/ Offline icon to go off-line again, and you can go back and read the articles you downloaded.

Honest — It's a Work of Art

Usenet allows exactly one kind of message: plain old text. (A few versions of news handle MIME messages, which were mentioned in Chapter 6, and there are versions for Japanese and Russian characters, but this chapter is confusing enough without worrying about them.) A few widely used conventions exist, though, for sneaking through other kinds of files.

Binary files

Some newsgroups consist partly or entirely of encoded binary files, most often executable programs for IBM PCs, Macs, or other personal computers, or GIF or JPEG bitmap files (see Chapter 18 for details about file formats) of, um, artistic images. (If you must know, the newsgroup with the largest amount of traffic, measured in megabytes per day, is called `alt.binaries.pictures.erotica`, and it contains exactly what it sounds like. It's an equal-opportunity group — it has about the same number of pictures of unclad men as of unclad women.) The usual way to pass around binary files of whatever type is called `uuencode`. You can recognize uuencoded messages because they start with a `begin` line followed by lines of what looks like garbage, as in the following:

```
begin plugh.gif 644
M390GNM4L-REP3PT45G00I-05[I5-6
M3OME,MRMK76OPI5LPTMETLMKPY
MEOT39I4905B05Y0PV3OIXKRTL5KWL
MJROJTOU,6P5;3;MRUO5OI4J5OI4
```

Spam wars

One of the worst innovations in recent Usenet history is *spamming,* which is sending thousands of copies of a message, invariably advertising something you don't want to buy, to thousands of newsgroups. It's a guaranteed way to let millions of people know that you're a jerk. There's even one fellow in New Mexico who styles himself the Spam King and will spam for you for a fee of several hundred dollars. (You provide the Internet account and take the flak when your provider finds out what you've done. He's no fool.) There's also a great deal of spam from commercial providers such as AOL, despite the efforts of the providers to prevent it. (Every day AOL sends out a list of accounts it has canceled for Net abuse.)

Usenet has always had a way to cancel articles, for the benefit of people who have second thoughts about something they've posted and for places that send out updated news articles to replace older ones. So some concerned users (or Net vigilantes, depending on your point of view) wrote *cancelbots,* which automatically send out cancellations for all the messages in a spam. The best-known cancelbot is the CancelMoose, run by an anonymous user who seems to be in Norway, and there are others all over the world. You can read all about who's canceling which spams in the newsgroups news.admin.net-abuse.announce and news.admin.net-abuse.misc.

There are also some e-mail spams, but they're less frequent because they take more work. (Why send e-mail to individuals when you can send news that will be seen by millions?) One of the most peculiar e-mail spams was the "Crusader" spam in mid-1995, which was a virulently racist neo-Nazi diatribe, mailed by an anonymous person who had broken in to and taken over some workstations in France, Germany, and Italy. The message was real to the extent that it was an actual piece written by a group in West Virginia, but it fairly quickly became apparent that the person sending it out wasn't a member of the group. Was he trying to discredit them (as though they needed much discrediting)? Trying to distract attention from someone else? No one seems to know.

One more cancel war involves the *cancelpoodle,* another anonymous user who cancels postings to the extremely contentious group alt.religion.scientology, a group that has sparked some real-world legal battles because the church claims that some of the messages, posted by a former church member, contain copyrighted and trade-secret church material. The poodle invariably cancels postings critical of the church, but again no one knows who's really behind it.

Extracting binary files

Free Agent handles uuencoded files with a single click. Click the Launch Binary Applications icon (the third one from the right, the one that looks like a lighthouse) to extract the encoded file and automatically run an appropriate program to view it. The appropriate programs are the same ones File Manager or My Computer uses. Some binary files are sent in several messages — highlight all the messages and click the lighthouse to glue the pieces back together. For example, if you read the `alt.binaries.pictures.fractals` newsgroup and see a set of messages with names such as "CUTE.GIF: Cute Fractal, Part 1 of 7," highlight the entire set of headers and click the lighthouse icon. Free Agent downloads the messages, uudecodes them to turn them into the original GIF (graphics) file, and
runs whatever program you have on your computer that can display a GIF graphics file.

For commercial providers such as AOL and CompuServe, check your provider's chapter in Part IV to learn the best way to unscramble uuencoded messages on your service.

What's in a Number?

Every Usenet message has a *message ID,* which is supposed to be different from the message ID of any other message ever, from the beginning to the end of time. (These people thought big.) A typical message ID looks like this:

```
<1994Jul19.055259.15278@chico.iecc.com>
```

The part after the @ is the name of the site where the article originated, and the part before the @ is some garbage made up to be unique and usually includes the date, time, phase of the moon, and so on.

Messages also have numbers, which are assigned in order at each newsgroup as articles arrive. So the first message in `rec.fooble` is number 1, the second is number 2, and so on.

An important difference distinguishes the IDs and the numbers: The IDs are the same everywhere, but the numbers apply to only *your local system.* So don't refer to articles' message numbers when you write a response, because people at other sites can't tell which articles you mean.

So You Want to Be Famous?

Sooner or later, unless you're an extraordinarily reticent person, you will want to send out some messages of your own so that people all over the world can at last find out just how clever you are. (This can be a mixed blessing, of course.) In this section, we look at general guidelines for responding to an article. For the details of how to do this stuff, look in your provider's chapter in Part IV.

Before posting a follow-up article, consider replying by e-mail to the article's author. For example, a response such as "Good point!" or "Nice article!" is of interest only to the author. Post a follow-up only if you are adding significant new information to the discussion.

That's a Roger, Roger

The easiest and usually most appropriate way to respond to an article is to send e-mail to its author in case you want to ask a question or offer a comment.

In Free Agent, write a mailed response to an article by pressing **R** or clicking the Post Reply Via Email icon, the little envelope icon that says Re: . Free Agent opens a new window in which you can edit the message and, if necessary, the headers. Then click Send Now to connect to your provider and send it immediately or, if you're off-line, Send Later to stash the message for later.

To send all your stashed messages after you are on-line, choose Online⇨Post Articles and Emails.

I'll follow you anywhere

If you have a comment about an article that is of general interest, you can post it as a Usenet article. In Free Agent, press **F** for Followup or click the Post Followup Article icon, the tiny picture of a page of paper with Re: over it. Again, when you're finished, you can send it now or stash it for later if you're off-line.

Many news systems reject messages that contain more quoted text than new material, to discourage lazy typists who quote an entire 100-line message and add a two-line comment. Some people are under the peculiar impression that if an article is rejected with too much quoted text, they should add garbage lines at the end to pad out the unquoted part. *Don't ever do that.* It instantly marks you as a pompous ass. Edit the text — your readers will thank you.

When you send your follow-up, the article in most cases is posted either immediately or in a few minutes (the next time a background posting program runs). Some groups are moderated, which means that you can't post to them directly. For moderated groups, your message is mailed to the group's moderator, who posts it if it meets the group's guidelines. Moderators are all volunteers and have work to do other than run their moderated groups, so it may take a while for your message to appear. Most moderators handle messages every day or two, but the slowest ones can take as long as two weeks. Remember: Patience is a virtue. As a newsgroup moderator (John runs one called `comp.compilers`, a technoid group that discusses techniques of translating one computer language to another), one of the authors of this book can assure you that writing cranky letters to a moderator — in which you complain that it's taking too long to process your pearls of wisdom — is utterly counterproductive.

Distributions Are Your Friends

Even though Usenet is a worldwide network, many times you're posting an article that doesn't really need to go to the whole world. If you're posting something to `misc.forsale.computers`, for example, to advertise an old disk drive you want to sell and you're in the United States, there's no point in sending the article outside the country because it wouldn't be worth the shipping and customs hassles to sell it overseas. Usenet distributions enable you to limit where an article is sent. A line like the following in your article header limits its distribution to the United States:

```
Distribution: usa
```

In Free Agent, while writing an article you have to click the <u>A</u>ll Fields button to open a subwindow in which one line says `Distribution`. Click that line to open a Distribution window in which you can type the distribution you want.

A long list of possible distributions exists. Some commonly used distributions are shown in this list:

- ✔ **world:** Everywhere (default)
- ✔ **na:** North America
- ✔ **usa:** United States
- ✔ **can:** Canada
- ✔ **uk:** United Kingdom
- ✔ **ne:** New England
- ✔ **ba:** Bay Area (California)

Unless you're sure that people on the other side of the world will be as fascinated by what you say as people next door, you should use the smallest appropriate distribution for any articles you post, both originals and follow-ups.

In practice, distributions are pretty leaky, and articles often get sent to places the distribution says that they shouldn't go because of peculiarities in the way news is passed from one system to the next. But it's a courtesy to faraway readers to at least *try* to avoid sending articles to places where the articles aren't interesting. Keep in mind that because international phone links are expensive, if you avoid sending an article to countries in which people aren't interested, you can save people some money.

All the News that Fits

Eventually you'll have your fill of news. Exit Free Agent in the usual Windows way, by choosing File⇨Exit or pressing Alt+F4. On the way out, it may ask whether it should compact its databases, a complicated way of asking whether it should free up space from old articles it deleted. (They go away after a week or so unless you specifically save them.) Unless you're in a big hurry, let it do so.

So What Is There to Read Already?

New newsgroups appear every day, old groups occasionally go away, and system managers can reject any groups they want to for lack of interest or other reasons. This book is getting fat, and it's easy to get a current and

---

Dying boy makes mailing list about modem tax

Back in Chapter 7, a sidebar lists well-known topics about which you should never, *never,* write to any mailing list. The same warning applies to Usenet news. For review, the top four topics *not* to write about are the following:

- ✔ Dying boy wants cards to set Guinness world record.

- ✔ FCC will pass modem tax and impoverish us all.

- ✔ Good Times Virus Erases Hard Disk.

- ✔ Make money fast with a chain letter.

See Chapter 7 for details about why nobody wants to hear about any of these things.

complete list from your newsreader, so we spend just a little space to give you a taste of what's out there. Trust us. If you can imagine a topic of interest to more than one person, there's probably a newsgroup about it already. In fact, there are newsgroups that may not even meet that criterion. Here, we first present some popular groups to get you acquainted with the mainstream hierarchies. Then we tell you about hierarchies that are a tad more obscure.

Subscribe to `news.announce.newgroups` to see the latest list of newsgroups and look for articles titled "List of Active Newsgroups, Part I" and "List of Active Newsgroups, Part II." For lists of the `alt` groups, look for articles with titles such as "Alternative Newsgroup Hierarchies, Part I."

The bare essentials

This section lists a few groups you should start with.

news.announce.newusers

Every new user should at least skim this group, which contains introductory material for new news users. One of the messages is pretty funny, but you have to read them to find out which one.

news.answers

This group contains all the periodic (weekly and monthly, mostly) postings to all the groups on the Net. Many of these have evolved into pithy and well-written introductions to their subjects. When you want to learn something fast about something that might have been discussed on the Net, start here.

rec.humor.funny

This highly competitive, moderated group contains jokes, most of which are pretty funny. Compare to `rec.humor`, which contains articles that the authors think are funny but that usually aren't.

comp.risks

The *Risks Digest* has lots of swell war stories about computer screw-ups.

comp.compilers

John thinks that it's interesting, but then he's the moderator.

alt.sex

Everybody reads it, but nobody admits to doing so. We certainly don't.

Computers, on computers, about computers

The largest set of newsgroups traditionally have been the computer-related ones under the hierarchy comp (a few of which are listed in Table 9-1). It's not surprising: If you listen in on ham-radio conversations, you realize that they're mostly about ham radio. So you may expect that when people used computers to create Usenet, they talked mostly about computers.

Table 9-1	Groups in the Comp Hierarchy
Name	*Discussion*
comp.ai.neural-nets	All aspects of neural networks
comp.ai.philosophy	Philosophical aspects of artificial intelligence
comp.answers	Repository for periodic Usenet articles (moderated)
comp.binaries.mac	Encoded Macintosh programs in binary (moderated)
comp.binaries.ms-windows	Binary programs for Microsoft Windows (moderated)
comp.binaries.os2	Binaries for use under the OS/2 ABI (moderated)
comp.human-factors	Issues related to human-computer interaction (HCI)
comp.internet.library	Electronic libraries (moderated)
comp.multimedia	Interactive multimedia technologies of all kinds
comp.patents	Patents of computer technology (moderated)
comp.society	The impact of technology on society (moderated)
comp.society.privacy	Effects of technology on privacy (moderated)
comp.speech	Research and applications in speech science and technology
comp.virus	Computer viruses and security (moderated)

The comp groups can tend toward the esoteric and the technoid, but they're also a treasure trove when your computer acts up and you need advice from people who have seen it all before.

Many groups offer usable computer programs. The ones under comp.binaries are the places to look for free programs for PCs, Macs, and other personal systems.

None of the above

Despite all the (sort of) careful arrangement of Usenet into meaningful hierarchies, some topics just didn't fit anywhere else; these topics ended up in `misc`, the miscellaneous hierarchy (Table 9-2 lists a few `misc` newgroups). Topics range from the totally staid to the hopelessly argumentative. The ultimate miscellaneous group is `misc.misc`, for discussions that don't fit *anywhere*.

Table 9-2	Groups in the Misc Hierarchy
Name	*Discussion*
misc.books.technical	Books about technical topics
misc.consumers	Consumer interests, product reviews, and so on
misc.consumers.house	Owning and maintaining a house
misc.education	The educational system
misc.entrepreneurs	Operating a business
misc.fitness	Physical fitness, exercise, and so on
misc.forsale	Short, tasteful postings about items for sale
misc.int-property	Intellectual property rights
misc.invest	Investments and the handling of money
misc.jobs.contract	Contract employment
misc.jobs.misc	Employment, workplaces, careers
misc.jobs.offered	Announcements of positions available
misc.jobs.offered.entry	Job listings only for entry-level positions
misc.jobs.resumes	Postings of resumes and "situation wanted" articles

Fun and games

Even computer weenies like to have fun. (Stop laughing. It's true.) Usenet has lots of recreational groups (in the `rec` hierarchy; some examples are listed in Table 9-3) for hobbies ranging from the strenuous, such as watching fish in an aquarium, to the totally relaxing — mountain climbing, for example. There are certainly a few here that you'll like.

Table 9-3	Groups in the Rec Hierarchy
Name	**Discussion**
rec.antiques	Antiques and vintage items
rec.arts.movies.reviews	Reviews of movies (moderated)
rec.arts.poems	For the posting of poems
rec.arts.startrek.info	Information about the universe of *Star Trek* (moderated)
rec.arts.tv	The boob tube, its history, and past and current shows
rec.autos.driving	Driving automobiles
rec.backcountry	Activities in the great outdoors
rec.birds	Birdwatching
rec.boats	Boating
rec.climbing	Climbing techniques, competition announcements, and so on
rec.crafts.brewing	The art of making beers and meads
rec.crafts.textiles	Sewing, weaving, knitting, and other fiber arts
rec.food.recipes	Recipes for interesting food and drink (moderated)
rec.food.restaurants	Dining out
rec.gardens	Gardening methods and results
rec.railroad	For fans of real trains
rec.running	Running for enjoyment, sport, exercise, and so on
rec.skiing	Snow skiing
rec.sport.football.pro	U.S.-style professional football
rec.travel	Traveling all over the world

Ask Dr. Science

Because many Usenetters are in university or industrial-research labs, you encounter a number of scientists in the sci hierarchy (both professional and amateur). You also find many computer-science types, although (despite its name) this area isn't really a science.

In this hierarchy, you find pretty much any kind of pure or applied science you can think of, from archaeology to zoology and everything in between. Table 9-4 shows you a choice few.

Table 9-4	Groups in the Sci Hierarchy
Name	**Discussion**
sci.aeronautics	The science of aeronautics and related technology (moderated)
sci.archaeology	The study of antiquities of the world
sci.astro	Astronomy discussions and information
sci.classics	The study of classical history, languages, art, and more
sci.crypt	Different methods of data encryption and decryption
sci.math	Mathematics and its pursuits
sci.med	Medicine and its related products and regulations
sci.skeptic	Skeptics discuss pseudoscience
sci.space	Space, space programs, space-related research, and so on

C'mon by and stay awhile

Usenet is a sociable place, so naturally a great deal of socializing goes on in the soc hierarchy. About half the soc groups are in soc.culture, where they discuss particular countries or ethnicities, and the other half are devoted to other sociable topics (Table 9-5 lists a few). This group is also where you find religious groups, ranging all the way from fundamentalist Christianity to paganism to Buddhism.

Table 9-5	Groups in the Soc Hierarchy
Name	**Discussion**
soc.couples	For couples (compare with soc.singles)
soc.history	Things historical
soc.men	Issues related to men and their problems and relationships

Name	Discussion
soc.religion.unitarian-univ	A hangout for Unitarians, Universalists, and their noncreedal friends
soc.religion.quaker	A quiet, friendly group
soc.singles	For single people and their activities
soc.women	Issues related to women and their problems and relationships

Blah, blah, blah

A few topics provoke running arguments that never, *never,* get resolved. Usenet puts these in the `talk` hierarchy, mostly to warn you to stay away (see Table 9-6). Most find these groups to be argumentative and repetitious and populated primarily by students. However, *you* may not mind this or you may feel differently — so take a look at any that seem interesting to you.

Table 9-6	Groups in the Talk Hierarchy
Name	**Discussion**
talk.abortion	All sorts of discussions and arguments about abortion
talk.answers	Repository for periodic Usenet articles (moderated)
talk.bizarre	The unusual, bizarre, curious, and often stupid
talk.rumors	For the posting of rumors

More hierarchies

Along with the standard hierarchies are a bunch of less widely distributed ones.

alt

This name designates so-called *alternative* groups. Setting up a group in a regular hierarchy is relatively difficult, requiring a formal charter and an on-line vote by its prospective readers and nonreaders. On the other hand, any fool can (and often does) set up an `alt` group. Often, after an `alt` has been around awhile, its proponents go through the procedure to create a corresponding mainstream group, and the `alt` group goes away. The quintessential stupid `alt` group is called `alt.barney.die.die.die.`

aol

These groups are for and about AOL users (they're accessible only from America Online).

bionet

This bunch of groups is of interest to *biologists,* with the latest news about fruit flies and the like. If you're not a biologist, don't bother.

bit

These BITNET mailing lists (see Chapter 8) are also available on some systems as Usenet news.

biz

Designates *business* groups that are more commercial than the generally noncommercial traffic in the mainstream groups.

clari

This one refers to ClariNet (see the sidebar "Listen to the ClariNet," later in this chapter).

compuserve

These groups are for and about CompuServer users (and are accessible only from CompuServe).

gnu

The *GNU project* develops freely available software, including, eventually, a complete reimplementation of the UNIX system. (GNU, by the way, stands for *G*NU'S *n*ot *U*NIX.)

hepnet

This is HEPnet(High Energy Physics). Like bionet, you know if you're interested.

ieee

IEEE is the professional organization for electrical and electronics engineers.

k12

The K-12 Net is for elementary and high school students and teachers. Students and teachers are welcome on all the other groups, of course, but these groups contain topics of particular interest.

relcom

These are Russian-language groups. They are unintelligible unless you have a newsreading program that handles Cyrillic characters. You have to be able to read Russian too.

vmsnet

Groups discuss the VMS system that runs on some Digital (DEC) computers. They are primarily for VMS fans.

Of all these hierarchies, only alt has many groups that are of general interest. A few of them can be found in Table 9-7. The character of alt groups varies wildly. Some, like alt.dcom.telecom, are just as staid as any comp group. Others, like alt.buddha.short.fat.guy, verge on the indescribable.

Table 9-7	Groups in the Alt Hierarchy
Name	**Discussion**
alt.activism	Activities for activists
alt.angst	Anxiety in the modern world
alt.backrubs	"Lower. To the right. Aaaah!"
alt.bbs	Computer BBS systems and software
alt.binaries.pictures.fine-art.d	The fine-art binaries (moderated)
alt.binaries.pictures.fractals	Nifty-looking fractal pictures, usually in uuencoded GIF format
alt.buddha.short.fat.guy	Religion and not religion; both, neither
alt.cobol	Relationship between programming and stone axes
alt.dreams	What do they mean?
alt.flame	Alternative, literate, pithy, succinct screaming
alt.paranormal	Phenomena that are not scientifically explicable
alt.save.the.earth	Environmentalist causes
alt.sex	Postings of a prurient nature
alt.tv.mash	Nothing like a good comedy about war and dying
alt.tv.mst3k	Hey, you robots! Down in front!
alt.tv.muppets	Miss Piggy on the tube
alt.tv.prisoner	*The Prisoner* television series from years ago

Listen to the ClariNet

It had to happen someday — Usenet meets real life. A guy named Brad (same guy who created `rec.humor.funny`, Usenet's most widely read group) had a simple goal for his computer: He wanted to get his weekly Dave Barry column in his electronic mail. How hard could that be, considering that newspaper features are all distributed by satellite, anyway? Pretty hard, it turned out, mostly because of the legal issues of who owns what on the satellite.

Brad kept at it, though, and ended up with the right to distribute by network not just Dave Barry but also the entire UPI newswire and many other features. That was *much* too much data to send out as e-mail, so Brad did the obvious thing and decided to use Usenet software instead. The result is a group of about 250 newsgroups known as ClariNet. Each group contains a particular category of news (actual newspaper-type news, not just Net news), such as `clari.news.economy` for stories about the economy.

If your system has a direct (not just dial-up) Internet connection, you can get ClariNet news about as fast as the news comes off the ticker. It costs money, of course, but for a site with dozens or hundreds of users, the price per user is low — on the order of a few dollars per user per month. For information, send e-mail to `info@clarinet.com`.

Brad also did get his e-mail Dave Barry, for about two years until the syndicate that distributed him decided that there was more copyright piracy of Dave's articles than they cared for. You can still get other syndicated columns, including Mike Royko, Miss Manners, and Joe Bob Briggs, for less than $10 per year (less than the cost of a Sunday paper each week). If your system gets ClariNet news, they may already be filed under `clari.feature.*`. If not, send e-mail to `info@clarinet.com` to get subscription details.

Chapter 10

Swiping Files by Using FTP

* *

In This Chapter

▶ Learning about FTP

▶ Using your Web browser to swipe files

▶ Using WS_FTP, a nice WinSock FTP program, to swipe files

▶ Using the UNIX FTP program to swipe files

▶ FTP-ing by e-mail, for the FTP-impaired

▶ Getting files from your Internet shell provider to your own computer

▶ Installing software you've swiped from the Net

* *

*F*irst, the fancy terminology: *File transfer* means to copy files from one system to another. You can copy files from other systems to your system and from your system to others. On the Internet, everyone uses the *FTP* (*f*ile-*t*ransfer *p*rotocol) system for transferring files.

Why copy a file from one system to another? Because lots of cool stuff is available out there on the Internet for free. You can download programs, pictures, and text to your computer by using FTP — it's quick, and the price is right. Much of the Internet software we use with PPP and SLIP accounts, for example, comes via FTP, and you can get nice clip art, recipes — you name it!

How FTP Works

Transferring a file requires two participants: an *FTP client program* and an *FTP server program*. The FTP client is the program that we, the Joe Six-Pack Users of the world, run on our computers. The FTP server is the program that runs on the huge mainframe somewhere (or these days, likely as not, on a PC under someone's desk) and stores tens of thousands of files. The FTP server is similar to an on-line library of files. The FTP client can *upload* (send) files to the FTP server or, more commonly, *download* (receive) files from the FTP server.

There are thousands of publicly accessible FTP servers, and they store hundreds of thousands of files. Many of the files are freeware or shareware programs. Some FTP servers are so popular that they can't handle the number of file requests they receive. When FTP servers are inundated, other FTP servers, called *mirrors,* with copies of the same files, are set up to handle the overflow traffic.

Hello, this is anonymous

To use an FTP server, you have to log in. But what if you don't have an account on the FTP server machine? No problem, if it's a publicly accessible FTP server. You log in as anonymous and type your e-mail address as your password. Voilà! You have access to lots of files! This method of using public FTP servers is called *anonymous FTP.*

When is a file not a file?

When it's a text file. The FTP definition specifies six different kinds of files, of which only two types are useful: ASCII and binary. An ASCII file is a text file. A binary file is anything else. FTP has two modes: *ASCII* and *binary* (also called *image* mode), to transfer the two kinds of files. When you transfer an ASCII file between different kinds of computers that store files differently, ASCII mode automatically adjusts the file during the transfer so that the file is a valid text file when it's stored on the receiving end. A binary file is left alone and transferred verbatim.

A few anonymous FTP tips

Some FTP servers limit the number of anonymous users or the times of day that anonymous FTP is allowed. Please respect these limits because no law says that the owner of the system can't turn off anonymous access.

Don't store files on the FTP server unless the owner invites you to do so. A directory called INCOMING or something similar is usually available where you can put stuff.

Some FTP servers allow anonymous FTP only from host computers that have names. That is, if you try to FTP anonymously from a host that has a number but no name, these hosts don't let you in. This problem occurs most often with SLIP and PPP accounts, which, because they generally offer no services that are useful to other people, don't always have names assigned.

Getting your FTP client

If you want to get files by FTP, you need an FTP client program. Luckily, you have several excellent ways to do so:

- ✔ Use your Web browser. Most Web browsers can handle anonymous FTP only for downloading files (no uploading). Prodigy and Microsoft Network users should try their Web browsers.

- ✔ If you have a SLIP or PPP account, use a WinSock or MacTCP FTP program. The most popular freeware FTP program that is WinSock compatible is WS_FTP, and you'll find out how to use it in this chapter. If you use a Mac, you can use a shareware program called Fetch. These programs can handle both uploading and downloading files by using both anonymous FTP or private accounts on an FTP server.

- ✔ If you have a UNIX shell account, you can use the UNIX ftp command to upload or download files, using either anonymous FTP or logging in to your own private account on a FTP server.

- ✔ If you use America Online (AOL) or CompuServe, it's easy to get files via anonymous FTP. On both services, use the keyword ftp. If you use CompuServe, see the section "Getting Files via FTP" in Chapter 12. If you use AOL, see the section "Grabbing Files from FTP Servers" in Chapter 13.

Get with the program

The basic steps you follow to FTP, no matter which program you use, are as follows:

1. If you use a UNIX shell provider and you want to upload files to an FTP server, first upload them from your own computer to the provider's computer.

2. Log in to the FTP server.

3. Move to the directory on the server that contains the files you want to download, or move to the directory to which you want to upload files.

4. Tell the program which kind of files (ASCII or binary) you will be moving.

5. Download or upload the files.

6. Log off the FTP server.

7. If you use a UNIX shell provider and you downloaded files, download the files from the Internet provider's computer to your own.

8. You're done!

The rest of this chapter describes how to use a Web browser, the WS_FTP program, and the UNIX `ftp` command to swipe files from FTP servers, in addition to how to send files to servers.

FTP-ing on the Web

Most Web browsers can do much more than just browse the Web — among other things, they can act as FTP client programs. You can use them only for downloading, and most work only for anonymous FTP.

Interestingly, Web browsers are smart enough to tell which files are ASCII and which are binary. You don't have to worry about it!

The URL of FTP

To tell your Web browser to log in to an FTP server, you tell it to load the URL of the FTP server. An FTP server's URL looks like this:

```
ftp://servername/directoryname/filename
```

You can leave out the directory name and filename if you want, and you'll get the top-level directory of that FTP server. For example, the URL of Microsoft's FTP server (at `ftp.microsoft.com`) is

```
ftp://ftp.microsoft.com/
```

Web browsers can only download files — they can't upload them to FTP servers. Most Web browsers can only handle anonymous FTP, although you can try including your account name, like this:

```
ftp://elvis@ftp.dummies.com
```

When it logs in to the server, your browser asks you to type the password.

Getting files over the Web

The following steps show you how to connect to an FTP server by using your Web browser:

1. Run your Web browser as usual.

2. **To tell your browser to load the URL of the FTP server, type the URL in the Address, URL, or Netsite box just below the toolbar, and press Enter.**

   If you use a browser in which you can't type a URL in that box, you must give a command to tell it which URL to go to. In older versions of Mosaic, for example, you choose File⇨Open (or press Ctrl+O) and then type the URL in the dialog box that is displayed.

   The browser logs in to the FTP server and displays its home directory. Each file and directory in the current directory appears as a link. Depending on the Web browser you use, the format may differ from the one shown in the figure.

3. **Move to the directory that contains the file you want by clicking the directory name.**

   When you click a directory name, you move to that directory and your browser displays its contents.

At this point, what you do depends on which browser you use.

If you use a version of Mosaic

After you have found the file you want to download (as described in the preceding section), here's how to grab it:

1. **Tell it that you want to save stuff on the disk rather than display it on the screen by choosing Options⇨Load to Disk from the menu.**

   Otherwise, Mosaic may try to display the file it downloads instead of storing it. (We call this "cruel-joke mode.")

2. **Download the file you want by clicking its filename.**

   Mosaic asks you for the filename to use, downloads the file, and stores it on your disk.

3. **When you finish downloading files and want to see Web pages again, choose Options⇨Load to Disk from the menu again.**

   This command turns off the "load to disk" mode you turned on in step 1.

If you hold down the Shift key while you click, Mosaic does a load to disk regardless of whether you've set it on the Option menu.

If you use Netscape

When you have found the file you want to download (as described in the section "Getting files over the Web," earlier in this chapter), follow these steps:

1. **Download the file you want by clicking its filename.**

   If you download a text file or another file your browser knows how to display, the browser displays it after it downloads. If you click the filename readme.txt, for example, the browser displays the text file. If you want to save it after you look at it, choose File⇨Save As from the menu and tell Netscape the filename to use.

   If you download a file your browser doesn't know how to display, such as a program, it asks what to do (see Figure 10-1).

2. **If Netscape asks what to do with the file, click Save to Disk and then choose the directory and filename in which to save it.**

   Netscape downloads the file.

Unknown File Type

No Viewer Configured for File Type: application/x-compress

How would you like to handle this file?

Save to Disk   Cancel Transfer   Configure a Viewer...

If you use another Web browser

Check your Web browser's documentation to learn how to save files that are downloaded. Or just try it — click the filename of a file that looks interesting and see what happens. If you don't like what happens, try holding down the Shift key and clicking again.

Using WS_FTP: FTP-ing Using a SLIP or PPP Account

If you use a SLIP or PPP account, you need a WinSock (for Windows users) or MacTCP (for Mac users) FTP client program. No problem! Many good freeware and shareware FTP programs are available right off the Internet. Our favorites are WS_FTP for Windows and Fetch for the Mac. This section describes how to use WS_FTP.

Cool features of WS_FTP include the ones in this list:

✔ Scrollable and selectable windows for the names of local and remote files and directories

✔ Clickable buttons for such common operations as connect and set binary mode

✔ Connection profiles, which save the host name, login name and password, and remote host directory of your favorite FTP sites; comes with a bunch of useful profiles already set

WS_FTP is good enough that even when we're using commercial WinSock packages which come with their own FTP programs, we still use WS_FTP because we like it the best.

Of course you can also use your Web browser to download files via anonymous FTP, as described in the earlier part of this chapter.

Getting WS_FTP

Our favorite WinSock FTP program is called WS_FTP, and it's available free of charge by FTP from a variety of places, including its "home," the United States Military Academy. And you thought that they only learned how to fight wars!

1. **In Windows File Manager (or Windows 95's My Computer or Explorer), make a directory in which to put WS_FTP.**

2. **Following the instructions earlier in this chapter, use your Web browser to FTP to this site:**

```
ftp://papa.indstate.edu/winsock-1/ftp/ws_ftp.zip
```

(That is, FTP to papa.indstate.edu, go to the /winsock-1/ftp directory, and download the file ws_ftp.zip.) If you can't find it on that FTP server, go to Stroud's Consummate WinSock Apps List Web page to find other locations that store the file, or use an Archie program to search for it. (See Chapter 21 for help.)

3. **Unzip the WS_FTP.ZIP file.**

You end up with a bunch of files, including the program, which is named WS_FTP.EXE.

4. **Make an icon for WS_FTP, to make it easy to run.**

In Windows 3.1, drag the WS_FTP.EXE file from File Manager into a Program Manager program group. In Windows 95's Explorer or My Computer, create a shortcut for the program by using the right mouse button to drag the filename to the Windows 95 desktop or into a folder.

You're ready to FTP by using WS_FTP!

Dialing for files

Here's how to use the WS_FTP program to swipe files from or put files on an FTP server:

1. **Run the WS_FTP program by double-clicking its icon.**

   You see the FTP Client Connect To dialog box, shown in Figure 10-2. This dialog box lets you enter information about the FTP server you want to connect to. After you've entered this information, WS_FTP saves it so that you can easily connect to the saved FTP server again.

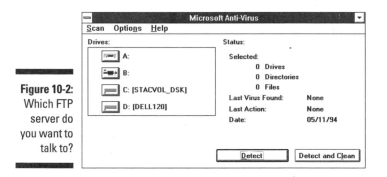

Figure 10-2:
Which FTP
server do
you want to
talk to?

2. **In the Config name box, enter the name you want to use for this FTP server.**

   If you want to FTP to `rtfm.mit.edu`, for example, which contains FAQs for all the Usenet newsgroups, you might enter **Usenet FAQ Central**.

3. **In the Host name box, enter the name of the FTP server.**

   This name can be a regular Internet name (such as `oak.oakland.edu`, another useful FTP server) or a numeric address.

4. **Leave the Host type box set to auto-detect.**

   This step tells WS_FTP to guess which operating system the FTP server is using.

5. **If you actually have a username on the FTP server, enter your username and password in the User ID and Password boxes.**

   Otherwise, click the Anonymous FTP box. WS_FTP asks for your e-mail address, which it uses as your password (this is the usual thing to do when you FTP anonymously).

6. **Enter your address and click OK.**

   WS_FTP fills in the User ID and Password boxes for you.

If you want WS_FTP to store the password in the Password box rather than ask you for it every time to connect to the FTP server, click the Save Password box so that it contains an ×.

Leave the account box blank, unless you have your own username on the FTP server and you know which account to enter.

7. **In the Remote Dir box, enter the directory you want to look in on the FTP server.**

   Alternatively, you can leave this box blank and look around yourself.

8. **In the Local Dir box, enter on your own PC the directory in which you want to store downloaded files.**

9. **Click the Save Config button to save this information.**

10. **Click OK.**

    WS_FTP tries to connect to the FTP server.

It won't speak to me!

If you have a problem connecting to the FTP server, messages appear in the two-line box at the bottom of the WS_FTP window. You can scroll this little window up and down to see what happened. For example, rtfm.mit.edu is frequently overloaded and won't let you log on. When this happens, it displays some helpful messages about other FTP sites that might have the information you want. You can see these messages in this box.

If you really want to see the messages the FTP server sent, double-click them. WS_FTP opens a big window so that you can see them better. To close it, click the Close button.

Do you copy?

After you're connected to the FTP server, you see the WS_FTP window, shown in Figure 10-3. WS_FTP displays information about the files on your own computer in the left side of the window (titled "Local PC info") and the directories and files on the FTP server on the right side (entitled "Remote host info"). On each side are buttons that enable you to change directories (ChgDir), make directories (MkDir), delete directories (RmDir), view files, and so on. Naturally, you don't have permission to delete or change anything on most FTP servers, so don't even try.

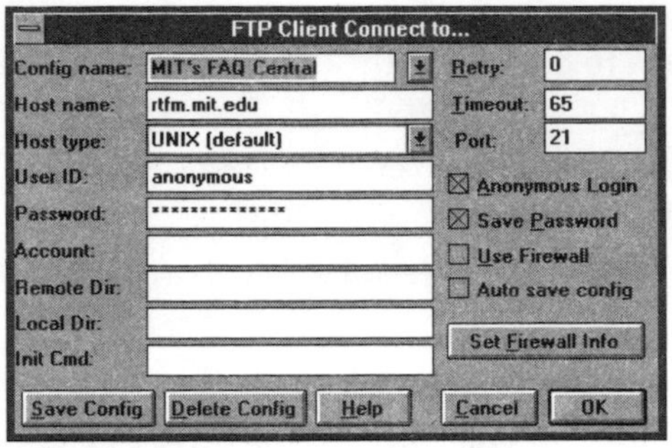

Figure 10-3:
Prepare to
receive
some files!

To move from directory to directory on the FTP server, choose directory names from the list box. Or you can click the ChDir button and enter the full pathname of the directory to go to.

Here's how to copy a file:

1. **Choose ASCII or Binary, using the buttons at the bottom of the window.**

   For files that consist entirely of text, choose ASCII. For anything else, choose Binary.

2. **Choose the file you want on the FTP server.**

3. **Choose the directory to put it in on your own computer.**

4. **Click the left-pointing arrow button in the middle of the window.**

   WS_FTP downloads the file. For large files, this step can take some time, and WS_FTP displays your progress as a percentage completed.

Hang up!

To disconnect from the FTP server after you're finished, click the Close button at the bottom of the WS_FTP window.

Connecting again

To call someone else, click the Connect button. You see the FTP Client Connect To window again. Fill in different information and click OK to make the connection.

To call an FTP server you've called before, click Connect. In the FTP Client Connect To window, click the arrow button to the right of the Config name box. You see a list of the configurations you entered before — choose one and then click OK.

For you Mac users

Fetch, an excellent Mac FTP program, gives you a choice between downloading files as raw data and MacBinary. The *MacBinary* format combines the parts (*forks*) of Macintosh files into one file so that they can travel together when they're being FTP'd. Use MacBinary for Mac-specific stuff that only other Macs can understand, such as Macintosh software. When you download Mac software from a Mac software archive, for example, use MacBinary. Don't use MacBinary for text files, graphics files, and other non-Mac-specific stuff. MacBinary formatted files usually have the filename extension .bin.

FTP-ing from a UNIX Shell Account

Almost every UNIX system has a program named ftp, an FTP client. You can use it for uploading and downloading, and it works both with anonymous FTP and for FTP-ing (Is that a verb? It is now!) to or from FTP servers on which you have your own account.

Remember that if you're calling into a UNIX account by using a terminal program on your PC or Macintosh, it takes *two* steps to get a file from an FTP server to your own computer. First, you use FTP to copy the files from the FTP server to your Internet provider's computer. Second, you still have to download it to your computer. We talk about that subject later in this chapter.

How hard can it be to copy a file from one place to another?

It's relatively simple to copy a file from one place to another (but don't forget — computers are involved). Here's how it works: Log in to the other computer for FTP and tell it what you want to copy and where you want it copied to.

Here's how to use the ftp program to download a file (that is, to copy a file from the FTP server to your computer):

1. **Run the ftp program, by typing the name of the FTP server on the command line.**

   To connect to the wuarchive.wustl.edu FTP server, for example, type this line:

```
ftp wuarchive.wustl.edu
```

You see a bunch of messages, confirming that you are connected and asking for your account name:

```
Connected to wuarchive.wustl.edu.
220 wuarchive.wustl.edu FTP server (Version wu-2.1b(1) Fri
Jun 25 14:40:33 CDT 1993) ready.
```

2. Type your username on the FTP server.

If you don't have one, type **anonymous**. Notice that your regular old username on your home account is not a username you can use on someone else's machine. Unless you're FTP-ing to a machine you regularly have access to, use **anonymous**.

If you log in as anonymous, you see a message like this:

```
331 Guest login ok, send your complete e-mail address as
password.
```

Next, the FTP server wants to know your password.

3. If you typed a username, type your password. If you logged in as anonymous **, type your e-mail address as your password.**

You see messages from the FTP server telling you what the rules of the server are, and then you see the ftp> prompt, which means that the FTP server is waiting for your command.

4. Go to the directory on the FTP server that contains the file you want, using the cd command, like this (this command moves to the docfiles **directory):**

```
cd docfiles
```

5. To see the files in the current directory, type dir.

You see a directory listing with filenames and sizes, like this:

```
200 PORT command successful.
150 Opening ASCII mode data connection for /bin/ls.
total 23
drwxrwxr-x  19 root      archive        512 Jun 24 12:09 doc
drwxrwxr-x   5 root      archive        512 May 18 08:14 edu
drwxr-xr-x  31 root      wheel          512 Jul 12 10:37 sys-
                tems
drwxr-xr-x   3 root      archive        512 Jun 25  1992
                vendorware
    ... lots of other stuff ...
226 Transfer complete.
1341 bytes received in 0.77 seconds (1.7 Kbytes/s)
```

6. **When you find the file you want, tell the FTP server what kind of file it is.**

   For text files, type **ascii**. For all other files, type **binary** or **image**.

7. **Use the** get **command to copy it to your computer.**

```
get README
```

   If you are using a UNIX shell account, the get command copies the file to your provider's computer, not to your own computer.

   You see messages like this:

```
150 Opening ASCII mode data connection for README (12686
          bytes).
226 Transfer complete.
local: README remote: README
12979 bytes received in 28 seconds (0.44 Kbytes/s)
```

8. **When you finish copying files, log off the FTP server by using the** quit **command.**

   You see a friendly message:

```
221 Goodbye.
```

That's basically how FTP works, but of course you need to know about 400 other odds and ends to really use FTP effectively.

The first directory you see on the FTP server may contain files with names such as read.me or index.txt. It's a good idea to download and view these files before continuing.

How to foul up your files in FTP

The most common error made by inexperienced Internet users (and by *experienced* users, for that matter) is transferring a file in the wrong mode. If you transfer a text file in binary mode from a UNIX system to an MS-DOS or Macintosh system, the file looks something like this (on a DOS machine):

```
This file
          should have been
                        copied in
                                ASCII mode.
```

Why is it called FTP?

We could say that FTP is short for *file-transfer program*, and you probably would believe us, but that would be wrong. It really stands for *file-transfer protocol*. Way back in 1971, the Internet Powers That Be decided on a *protocol*, a set of conventions for copying files from one place to another on the Net. Then many people wrote programs that implemented the protocol and called them all FTP. Is this clear? Never mind.

On a Mac, the entire file looks like it's on one line. When you look at the file with a text editor on a UNIX system, you see strange ^M symbols at the end of every line. You don't necessarily have to retransfer the file. Many networking packages come with programs that do ex-post facto conversion from one format to the other.

If, on the other hand, you copy something in ASCII mode that isn't a text file, it gets scrambled. Compressed files don't decompress; executable files don't execute (or they crash or hang the machine); images look unimaginably bad. When a file is corrupted, the first thing you should suspect is the wrong mode in FTP.

If you are FTP-ing files between two computers of the same type, such as from one UNIX system to another, you can and should do all your transfers in binary mode. Whether you're transferring a text file or a nontext file, it doesn't require any conversion, so binary mode does the right thing.

The directory thicket

You use the `dir` command to see what's in a directory. Most FTP servers run an operating system called *UNIX*. When you use the FTP `dir` command, you see a standard UNIX directory listing, in which the first letter on the line tells you whether something is a file or a directory. *d* means that it's a directory — anything else is a file.

If you want to see some of but not all the files in the current directory, you can type a filename after the *dir*, and you can use * in the filename to match any character or characters. For example, to see a listing of files that begin with z, you type:

```
dir z*
```

WARNING!

Patience is a virtue

The Internet is pretty fast, but not infinitely so. When you're copying stuff between two computers on the same local network, information can move at about 200,000 characters per second. When the two machines are separated by a great deal of intervening Internet, the speed drops — often to 1,000 characters per second or fewer. So if you're copying a file that's 500,000 characters long (the size of your typical inspirational GIF image; see Chapter 18), it takes only a few seconds over a local network, but it can take several minutes over a long-haul connection.

It's often comforting to get a directory listing before issuing a get or put command so that you can have an idea of how long the copy will take.

If you see any directories in the current directory, the cd command changes directories. It changes the current directory on the FTP server but doesn't affect the current directory on your UNIX system. You can also change the directory on your own computer, using the lcd command. (You might expect cd to change directories correspondingly on both machines, but it doesn't.)

To move up to the directory that contains the current directory (the *parent* directory, as they say), type:

```
cd ..
```

What's in a name?

You can change the name of a file when you download it. Because some UNIX filenames aren't permitted on Windows PCs, you may have to use a different name for the file when you download it. To store the file by using a different name from the one it has on the FTP server, type the name you want to use at the end of the get command, like this:

```
get rose-photograph rose2.gif
```

This command downloads the file named rose-photograph and names it rose2.gif.

Grabbing a buncha files

Suppose that you want to get a bunch of the files that begin with ru. In that case, you can use the mget (which stands for *m*ultiple *GET*) command to retrieve them. The names you type after mget can be either plain filenames or wildcard patterns that match a bunch of filenames. For each matching name, FTP asks whether you want to retrieve that file, as in the following:

```
ftp> mget ru*
mget ruby? n
mget ruby2? n
mget ruger_pistol? n
mget rugfur01? n
mget rush? y
200 PORT command successful.
150 Opening BINARY mode data connection for rush (18257
        bytes).
226 Transfer complete.
local: rush remote: rush
18257 bytes received in 16 seconds (1.1 Kbytes/s)
mget rush01? y
200 PORT command successful.
150 Opening BINARY mode data connection for rush01 (205738
        bytes).
local: rush01 remote: rush01
205738 bytes received in 200.7 seconds (1.2 Kbytes/s)
mget rush02?
```

Note: If you find that mget matches more files than you expected, you can stop it with the usual interrupt character for your system — typically Ctrl+C or Delete. You can even interrupt in the middle of a transfer if a file takes longer to transfer than you want to wait.

This game of 20 Questions is OK for three or four files, but it can get darned tedious if you want to copy a bunch of them. Fortunately, you also can do an *express mget*, which doesn't ask any questions and enables you to find exactly the files you want. Suppose that you use the dir command to see information about a bunch of files you might want to download:

```
ftp> dir 92-1*
200 PORT command successful.
150 Opening ASCII mode data connection for 92-1*.
-rw-rw-r—   1 johnl     staff        123728 Jul  1 20:30 92-10.gz
-rw-rw-r—   1 johnl     staff        113523 Jul  1 20:30 92-11.gz
-rw-rw-r—   1 johnl     staff        106290 Jul  1 20:30 92-12.gz
226 Transfer complete.
remote: 92-1*
192 bytes received in 0.12 seconds (1.5 Kbytes/s)
```

Now suppose that you want all those 92-1 files and don't feel like hammering on the y key to tell FTP to get all the files. Use the prompt command, which tells FTP not to ask any questions in mget but to just do it:

```
ftp> prompt
Interactive mode off.
ftp> mget 92-1*
200 PORT command successful.
150 Opening BINARY mode data connection for 92-10.gz (123728
          bytes).
226 Transfer complete.
local: 92-10.gz remote: 92-10.gz 123728 bytes received in 2.8
          seconds (43 Kbytes/s)
200 PORT command successful.
150 Opening BINARY mode data connection for 92-11.gz (113523
          bytes).
226 Transfer complete.
local: 92-11.gz remote: 92 11.gz 113523 bytes received in 3.3
          seconds (34 Kbytes/s)
200 PORT command successful.
150 Opening BINARY mode data connection for 92-12.gz (106290
          bytes).
226 Transfer complete.
local: 92-12.gz remote: 92-12.gz 106290 bytes received in 2.2
          seconds (47 Kbytes/s)
```

About face!

OK, now you know how to retrieve files from other computers. How about copying the other way? It's just about the same procedure except that you use put rather than get. That is, you log on to the FTP server and use the cd and dir commands to find the directory to which you want to upload the file. Then you use put to copy the file to the FTP server, and quit to log off. Simplicity itself!

The following example shows how to copy a local file called rnr to a FTP server and rename the file rnr.new on the server:

```
ftp> put rnr rnr.new
200 PORT command successful.
150 Opening ASCII mode data connection for rnr.new.
226 Transfer complete.
local: rnr remote: rnr.new
168 bytes sent in 0.014 seconds (12 Kbytes/s)
```

(As with get, if you want to use the same name when you make the copy, leave out the second name.)

The `mput` command works just like the `mget` command does, only in the other direction. If you have a bunch of files whose names begin with `uu` and you want to copy most of them, issue the `mput` command, as in the following example:

```
ftp> mput uu*
mput uupick? y
200 PORT command successful.
150 Opening ASCII mode data connection for uupick.
226 Transfer complete.
local: uupick remote: uupick
156 bytes sent in 0.023 seconds (6.6 Kbytes/s)
mput uupoll? y
200 PORT command successful.
150 Opening ASCII mode data connection for uupoll.
226 Transfer complete.
local: uupoll remote: uupoll
200 bytes sent in 0.013 seconds (15 Kbytes/s)
mput uurn? n
```

(As with `mget`, you can use `prompt` to tell it to go ahead and not to ask any questions.)

Most systems have protections on their files and directories that limit where you can copy files. You generally can use FTP to put a file anywhere that you could create a file if you were logged in directly by using the same login name. If you're using anonymous FTP, you generally cannot `put` any files.

Other FTP shenanigans

A bunch of other file-manipulation commands are sometimes useful, as in the following example of the `delete` command:

```
delete somefile
```

This command deletes the file on the remote computer, assuming that the file permissions enable you to do so. The `mdelete` command deletes multiple files and works like `mget` and `mput`. The `mkdir` command makes a new directory on the remote system (again assuming that you have permissions to do so), as in the following example:

```
mkdir newdir
```

After you create a directory, you still have to use cd to change to that directory before you use put or mput to store files in it.

If you plan to do much file deleting, directory creating, and the like, it's usually much quicker to log in to the other system by using telnet to do your work and using the usual local commands.

An FTP cheat sheet

Table 10-1 gives a short list of useful FTP commands, including a few not otherwise mentioned.

Table 10-1	Useful FTP Commands
Command	*Description*
get old new	Copies remote file old to local file new; can omit new if same name as old
put old new	Copies local file old to remote file new; can omit new if same name as old
del *xxx*	Deletes file *xxx* on remote system
cd newdir	Changes to directory newdir on the remote machine
cdup	Changes to next higher directory
lcd newdir	Changes to directory newdir on the local machine
asc	Transfers files in ASCII mode (use for text files)
bin	Transfers files in binary or image mode (all other files)
quit	Leaves FTP
dir pat	Lists files whose names match pattern pat; if no pat, lists all files
mget pat	Gets files whose names match pattern pat
mput pat	Puts files whose names match pattern pat
mdel pat	Deletes remote files whose names match pattern pat
prompt	Turn name prompting on or off in mget and mput

What's with all these three-digit numbers?

You may notice that whenever you give a command to FTP, the response from the remote host begins with a three-digit number. (Or you may not notice, in which case never mind.)

The three-digit number is there so that the FTP program, which doesn't know any English, can figure out what's going on. Each digit means something to the program.

Here's what the first digit means:

- 1 means that it has begun to process your request but hasn't finished it.

- 2 means that it has finished.

- 3 means that it needs more input from you, such as when it needs a password after you enter your username.

- 4 means that it didn't work but may if you try again.

- 5 means "you lose."

The second digit is a message *subtype,* namely, a digit that distinguishes this message from other, similar ones.

The third digit distinguishes messages that otherwise would have the same number (something that in the computer world would be unspeakably awful).

If a message goes on for multiple lines, all the lines except the last one have a dash rather than a space after the number.

Note: Most FTP users have no idea what the numbers mean, by the way, so now that you're one of the few who does know, you're an expert.

Waaahh! I Can't FTP!

Oh, no! You only have an e-mail connection to the Internet, so you can't FTP any of this swell stuff! Life isn't worth living!

Wait. There's hope even yet. Several kind-hearted Internet hosts provide FTP-by-mail service. You e-mail a request to them, and a helpful robot retrieves the file and mails it to you. It's not as nice as direct FTP, but it's better than nothing. Only a few FTP-by-mail servers exist, so treat them as a precious resource. In particular, observe the following:

- **Be moderate in what you request.** When it mails you a nontext file (remember that compressed or archived files are nontext for FTP purposes, even if what they contain is text), it has to use a textlike encoding that makes the mailed messages 35 percent larger than the file itself. So if you retrieve a 100KB file, you get 135KB of mail, which is a great deal of mail. If you use a commercial system in which you pay for incoming mail, you probably will find FTP by mail to be prohibitively expensive. (In that case, try a service such as AT&T Mail or MCI Mail that doesn't charge for incoming mail or a public Internet provider that provides direct FTP access.)

- ✔ **Be patient.** Nearly all FTP-by-mail systems ration their service. This means that if many people are using them (which is always true), there may be a delay of several days until they can get to your request. If you send in a request and don't hear back right away, *don't send it again.*

- ✔ **Do some research.** Before you use a general-purpose FTP-by-mail server, check to see whether the system from which you want to retrieve stuff has a server of its own that can send you files from just that system. If it does, use it because that is much quicker than one of the general servers.

The most widely available FTP-by-mail server is known as *BITFTP.* It was originally intended for users of *BITNET,* an older, mostly IBM network, which has great mail facilities but no FTP. In the United States, a BITFTP server is at Princeton University at bitftp@pucc.princeton.edu. European users should try bitftp@vm.gmd.de in Germany.

Table 10-2 lists other FTP-by-mail servers. To minimize expensive international network traffic, please use one in your own country.

Table 10-2	FTP-by-Mail Servers
E-mail Address	*Location*
ftpmail@decwrl.dec.com	California
ftpmail@sunsite.unc.edu	North Carolina
ftpmail@cs.uow.edu.au	Australia
ftpmail@ieunet.ie	Ireland
bitftp@plearn.edu.pl	Poland
ftpmail@doc.ic.ac.uk	Britain

Before you send any requests to an FTP-by-mail server, send a one-line message containing the word *help.* You should do this for two reasons: to see whether the help message contains anything interesting and to verify that you and the server can send messages to each other. Don't try to retrieve any files until you get the help message.

The message you send to a BITFTP server is more or less the sequence of commands you would issue in an interactive FTP session. For example, to retrieve a text file with the index of FYI notes from InterNIC (Internet Network Information Center), send this message to BITFTP:

```
FTP ftp.internic.net
USER anonymous
cd fyi
get fyi-index.txt
quit
```

You can enter multiple `cd` and `get` commands if necessary, but keep in mind that you don't want to overwhelm your mailbox with huge numbers of incoming messages full of files.

How am I supposed to know what files to ask for?

An excellent question. We're glad you asked. When you use FTP-by-mail, you can't see what files the FTP server has. If you're lucky, someone has sent you a note that tells you what to look for. Failing that, you can get a directory listing and then ask for a file in a later request, like this:

```
FTP ftp.internic.net
USER anonymous
cd fyi
dir
quit
```

Many systems have a complete directory listing available as a file in the top-level directory. The file is usually called something like `ls-lR` or `ls-lR.Z`. (The odd name comes from the name of the UNIX command used to create it.) If such a file exists, try getting it instead of doing a zillion `dir` commands. If no `ls-lR` is available but the file `README` is, get that because it often tells you where the directory listing is hidden.

If u cn rd ths u mst b a cmptr

So far we've considered retrieving text files by mail. But what about the 95 percent of available files that aren't text? For those files, there's a subterfuge called uuencode. (We mentioned this subject in Chapter 9 because it's the same way binary files are sent as Usenet news.) The uuencode program disguises binary files as text, something like this:

```
begin plugh.exe 644
M390GNM4L-REP3PT45G00I-05[I5-6M3OME,MRMK760PI5LPTMETLMKPY
MEOT39I4905B05YOPV3OIXKRTL5KWLJROJTOU,6P5;3;MRUO5OI4J5OI4
...

end
```

Because Eudora and Agent (the payware version of Free Agent, which handles mail in addition to news) automatically decode uuencoded messages, most Windows users can unscramble uuencoded messages easily enough.

Otherwise, you have to feed the message through the program *uudecode* (or, for Windows users, WinCode) to get back the original file. If a file is really big, its uuencoded version is sent as multiple mail messages, in which case you have to save to a file all the messages in the correct order and then uudecode that file. (Agent handles multiple parts, but Eudora doesn't.)

For UNIX users, you can pass a message directly to uudecode. In Pine or Elm, after the message is on your screen, press | (a vertical bar) and then type **uudecode** and press Enter. This command uudecodes the message directly, leaving the file on the UNIX system's disk. (Dial-in users then have to download the file, as discussed in Chapter 10.)

To retrieve a binary file by mail, you give both a uuencode *keyword* on the FTP line to tell it to uuencode what it retrieves and, as always, a binary command to tell it to FTP the file in binary mode. For example, to retrieve the compressed directory listing from /INFO on wuarchive.wustl.edu, send this message to BITFTP:

```
FTP wuarchhive.wustl.edu uuencode
USER anonymous
binary
cd info
get ls-1R.Z
quit
```

After you've uudecoded this file, you uncompress it (just like a file you FTP-ed directly) to get the file listing.

Meanwhile, Back at the Ranch

"All this FTP stuff is fine and dandy and works just great for getting stuff from one UNIX machine to another, but how about all us other folks out here who just plan to dial in to UNIX shell accounts — what about us? Huh? Huh?" You should ask this question because, just as we warned you, it ain't over yet.

Down and dirty

To get stuff to your very own PC or Macintosh, you have to *download* it. For this process to work, you have to have matching software on your PC or Mac and on your Internet service provider. The program on your PC or Mac and the program on your Internet provider have to use the same *protocol,* that is, the same system for transferring the file and checking it for errors. Commonly used protocols include Kermit, Xmodem, Ymodem, Zmodem, and MacTerminal.

Most service providers have a range of programs to choose from, and the software that came with your modem probably has something to do the trick. Most UNIX providers have programs called `sx` to send files by using the Xmodem protocol, `sz` to send files by using the Zmodem protocol, and `kermit` to send files by using Kermit. Look at the documentation or on-line help for the terminal program you use to find out which protocols it can deal with.

For PCs, a good hunch is that Zmodem is around on the provider's side. One way you can check is to type this command to find out about the `sz` program:

```
man sz
```

If Zmodem is present, the directions for how to use it are displayed.

A great deal of MacTerminal software, such as Microphone, supports Zmodem. If you have it, use it the same way the PC users do. If your terminal software doesn't support Zmodem, you can check your provider's support for MacTerminal by typing this line:

```
man macput
```

If MacTerminal is present, the directions for how to use it are displayed.

Because downloading varies from provider to provider, you may have to call your service to get the scoop on how to download from its system. Generally speaking, though, you have to go through these basic steps:

1. **Prepare your computer to receive data.**

   This step may not be anything other than ensuring that your terminal program's file-transfer settings are appropriate to the program you'll be using from your Internet service provider.

2. **Tell the Internet service provider's computer to send stuff.**

   For example, if you want to send a file called `wiggle.txt` by using zmodem, you type **sz wiggle.txt**.

3. **Wait.**

What goes down goes up

If you want to share something of yours with other users on the Net, you have to upload it. *Uploading,* as you probably have guessed, is just the reverse of downloading. Uploading, just like downloading, varies from system to system, but here's the basic plot (it works on The World, our local UNIX shell provider, and something similar will work on whatever system you're on):

1. **Prepare your computer to send data.**

   This step may not be anything other than ensuring that its file-transfer settings are appropriate to the software you'll be using from your Internet service provider.

2. **Tell the Internet service provider's computer to prepare to receive stuff.**

   Chances are that your Internet provider has the `rx`, `rz`, or `kermit` program that can receive information by using the Xmodem, Zmodem, and Kermit protocols, respectively.

3. **Tell your computer to send the data.**

4. **Wait.**

For PCs, a good hunch is that Zmodem is around on the provider's side. One way you can check is to type this command:

```
man rz
```

If Zmodem is present, the directions for how to use it are displayed.

For Macs, if your terminal program supports Zmodem, use its `send` command. You probably don't have to do anything on the provider's side as long as it has Zmodem support. If you don't have Zmodem on both ends, check your provider's MacTerminal availability by typing this line

```
man macget
```

If MacTerminal is present, the directions for how to use it are displayed.

For helpful hints about rooting around on UNIX machines to find useful stuff, see *UNIX For Dummies,* 2nd Edition, by John R. Levine and Margaret Levine Young (IDG Books Worldwide). For more information about uploading and downloading, see *Modems For Dummies,* 2nd Edition, by Tina Rathbone (IDG Books Worldwide).

It's Not Just a File — It's Software

Using FTP, you can download freeware and shareware programs, install them, and use them. You'll need a few well-chosen software tools, including a program to uncompress compressed files. (Useful little programs like this are usually called *utilities* in the jargon.)

Installing FTP'd software usually requires three steps:

1. **Using FTP, download the file that contains the software.**
2. **The software is usually in a compressed format, so uncompress it.**
3. **Run the installation program that comes with it, or at least create an icon for the program.**

The first part of this chapter described how to do step 1, the FTP part. The rest of this chapter describes steps 2 and 3: uncompressing and installing. Here goes!

Decompressing and unzipping

Most software is stored on FTP servers in a compressed format, to save both storage space on the server and transmission time when you download the file. You need a program to deal with compressed files, specifically those with the file extension .zip (these are called, amazingly, *ZIP files*). Programs with names such as PKZIP, PKUNZIP, and UNZIP have been around for years for DOS users. UNZIP and its brethren work fine, but they are DOS programs and not really convenient to use from Windows. It's annoying to use the MS-DOS icon every time you want to run one. Luckily, someone (a guy named Nico Mak) wrote a nice little Windows program called WinZip that can both unzip and zip things for you, right from Windows. Mac users can get a program named UNZIP.

If you already have WinZip (which is also available through the mail or from various shareware outlets), skip this entire section. If you have and love PKZIP and PKUNZIP or UNZIP and don't mind running them from DOS, you can skip it too.

To get WinZip, FTP it from ftp.winzip.com in the /winzip directory. On the Web, go to http://www.winzip.com/. As of this writing, the version for Windows 3.1 is in a file called WZ60WN16.EXE. The version for Windows 95 is in a file called WINZIP95.EXE.

To install WinZip:

1. **Create a directory for the program.**

   Use File Manager (in Windows 3.1) or My Computer or Explorer (in Windows 95) to create a directory or folder.

2. **Move the file you just downloaded into the directory or folder you just created.**

   Again, use Windows File Manager or Windows 95's My Computer or Explorer.

3. **Run the file you just downloaded, but double-click its filename in File Manager, My Computer, or Explorer.**

   The file magically unzips itself, creating a bunch of files in the directory or folder you just made. One of the files contains installation instructions.

4. **Follow the installation instructions that came with WinZip.**

Mac Users Say Stuffit

Mac users can download an unzip program from `ftp.uu.net` in the `/pub/archiving/zip/MAC` directory or from `ftp.doc.ic.ac.uk` in the `/packages/zip/MAC` directory or from `quest.jpl.nasa.gov` in the `/pub/MAC` directory. The file that contains the unzip program is called something like `unz512x.hqx`.

More popular than ZIP and UNZIP for the Mac crowd is a shareware program, by Raymond Lau, known as Stuffit. Stuffit comes in many flavors, including a commercially available version called Stuffit Deluxe. Stuffit files of all varieties generally end with .SIT.

For decompression, you can use the freeware programs UnStuffit, Stuffit Expander, or Extractor.

Running WinZip

Give it a try! Double-click that icon! WinZip looks like Figure 10-4.

To open a ZIP file (which the WinZip folks call an *archive*), click the Open button and choose the directory and filename for the ZIP file. Poof! WinZip displays a list of the files in the archive, with their dates and sizes.

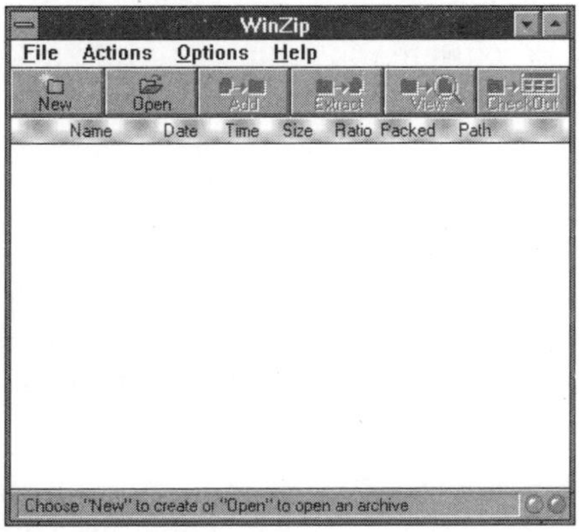

Figure 10-4:
WinZip is
ready to
deal with
your ZIP
files.

Unzip it!

Sounds suggestive, we know, but it's not as much fun as it sounds. If you want to use a file from a ZIP file, after you have opened the ZIP file you *extract* it — that is, you ask WinZip to uncompress it and store it in a new file.

To extract a file:

1. **Choose it from the list of files.**

   You can choose a group of files that are listed together by clicking the first one and then Shift-clicking the last one. To select an additional file, Ctrl+click it.

2. **Click the Extract button.**

   A dialog box asks which directory you want to put the file in and whether you want to extract all the files in the archive or just the one you selected.

3. **Select the directory in which to store the unzipped files.**

4. **Click OK.**

   WinZip unzips the file. The ZIP file is unchanged, but now you have the uncompressed file (or files) also.

Zipped out?

When you are all finished zipping and unzipping, quit WinZip by choose File⇨Exit.

WinZip can do a bunch of other things too, such as add files to a ZIP file and create your own ZIP file, but you don't need to know how to perform these tasks in order to swipe software from the Net, so we'll skip them. (We bet that you can figure them out just by looking at the buttons on the WinZip toolbar.)

Now that you know how to unzip software you get from the Internet, you're ready for the next topic: safe software.

Scanning for viruses

We all know that you practice safe software. That is, you check every new program you get to make sure that it doesn't contain any hidden software viruses that might display obnoxious messages or trash your hard disk. If this is true of you, you can skip this section.

For the rest of you, it would be a good idea to use a virus-scanning program. You never know what naughty piece of code you might otherwise unwittingly FTP to your defenseless computer!

If you use Windows 3.1 with DOS 6.2, you have a virus checker built right into File Manager. Here's how to use the virus checker:

1. **Run File Manager.**

2. **Choose Tools⇨Antivirus from the menu.**

    You see the Microsoft Anti-Virus window, shown in Figure 10-5.

3. **Choose a disk drive by clicking it in the Drives box.**

4. **Click the Detect and Clean button.**

    If you are scanning a large hard disk for viruses, this step can take several minutes.

TIP

It's a good idea to run Anti-Virus after you have obtained and run any new piece of software. The FTP servers on the Internet make every effort to keep their software archives virusfree, but nobody is perfect. Don't get caught by some prankster's idea of a joke!

Windows 95 doesn't come with a virus checker, but several commercial ones are available.

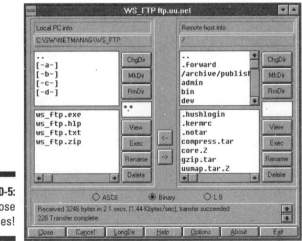

Figure 10-5:
Evict those
viruses!

Installing the program

Now you've downloaded the software, unzipped it (if it's a ZIP file), and the program is ready to run, but there is no icon for it. Here's how to make one in Windows 3.1:

1. **Open both Program Manager and File Manager and arrange the screen so that you can see the program group you want to put the icon in (in Program Manager) and the program name (in File Manager).**

2. **Drag the program name from File Manager into Program Manager, and place it in the program group where you want it.**

   You see a new icon in the program group.

To run your new program, you can just double-click the icon. Cool!

In Windows 95, follow these steps:

1. **Run either My Computer or Explorer, and select the program file (the file with the extension EXE, or occasionally COM).**

2. **Use your right mouse button to drag the filename out onto the desktop or into an open folder on the desktop.**

   An icon for the program appears.

For information about other cute things you can do in Windows 95 (such as add the program to the Start button's menu), see *Windows 95 For Dummies*, by Andy Rathbone (IDG Books Worldwide).

Configuring the program

Now you can run the program by double-clicking its icon. Hooray!

You may have to tell the program, however, about your Internet address or your computer or who knows what before it can do its job. Refer to the text files, if any, that came with the program or choose Help from the program's menu bar to get more information about how to configure and run your new program.

Where Is It?

"The world of FTP sounds fine and dandy," you may say, "but what's out there, and where can I find it?" See Chapter 11 to learn how to find which files are available by anonymous FTP and on which FTP server the files are stored.

Chapter 11

Finding Stuff on the Net

● ●

In This Chapter

▶ Finding stuff on the Web

▶ Finding stuff on Gopher

▶ Finding stuff on FTP servers

▶ Finding stuff by e-mail

▶ Finding stuff in Usenet newsgroups

● ●

*O*K, all this great stuff is out there on the Net. How do you find it? That's an excellent question. Thanks for asking that question. Questions like that are what makes this country strong and vibrant. We salute you and say, "Keep asking questions!" Next question, please.

Oh, you want an *answer* to your question. Fortunately, there's quite a bit of (technical term follows) stuff-finding stuff on the Net. More particularly, there are indexes and directories of much of the interesting material available on the Net.

There are different kinds of indexes and directories for different kinds of material. Unfortunately, because they tend to be organized by the kind of Internet service they provide rather than by the nature of the material, you find Web resources in one place, Gopher resources in another place, and so on. Because most of the good stuff is on the Web or on Gopher, they are the main places we discuss in this chapter.

Wending Your Way through the Web

When we're looking for stuff on the Net, we always begin with one of the Web guides discussed in this section.

You use them all in more or less the same way:

1. Start your Web browser, such as Netscape.

2. **Tell it to go to the index or directory's home page.**

We list the URLs (page names) of the home pages later in this section.

After you get there, there are two approaches.

3A. **If there's a Search box, type some keywords in the box and click Search, or. . .**

This is the "index" approach, to look for topic areas that match your keywords.

After a perhaps long delay (the Web is pretty big) it returns an index page with links to pages that match your keywords.

3B. **If there's a list of links to topic areas, click a topic area of interest.**

The "directory" approach is to begin at a general topic and get more and more specific. Each page has links to subpages, which get more and more specific until they link to actual pages likely to be of interest.

After some clicking around to get the hang of it, you'll find all sorts of good stuff.

You hear a great deal of talk around the Web about *search engines*. Search engines is a fancy way to say stuff-finding stuff. All the directories and indexes we're about to describe are in the broad category called search engines. So don't get upset by some high falutin'-sounding terms. They is what they is.

Yahoo

Yahoo is a large, well-indexed directory of Web pages. It began as a student project at Stanford and is now commercially supported. It organizes its information in categories and subcategories, like a library, although you can also do keyword searches. It's one of the best places to begin any search. It now also includes Reuters headlines and some other "real world" information.

Yahoo's URL is

```
http://www.yahoo.com
```

You can either click down through categories starting from the Yahoo home page or search for categories by keyword. (You're searching the categories, not the Web pages themselves.)

Yahoo pages contain a mixture of references to information pages out in the rest of the Web, and references to subpages (and sub-sub and sub-sub-sub and so on) within Yahoo. You can also go back up to more general categories by clicking the category titles that appear at the top of each page.

Index, directory, what's the difference?

When we talk about a *directory,* we mean a listing that's divided up into named categories with the entries assigned to categories partly or entirely by humans. You look things up by finding a category you want and seeing what it contains. In this book, we would think of the Table of Contents as a directory.

An *index,* on the other hand, simply collects all the items, extracts keywords from them (often by taking all the words except for *the, and,* and the like), and makes a big list. You search it by giving some words that seem likely and it finds all the entries that contain that word. The index in the back of the book is more like an index.

Each has its advantages and disadvantages. Directories are organized so that when you find a category of interest, all the items in that category are likely to be related to what you want. Because indexes, on the other hand, don't know what the words mean, if you look for *program,* for example, it finds computer programs, educational programs, theater programs, and anything else that contains the word. But because indexes can be created largely or completely automatically, indexes on the Net tend to contain many more entries and to be updated more often.

There's some overlap between the two — Yahoo, the best-known Web page directory, lets you search by keyword, and many indexes divide their entries into general categories that let you limit the search.

Lycos

Lycos is a largely automated "Web crawler" that collects pages from all over the Net that you can search by keyword. It began as a project at Carnegie-Mellon University and has also gone commercial.

Lycos' URL is

```
http://www.lycos.com/
```

Webcrawler

Webcrawler is an automated indexer that crawls around the Web cataloging and indexing every page it comes across. It's owned by America Online (AOL), but you don't have to have an AOL account to use Webcrawler.

Webcrawler's URL is

```
http://www.webcrawler.com/
```

InfoSeek

InfoSeek is an index rather than a directory: You give it some keywords to look for, and it finds the pages that match the best. InfoSeek has a smaller database than do some of the other indexes, but because it searches it faster, it's often the quickest way to find a page.

You can get limited access free of charge, or subscribe for either a monthly or per-search fee. (The per-search fee is currently 20 cents, or less if you get a monthly plan.) With the subscription plan you can also search Usenet postings, articles from computer magazines, and some investment reports.

InfoSeek's URLs are

```
http://www.infoseek.com/ (paid)
http://www2.infoseek.com/ (free)
```

Other Web guides

There are lots of other Web guides, including many specialized guides put together for particular interests. (For example, there's Femina, a feminist guide at http://www.femina.com/.)

Yahoo has an directory of other guides: Start at the Yahoo page (http://www.yahoo.com/), choose WWW (which appears under Computers), and then choose Indices to Web Documents or Searching the Web.

Archie Finds That Missing File

Archie is a rarity on the Net, a tool that does only one thing, but it does that one thing well: It helps you find files available on anonymous FTP servers.

If you know the name of a file you're looking for — or kind of know the name, enough so that you can come up with a reasonable guess — Archie goes running around the world, checking database after database and looking for files that match your description.

Archie servers exist all over the world, but you should choose one close to home to help minimize traffic on the Net. Different Archie servers get different amounts of use, so you may have to try a few before you find one with a reasonable response time. If everything you try seems painfully slow, try early in the morning or late at night, or try sending your Archie request by e-mail (see the section "E-mail Archie," later in this chapter).

Table 11-1 lists several Archie servers you can try. If you try one and it doesn't let you on because it's too full, chances are that it provides you with another list of Archie servers you can try. Eventually, you'll get on.

Table 11-1	Archie Servers
Server Name	*Location*
archie.rutgers.edu	New Jersey
archie.sura.net	Maryland
archie.unl.edu	Nebraska
archie.ans.net	New York
ds.internic.net	U.S.A. (run by AT&T)
archie.mcgill.ca	Canada
archie.au	Australia
archie.th-darmstadt.de	Europe (Germany)
archie.funet.fi	Europe (Finland)
archie.luth.se	Europe (Sweden)
archie.univie.ac.at	Europe (Austria)
archie.doc.ic.ac.uk	U.K. and Europe
archie.cs.huji.ac.il	Israel
archie.ad.jp	Japan
archie.kuis.kyoto-u.ac.jp	Japan
archie.sogang.ac.kr	Korea
archie.nz	New Zealand
archie.ncu.edu.tw	Taiwan

You can access Archie servers in several ways:

- If you have *Archie client software* (`archie` or `xarchie`), you can run directly from your machine (see the sections "Straight Archie" and "Xarchie," later in this chapter).

- You can telnet to an Archie server (see the following section, "Telnet Archie").

- You can e-mail your request to an Archie server (see the section "E-mail Archie").

Telnet Archie

Unless you have Archie client software available to you locally (try using the command `archie` or, on a machine with X Windows or one of its variants such as Motif, `xarchie`), you probably want to telnet to an Archie server. Before you do, however, if you can, you probably will want to start a *log file* (a file in which all the text displayed in your window is captured) because Archie's output may come fast and furiously, gushing filenames, hostnames, and Internet addresses you really don't want to have to copy down by hand if you can avoid it. If you're running on a machine with X Windows or one of its variants such as Motif, hold down Ctrl, press the left mouse button, and choose Log to File from the Main Options window. If you're not running X, it's worth asking around to see whether some locally available program can capture the text on the screen to a file. Windows users have `wsarchie`, which we consider later.

For now, choose a server, use telnet, and log in as `archie`:

```
% telnet archie.ans.net
Trying...
Connected to forum.ans.net.
Escape character is '^]'.Archie
AIX telnet (forum.ans.net) IBM AIX Version 3 for RISC System/
        6000
(C)   Copyrights by IBM and by others 1982, 1991.
login: archie
```

Archie returns with an Archie prompt:

```
archie>
```

Telling Archie how to behave: The set and show commands

Every Archie server is set up with features you can tune to suit your needs. You may have to change them to make Archie do what you want. Not all Archie servers are alike, and you have to pay attention to how things are set up on the server you land on.

To see how the server you're on is set up, use the `show` command:

```
archie> show
# 'autologout' (type numeric) has the value '15'.
# 'mailto (type string) is not set.
# 'maxhits' (type numeric) has the value '100'.
# 'pager' (type boolean) is not set.
# 'search' (type string) has the value 'sub'.
# 'sortby' (type string) has the value 'none'.
# 'status' (type boolean) is set.
# 'term' (type string) has the value 'dumb 24 80'.
```

You can also use show to see specific values one at a time (try typing show term, show search, and so on). Although all these values are explained next, the variables you need to pay careful attention to are search and maxhits. We also suggest setting the *pager,* which tells Archie to stop after every screen full of text and wait for you to press the spacebar, to avoid the extremely irritating situation in which you wait 15 minutes for an Archie search and then the output flies off the screen before you can read it.

Searching is such sweet sorrow, or something

Archie normally searches for a name that contains the string you type, disregarding uppercase and lowercase. If you search for *pine,* for example, it matches *PINE, Pineapple,* and *spineless,* among other things. If you use Archie much, you'll want more control over the searching process, so you probably will want to use one of the other search methods for matching what you type. How much you know about the name of the file you're looking for should determine the search method you use.

To set the search method, use the set command:

```
archie> set search sub
```

The search methods Archie supports are called *sub, subcase, exact,* and *regex:*

- ✔ **Sub method:** Searches to match the substring anywhere in the filename. This search is case insensitive (case doesn't matter). If you have an idea of a character string that's likely to be contained in the filename, choose sub.

- ✔ **Subcase method:** Searches to match the substring exactly as given anywhere in the filename. This search is case sensitive. Use this method only if you are sure about the case of the characters in the filename.

- ✔ **Exact method:** Searches for the exact filename you enter. This type of search is the fastest, and you should use it if you know exactly what file you're looking for.

- ✔ **Regex method:** Uses UNIX *regular expressions* to define the pattern for Archie's search — see the following section for a description.

Using advanced searching tactics

If you want to look for filenames that begin with *x* and end with *gif* and have exactly three letters in between, regex searchers are for you. (The rest of you can skip this section.) This is a particular kind of substring search, and Archie tries to match the expression to a string anywhere in the file's name. In regular expressions certain characters take on special meaning, and regular expressions can get absurdly complicated, if you want them to be.

- ✔ If you know that the string begins the filename, start your string with the ^ (caret) to tie the string to the first position of the filename.

- ✔ If you know that the file ends with a particular string, end your string with the $ (dollar sign) to tie the string to the end of the filename.

- ✔ The . (period) is used to specify any single character.

- ✔ The * (asterisk) means zero or more occurrences of the preceding regular expression.

- ✔ Use [and] (square brackets) to list a set of characters to match or a range of characters to match. Combined with ^ (caret) in the first position, square brackets list a set of characters to exclude or a range not to include.

- ✔ You can specify more than one range in the same search. To use a special character as part of your string, put a \ (backslash) in front of it.

To find any files that contain the string *birdie* and end with *txt,* for example, type this line:

```
prog ^birdie.*txt$
```

To find filenames that contain numeric digits, type:

```
prog [0-9]
```

To exclude filenames that contain lowercase letters, type this line:

```
prog [^a-z]
```

How long do you want to look?

The maxhits variable determines how many matches Archie tries to find. On many servers the default for this number is 1000 — but for most searches that's ridiculous. If you know the name of the file you want, how many copies do you want to choose from? Ten or 20 should give you sufficient choice. But if you don't reset maxhits, Archie continues traveling around the Net looking for as many as 1,000 matches.

Remember too that Archie's output is going to your screen and maybe to your log file — so think about how much data you can handle. After you decide just how much you want to know, set maxhits equal to that number (suppose that it's 100):

```
archie> set maxhits 100
```

Table 11-2 lists more `set` settings.

Table 11-2	Other Nifty Features to Set from Set
Variable	**What It Does**
autologout	Sets how long Archie waits around for you to do something before kicking you off.
mailto	Sets the e-mail address used by the `mail` command.
pager	When set, sends Archie's output through the pager program `less`, which stops after each screen full of output and waits for you to press the spacebar. Using the command set pager switches the pager from off to on or from on to off, so do a show before you change the pager setting so that you don't do the opposite of what you intend.
sortby	Sorts Archie's output in one of the following orders: by *hostname* in alphabetical order or reversed (*rhostname*); by most recently modified (*time*) or oldest (*rtime*); by *size,* largest first, or smallest first (*rsize*); by *filename* in lexical order, or reverse (*rfilename*); or *unsorted* (usually the default). You type something like **set sort by time**.
status	If set, Archie shows the progress of the search. Can be reassuring when Archie is very slow.
term	Sets the type of terminal you're using so that Archie can tailor your output (try vt100 if you're not sure).

Find it!

Archie's basic command is the `prog` command, and it takes this form:

```
prog searchstring
```

That's it. That command launches the whole search. The nature and scope of the search are determined by the variables you set or didn't set.

Here's an example. Suppose that you want to find out what kind of font software is around:

```
archie> prog font

Host csuvax1.murdoch.edu.au   (134.115.4.1)
Last updated 00:23 31 Jul 1993

    Location: /pub/mups
       FILE      rw-r--r--      4107  Nov 16  1992     font.f
       FILE      rw-r--r--      9464  Nov 16  1992
          fontmups.lib

Host sifon.cc.mcgill.ca   (132.206.27.10)
Last updated 04:22 11 Aug 1993

    Location: /pub/packages/gnu
       FILE      rw-r--r--    628949  Mar  9 19:16   fontutils-
          0.6.tar.z

Host ftp.germany.eu.net   (192.76.144.75)
Last updated 05:24  7 May 1993

    Location: /pub/packages/gnu
       FILE      rw-r--r--    633005  Oct 28  1992    fontutils-
          0.6.tar.z
    Location: /pub/gnu
       FILE      rw-r--r--   1527018  Nov 13 16:11
          ghostscript-fonts-2.5.1.tar.z

Host ftp.uu.net   (192.48.96.9)
Last updated 08:17 31 Jul 1993

    Location: /systems/att7300/csvax
       FILE      rw-r--r--   1763981  Mar  5 23:30    groff-
          font.tar.z

Host reseq.regent.e-technik.tu-muenchen.de
          (129.187.230.225)
Last updated 06:26 10 Aug 1993

    Location: /informatik.public/comp/typesetting/tex/
          tex3.14/dev
FILE      rw-r--r--        51  Sep 24  1991    fontdesc

Host nic.switch.ch   (130.59.1.40)
Last updated 04:48  7 Aug 1993


Host nic.switch.ch   (130.59.1.40)
Last updated 04:48  7 Aug 1993

    Location: /software/unix/TeX/dviware/umddvi/misc
       FILE      rw-rw-r--      607  Oct  2  1990    fontdesc
```

As you quickly find out, a great deal of duplication is out there. If you're looking for variety, you can make a series of inquiries that eliminate the stuff you've already found and make subsequent queries more fruitful.

After you have found it, or some of it . . . what is it?

There sure is a great deal of *stuff* out there. But what the heck is it? Sometimes Archie can help you to figure that out. We say "sometimes" because Archie's information is only as good as that provided by the folks who hung the stuff out there in the first place. The whatis command lets you search through file descriptions contributed by the people who run FTP archives.

For example, if you use whatis rather than prog in the search for font software, you get the following:

```
archie>   whatis font
afm2tfm           Translate from Adobe to TeX
gftodvi           Converts from metafont to DVI format
gftopk            Converts from metafont to PK format
gftopxl           Converts from metafont to PXL format
her2vfont         Hershey fonts to 'vfont' rasterizer
hershey           Hershey Fonts
hershey.f77       Hershey Fonts in Fortran 77
hershtools        Hershey font manipulation tools and data
hp2pk             HP font conversion tool
jetroff/bfont     Jetroff Basic Fonts
jis.pk            The JTeX .300pk fonts (Japanese language
                  support)
k2ps              Print text files with Kanji (uses JTeX fonts)
                  (Japanese language support)
mkfont            Convert ASCII font descriptions <-> device-
                  independent troff (ditroff) format
ocra-metafont     METAFONT sources for the OCR-A
"Alphanumeric Character Sets for
Optical Recognition"
```

Note: The string font appears in some of these filenames, but only in the description of others.

You can't get there from here

Archie is great for *finding* stuff but no help at all in *retrieving* stuff for you. To get stuff off the Net, you have to do what Archie did to find it in the first place: Use *FTP* (*f*ile-*t*ransfer *p*rotocol) to copy it from the archive where it lives back to your computer. Use *anonymous FTP* and log in as the generic user anonymous, using your e-mail address as the password. After you've logged in for FTP, you use the cd command to move to the appropriate directory and get or mget to retrieve the files (see Chapter 6 for details). Some Windows clients, such as the popular WS_ARCHIE, can hook to an FTP program and retrieve stuff automatically; it's obvious when they're able to do that.

If you're on a quest for related software, after you have FTP'd to a host that has relevant stuff, you might want to look around in the directory containing the file you know about (use the FTP dir command to list the contents of a remote directory) and in any subdirectories near it.

Straight Archie

If you use a shell provider and try to type the archie command directly and it returns a comment telling you how to use it, you're in luck. You can use the Archie client software directly without telnetting to an Archie server. One big advantage of using Archie from a command line is that you can easily redirect its output to a file, as in the following:

```
$ archie -ld font > fontfiles
```

(This line stores the result of the search in a file called fontfiles, which you can peruse later at your leisure by using any text editor or file viewer.) Be aware, however, that the client software is limited and that you may want to telnet to an Archie server to take advantage of more of Archie's capabilities. For one, you can't set all the tuning variables described in the section "Telnet Archie," earlier in this chapter. Also, you cannot use the whatis command.

Using Archie directly means using a command line that may get complex. You can specify the kind of search and the Archie server you want to use and format the output to a limited extent. If you supply the search string and no modifiers, Archie defaults to an exact search with a maximum of 95 matches. For details about choosing a search method and other available options, see the section "Telnet Archie," earlier in this chapter.

Table 11-3 lists the modifiers you can supply.

Table 11-3	Search-String Modifiers	
Archie Modifier	Telnet Equivalent	Archie Meaning
-c	subcase	Sets search mode for a case-sensitive substring
-e	exact	Sets search mode for an exact string match (default)
-r	regex	Sets search mode for a regular expression search
-s	sub	Sets search mode for a substring search
-l		Lists one match per line
-t	sortby	Sorts Archie's output by date, newest first

Archie Modifier	Telnet Equivalent	Archie Meaning
-m#	maxhits	Sets the maximum number of matches to return (default 95)
-h		Specifies the Archie server to use
-L		Lists the known Archie servers and the current default

For example, to use the server archie.ans.net to do a regular expression search for no more than 50 files that contain digits in their names, type this line:

```
$ archie -r -m50 -h archie.ans.net "[0-9]"
```

(Note that the pattern [0-9] is enclosed in double quotation marks to avoid having it misinterpreted as the name of a file to match locally. In general, put your patterns in quotation marks if they contain anything other than letters and digits.)

Windows Archie

A couple of Archie clients are available in Windows, the nicest of which is David Woakes' wsarchie.

You start it up by clicking its icon. Then fill in the search for string, choose a server if you don't like the default one, and click Search. It contacts the server and comes back with an optimistic estimate of how long you have to wait. (At the bottom of Figure 11-1, Queue 2 means that we're second in line, and Time 18s means 18 seconds to wait. Ha!)

When the results come back, you can scroll through the lists of matching hosts, directories, and files. If you find a file you like, double-click its name, and wsarchie starts up an FTP program and automagically retrieves it for you. Pretty cool.

One of the nicest things about running Archie under Windows is that you can start your query and then shrink wsarchie to an icon and go do something else until the answer comes back.

E-mail Archie

If you're unable to telnet to an Archie server either because of the limitations of your network connection or because you have been unsuccessful in logging in to an Archie server, you can send your request to Archie by using e-mail. If

Figure 11-1:
Wsarchie is
a Windows
program
that helps
you find files
in FTP
archives.

you're planning to launch a major search and don't want to wait for the response, using Archie from e-mail is a good way to go.

Not all of telnet Archie's capabilities are available to you through e-mail, but you
can still carry out a substantial search. To send a request to Archie, send mail
to `archie@servername`, where `servername` is any of the Archie servers
mentioned at the beginning of this chapter.

The body of the e-mail message you send contains the commands you want to
issue to Archie. Enter as many commands as you like, each beginning in the first
column of a line. Choose from the available commands, which are listed in
Table 11-4.

The most common commands are `prog` and `whatis`, which take exactly the
same form you use in telnet Archie, as shown in this example:

```
prog font.*txt
whatis font
```

Archie has become extremely popular, so popular that it's common for each
server to be handling several dozen requests at a time, all the time, all day. That
means that telnet or command-line Archie can be *sssllllooowww,* like 10 or 15
minutes to do a search. If it's going to be *that* slow, you may as well send in your
request by e-mail and go do something else. As soon as Archie finishes your
request, it drops its answer in your mailbox, where you can peruse it at your
leisure. An added advantage of e-mail is that, if the response turns out to be 400
lines long, it's much easier to deal with a 400-line e-mail message than with 400
lines of stuff flying off your screen.

Table 11-4	Commands to Send to E-Mail Archie Servers
Command	**What It Does**
prog	Searches for matching names; assumes a regular expression search (regex)
whatis	Supplies the keyword for the software-description database search
compress	Sends the reply in a compressed and encoded format
servers	Returns a list of Archie servers
path	Gives the e-mail address you want Archie to use to respond to your mail request, if the automatically generated return address on your e-mail isn't correct
help	Returns the help text for e-mail Archie
quit	Ends the request to Archie

Veronica, My Darling

Gopher, the menuing system discussed in Chapter 11, lets lots and lots of people set up Gopher servers and create menus full of interesting stuff.

Gopher quickly became a victim of its own success. So many Gopher servers are out there that finding the Gopher menu you want has itself become difficult. *Veronica* comes to the rescue. Like Archie, Veronica has a big database of available services. Veronica tracks all the Gopher menus that can be accessed directly or (often very) indirectly from the Mother Gopher in Minnesota.

Finding stuff with Veronica

Using Veronica is easy — it's just a search item. You can find Veronica under Other Gophers or a similar name in most public Gopher systems. If you, like most people, use Gopher through a Web server, you can find links to a bunch of Veronicas at

```
gopher://gopher.scs.unr.edu/11/veronica
```

There are two slightly different "flavors" of Veronica-searching. One is a menu search, which searches through the names of existing Gopher menus and returns a menu of menus whose names include the words you want. The other is an item search, which searches through every Gopher menu item and creates a menu of all the items that match the words you selected. An item search generates a really huge menu unless you choose some really obscure terms, so we suggest that you try a menu search first.

To search, click a link for a Veronica server, either a menu search or an item search. (Because the servers tend to be pretty busy, you may have to try several to get one that's able to give you a response.) Then your Gopher or Web program invites you to type some search words. Do so; try to come up with two or three words that describe what you want. Then press Enter and see what it finds.

One time we wanted to find the on-line computerized *Jargon Dictionary,* which has been around in various forms since the late 1960s. We picked a Veronica Gopher item and, for the search string, entered `jargon dictionary`. Veronica constructed for us a custom menu that contained only entries that matched our search string (this is the response displayed by the simple UNIX Gopher client; if you have something fancier, such as Netscape, the display is prettier, but the items are the same):

```
 ->     1.  The Jargon Dictionary File/
        2.  The Jargon Dictionary File/
        3.  The Jargon Dictionary File/
        4.  The Jargon Dictionary File/
        5.  The New Hacker's Dictionary (computer jargon) <?>
        6.  jargon: The New Hacker's Dictionary <?>
        7.  jargon: The New Hacker's Dictionary <?>
        8.  Fuzzy search in "The New Hackers Dictionary"
               (jargon.txt) <?>
        9.  The Jargon Dictionary <?>
       10.  Computer Jargon Dictionary <?>
```

Redundant items mean that a resource is available at more than one place. It usually doesn't matter which one you use.

Jughead?

Veronica is a handy searching system, but she can be unwieldy to use because there are so many possible places she looks. Jughead is a similar search system that looks for Gopher menus on a single server, so it's both faster and more specific. If a site offers Jughead, there's an item for it in the top-level Gopher menu at the site.

You use Jughead in the same way as you use Veronica: Select the item, type some search words, and get back a Gopher menu with the items that match.

WAIS and Means

WAIS (which stands for *wide-area information service*) is a full text-search system available on the Net. Full text means that, for the documents it handles, it looks through the entire document to match search words you specify. Because WAIS uses a clever statistical matching technique, unlike other search programs, it works better if you give more terms rather than fewer.

The set of databases you can search via WAIS is, even by Net standards, pretty miscellaneous. There are collections of scholarly papers (particularly in the biosciences), archives of some Usenet groups, and lots of other document collections that someone decided to offer on-line. As is always the case on the Net, there are some nuggets of great stuff, but it can take some guessing to find a good database to search.

There are specialized WAIS client programs for UNIX and Windows, but unless you plan to do an awful lot of WAIS searching, it's easier to go in through the World Wide Web. Several different WAIS-to-Web gateways are available, but the one at WAIS, Inc. is the most reliable.

To do a WAIS search, point your Web browser at `http://www.wais.com/directory-of-servers.html`. You'll find a Web page with a search field at the top, and a list of links to individual WAIS databases. You can either click one of the databases to select it or use WAIS itself to find a database to search. To do that, type in the search box at the top of the page some words describing the kind of information you're looking for and select Search. (If you're looking for a recipe for pot roast, for example, you need to find databases of recipes, so use search words such as *food, cooking,* and *recipes*). WAIS returns a page of links to databases that best match what you're looking for. Click one of them to select it.

Whether you chose a database directly or by searching, now you've arrived at a page that lets you search a particular WAIS database. Type some words describing what you want to read about. (Here's where you type **pot roast**.) Click Search, and you get back a list of matching documents, ranked by how well they matched. To read any that look interesting, click on them.

Why did they name it Veronica?

According to Veronica's authors, the name is just a coincidence, unrelated to Archie, because it's an acronym for the true name, which *is Very Easy Rodent-Oriented Net-wide Index to Computerized Archives.*

But the next index searcher is called Jughead, which is supposed to stand *for Jonzy's Universal Gopher Hierarchy Excavation And Display.* How gullible do they think we are? And what about Betty? And Moose?

Where did WAIS come from?

WAIS began at Thinking Machines, a high-tech computer company down the street from M.I.T. in Cambridge, Massachusetts. (Not surprisingly, the kind of computers that Thinking Machines makes are really good at WAIS searches.) The WAIS project got big enough that it spun off into a separate company called WAIS, Inc. Some commercial business-information services, notably Dow Jones (which publishes the *Wall Street Journal* and has a large on-line news subsidiary) chose WAIS for searching through their databases, although WAIS never became as popular on the Net as other search schemes.

In mid-1995 AOL bought WAIS, Inc., presumably to fold it into services it plans to offer. As of late 1995, WAIS, Inc. still seemed to be doing pretty much the same things it always had.

What's in the News?

In among the mountains of dross in Usenet news is some good stuff. This section lists some tips for finding what you want:

- ✔ Most newsgroups have FAQ (frequently asked questions) messages posted regularly to the group. These FAQs are a treasure trove of useful and interesting information. You can find all the FAQs in the newsgroup `news.answers`. The `comp.answers` newsgroup also contains FAQs for the `comp` newsgroups, `misc.answers` contains FAQs for `misc` groups, `alt.answers` contains FAQs for `alt` groups, `rec.answers` has FAQs for `rec` groups, and `soc.answers` has FAQs for `soc` groups. There's also an FTP archive of the FAQs at `rtfm.mit.edu`.

- ✔ Some newsgroups are archived and have WAIS indexes (see the preceding section) to search them. This is a good way to look for articles about particular topics.

- ✔ A couple of on-line search systems let you search through news postings. Look at `http://www.dejanews.com` for a public news-search system. If you subscribe to InfoSeek, described earlier in this chapter, one of the optional databases you can search is news articles from the past seven weeks.

Mail, One More Time

Mailing lists are another important resource. Most lists (but not all — check before you ask) welcome concrete, politely phrased questions related to the list's topic. See Chapter 8 for more information about mailing lists. The section "Finding Other Mailing Lists" in Chapter 8 tells you how to look for lists of particular topics of interest to you.

Part IV
Four Entrance Ramps

The 5th Wave   By Rich Tennant

"SINCE WE GOT IT, HE HASN'T MOVED FROM THAT SPOT
FOR ELEVEN STRAIGHT DAYS. ODDLY ENOUGH THEY CALL
THIS 'GETTING UP AND RUNNING' ON THE INTERNET."

In this part . . .

Millions of Internet users use a commercial provider as their entrance ramp to the Information Superhighway (known in some circles as the Information Supercollider or the Information Supersoaker.) We look in detail at the most popular ones: CompuServe, America Online, and Microsoft Network — as well as at UNIX shell providers, which let you use the Internet with the simplest of computer hardware and software.

Chapter 12

Using the Internet via CompuServe

● ●

● ●

CompuServe is a very successful on-line service that caters to business and professional users. It has lots of information about computer hardware and software, including support forums for hundreds of software and hardware vendors. Since CompuServe created WinCIM and MacCIM — easy-to-use access programs — a CompuServe account has become as user-friendly as some of the more recent on-line services, such as America Online and Prodigy.

To provide access to Internet services such as the World Wide Web, CompuServe created another way to use your CompuServe account. By using its NetLauncher program, you can dial in to CompuServe as though it were a PPP Internet account and use Internet software such as Mosaic. In fact, NetLauncher comes with a version of Mosaic called Spry Mosaic. It's a little confusing because, if you want to use CompuServe's regular services, you run one program (WinCIM or MacCIM). If you want to use CompuServe for Internet services, you run a different program (NetLauncher).

This chapter describes CompuServe's Internet-related abilities, including e-mail and the World Wide Web. For the complete scoop about CompuServe, take a look at *CompuServe For Dummies*, 2nd Edition, by Wallace Wang (IDG Books Worldwide).

This chapter describes how to use CompuServe with its Windows software: the CompuServe Information Manager (CIM) for Windows, better known as WinCIM (version 1.4). If you're using its Macintosh software, MacCIM, or a different version of WinCIM, your screens will look a little different from those shown in this chapter. It also describes NetLauncher, the program that lets you use your CompuServe account as an Internet PPP account.

Signing Up for CompuServe

To sign up for a CompuServe account, get hold of one of its little disk packages (call 1-800-487-0453 to get yours). It contains a disk and instructions for installing it. Make sure that you have the right disk for your computer — a sticker on the outside says "WIN" for Windows or "MAC" for Macintoshes. The WIN version works with both Windows 3.1 and Windows 95.

The disk contains both the CompuServe Information Manager (CIM) software, which lets you connect to and use CompuServe, and an automated sign-up program that lets you sign up for a new CompuServe account over the phone. You need a credit card to make this process work. You get 15 free hours when you sign up for a new account, so you can figure out whether CompuServe is for you before spending too much dough.

The pros and cons of CompuServe

CompuServe has been around for a while and has lots of fascinating forums available only to CompuServe subscribers. If you're a serious PC user, you'll love the many technical-support forums provided by hundreds of hardware and software vendors.

Another big plus about CompuServe is that its phone network extends around the world. If you travel frequently, especially overseas, you'll find this feature invaluable.

On the other hand, CompuServe hasn't integrated its Internet offerings with its other services. If you want to use CompuServe's own features, you connect by using WinCIM (or MacCIM). If you want to use CompuServe as your Internet provider, you connect by using NetLauncher. It's more confusing than America Online, which bundles everything together.

My user ID is what?!

Unlike most other on-line services and Internet providers, CompuServe assigns a number to each user. Rather than a username that's easy to remember (such as ElvisLives or HeartThrob117), you get a number that looks like this:

77777,7777

The exact number of digits varies, but your user ID is always a number with a bunch of digits and a comma somewhere in the middle. Users in the U.S. and Canada usually have numbers that begin with a 7, and overseas users usually have numbers that begin with 1. (This numbering scheme dates back to the stone age of computing, in the late 1960s. The numbers are base 8, by the way.)

Your Internet e-mail address is not the same as your CompuServe ID — you have to modify it to include the information that it is a CompuServe account number. To figure out your e-mail address, change the comma in your user ID to a period, and add @compuserve.com to the end. If your CompuServe ID is 77777,7777, for example, your Internet e-mail address is

77777.7777@compuserve.com

If you use a Mac

This chapter describes the way CompuServe looks when you use the Windows version of the CompuServe Information Manager (CIM) software, WinCIM. The Mac version is similar, so the instructions should help Mac users too.

As of October 1995, the NetLauncher program was not yet available for the Mac. Check with CompuServe to find out whether a Mac version has been released.

Installing WinCIM by using Windows 95

To install the WinCIM software, follow these steps:

1. **Start Windows 95.**

2. **Click the Start button and choose Settings⇨Control Panel.**

3. **Double-click the Add/Remove Programs icon.**

   You see the Add/Remove Programs Properties dialog box as shown in Figure 12-1.

4. **Click the Install button.**

   Windows asks you to put the program disk in your disk drive.

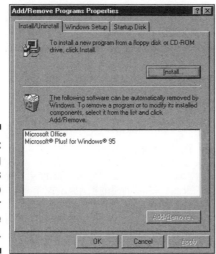

Figure 12-1:
This dialog
box allows
you to
install your
CompuServe
software.

5. **Stick the CompuServe disk in the drive and click Next.**

   Windows finds the setup program on the CompuServe disk — it's called SETUP.EXE.

6. **Click Finish.**

   "Finish"? You've hardly begun! But click it anyway.

   WinCIM asks where to install the software. It suggests a directory named C:\CSERVE, but you can change it to another directory.

7. **If you want to install WinCIM somewhere else, change the path. Then click OK.**

8. **Tell the setup program whether you want it to install the sign-up program and click OK.**

   If you want to sign up for a new CompuServe account, choose Yes. If you already have an account and are installing a new version of the software, choose No.

   WinCIM copies the program files to your disk. When it's finished, if you already have a CompuServe account, you're done — skip to step 11. If you want to sign up for a new account, WinCIM asks whether you want to sign up now.

9. **Click Yes to sign up for a new account.**

10. **Follow the instructions on the screen to open a new account.**

    You need the folder your CompuServe disk came in, because it contains two magic numbers: the Agreement Number and the Serial Number. You also need your credit-card number (and what number could be more magic than that?).

11. **You're done!**

When you finish, Windows 95 creates a window called, not surprisingly, CompuServe. It also adds CompuServe to the <u>P</u>rograms menu you see when you click the Start button.

You're ready to roll! You should take the CompuServe disk out of the drive and stash it somewhere in case you ever need to install it again. If you have trouble, call CompuServe at 1-800-609-1647 (or 614-529-1340).

Windows leaves the Control Panel and CompuServe windows open — they appear on the taskbar (the bar at the bottom of the screen). Might as well close 'em, by clicking the program name on the taskbar and then clicking the Close button in the upper right corner of the program window.

Installing the WinCIM by using Windows 3.1

To install the WinCIM software, follow these steps:

1. **Start Windows and stick the disk in the drive.**

2. **From Program Manager, choose <u>F</u>ile⇨<u>R</u>un from the menu.**

3. **Type** a:setup.exe **and click OK.**

If your disk drive is drive B:, type b:setup.exe. Either way, the CompuServe setup program runs.

4. **Tell the setup program where to install the software and click OK.**

It suggests installing the CompuServe Information Manager software in a directory named C:\CSERVE, but you can change it to another directory if you want.

5. **Tell the setup program whether you want it to install the sign-up program, and click OK.**

If you need to sign up for a new CompuServe account, choose <u>Y</u>es. If you already have an account and are installing a new version of the software, choose <u>N</u>o.

6. **Follow the instructions on-screen.**

Be sure that you have the folder the CompuServe disk came in (because it contains two numbers you need to type) and your credit-card number. When the setup program finishes, it creates a Program Manager program group named CompuServe that contains an icon for the CompuServe Information Manager, better known as WinCIM.

If you have trouble installing the CompuServe Information Manager, call 1-800-609-1674 or (614) 529-1340.

 If you want the CompuServe Information Manager icon to appear in another program group in Program Manager, hold down the Ctrl key while you drag it to the group in which you want it to appear. Program Manager copies the icon into the new group.

You can also change the name of the icon. Click once on the CompuServe Information Manager icon and then press Alt+Enter. You see the Program Item Properties dialog box (yikes — don't panic!). Change the Description, perhaps to the terser "WinCIM," but don't change anything else in the dialog box. Then click OK.

Revving Up CompuServe

Now you're ready to run WinCIM and use your CompuServe account. Here's how:

1. **Click the Start button and then choose Programs⇨CompuServe⇨ CompuServe Information Manager from the menu.**

   (Windows 3.1 users can just double-click the CompuServe Information Manager icon in Program Manager.)

   The first time you run WinCIM, it may display a message and terms and conditions. If it does, read the message and, if you can stand the terms, click OK.

   WinCIM asks whether you want it to connect to CompuServe as soon as you load the program. We recommend that you turn this option off so that you spend as little time as possible connected to CompuServe. (You pay by the minute, remember?)

2. **Just the first time, click the Show at Startup box, to remove the ×. Then click Continue.**

   You see the WinCIM window, in which several windows can be open at the same time. When WinCIM starts up, it shows the Services dialog box, with buttons for some of the more popular services. The Basic Services button doesn't do much (it usually displays a message about rates for using CompuServe services), but the other buttons take you to interesting CompuServe services.

3. **To call up CompuServe and do something, click the button for what you want to do.**

The rest of this chapter contains ideas for things you might want to do, primarily Internet-related things. As soon as you click a button that tells

WinCIM what you want to do, it calls up CompuServe on the phone, logs you in, and displays the information you want.

The Services window has lots of handy buttons. If it's not visible, click the globe icon on the toolbar to display it.

Hang Me Up!

When you finish using your CompuServe account, choose File⇨Disconnect from the menu or press Ctrl+D or click the Disconnect icon on the toolbar. You pay for the time you're connected to CompuServe, so be sure to disconnect before wandering off for a bite to eat. (CompuServe thoughtfully displays the amount of time you've been on-line on the toolbar, just to the right of the big yellow question-mark icon.)

To leave the CompuServe Information Manager program, choose File⇨Exit from the menu or click the EXIT icon on the toolbar.

Go, CompuServe!

CompuServe has hundreds of *forums,* or *services* — that is, material on a particular topic. Some services contain ongoing discussions, some have libraries of files you might find useful, and some let you ask questions to technical experts.

Going places

In the old days, before WinCIM, when you had to type lots of commands to get to places in CompuServe, the command you used the most was *go*. To get to information about your CompuServe bill, for example, you typed **go billing**. Documentation about CompuServe still frequently tells you "go support" rather than "go to support," because that's the command you had to type. Each CompuServe service has an official name — the one you type after the Go command.

In this modern age of pointing and clicking, you don't have to type *go* anymore to get places. Instead, you can click the Go icon on the toolbar, the one that looks like a traffic light. CompuServe asks for the service you want to go to — just type the official name of the service and click OK.

The easy way to get places is to click one of the buttons on the Services window. If you want to send or receive e-mail, for example, you can click the Communicate button. One of the choices it gives you is e-mail.

When you tell CompuServe where you want to go, if you're not already on-line, WinCIM dials the phone and logs you in. Then it displays the information you asked for.

Other WinCIM tips

This section lists some other cool moves you can make with WinCIM:

✔ You can see lots of windows at the same time within the WinCIM window. For example, you can keep windows about e-mail, the Internet, and Usenet newsgroups open at the same time.

✔ Use the Minimize, Maximize, and Close buttons in the upper right corner of the window to shrink, expand, or close it. (Windows 3.1 users don't see a Close button — double-click the Control-menu box instead, in the upper left corner of the window).

✔ To move a window around, drag its title bar (the top part of the window) with your mouse.

Go, Internet!

Beginning with WinCIM 1.4, WinCIM has a button labeled Internet right on the Services dialog box. When you click it, CompuServe (after dialing up and logging in, if necessary) displays the Internet window. This window lists all of CompuServe's Internet-related services in one handy spot — be sure to add it to your Favorite Places list.

In the next few sections of this chapter, you find out how to use CompuServe's Internet stuff.

Go, E-Mail!

CompuServe has a mail service for sending messages to and from other CompuServe users. The same mail service works for sending and receiving e-mail to Internet addresses.

Do I have mail?

When you start WinCIM and connect to CompuServe, the status bar at the bottom of the WinCIM window tells you how many messages you have waiting for you to read. If any messages are waiting, an extra icon appears on your toolbar — a little mailbox icon to the far right of the toolbar. Click it to read your incoming mail.

Reading your mail the cheap and easy way

The most efficient way to read your mail is to read it off-line, that is, while you're not connected to CompuServe. You don't have to pay for connect-time while you're reading and composing messages. Here's how it works:

✔ You use the Mail➪Send/Receive All Mail command on the menu. This command grabs all your mail and downloads it (copies it) from CompuServe into your In Basket, a storage area on your hard disk.

✔ You disconnect from CompuServe.

✔ While you're disconnected (and therefore not paying connect-time charges), you read your e-mail at a leisurely pace. You can even write replies or compose messages to other people. Messages you write are stored in your Out Basket, which is also on your hard disk.

✔ When you finish reading your mail, you use the Mail➪Send/Receive Mail command again to send the messages in your Out Basket and pick up any additional messages in your In Basket.

The result is that you're on-line only long enough to download your incoming mail and upload your outgoing mail.

Ready to try it? Follow these steps:

1. **In WinCIM, choose Mail➪Send/Receive All Mail from the menu.**

   WinCIM asks whether you want it to hang up when it finishes getting your mail.

2. **Click the Disconnect when Done box so that it has an X in it and then click OK.**

   WinCIM dials CompuServe, logs on, grabs your mail, stores it in the In Basket on your hard disk, and hangs up. There! You stop paying connect charges. WinCIM tells you how many messages it sent (messages you have composed since the last time you connected to CompuServe) and how many incoming messages it received.

3. **To read your messages, choose Mail⇨In-Basket from the menu.**

   You see your In Basket.

4. **To read a message in your In Basket, double-click it (or select it and click Open).**

5. **To reply to a message, click the Reply button, compose a response, and click Send Now (if you want to connect to CompuServe and send it right now) or Out-Basket (to put the message in your Out Basket, to be sent the next time you connect to CompuServe).**

   When you reply to a message, WinCIM addresses the message for you. All you have to do is type your response.

6. **To forward a message to someone else, click Forward, address the message, and click Send Now or Out-Basket.**

   See the section "Using your little black book," later in this chapter, to learn how to use the Recipient List dialog box to address a CompuServe message.

7. **To see the next message in your In Basket, click Next.**

8. **Compose any new messages by choosing Mail⇨Create Mail from the menu.**

9. **When you finish reading and composing mail, choose Mail⇨Send/ Receive All Mail from the menu.**

   WinCIM calls CompuServe again, sends all the mail in your Out Basket, and checks for any mail that has arrived since you last checked it.

You can see the messages in your Out Basket by choosing Mail⇨Out-Basket from the menu. You see a list of the messages you have written but that have not yet been sent to CompuServe. If you want to change a message (perhaps you thought better of that snappy retort in a message to your boss), you can edit the message by clicking Open. To send all the messages in your Out Basket right away, click Send All.

In addition to your In Basket and Out Basket, WinCIM provides you with a filing cabinet in which to file your messages. When you read a message, you can click File It to store it in your filing cabinet. See that little filing cabinet icon on the toolbar? Click it to see what's in your filing cabinet.

Using your little black book

When you send mail to another CompuServe user, you address a message to that person's CompuServe ID (the one that looks like 77777,7777). When you send mail to someone on the Internet, you address the message to:

INTERNET:*username@host*

For example, you can send a test message to us authors here at Internet For Dummies Central by addressing it to:

INTERNET:ninternet@dummies.com

When you create a new e-mail message or forward a message to someone, you have to address it. Whether you're connected to CompuServe or not, choose Mail⇨Create Mail. You see the Recipient List dialog box, as shown in Figure 12-2.

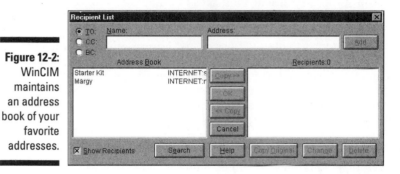

Figure 12-2:
WinCIM
maintains
an address
book of your
favorite
addresses.

The Recipient List dialog box shows two lists of addresses: On the left are the addresses in your address book, and on the right are the addresses to which this particular message is addressed. At the top are boxes for you to enter the Name and Address to send a message to.

Here are some things you can do:

✔ To address the message to someone in your address book, choose the name from the Address Book list and click the Copy>> button. The address appears in the list on the right side.

✔ To address the message to someone who isn't in your address book, type the person's name in the Name box and her e-mail address in the Address box. Click the Add button to move the name and address into the list on the right so that the message will go to her. If you want to add the name to your address book too, for use in addressing other messages, choose the name in the list on the right side and click the <<Copy button. WinCIM lets you enter comments about the person — do so, if you want, and then click OK.

✔ If you decide that you don't want to send the message to someone after all, choose her name from the list on the right and click Delete.

✔ If you want to send a copy of the message to someone (or a blind copy), click the CC (or BCC) option. Then either choose an address from your address book or enter the person's information in the Name and Address boxes. In the list on the right side, each address is preceded by To:, CC:, or BC: to show how the message will be addressed to that person.

When you finish addressing the message, click OK. You see the Create Mail dialog box. Enter the subject in the Subject box and the text of the message in the big box. When you finish, click Out Basket to park the message in your Out Basket until the next time you send messages to CompuServe or click Send Now to connect to CompuServe and send it right away.

You can use the Windows Clipboard to copy text from another Windows program into a mail message. To include text from a word-processing document, for example, select the text in your word processor, copy it to the Clipboard (in most programs you use the Edit⇨Copy command), place your cursor where you want the text to appear in your message in WinCIM, and choose Edit⇨Paste from the menu (or press Ctrl+C).

Send along this file, too

The Create Mail dialog box enables you to attach a file to a message. If it's a text file, you can send it to anyone. If it's not text, you can send it only to other CompuServe users. (This limitation may change when CompuServe supports one of the standard methods of attaching nontext files to e-mail, such as uuencoding or MIME).

To attach a file to a message, just click the Attach button. You see the File Attachment dialog box, as shown in Figure 12-3.

Figure 12-3:
Attach a file
to your
e-mail
message.

Click the File button to choose the file you want to send along with the message. When you select it, the pathname of the file appears in the box next to the File button. Set the FileType to the type of file you're sending:

- ✔ **Binary:** Any file other than text
- ✔ **Text:** Text only, with no formatting or special characters (the only kind of file you can send to Internet addresses)
- ✔ **GIF:** Graphics file in Graphics Interchange Format
- ✔ **JPEG:** Graphics file in Joint Photographic Experts Group format

Type any other information you want to send along with the file, and then click OK. Send the e-mail message as usual.

When you receive a file attached to an e-mail message, you receive a separate message with the same subject line as the message to which it was attached. (Sounds to us like attached text files get detached, but as long they arrive, it sounds good to us.) The message announces that a file awaits your attention. Click Retrieve to download the file to your computer, after WinCIM asks you where to store it.

If you want to practice mailing messages, go to the Practice Forum, (click the Go icon, type **practice**, and click OK). Connect-time is free while you're using this service, and the forum gives you someone to write to while you practice.

Reading Newsgroups

E-mail isn't the only Internet service you can use via WinCIM. Usenet newsgroups are also available, for when you need a good dose of gossip and innuendo. See Chapter 9 for general information about Usenet, like what the heck it is.

To read Usenet newsgroups, click the Internet icon on the Services window to display the Internet window, and then click the Usenet Newsgroups button. Or click the Go icon and type **newsgroups**. You see the Usenet Newsgroups window.

If you're new to Usenet newsgroups, try choosing the introductory topics on this list. When you're ready to read some newsgroups, click Usenet Newsreader (CIM). You see another Usenet Newsgroups window that looks like Figure 12-4.

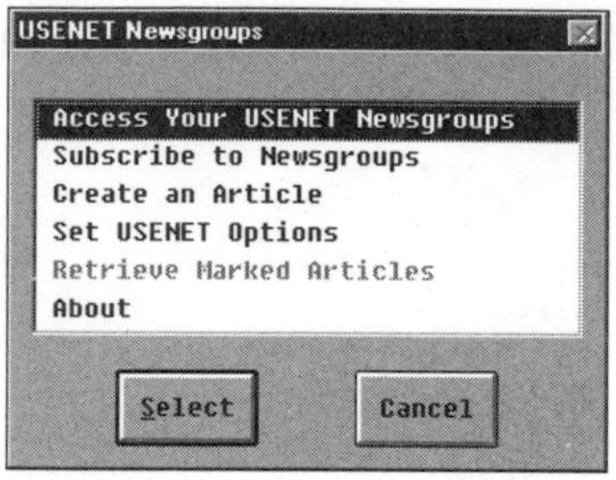

Figure 12-4:
The CIM
Usenet
newsreader
lets you
read and
post articles
to Usenet
newsgroups.

This menu is Mission Control for reading and posting newsgroup articles. It's not really part of WinCIM — it's a separate program, called the CIM Usenet Newsreader, and the toolbar and menu bar choices change while you're running it. All the other windows you have open within WinCIM are minimized (they shrink to icons at the bottom of the WinCIM window) while you're running the CIM Usenet Newsreader.

When you finish reading newsgroups, exit from the newsreader program by clicking the Cancel button.

Finding a newsgroup

The first step to reading newsgroups is to subscribe to newsgroups that interest you. Double-click Subscribe to Newsgroups on the Usenet Newsgroups window (refer to Figure 12-5). You see the Subscribe to Newsgroups window.

Here are ways to find the newsgroups you want:

✔ The dialog box lists newsgroups by the first part of the newsgroup *name* (comp, rec, and soc, for example). To see the newsgroups in a group, double-click the type of newsgroup. To see recreational newsgroups (those with names beginning with rec), for example, double-click Recreational (rec.*) on the list. You see a list of the newsgroups of that type. To subscribe to one, select it, and an × appears in the little box to the left of the newsgroup name. When you've chosen the newsgroups you want, click Subscribe. (To take a peek at the newsgroup without subscribing, click Preview.)

✔ To search for a newsgroup on a particular topic that interests you, type a word or phrase in the Keyword box and click Search. CompuServe searches for newsgroups that contain the word or phrase in the newsgroup name or description. On the list that results, you can choose the groups to which you want to subscribe.

> ✔ If you know the exact name of the newsgroup you want, click Subscribe by Name, type the name of the newsgroup in the box, and click OK.

When you finish, click Close.

Reading newsgroup messages

To see the newsgroups you are subscribed to — whether you want to read an article or post your own — double-click Access Your Usenet Newsgroups on the Usenet Newsgroups window. You see a list of the groups you are subscribed to. For each newsgroup, you see the number of articles you haven't yet read (a daunting number, in most cases).

To read the articles in a newsgroup, double-click the newsgroup name. You see a list of the threads (articles grouped by topic) in the newsgroup, as shown in Figure 12-5.

Figure 12-5:
Each thread listed is a group of articles, starting with a post and including all the responses to that post.

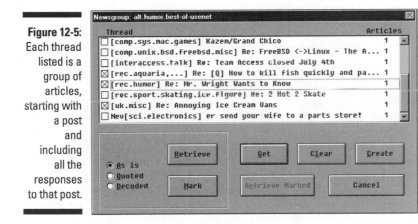

> ✔ To read articles on the spot, while connected to CompuServe, choose the threads that look interesting and click Get.
>
> ✔ To save money and download the threads to your hard disk so that you can read them after disconnecting from CompuServe, choose the threads you want and click Retrieve. CompuServe asks whether to save the articles in separate files by article or by thread, or in one big file, and then asks where to put each file. The program suggests the DOWNLOAD directory of your WinCIM program directory (usually C:\CSERVE\DOWNLOAD).

✔ To respond to an article, either by e-mail or by posting an article, click Reply. (See the section "Mouthing off," later in this chapter.)

✔ To write a new article for this newsgroup, click Create. (Again, see the section "Mouthing off.")

When you finish reading the articles in the newsgroup, click Cancel.

Telling the CIM newsreader who you are

Before you can post articles to Usenet newsgroups by using the CIM newsreader, you have to tell it who you are. It's just one of those rules — the program balks otherwise. To make it feel better, double-click Set Usenet Options on the Usenet Newsgroups window. When you see the Options dialog box, fill in the blanks. For the signature, type as many as three lines of text to be added to the end of every article you post to Usenet. Be sure to include your name and e-mail address. (Remember that your e-mail address is your CompuServe ID, with the comma changed to a period, followed by @compuserve.com.) Click OK when you're done.

Tell that jerk to shut up!

There are jerks in almost every newsgroup, and it doesn't help at all to tell them to shut up. They just send *more* messages, in fact, pointing out to you why they are right and you are wrong. The intelligent tack is to *ignore* them. CompuServe makes this easy — it ignores people for you!

Here's how it's done:

1. Double-click Set Usenet Options on the Usenet Newsgroups window.

2. Click the Set Ignore Options button.

3. You see a list of the newsgroups to which you're subscribed. Double-click the one that contains the jerk in question.

4. You see the Ignore Criteria dialog box. Click Author for the Ignore By setting (that is, ignore articles based on their author), and then click OK.

5. Click Insert to enter the name of the jerk whose articles you want to ignore.

6. Type the Internet address of the jerk and the number of days you want to ignore his articles, or click Non-Expiring to ignore all additional articles from this person. Then click OK.

7. The information about whom you're ignoring, and for how long, is displayed in the dialog box.

8. Click Close, Cancel, and then OK to back out of the dialog boxes you have open.

You can use the same system for ignoring all articles on a particular topic. If the folks in a newsgroup are talking endlessly about a pointless, boring subject, you can ignore all the articles on that subject. Click Subject and then OK on the Ignore Criteria dialog box, and enter the subject you want to ignore.

Mouthing off

The best way to respond to a newsgroup article is by sending e-mail to the person who wrote the article. After all, not everyone who reads the newsgroup may be interested in your response. Sometimes you just can't restrain yourself from posting an article, however, even though you take the chance of making a fool of yourself in front of tens of thousands of people around the world.

When you read an article that demands a response, whether you're determined to post an article or have wisely decided to respond by e-mail, you can use the same button: Click Reply. If you decide to post an article on a new subject, not in response to another article, double-click Create an Article from the Usenet Newsgroups window or display the list of threads in the newsgroup and click Create.

You see the Reply to Usenet Message or Create Usenet Message window. You can use this window for posting articles to newsgroups or for sending e-mail.

Here's how to proceed:

1. **Type the subject of the e-mail or article in the Subject box.**

2. **If you want to post an article to a newsgroup, click Post to Newsgroup(s), and choose the newsgroup (or newsgroups) from the Newsgroups list. If you want to send an e-mail message, click Send via E-mail.**

   The Newsgroups list contains the list of newsgroups to which you subscribe. (It's not polite to post articles to newsgroups you don't subscribe to — how do you know what they're talking about?)

3. **Type the article or message in the Message Contents box (the big one).**

   If you want to include text you have stored on your hard disk, you can upload it (copy the text from a file on your hard disk into the Message Contents box). Just click Upload and click the File button to choose the text file you want to include in the message. You can upload only text files — other types of files don't work.

4. **Click Send.**

   When you click Send, if you're sending the message via e-mail, the program prompts you for the e-mail address to which to send the message. Type it and click OK. You *don't* have to type *INTERNET:* before Internet addresses. Because Usenet is part of the Internet, all addresses are Internet addresses. To send a message to a CompuServe user, use her Internet address (change the comma in her user ID to a period, and add @compuserve.com to the end).

If you're posting a newsgroup article, the program confirms that the article was posted.

Remember never to post in anger! Take a walk instead!

Dealing with boring newsgroups

If you *don't* want to continue subscribing to a newsgroup, you can unsubscribe from it. (Yes, *unsubscribe* is now a word.) In the Usenet Newsgroups window (refer to Figure 12-4), double-click Access Your Usenet Newsgroups. Choose the newsgroup you're sick of, and click Remove. The program asks whether you're absolutely, positively sure that you want to unsubscribe. Click Yes to go for it. Poof! The newsgroup disappears from your list of newsgroups, never to return (unless you resubscribe).

Getting Files via FTP

CompuServe has oodles of files you can download. But so does the Internet. FTP (file-transfer protocol) is the Internet service that enables you to transfer files from one computer to another, usually from large public file archives to your own PC. See Chapter 10 for more information about FTP, including what kinds of files you're likely to find and likely places to look for them.

To use FTP to download files to your computer, click the Go icon on the toolbar, type **ftp**, and click OK. Or start at the Internet window and click the FTP: File Transfer Protocol button.

Either way, CompuServe displays a serious-looking warning message, indicating that CompuServe Information Services is not responsible for what's in the files you might or might not download and that they *don't* want to hear about it if you *don't* like what you find. Fair enough: FTP isn't a CompuServe service, after all. Click Proceed to continue. You see the File Transfer Protocol window.

To download a file from the FTP archive that has the file you want, follow these steps:

1. **Click the Access a Specific Site button.**

   You see the Access a Specific Site window.

2. **In the Site Name box, enter the Internet host name of the FTP archive in which the files you want are stored.**

   If you want to download a file from Microsoft's FTP server, for example, enter **ftp.microsoft.com**.

3. **If you know the directory on the FTP server in which the file is stored, enter it in the Directory box.**

   If you know that the file is in /pub/clip-art, for example, enter that.

4. **If you're using anonymous FTP (that is, you don't have your own account on the FTP server), leave the User Name as** anonymous. **If you have your own account, type it in the User Name box.**

Publicly accessible FTP servers require you to log in as anonymous.

5. **If you're using anonymous FTP, leave the Password box set to your Internet address. If you have your own account, enter the password.**

When you use anonymous FTP, you're supposed to enter your Internet e-mail address as the password. WinCIM fills it in for you.

6. **Click OK.**

CompuServe contacts the FTP server and tries to log you in. The server may be busy, or down, in which case you see an error message — try again later.

If you are able to log in to the FTP server, you see a message welcoming you to the server. You may also see information about the server.

7. **Click OK.**

WinCIM displays a directory listing of the current directory on the FTP server, as shown in Figure 12-6. The list on the left side of the window contains the subdirectories of the current directory, and the list on the right shows the files in the current directory.

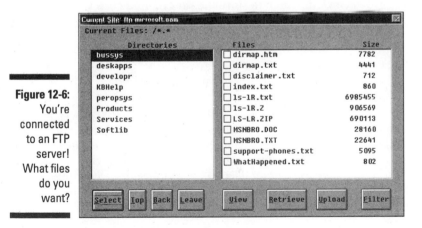

Figure 12-6:
You're
connected
to an FTP
server!
What files
do you
want?

8. **Read the instructions.**

The first directory you see may contain a list of the files on the FTP server, in a file with a name such as read.me or index.txt. If is does, take a look at it, by clicking the filename and then clicking the View button.

Why use FTP if you can get the file from CompuServe?

CompuServe has libraries with tens of thousands — perhaps hundreds of thousands — of files. You might want to check whether the file you want is available from CompuServe itself before going to the trouble of using FTP. To look

for a file in CompuServe's many libraries, click the Access CompuServe's File Finders option in the File Transfer Protocol window, or click the Go icon on the toolbar and type **filefinder**.

---

9. **Move to the directory that contains the file (or files) you want.**

   To move to a subdirectory of the current directory, double-click the directory name in the list on the left. To move back to the preceding directory, click the <u>B</u>ack button. To move back to the directory from which you started, click the <u>T</u>op button.

10. **When you see a file you want, click the filename so that an × appears in its little box. Then click the Retrieve button.**

    You can choose more than one file, if you want. WinCIM asks where you want to store the file (or files).

11. **Choose a directory in which to store the files in, and click OK.**

    WinCIM downloads the file from the FTP server to CompuServe to your own computer.

12. **When you finish, click <u>L</u>eave.**

    WinCIM logs you off the FTP server.

WinCIM's File Transfer Protocol window lets you log in to an FTP server, look around, and download some files. The Selected Popular Sites and List of Sites buttons on the window display lists of popular FTP servers — choose an FTP server from one of these lists, and you see the Access a Specific Site window with the host name of the FTP server filled in for you. The Site Descriptions button lets you see descriptions of some popular FTP servers, including the types of files stored on each server.

If you use NetLauncher, described in the section "NetLauncher: Using CompuServe as a PPP Account," later in this chapter, you can use Spry Mosaic (or another Web browser) to download files from FTP sites too. Chapter 10 tells how to use a Web browser for FTP.

Telnetting to Other Computers

WinCIM lets you use one other Internet service: telnet. Telnet lets you log in to other Internet host computers.

To use telnet to log in to another computer on the Internet, click the Internet button on the Services window and then click the Telnet: Remote Login button. Or you can click the Go icon on the toolbar and type **telnet**. Either way, you see the CompuServe Telnet Access window. Here's how:

1. **If you know exactly which computer you want to log in to, click Access a Specific Site. To browse a list of publicly available computers, click List of Sites and choose a site.**

   Either way, CompuServe warns you that you're about to leave the world of CompuServe and use another computer. "Don't blame us if something goes wrong!" they imply.

2. **Click ᴘroceed.**

   WinCIM displays a terminal-emulation window (a window in which it runs a program which pretends that you're using a plain old terminal rather than a PC or Mac). It logs in to the computer you chose.

3. **Follow the instructions given by the computer you're using.**

   Remember that although the information you see flows through CompuServe, it comes from another computer entirely. Figure 12-7 shows a telnet session with NASA Spacelink.

Figure 12-7:
WinCIM pretends to be a terminal and lets you talk to another computer on the Internet.

4. When you finish, log off from the other computer.

How you log off depends on the other computer. When you disconnect from the other computer, WinCIM closes the Terminal Emulation window.

Telnet is great for using a few services that provide information by letting you log in. Many libraries, including the Library of Congress, let you log in and search for books by using telnet.

NetLauncher: Using CompuServe As a PPP Account

Internet e-mail, Usenet newsgroups, FTP, and telnet are a good start, but that's not the whole Internet. Aside from e-mail, the most popular Internet service is, of course, the World Wide Web. WinCIM doesn't have a built-in Web browser — unlike America Online's software, which does. Instead, CompuServe decided to take a different approach: You can use your CompuServe account as though it were a SLIP or PPP account, using Internet access software (not WinCIM). If you use Windows, you can then use any WinSock-compatible program to access Internet services. You can use Netscape or Mosaic, for example, to browse the Web.

What do we mean, you ask, by special Internet software? We mean the same software you would use to connect to a PPP account at any Internet provider. Chapter 2 describes this software, which is usually called a *TCP/IP stack.* Luckily, CompuServe provides Internet (TCP/IP) software you can use free of charge. It's called NetLauncher. NetLauncher even comes with a Web browser, Spry Mosaic.

If you use NetLauncher (or other TCP/IP software), you have two (count 'em) ways to connect to your CompuServe account:

- ✔ Run WinCIM to use all the Internet services you've read about so far in this chapter and to use CompuServe's non-Internet-related services, such as all those great technical-support forums.

- ✔ Run NetLauncher to use WinSock programs to access Internet servers. You can use a WinSock browser, in addition to other WinSock software, to look at the Web.

Note: You can use a WinSock newsreader such as Agent to read Usenet newsgroups, if you like Agent better than WinCIM's newsreader (who wouldn't?). But you can't use a WinSock e-mail program such as Eudora to get your mail because CompuServe doesn't support the POP (Post Office Protocol) system that Eudora requires for getting your mail, at least not yet.

So where do you get NetLauncher, and how do you use it? We thought you'd never ask. Read on!

Although it's convenient to use your CompuServe account as a PPP account, it's not cheap — it costs about $3 an hour. If you spend a great deal of time using CompuServe as a PPP account, it would be cheaper to get a real PPP account with an Internet provider because most charge much less than $3 an hour.

But what is NetLauncher?

Good question. We ourselves asked the very same question. Ahem. NetLauncher consists of three programs that run under Windows:

- ✔ **CompuServe Internet Dialer:** A program you use to call up CompuServe and connect to it as your Internet account. For you technoids, it's a TCP/IP stack that connects to CompuServe via PPP.

- ✔ **Spry Mosaic:** A Web browser. If you're not logged in to CompuServe when you run Spry Mosaic, it tells the CompuServe Internet Dialer to log you in (very convenient!).

- ✔ **ImageView:** A program that lets you look at the graphic files you run across while browsing the Web.

When you install NetLauncher, these three programs appear on your computer.

Launching NetLauncher

NetLauncher is available free of charge from none other than CompuServe. It runs with Windows — if you use a Mac or DOS, you have to provide your own TCP/IP software (see the following sidebar, "For Mac users").

Here's how to download and install NetLauncher so that your Windows computer can connect to CompuServe as though it were an Internet PPP account:

1. **Log in to CompuServe by using WinCIM.**

2. **Click the Internet button on the Services window, and then double-click the Direct Internet Access (Dial PPP) item on the Internet window. Or click the Go icon on the toolbar and type** ppp.

   Either way, you see the Dialup PPP window. It wouldn't be a bad idea to read some of the informational topics listed in this window, in case a brand-new version of NetLauncher has appeared.

TIP

For Mac users

NetLauncher is available only for Windows, at least as of this writing (late 1995). Bummer. Luckily, you can use any Mac TCP/IP program with CompuServe's PPP service. You need Mac Internet dial-up software (the core parts of TCP/IP are included with System 7.5, but the dial-up parts and the applications aren't). Then you have to configure your software to dial CompuServe and connect to its PPP service. Contact CompuServe for details — they're not difficult, but they can be tedious.

3. Double-click Download NetLauncher.

An informational window crops up, warning you about the usual legal warranty stuff.

4. Click Retrieve.

The Save As window appears, asking you where to put the program file, CNL.EXE. WinCIM suggests putting it in your WinCIM download directory (which is usually C:\CSERVE\DOWNLOAD). Sounds like a good place to put it!

5. Click OK.

WinCIM downloads the NetLauncher program file, CNL.EXE. It's larger than 1MB, so it takes a few minutes. (If you use a 2400 baud modem, it takes closer to 30 minutes.)

6. Disconnect from CompuServe.

There's no point in paying connect-time charges while you install the NetLauncher program!

7. Run the CNL.EXE program to install NetLauncher.

If you use Windows 95, double-click the My Computer icon, double-click the hard disk on which you installed WinCIM (probably C:), double-click the folder in which you installed it (probably Cserve), double-click the Download folder, and double-click the Cnl.exe icon. Or click the Start button, choose Run, and type the command **C:\CSERVE\ DOWNLOAD\ CNL.EXE**.

If you use Windows 3.1, go to Program Manager, choose File⇨Run from the menu, and type the command C:\CSERVE\CNL.EXE in the Command Line box (modify the command if you downloaded the NetLauncher program to another directory).

In either case, the CNL.EXE program asks for the name of a directory in which it can create a temporary directory in which to store some files. It suggests C:\WINDOWS.

8. **Change the directory name if you want CNL to create a temporary directory in another directory, and then click OK.**

   CNL.EXE creates a temporary directory called WCINST0 in the directory you specify. It sticks a bunch of files in the new directory, including its setup program. Then it runs the setup program, and you see the Installing CompuServe NetLauncher screen.

9. **Click Proceed.**

   The setup program asks for the name of the directory in which you installed WinCIM. (NetLauncher doesn't work unless you already have some version of CIM installed on your computer, because it uses information from CIM — your access number, user ID, and password, among other things — in configuring the CompuServe Internet Dialer program.) It suggests C:\CSERVE, which is where most people install WinCIM.

10. **Correct the directory, if necessary, and click OK.**

    If you already have a file named WINSOCK.DLL on your hard disk, the Setup program warns you that it must rename the existing WINSOCK.DLL file to become WINSOCK.000. (It plans to install its own WINSOCK.DLL in its place). If you see this message, click OK to proceed.

    The setup program installs NetLauncher, including the CompuServe Internet Dialer, Spry Mosaic, and ImageView. When it finishes, it creates a new folder (in Windows 95) or program group (in Windows 3.1) for the new programs, as shown in Figure 12-8.

Figure 12-8:
NetLauncher comes with three — no, eight — programs.

11. **When the setup program asks whether you want to run Spry Mosaic now, click Yes.**

    Sure — why not?

NetLauncher is ready to run! You now have the CompuServe Internet Dialer (CID), which is ready to connect to CompuServe as your Internet account, you have Spry Mosaic ready to browse the Web, and you have ImageView ready to display any cool images that run across while you're browsing!

The CNL.EXE program remains in your WinCIM Download directory. If you're the kind of person who saves all your program installation disks in a neat, plastic box with dividers, you may want to copy this file to a disk to add to your collection.

Starting the Web browser

This section shows you how to fire up your new Web browser:

- ✔ If you use Windows 95, to connect to CompuServe as an Internet provider and run Spry Mosaic, click Start and then choose Programs⇨CompuServe⇨ Spry Mosaic. If the CompuServe folder appears on your desktop, open it and double-click the Spry Mosaic icon.

- ✔ If you use Windows 3.1, double-click the Spry Mosaic icon in the CompuServe program group.

What is WINSOCK.DLL, and why do I care?

If you don't care, you may learn to care! The WINSOCK.DLL file contains a program used by programs that connect to the Internet. On a computer running Windows (3.1 or 95), every program that dials up an Internet SLIP or PPP account and logs you in comes with a WINSOCK.DLL program. NetLauncher comes with WINSOCK.DLL, for example. Windows 95 also comes with a WINSOCK.DLL program, as part of its built-in Internet support. WINSOCK.DLL is stored in your Windows program directory, which is usually C:\WINDOWS. You can also store it in the program directories for your Internet program, for example, in the NetLauncher program directory.

Here's the problem: What if you have two different programs for connecting to the Internet, each of which comes with its own WINSOCK.DLL file? What if you run Windows 95, for example, and you install NetLauncher? They have a little argument about it, that's what happens.

When you install NetLauncher, it notices whether you already have a file named WINSOCK.DLL in your Windows program directory and displays a message. It says that it's going to rename the file as WINSOCK.DLL file, unless you have a better idea.

If you run into a situation in which you have more than one version of WINSOCK.DLL, one solution is to copy the WINSOCK.DLL that comes with NetLauncher into the CompuServe and NetLauncher program directories. That is, right after you install NetLauncher, copy the WINSOCK.DLL file from your Windows program directory into the CompuServe program directory (which is usually C:\CSERVE) and the NetLauncher program directory (which is usually C:\CSERVE\CID). This step ensures that NetLauncher will be able to find its own WINSOCK.DLL program.

Either way, Mosaic fires up and loads the CompuServe home page. For information about using Mosaic, see Chapters 4 and 5.

Using other Internet software

Now that you have NetLauncher up and running, you can use lots of other nifty Internet software. In fact, you can use almost any WinSock-compatible programs. If you don't like Spry Mosaic, you might want to try using Netscape as your Web browser instead (see Chapter 4). If you don't like CompuServe's Usenet Newsgroups window, you can use Free Agent or another newsreader instead (see Chapter 9).

How to run WinCIM and NetLauncher at the same time

If you use WinCIM to dial up your CompuServe account, you can't run NetLauncher (that is, Spry Mosaic and other WinSock programs) at the same time. The problem is that the CompuServe Internet Dialer can't call up CompuServe and connect as an Internet account because the phone is already in use by WinCIM.

There is a way around this, however. The secret is to configure WinCIM to be a WinSock-compatible program! Confusing, but true! Here's what to do:

1. Connect to CompuServe using the CompuServe Internet Dialer or Spry Mosaic. Now you're logged in as an Internet PPP account.

2. Fire up WinCIM.

3. Choose Special⇨Session Settings from the WinCIM menu bar. You see the Setup Session Settings dialog box. The Connector setting is set to the COM port to which your

modem is attached, probably COM1 or COM2.

4. Set the Connector setting to WINSOCK, to tell it to use the Internet connection.

5. Click OK to make the Setup Session Settings dialog box go away.

6. Use WinCIM as usual. When you choose a service and WinCIM needs to connect to CompuServe, rather than dial the phone, it connects via the existing CompuServe Internet Dialer session that is already in progress.

Now you can use WinCIM at the same time as Spry Mosaic and other WinSock-compatible programs. You always connect to CompuServe as an Internet account. Keep in mind, however, that you're paying about $3 an hour for the privilege, so don't stay connected any longer than you have to!

Chapter 13

Using the Internet via America Online

. . . .

In This Chapter

▶ Signing up for AOL

▶ Setting up your communications program to call AOL

▶ Calling America!

▶ Typing commands

▶ Hanging up

▶ Sending e-mail

▶ Browsing the Web

▶ Reading newsgroups, including downloading uuencoded files

▶ Downloading files from FTP servers

▶ Using America Online as your SLIP account

▶ Doing other things

. . . .

merica Online (AOL, to its friends) is a widely used information system that includes Internet access. It comes with a nifty Windows-, DOS-, or Macintosh-based access program, so you can do lots of pointing and clicking and not so much typing of arcane commands. AOL has more than 3 $\frac{1}{2}$ million users and is still growing. This chapter describes its Internet-related capabilities, including e-mail and the World Wide Web.

This chapter describes AOL software version 2.5. AOL updates its software and the graphics that appear in its dialog boxes all the time, so your screen may not exactly match the figures in this chapter.

The pros and cons of AOL

AOL is easier to use than most commercial on-line services and Internet accounts because one big AOL access program does it all for you. AOL also does a nice job of providing users with on-line software updates –– it can update your AOL access software for you right over the phone, and connect-time is usually free of charge when it does so.

AOL also has lots of discussion groups and information that is available only to AOL subscribers.

On the other hand, if you frequently connect to the Internet (a half-hour or more a day), AOL is more expensive than many other services. Its pricing includes five hours a month, and you pay by the hour after that.

Signing Up for America Online

No problem! Just call 1-800-827-6364 and ask for a trial membership. Specify that you want the Windows version of the software (unless, of course, you have a Mac or a computer running DOS). These folks will send you an introductory package with instructions and a disk containing the AOL access program, America Online for Windows. While you're at it, ask about pricing because, after you use up your free introductory hours, you pay by the hour.

If you're using Windows 95

Still no problem! America Online for Windows version 2.5 or later works just fine with Windows 95. Put the disk in the drive, use the Microsoft Explorer or My Computer icon to see the files on the disk, and double-click the file SETUP.EXE. The AOL Setup program starts and runs, just as described in the following sections.

If you're using a Mac

In this chapter we discuss the Windows version of AOL software. The Mac version is similar enough that you should be able to follow along and make a few adjustments for the Mac.

Installing your AOL software

To install the America Online for Windows software on a PC running Windows 3.1, follow these steps:

1. **Start Windows and stick the disk in the drive.**

2. **Choose File⇨Run from the Windows Program Manager's menu bar.**

3. **For the command line, type the following:**

```
a:setup
```

(If your disk is in drive B, substitute b for a.)

4. **Choose OK.**

    The setup program is very friendly and tells you what to do.

5. **Choose Continue when it asks.**

    When the program asks in which directory you want to install the program, it suggests a reasonable directory name, such as C:\AOL25 (for version 2.5 of the software).

6. **Change the directory name if you have another idea and then choose Continue.**

    It copies the program into the directory it has created and then tells you that the installation is complete.

7. **Click OK to make the message go away.**

The installation program creates a Program Manager program group named America Online that contains a cute triangular icon *also* named America Online. The icon's full name is "America Online – Double-click here to start," which is a heck of a name. (Press Alt+Enter to change the name of the icon, maybe to a more succinct "AOL"). If you want to move the America Online icon to another program group, just drag it there. To copy the icon, hold down the Ctrl key while you drag it. If you put the icon in another program group, you then can delete the America Online program group — after all, it seems silly to have an entire program group that contains just one icon. To delete the program group, select the title bar of the program group (which must be empty) and press Del.

If you have trouble installing the AOL software, call AOL at 1-800-827-3338 or follow the directions on the disk.

Setting up your AOL account

The first time you use your trial package, you have to tell it which username you want to use and how you want AOL to bill you after you have used up your free hours.

Follow these steps to set up your account:

1. **Click the America Online icon.**

2. **Follow the instructions on-screen.**

   First, AOL calls up an 800 number to find out the closest local access number to you. You type your area code, AOL shows you the access phone numbers in your area, and then you choose the ones you want to use (in case you don't know, you should choose numbers that are local calls).

   If you received a *registration certificate* with your trial membership, you are prompted for it — it's a long number with a couple of dashes.

3. **Type the number and the password that appears under the number on the certificate.**

   (We love it — ours was *SPECS-RICHES*, and our editor's was *ANGER-PASTRY.* Who thinks these things up?)

4. **Choose a username (which AOL calls a *screen name* — sounds glamorous) for yourself.**

   Your screen name can be as long as ten characters and can contain spaces. You can use a combination of capital and small letters, as in MargyL or J Levine. When AOL asks you to enter the username, it checks its list of existing usernames. If someone is already using that name (John Smith, for example), you have to invent another one. You can use a fanciful screen name, such as Dark Wolf or Queen Bee, if you prefer.

   If the screen name you want is already taken, just add a number to the end to make it unique. For example, if *BigBoy* is taken (and we're sure that it is), you can be BigBoy326.

5. **Pick a password.**

   AOL asks you to type your password twice to make sure that you don't make a typo. The password doesn't appear on-screen — you just see asterisks.

   Yes, here's the part you knew was coming. AOL asks how you want to pay after you use up your ten free hours.

6. **Enter a credit-card number and expiration date.**

   Bummer. The good news is that the time you spend completing this registration doesn't count as part of your ten free hours. When you finish, you see the "Welcome!" window in the America Online window.

The America Online window always displays the menu bar and, underneath it, the *Flashbar* (a row of cute little icons).

Calling America Online!

To connect your computer to AOL:

1. **Type your password in the Password box.**

2. **Click the Sign On button.**

   A window appears that shows you the progress of the connection. The graphic changes as the AOL program dials the phone, establishes a connection with the big AOL computer in the sky, and logs you in.

   You see the Welcome window and behind it the Main Menu window (its edges peek out from behind the Welcome window).

   Now you're connected to AOL. You can click the buttons to read the day's news stories. If e-mail is waiting for you, you can click the You Have Mail button.

3. **Click the Go To Main Menu button at the bottom center of the Welcome window.**

   You see the Main Menu.

If your PC has a sound board or you're using a Mac, don't be surprised if your computer suddenly says "Welcome!" when you log on to AOL. If you have e-mail, it says "You have mail!" Try not to jump right out of your chair when this happens.

Hang Me Up!

With all the friendly little pictures on the screen, you would think that one of them would show a door or an EXIT sign or something. But no. To get out of AOL (and stop using connect-time), choose File➪Exit from the menu bar or press Alt+F4. AOL asks whether you really, truly want to leave. Choose Yes to sign off from AOL but remain in the America Online for Windows program (unlikely) or choose Exit Application to end everything.

We can't help but feel that this is a sleazy maneuver on the part of AOL to keep us on-line (and paying) for as long as possible. Tacky, no?

Calling Again

The next time you want to use AOL, follow these steps:

1. **Double-click the AOL icon.**

   You see the Welcome window.

2. **Enter your America Online screen name in the Screen Name box.**

   In fact, your screen name probably already appears in the box.

3. **Press Tab to move to the Password box and then type your password.**

4. **Click the Sign On button or just press Enter.**

   Poof! You see some messages about how it's initializing your modem and making the call. You're ready to surf the Net when you see the on-line Welcome window.

5. **If you want to read the day's headlines, click the buttons in the Welcome window. If you have mail and want to read it, click the You Have Mail button.**

   See the "Mail It, AOL" section, later in this chapter, to learn how to read and send e-mail.

6. **When you want to use the Internet or other AOL services, click the Go To Main Menu button at the bottom center of the Welcome window.**

   You see the Main Menu.

Now you're ready to use AOL!

Internet, Ho!

AOL has organized its Internet services in one dialog box so that they're easy to find. To get at AOL's Internet services, click the Internet Connection button on the Main Menu. Alternatively, you can choose <u>G</u>o To⇨Keyword from the menu (or press Ctrl+K) and enter the keyword **internet**. You see the Internet Connection window.

The Internet Center has the following icons you can use:

- ✔ **World Wide Web:** Lets you browse the Web

- ✔ **Gopher and WAIS Databases:** Enables you to search the Internet for the information you want

- ✔ **FAQs:** Frequently asked questions (and their answers) about the Internet Connection; this free area contains lots of useful information about how to use Internet services from your AOL account — highly recommended!
- ✔ **FTP:** Lets you download (copy) files from archives (FTP servers) to your own computer
- ✔ **News Groups:** Enables you to read Usenet newsgroups

In addition, the right side of the Internet Connection lists other Internet-related departments, including information about how to join Internet mailing lists and download Internet-related programs.

When you finish using the Internet Center, double-click the little box in the upper left corner of its window to close the window.

Mail It, AOL

America Online has a mail system by which AOL members can send messages to each other in addition to the rest of the Internet.

Your Internet address is your username (omitting any spaces) plus @aol.com. If your username is John Smith, for example, your Internet address is JohnSmith@aol.com.

Do I have mail?

When you sign on to AOL, it tells you whether you have any mail. On the left side of the Welcome! window you see either the message No New Mail or the message You Have Mail. Another way to tell whether mail is waiting for you is to look at the List Unread Mail icon on the Flashbar — it's the first one, a picture of a little mailbox. If the little red flag is *up,* you have mail.

Reading your mail

You probably *do* have mail, in fact, because every new member gets a nice note from the president of AOL. To read your unread mail, follow these steps:

1. **Click the leftmost icon on the Flashbar, the one just below the world** *File.*

This is the Read New Mail icon. Alternatively, you can choose Mail⇨Read New Mail from the menu or press Ctrl+R.

You see the New Mail dialog box. Each line on the list describes one incoming mail message with the date it was sent, the sender's e-mail address, and the subject.

2. **To read a message, highlight it on the list and click Read or press Enter.**

    You see the text of your message in another cute little dialog box.

3. **To reply to the message or forward it, see the following sections.**

4. **To see the next message, click the Next button.**

5. **When you finish, double-click the little box in the upper left corner of each window you're finished with.**

From the Welcome window you can click the You Have Mail icon to see your new mail.

Keeping messages

When you have read your mail, AOL keeps each message for a few days and then throws them away. If you want to keep a message around, select it from your list of mail and click the Keep As New button.

It's not always a good idea to respond to messages right away. You might have to get some information or you may have to cool off after reading the brainless message some jerk sent you.

Sending a reply

To reply to a message you have received, display it as described in the preceding two sections. Then follow these steps:

1. **Click the Reply button.**

    In the dialog box, the To address is already filled in with the address from which the original message came, and AOL suggests a subject line.

2. **Type the text of your message in the box in the lower part of the dialog box.**

3. **To send the message, click the Send icon.**

Composing a new message

You don't have to reply to other messages — you can start an exchange of messages, assuming that you know the e-mail address of the person you want to write to:

1. **Click the second icon from the left on the Flashbar, the picture of a pen at an angle.**

   Alternatively, you can choose Mail from the menu and then choose Compose Mail. Or just press Ctrl+M. You see the Compose Mail dialog box.

2. **Enter the recipient's address in the To box.**

   For AOL members, just enter the username. For others on the Net, type the entire Internet address.

3. **In the CC box, enter the addresses of anyone to whom you want to send a copy.**

   You don't have to send a copy to yourself — AOL keeps copies of mail you have sent.

4. **Enter a brief subject line in the Subject box.**

5. **In the box with no name, type the text of your message.**

   Don't use the Tab key because it moves your cursor from one box to the next in the dialog box. You can press Enter, though, to begin a new paragraph.

6. **When you like what you see, click the Send button.**

   AOL confirms that the mail is winging on its way.

7. **Click OK to make the message go away.**

Attaching a file to your message

If you want to send a file from your PC to someone as an e-mail message, AOL makes this process easy. When you're writing the message, click the Attach button. The Attach File dialog box is displayed, which lets you choose any file from your PC. Select a file and click OK.

When you send an attached file to an Internet address, AOL turns it into an Internet MIME-format message. If your recipient uses an Internet mail program that handles MIME, such as Pine or Eudora, you're all set. If not, the following steps show you how to send text files as plain text messages, utilizing the Windows Clipboard. These steps work only for sending text:

1. **Run Windows Notepad, your word processor, or any other program that can display the text you want to send.**

2. **Using that program, copy the text to the Windows Clipboard.**

   In most programs, you copy by highlighting the text and choosing Edit⇨Copy from the menu. Most Windows programs let you copy highlighted text by pressing Ctrl+Ins or Ctrl+C.

3. **In America Online, begin a new message by replying to a message or by composing a new message (see the preceding few sections).**

4. **Place your cursor in the text box where you type the text of the message.**

5. **Choose Edit⇨Paste (or press Ctrl+V).**

   The text appears.

6. **Send your message as usual.**

There *is* a limit to how much text you can copy at a time into the Windows Clipboard, but it's big. If you have trouble, copy the text a piece at a time. Also, this method works only for text, not for pictures or data files.

Saving a message on your PC

If you get a message on AOL that you want to download to your PC, display it on the screen as described in the section "Reading your mail," earlier in this chapter. Then choose File⇨Save As from the menu bar. AOL lets you choose the directory and filename in which to save the file on your computer. When you click OK, it saves the e-mail message as a text file. Nice and easy!

Other mail tricks

AOL lets you make an address book of the e-mail addresses of your friends and coworkers, forward messages, and other nice things. They have nothing to do with the Internet, however, and they're easy to figure out. If you run into trouble, choose Help from the menu bar.

You can also compose messages off-line, when you're not logged in to AOL, to save money. You can also read your e-mail off-line. See the section "A Cheaper Way to Use AOL," later in this chapter.

NAVIGATE

AOL mail shorthand

AOL lets you abbreviate the Internet addresses of people on some other services:

Messages to MCI Mail users can be addressed to name@mci rather than to the complete address, name@mcimail.com. (You can replace *name* with the person's MCI Mail name *or* number.)

Messages to CompuServe users can be addressed to 7654.321@cis rather than to the complete address, which is 7654.321

@compuserve.com. (Use the person's actual CompuServe ID rather than *7654.321*, and be sure to type a period, *not* a comma, in the middle of the number.)

Messages to AT&T Mail users can be addressed to name@att rather than to the complete address, name@attmail.com.

Messages to AppleLink users can be addressed to name@apple rather than to the complete address, name@applelink.apple.com.

Browsing the Web from AOL

AOL was among the last on-line services to add a Web browser. Unlike some other on-line services we can name, the Web browser works the same way the rest of the AOL program works, so it's easy to learn how to use it. You can add Web pages to your Favorite Places list. And you can have a Web browser window open at the same time that other AOL windows are open.

The Web browser requires that you use AOL software version 2.5 or higher. The Web browser doesn't come with version 2.5: You have to download the Web browser over the phone. The good news is that it's easy and that AOL doesn't charge you for the connect-time while you're downloading the Web browser program. The bad news is that it takes a while (several minutes to half an hour, depending on your modem speed) to download the program.

Getting the Web browser program

The first time you want to use the World Wide Web, you may have to download the AOL Web browser program. If you have a version earlier than 2.5 (for Windows users) or 2.6 (for Mac users), you must upgrade to more recent software. Press Ctrl+K to see the Keyword dialog box (refer to Figure 13-1), type **upgrade**, and click Go. You see instructions for upgrading to version 2.5, including the Web browser.

If you already have version 2.5 (Windows) or 2.6 (Mac), you have to download only the Web browser. Press Ctrl+K to see the Keyword dialog box, type **web**, and click Go. If you have already installed the AOL Web browser, it runs the browser. If not, AOL asks you whether you want to download and install it.

Starting the Web browser

Here are three ways to start the AOL Web browser:

- ✔ Choose Internet Connection from the Main Menu. You see the Internet Connection window. Click the World Wide Web button.
- ✔ Press Ctrl+K to see the Keyword dialog box, type **internet**, and click Go.
- ✔ Press Ctrl+K to see the Keyword dialog box. Type the URL of the Web page you want to see and click Go.

Whichever method you use, AOL runs its Web browser. Unless you configured it otherwise, it displays the AOL home page on the Web.

To use the browser, click on any picture that has a blue border or any button or any text that appears underlined. (See Chapters 4 and 11 for information about how to find information on the World Wide Web.)

Creating your own Web page

It's fun to look at Web pages that other people have created, but what about making your own? AOL lets you create your own *home page* (a page about you).

Press Ctrl+K, type **html**, and click OK to go to the Web Page Toolkit window. Follow the instructions to create your own home page on the Web. Click Go to Personal Publisher for the less ambitious method of creating a Web page or Go to NaviSoft for the fancy stuff!

Reading Newsgroups

AOL has some interesting departments, but in our minds Usenet newsgroups are where the action is. (We're probably just old-fashioned.) Chapter 9 describes how newsgroups work — in a nutshell, they're a large collection of bulletin boards, each on a particular topic. Topics range from recipe swaps (`rec.food.cooking`) to arguments about abortion issues (`talk.abortion`) to technical discussions of multimedia computing (`comp.multimedia`).

To use newsgroups from AOL, click the News Groups button in the Internet Center window. Or press Ctrl+K to see the Keyword dialog box, type **newsgroups**, and click OK. You see the Newsgroups window.

There are thousands of newsgroups, so you aren't going to read all of them. The idea is to find the ones which discuss subjects that interest you. After you've chosen one or more newsgroups, you still have to sift through the messages (also known as *postings*) to find the ones you want to read — some newsgroups get hundreds of postings a day.

Reading newsgroup messages

AOL remembers which newsgroups you're interested in. To get you started, those nice AOL folks even suggest a few. When you click the Read My Newsgroups icon in the Newsgroups window, you see the list of "your" newsgroups (see Figure 13-1).

If you aren't interested in the newsgroups AOL has suggested, don't worry. You can delete them from your list of newsgroups.

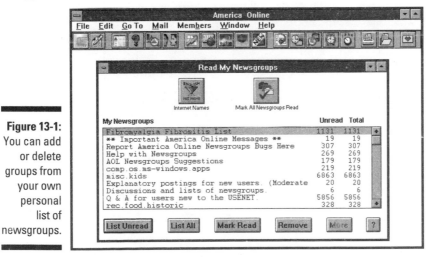

Figure 13-1:
You can add or delete groups from your own personal list of newsgroups.

For each newsgroup on your list, you can see the total number of messages in addition to the number you haven't read yet. Yikes!

For some mysterious reason, AOL uses different newsgroup names from the rest of the Internet. It replaces the dots within newsgroup names with dashes so that `rec.gardens` becomes `Rec-Gardens`. For some widely read newsgroups, AOL has invented its own names. For example, the `news.announce.newusers`

group is listed as `Explanatory postings for new users`. Anyway, if you want to see the actual Internet name of a newsgroup on AOL's list, click the Internet Names icon in the Read My Newsgroups window.

To read the messages in a newsgroup, follow these steps:

1. **Choose the newsgroup from the list in the Read My Newsgroups window.**

   If the newsgroup isn't on that list, see the section "Finding a newsgroup," later in this chapter.

2. **Click the List Unread button to see a list of the subjects of all the messages in that newsgroup you haven't read yet.**

   Figure 13-2 shows the messages in `rec.food.historic`. There may be several messages on the same topic (an exchange of messages on the same topic is called a *thread*), and the number of messages is shown for each subject.

3. **Choose a subject that looks interesting.**

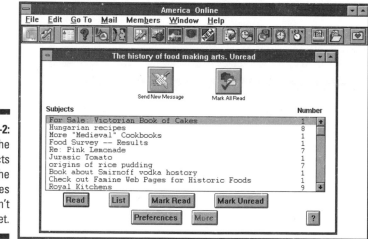

Figure 13-2:
Here are the subjects of the messages you haven't read yet.

4. **Click the Read Messages button.**

   The message appears in its own little window.

5. **Click the Next and Previous buttons to read the other messages for this subject, if there are any.**

6. **When you have read the messages, double-click in the upper left corner of the window to make it go away.**

In the window that lists the subjects of the messages in the newsgroup, after you have read the messages that interest you, you can "dismiss" the rest of them. Click the Mark All Read button to mark all the messages in this newsgroup as having been read by you. The next time you read this newsgroup, those moldy old messages don't appear.

Mouthing off

Always read a newsgroup for at least a week before you send anything to it. AOL users have a reputation (well-earned, unfortunately) of barging into newsgroups and having no idea of what the group is about or what people on it are discussing. So *please* restrain your creative impulses for a few days before contributing to a group. The rest of Usenet will thank you.

After you have read a message, you can send a response. Make sure, however, that you read all the existing responses first! Someone may already have made the excellent point you want to make.

Instead of replying to the newsgroup, consider sending e-mail to the person who posted the original message. If the information in your response will be of interest mainly to the original poster, send e-mail. If you're sure that it will interest lots of people in the newsgroup, post it.

To reply by e-mail to the person who posted the original article, click the Email to Author button. To post a response to the newsgroup, click Reply to Group. Either way, you see a Reply dialog box, which lets you enter the text of your

---

What's all that garbage in this article?

Some newsgroups' articles contain *uuencoded information*, which is nontext information that has been encoded as text. (See Chapter 18 for a more in-depth explanation of uuencoding.) For example, the `alt.binaries.pictures.fractals` group contains lots of beautiful GIF (graphic) files that have been uuencoded.

AOL has a feature it calls FileGrabber that helps you download these files (even large files that have been split up into several messages) and

uudecode them to re-create the original file. When you read a post that contains uuencoded information, AOL notices and displays a message from FileGrabber. If you click the Download File button, AOL asks where you want to store the file on your computer. Then it downloads and displays the file. If the file uses a graphics format that AOL can't handle, it only downloads the file. (For you graphic aficionados, AOL can handle GIF, JPEG, and PCX files on Windows systems and GIF, JPEG, and PICT files on Macs.)

message. If you're changing the subject, be sure to change the Subject of the posting also. When you've written your message, click the Send button.

In addition to making sure that you're not repeating what someone may have already said, be sure to write clearly, proofread your message, stay calm rather than get emotional (emotional responses don't work well in newsgroups), be polite (Net surfers are people too), and keep it brief. After all, tens of thousands of people are likely to read your posting, so don't waste their time!

If you begin to compose a reply and then think better of it, you can cancel sending the reply. Double-click the button in the upper left corner of the Reply dialog box rather than click the Send button.

Removing boring newsgroups

You cannot get rid of a newsgroup (what would all those people who *like* it do?), but you can delete it from your own list of newsgroups. Out of sight, out of mind.

To delete a newsgroup from your list, choose it from the list on the Read My Newsgroups dialog box and click the Remove button. The newsgroups don't disappear from the list immediately (who knows why not?), but the next time you choose the Read My Newsgroups button from the Newsgroups window, they don't appear.

Finding a newsgroup

AOL's kindly suggestions about newsgroups are certainly helpful, but you will want to choose your own. After all, what's the point of Internet access if you can't read the newsgroup devoted to your favorite musical group, television show, or sports team?

To find a newsgroup and add it to the list of newsgroups you read, follow these steps:

1. **In the Newsgroups window, click the Add Newsgroups button.**

2. **In the window that's displayed, browse down through the list and look for the type of newsgroup you want.**

   The list is so long that AOL sends it to you a section at a time. When you get to the end of the list, click the More button for the next section. You've really seen all of them when the More button is gray.

   For suggestions about which categories to try, see the following sidebar, "The usual suspects."

3. **Double-click a likely-looking category.**

   AOL displays — no, you're not finished yet! — the list of *topics* within that category. To the right of each topic is the number of newsgroups on that topic.

4. **Double-click a topic that interests you.**

   You see a list of the newsgroups about that topic (see Figure 13-3).

5. **Look at the subjects of the messages in each newsgroup and read the messages, just as we described in the section "Reading newsgroup messages," earlier in this chapter.**

   Before subscribing to the newsgroup, you might as well take a look at the articles in the newsgroup to see whether they're what you're looking for. When you finish, close the windows that display the individual messages and the list of articles in the newsgroup.

6. **If you plan to read the newsgroup regularly, click the Add button to add it to your list of newsgroups.**

   The newsgroup now appears on the list of newsgroups you get when you click the Read My Newsgroups button in the Newsgroups window.

7. **When you finish, double-click the little box in the upper left corner of each window you're finished with.**

To see the actual Internet names for the newsgroups that are listed, click the Internet Names button.

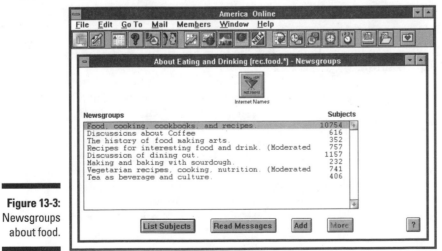

Figure 13-3:
Newsgroups
about food.

The usual suspects

AOL carries all the standard newsgroups discussed in Chapter 9. It also has a category not found elsewhere: Mailing Lists Echoed to Usenet (*list.**). These newsgroups are mailing lists. You may find it more convenient to read mailing-list messages as though they come from a newsgroup rather than have them clutter up your mailbox. (These aren't real newsgroups available anywhere except on AOL — they're a convenience provided by AOL for its users.)

Finding a newsgroup if you know its name

Finding a newsgroup by using the procedure described in the preceding section can take all day, although it's nice to be able to browse around and see what's there.

If you already know the name of the newsgroup you want to read, however, there's a faster way:

1. **Click the Expert Add button in the Newsgroups window.**

   AOL asks you for the Internet name of the newsgroup (that's the newsgroup name with dots between the words, usually all in small letters).

2. **Enter the newsgroup name and click the Add button.**

3. **When AOL asks you to confirm the addition of the newsgroup, do so.**

4. **When you finish, double-click the little box in the upper left corner of the window.**

AOL offers every newsgroup in the known universe — even the notably uncensored ones, such as `alt.sex.spanking`. If you know the name of the group you want, you can add it to your list, even if it's not in the list that AOL displays. Complete lists of newsgroups are posted in the group `news.lists` (or in AOL-ese, `news-lists`) on the first day of each month under the titles List of Active Newsgroups and Alternative Newsgroup Hierarchies. Some of them can get pretty raunchy, so if you or your family members who use AOL are young, impressionable, or easily offended, don't say that we didn't warn you. If you stick to the groups in AOL's lists, the worst thing you will find, other than some incredibly bad spelling, is an occasional rude word uttered (typed, actually) in frustration.

Searching for a newsgroup

If you don't know the name of the newsgroup you want to read, another way to find it is to click the Search All Newsgroups button in the Newsgroups window. You can then enter a word in the Search Newsgroups dialog box that is displayed, and AOL shows you the newsgroup names which contain that word.

A Cheaper Way to Use AOL

AOL has a nice feature that lets you read your e-mail and newsgroup messages off-line (when you're not connected to AOL). This feature, called *FlashSessions,* can save you big bucks in connect-time.

FlashSessions enable you to tell AOL to log in to your account, send e-mail messages you have composed, get the new mail, and log off as fast as it can. You can also tell AOL to perform this series of steps at a preset time each day, such as in the middle of the night when your computer isn't doing anything else.

Setting up FlashSessions

Here's how to tell AOL that you want to use FlashSessions:

1. **Choose Mail⊏❯FlashSessions from the menu bar.**

    You see the FlashSessions dialog box, shown in Figure 13-4.

Figure 13-4:
FlashSessions
grab your
incoming
e-mail,
download
messages,
send
messages
you've
composed,
and log you
right off.

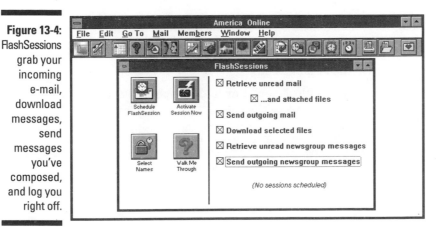

2. **If each of the boxes in this dialog box does not already contain an ×, click in the boxes.**

   These boxes control what AOL does during FlashSessions. Make sure that all the boxes have an × in them so that AOL will upload and download all the e-mail messages, files, and Usenet articles that are waiting to be transmitted.

   If you want AOL to run FlashSessions automatically on a schedule, keep following these steps. If you want to perform FlashSessions only when you give the command, skip to step 9.

3. **Click the Schedule FlashSessions button.**

   In the Schedule FlashSessions dialog box that's displayed, tell AOL how often to log on and get your e-mail.

4. **Choose which days you want AOL to get your mail.**

   Click the boxes for days you want to skip, to remove the × from the box. If you use AOL at work, for example, you might want to skip getting your mail on Saturday and Sunday.

5. **Click the How Often box to choose how often during the day you want AOL to get your mail.**

   To get your mail during the night, for example, choose Once each day.

6. **Click the up and down arrows for the Starting Time to see the time you want the downloads to begin.**

   If you choose Once each day for How Often, the Starting Time is the time that the download begins each day. To get your mail at 5:00 a.m. every day before you get to work, for example, set the first Starting Time (the hours) to 5 and the second number (the minutes) to 0. Notice that AOL uses a 24-hour clock: To get your mail at 2 o'clock each afternoon, set the hours to 14.

7. **Click the Enable Scheduler box so that it contains an ×.**

8. **Click OK.**

   You return to the FlashSessions dialog box.

9. **Double-click the Control-menu box in the upper left corner of the FlashSessions dialog box to close it.**

Now AOL will log on to AOL following the schedule you set. It sends any e-mail you composed, gets any incoming e-mail for you, gets any articles in Usenet newsgroups to which you are subscribed, and posts any Usenet newsgroup articles you've written.

Telling AOL which newsgroups to download

If you read Usenet newsgroups (described in the section "Reading News-groups," earlier in this chapter), you can tell AOL to download the messages from selected newsgroups so that you can read them off-line. Here's how:

1. **Log on to AOL.**

2. **Go to the Newsgroups window (by clicking Internet Connection on the Main menu and then clicking News Groups).**

   Alternatively, press Ctrl+K, type newsgroups, and click Go.

3. **Click Read Offline.**

   The Choose Newsgroups dialog box that's displayed lists the newsgroups you're subscribed to.

4. **For each group you want to read off-line, select the group and click Add.**

   If you want to read off-line all the groups to which you are subscribed, click Add All.

5. **Click OK.**

When you run a FlashSession, AOL downloads all the unread articles in the newsgroups you chose.

Composing e-mail off-line

If you use FlashSessions, you can compose your e-mail when you're not connected to AOL. Choose Mail⇨Compose Mail from the menu bar or press Ctrl+M. You see the Compose Mail dialog box. Address and write your e-mail message as usual. When you finish, click the Send Later button. AOL saves the message to be sent the next time you run a FlashSession.

Flashing on AOL

To run a FlashSession, just choose Mail⇨Activate FlashSession Now. You see the Activate FlashSession Now dialog box, as shown in Figure 13-5. Click Begin to start the FlashSession. Now AOL works like a player piano, or a program being controlled by an invisible robot. It logs on, transmits to AOL the e-mail you composed, downloads your incoming e-mail, downloads articles in the Usenet newsgroups you chose, and logs off, recording its actions in a FlashSession Status dialog box so that you can see what it has done.

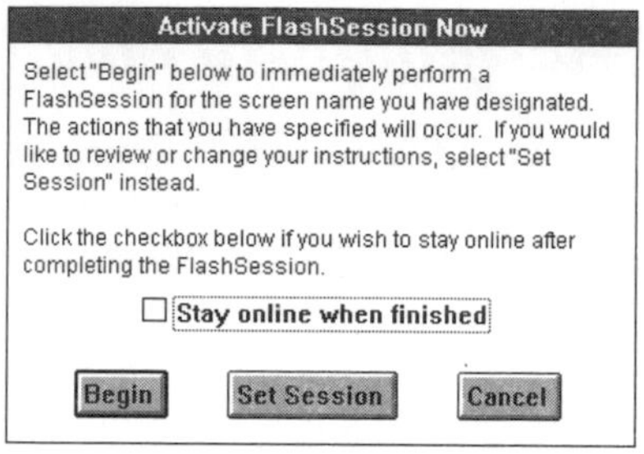

Figure 13-5:
Click Begin
to tell AOL
to log in and
get your
e-mail.

Activate FlashSession Now

Select "Begin" below to immediately perform a
FlashSession for the screen name you have designated.
The actions that you have specified will occur. If you would
like to review or change your instructions, select "Set
Session" instead.

Click the checkbox below if you wish to stay online after
completing the FlashSession.

☐ **Stay online when finished**

[Begin]   [Set Session]   [Cancel]

Reading flashed mail

After you have used a FlashSession to download your e-mail, read it by choosing Mail⇨Read New Mail (or press Ctrl+R). To see a list of all the mail you've downloaded, not just your new mail, choose Mail⇨Read Incoming Mail. You can reply to mail and forward messages — click the Send Later icon when you finish editing the messages.

Reading and composing flashed newsgroup articles

To read a Usenet newsgroup off-line (notice that you don't have to be logged in to follow these steps):

1. **Choose Mail⇨Personal File Cabinet from the menu bar.**

   You see your Personal Filing Cabinet window, where AOL stores your incoming and outgoing e-mail messages, files you've downloaded, and other information connected to your account.

2. **Scroll down to the Newsgroups section of the listing.**

3. **Double-click articles to read them.**

   AOL displays each article in a window. You can reply by sending an e-mail message to the author of an article by clicking the Reply to Author button.

4. **To send a new message to the newsgroup, click the Send New Message button, type the text of your article, and click the Send Later button.**

   The next time you run a FlashSession, the article is posted to the newsgroup.

5. **When you finish reading newsgroup articles off-line, double-click the button in the upper left corner of the Personal Filing Cabinet dialog box to close it.**

You can spend as long as you want perusing newsgroup articles and carefully crafting your replies because you aren't paying by the minute!

Grabbing Files from FTP Servers

AOL lets you download files from FTP servers on the Internet. AOL can do anonymous FTP (in which you connect to an FTP server you don't have an account on) or FTP-ing in which you do have an account. To use the AOL FTP service, you have to know which file you want to download, which FTP server has it, and which directory the file is in. For information about FTP, see Chapter 10.

To download a file:

1. **Go to the File Transfer Protocol dialog box.**

   Click Internet Connection on the Main Menu and then the FTP button in the Internet Connection dialog box. Or press Ctrl+K to see the Keyword dialog box, type **ftp**, and click Go. The File Transfer Protocol dialog box is displayed.

2. **Click the Go To FTP button.**

   Another dialog box, also named File Transfer Protocol, appears.

3. **If the FTP server that has the file you want is listed, select it and click Connect. If not, click Other Site, type the Internet name of the FTP server, and click Connect.**

   When you've connected to the FTP server of your choice, AOL may display an informational message about it — click OK when you've read it. Then you see a list of the contents of the current directory on the FTP server (see Figure 13-6).

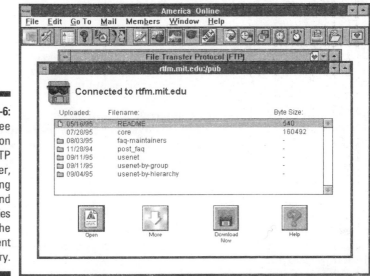

Figure 13-6: You can see what's on the FTP server, including the files and subdirectories in the current directory.

4. **To move to the directory that contains the file you want, double-click the directory names.**

AOL shows little file-folder icons by directory names and little sheet-of-paper icons by filenames. For files, look at the size of each file (in bytes, or characters) — the larger the file, the longer it takes to download.

5. **To download a file to your computer, choose the file and click Download Now.**

The Download Manager dialog box appears, asking where to put the file on your computer.

6. **Choose the directory in which you want to put the file on your own computer, and edit the filename. Then click OK.**

AOL downloads the file to your computer's disk. Depending on the size of the file and the speed of your modem, this step can take seconds, minutes, or hours.

7. **Close dialog boxes in AOL when you're finished.**

You can even close dialog boxes while AOL is transferring the file. If you have an account on the FTP server (and therefore have access to files not available to the public), use the Other Site button and click the Ask for login name and password button.

Some FTP servers are extremely busy, and you may not be able to connect. Try again during off-hours, or try another server. AOL keeps copies of most or all of the files on some of the busiest servers, to alleviate the traffic jams on-line.

Using AOL As a SLIP Account

It's a tough decision, choosing between a commercial on-line service such as America Online and an Internet account. America Online has lots of AOL-only information, but an Internet SLIP account lets you use all that snazzy, new WinSock software, such as Netscape. What's a cybernaut to do?

Now you don't have to choose — you can have it all. AOL has created a special version of the WINSOCK.DLL program that all WinSock programs use to talk to your SLIP account. (Refer to Chapter 2 for an explanation of WinSock and SLIP accounts.) If you use AOL's WINSOCK.DLL program, your WinSock programs talk to your AOL account.

Confused? So were we. Here's how it works:

1. If you have an existing WINSOCK.DLL program and you still want to use AOL's, you have to move the old one out of the way so that it doesn't interfere with AOL's.

2. Using AOL, you download its version of the WINSOCK.DLL file.

3. You install AOL's WINSOCK.DLL program.

4. You get a cool WinSock program you want to use, such as Netscape.

5. You log in to AOL as usual.

6. You run the WinSock program. Voilà! It works just as though you had a SLIP or PPP account, communicating with the Internet via your AOL phone connection.

If you already have a WINSOCK.DLL program, see the following sidebar, "But I already have WINSOCK.DLL!" You may not want to use AOL's.

You pay AOL connect-time charges for the time you're logged on. At about $3 an hour, AOL is a relatively expensive SLIP account. If you're spending too much time using AOL with WinSock programs, consider getting a regular Internet SLIP or PPP account.

Installing the AOL WinSock program

Follow these steps to install the software necessary to use AOL while you're running WinSock programs:

1. **Don't log in to AOL yet.**

   You have to do a few things first, and there's no point in paying AOL connect-time while you do it!

2. **Run the Windows File Manager.**

   Double-click the File Manager icon in the Program Manager window. It's usually in your Accessories program group.

3. **Choose File⇨Search from the menu bar.**

   You see the Search dialog box.

4. **In the Search For box, type** winsock.dll. **In the Start From box, type** c:\. **(If your hard disk is not drive C:, substitute the drive letter of the drive on which you store your programs.)**

5. **Click OK.**

   File Manager looks all over your hard disk for files named WINSOCK.DLL. If it finds any, it lists them with their full pathnames so that you can see where they are. If you already have one or more files named WINSOCK.DLL, see the following sidebar, "But I already have WINSOCK.DLL!"

6. **Now log on to AOL.**

7. **Go to the WinSock Central window.**

   Press Ctrl+K, type **winsock**, and click Go. WinSock Central contains information about WinSock programs and how to use them with your AOL account, just like this section of the chapter!

But I already have WINSOCK.DLL!

If you have Internet Chameleon, Internet in a Box, NetLauncher, or any other set of programs that enables you to connect directly to an Internet account, you already have a file named WINSOCK.DLL. It's in the program directory of the Internet programs, your Windows program directory (usually C:\WINDOWS), or some other directory included in your path (the list of directories Windows searches when it looks for programs). Windows 95 also comes with a WINSOCK.DLL program.

Now you have a decision to make: Do you want to use AOL's WinSock or keep the one you have? If you already have an Internet account, you probably should keep the existing WinSock. Why? Because it's almost certainly cheaper and, in most cases a local Internet provider offers snappier response time than AOL does.

If you have an existing flat-rate Internet account, you can use AOL and your WinSock software at the same time without installing any new software. You do that by making AOL itself run over the Internet. Rather than use your AOL account as a SLIP account, you can use your AOL software as WinSock software.

Start up the AOL software, but *don't* connect yet. Then go to the Modem menu and choose a "WinSock" modem. Connect to your Internet provider in the usual way, and after that connection is made connect to AOL. AOL connects via your Internet provider as just another WinSock program, and you can start any other Internet programs you want and click back and forth between AOL and the other programs. When you're finished with AOL, disconnect from AOL and then disconnect from your AOL provider.

If you have an Internet provider that charges by the hour, you probably don't want to do this because you'll pay both AOL and provider hourly charges. But if your provider has a flat rate or nearly so (a large number of free hours are included each month), it can be the best way to go. Notice that many Internet providers offer 28.8kbps connections and that AOL is limited to 14.4 in some areas, so a WinSock connection can be *faster* than a regular one.

But if you already have a WINSOCK.DLL program and you really do want to switch to AOL's, you have to get rid of it before using AOL's version. No! Don't delete it! You might want it again later! Instead, do one of two things:

✔ Rename your WINSOCK.DLL file so that any program looking for a file named WINSOCK.DLL can't find it

✔ Move it to a directory that you're sure is not in your path.

For example, if you already have a WINSOCK.DLL file that is part of your Internet Chameleon program (a set of programs for connecting to an Internet provider), you can rename it WINSOCK.CHA (use the File Manager's File➪Rename command to rename the file). Or create an UNUSED subdirectory of your Windows program directory, and move WINSOCK.DLL there.

After you use AOL's WinSock program, you may want to switch back to using the WINSOCK.DLL you already have. In that case, you have to rename or move the AOL version of WINSOCK.DLL. For example, rename AOL's version of WINSOCK.DLL to be named WINSOCK.AOL. Then move or rename your original WINSOCK.DLL file back to its original name and location.

We use Internet Chameleon, so we like to keep the Chameleon version of WINSOCK.DLL as WINSOCK.CHA, the AOL version as WINSOCK.AOL, and whichever one we are currently using as WINSOCK.DLL.

If you're not sure what you're doing, you may want to consult someone who knows about your computer system or who installed your existing Internet software before messing around with your WINSOCK.DLL file.

8. **Click the button labeled Click here to automatically download WinSock.**

   AOL displays a dialog box with information about its version of WinSock.

9. **Click Download Now to download the file.**

   AOL downloads it into your download directory, which is usually C:\AOL25\DOWNLOAD.

10. **When the file has been downloaded, exit from AOL.**

11. **Using File Manager, move into your Windows program directory the WINSOCK.DLL file you just downloaded.**

   Find the WINSOCK.DLL file in your download directory and highlight it. Drag it to your Windows program directory, which is usually C:\WINDOWS.

12. **Exit from Windows by choosing File⇨Exit from the menu bar.**

   This step makes sure that Windows forgets all about any other versions of WINSOCK.DLL it might have seen.

13. **Restart Windows by typing win and pressing Enter.**

   Now you are ready to use the AOL WinSock program.

Getting WinSock-compatible programs

Lots of freeware and shareware WinSock software is available from AOL and from the World Wide Web! Here are places to look for WinSock programs:

✔ Go to WinSock Central in AOL (keyword "winsock") and click the Software Library button. You see a long list of programs that work with your new WinSock program. However, the most popular WinSock applications are now listed (late 1995).

✔ Look at Forrest Stroud's "Consummate WinSock Apps List" on the World Wide Web (see Chapter 21). Press Ctrl+K and type the URL (address) of the Web page:

```
http://cwsapps.texas.net/
```

When you click Go, the AOL Web browser is displayed (see the section "Browsing the Web from AOL," earlier in this chapter) and it displays an extensive list of WinSock programs. Click the type of program you want (Web browsers or newsreaders, for example) and you'll see names, descriptions, and even reviews of the programs. Click on the Location section of the program description to download the program.

Using a WinSock Program

Suppose that you want to use Netscape Navigator rather than AOL's Web browser. Assuming that you've followed the steps earlier in this section to install the AOL WinSock program and to download the Netscape Navigator program (or bought a commercial version), here's all you have to do to use Netscape:

1. **Run it.**

   That's it. That's all you do. To be specific, run AOL and log in to your account. Then run Netscape (or any other WinSock-compatible program). It works, using your AOL account as its connection to the Internet.

When you finish, exit from the WinSock program. Then log off from AOL.

For more information about where to get nifty WinSock programs you might want to use, see Chapter 21.

Doing Other Things

America Online offers tons of information that has nothing to do with the Internet, so after you sign up, you might as well check it out. The Computing and Software department lets you exchange messages with others about the software you use or download shareware. The Learning and Reference department offers all kinds of on-line reference materials, including the Library of Congress database of books, Compton's Encyclopedia, Webster's dictionary of computer terms, and information about educational software. The Travel and Shopping department lets you use EAASY SABRE to make and check your own airline reservations.

AOL doesn't provide all the Internet services — it doesn't support telnet, for example, and its FTP service can be used only for downloading, not uploading. But by using the AOL WinSock program, you can use any WinSock program with your account, including WinSock telnet and FTP programs.

Overall, AOL has one of the nicest *front ends* (as we say in the software biz — it means the way a human being actually uses the system) of any of the Internet shell providers. For everyone except the most seasoned hackers, these nice icons and menus make the system easy to use! AOL can be slow at times, especially evenings and weekends, but it keeps promising to speed things up soon. The trial membership is free — try it out!

We've heard lots of complaints about how difficult it is to *cancel* an AOL account if you decide that you don't want it. You may have to call or write AOL and let your credit-card company know, several times, that you refuse any additional charges from AOL. Here's a friendly tip: Don't let AOL automatically deduct charges from your bank account.

For More Information

If you want to know more about America Online, we recommend *America Online For Dummies,* 2nd Edition, by John Kaufeld (IDG Books Worldwide). Alternatively, you can use the Members department (click the big, red question-mark button on the Flashbar) to read the answers to frequently asked questions and to ask your own.

Chapter 14

Using the Internet via Microsoft Network

• •

In This Chapter

▶ Signing up for an MSN account

▶ Climbing on-line

▶ Telling MSN where to go

▶ Hanging up

▶ Sending e-mail

▶ Browsing the Web

▶ Reading newsgroups

▶ Getting files using FTP

▶ Doing other things

▶ Finding out more about MSN

• •

*M*SN, or the Microsoft Network, is the new kid on the block on-line, service-wise. It debuted on the same day that Windows 95 was shipped, if you don't count the yearlong beta test phase with more than 100,000 test users. MSN tries to be the Cadillac of on-line services — the jury is out about whether Microsoft will succeed.

The MSN access software comes with Windows 95 — you can use it only from Windows 95, in fact, not from Windows 3.1, DOS, Macs, or any other computer systems. When you install Windows 95, an attractive icon for MSN appears right on your desktop, just begging to be clicked. Lots of other commercial on-line services complained, saying that it gave MSN an unfair advantage, but the courts didn't see it that way. So thousands of new Windows 95 users are signing up for MSN — you may want to be one of them.

This chapter talks about the Internet services MSN offers: e-mail, the World Wide Web, and Usenet newsgroups. There's lots more to MSN than the Internet, and you may want to pick up *Microsoft Network For Dummies,* by Doug Lake (IDG Books Worldwide), to learn about other great MSN features.

The pros and cons of MSN

MSN is easy to sign up for, at least if you use Windows 95. It includes good access to the Internet. On the other hand, you can't use MSN if you don't use Windows 95. Many people are reluctant to turn over yet another important part of the computer industry to Microsoft, and, for that reason, they don't use MSN. Also, like other large commercial providers, it can be expensive if you use it much.

Signing Up for MSN

To sign up for an MSN account, you need a credit card and a few minutes. Start Windows 95 and follow these steps:

1. **Double-click the Microsoft Network icon on your Windows 95 desktop.**

   You see a Microsoft Network window that tells you a little about the service.

2. **Click OK.**

   Microsoft asks for your area code and the first three digits of your phone number (telephone prefix), for U.S. users, anyway. (This part of the process works differently in different countries.) MSN needs to know so that it can figure out the closest MSN phone number.

3. **Enter your area code and phone exchange and click OK.**

   MSN tells you what the closest phone number is, according to the list of phone numbers available when you installed Windows 95. (Closer phone numbers may have been installed since the Windows 95 program was shipped.)

   MSN is ready to call in, update its list of phone numbers, and sign you up, although you can still back out later.

4. **Click Connect.**

   The MSN program connects to MSN. When it's finished, it hangs up and you see another Microsoft Network window with buttons for signing up for an account (see Figure 14-1).

5. **Click each of the big buttons to tell MSN your name and address (for billing purposes and to send you information and upgrades), to tell MSN how you'll pay for the account, and to read the rules you have to follow to use MSN.**

   When you have done so, the Join Now button no longer appears gray — it's ready to go.

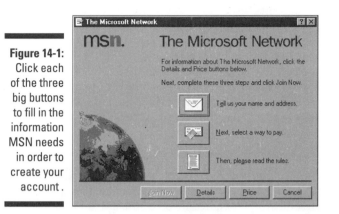

Figure 14-1:
Click each
of the three
big buttons
to fill in the
information
MSN needs
in order to
create your
account.

6. **Click the Price button to find out what you're agreeing to pay.**

MSN displays a window explaining the price per month, how many free hours that price includes, and how much you have to pay per hour. MSN offers several different pricing plans — different plans are attractive to different people depending on how many hours per month they use MSN.

7. **Click Close to clear away the information about prices.**

If you're curious about what you're getting into, you might want to click the Details button, too.

8. **If you want to go ahead and sign up, click Join Now. Otherwise, click Cancel (and skip the rest of this chapter!).**

MSN displays the two phone numbers it thinks are the closest to where you are (see Figure 14-2). If you want to look at the list of access phone numbers and choose a closer one, if there is one, click the Change button next to the Primary or Secondary phone number.

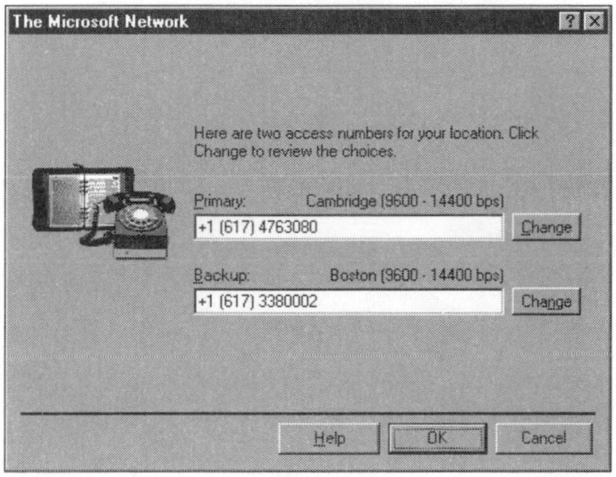

Figure 14-2:
Who ya
gonna call?

9. **Click OK.**

The MSN program displays a message to tell you that it's ready to connect to MSN again, this time to set up your new account.

10. **Click Connect.**

The program makes the call and asks you to enter a member ID (the name to use for your account) and a password. The member ID is the first part of your e-mail address (followed by @msn.com).

11. **Type a member ID and password, and click OK.**

The member ID cannot include spaces or most punctuation — stick with letters, numbers, and underscores (which look a great deal like spaces). Write down the member ID you enter, because you have to know it later. Don't write down the password, because if someone else knows your member ID and password, he can sign on to your account and spends lots of money — instead, choose a password you can remember.

If someone else is already using the member ID you entered, MSN tells you to try another one.

After you click OK, MSN creates your account, and you're finished! You have a new on-line account!

12. **Click Finish to close that last sign-up window.**

You see the MSN Sign In window, the window you use every time you log on to MSN. Read on to find out how to use it!

If you get interrupted and can't finish signing up for your account, you can start over later by double-clicking the My Computer icon on the desktop, opening the Program Files folder, opening the Microsoft Network folder, and double-clicking the Signup icon.

Calling MSN

When you're all signed up, here's how you can call MSN at any time:

1. **Double-click the Microsoft Network icon on your Windows 95 desktop.**

You see the MSN Sign In window, as shown in Figure 14-3. This window is the same one you saw when you finished signing up for your account.

2. **Enter your member ID and password, and click Connect.**

When you type the password, it appears as asterisks so that if someone is looking over your shoulder, she can't read it.

Figure 14-3:
You use the MSN Sign In window to call up MSN.

If you want MSN to remember your password so that you don't have to type it every time you sign in, click the box in the lower left corner of the window before clicking OK. If you do this, though, anyone can log in to your MSN account by double-clicking the MSN icon on your computer. Do you trust your cleaning people? Do you trust your roommate, or your little brother?

The first time you call MSN, you see a friendly welcome message from Bill Gates. Click the Close button after you read it. (Nice touch, Bill!)

When you have logged in, you see the MSN Central window, as shown in Figure 14-4. You also see the MSN Today window, as shown in Figure 14-5.

If you have received e-mail you haven't read yet, you see a message like the one in Figure 14-6.

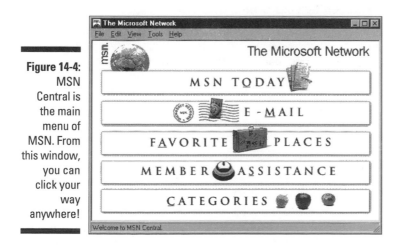

Figure 14-4:
MSN Central is the main menu of MSN. From this window, you can click your way anywhere!

3. If MSN suggests opening your in-box, click Yes.

Microsoft Exchange, the e-mail in-box program that comes with Windows 95, runs, and you see its window. (See the section "Sending Love Letters to Bill," later in this chapter, to learn how to use Microsoft Exchange to do things with your e-mail.)

Now you're logged in and ready to use MSN.

If you have trouble with MSN, call (800) 386-5550.

Hang Me Up!

Be sure to hang up when you finish using MSN or if you have to step away from your computer for a while. *Remember:* You pay by the minute! To hang up, choose File➪Sign Out from the MSN Central window. Or close the MSN Central window, and it gets the hint.

Here's another way to hang up: When you are connected to MSN, a teeny-tiny MSN logo is displayed at the right end of the taskbar (which usually runs along the bottom of your screen). Double-click the MSN logo, and MSN asks whether you want to hang up.

Up and Running with MSN

You have an account, you're ready to roll. . .but how do you use MSN? This section gives you some information about what you see and how to get to where you want to go.

When you log in to MSN, you see two windows: MSN Today and MSN Central.

On-line today

MSN Today is MSN's daily front page, with icons for about four news stories, links to one or two MSN services, and an ad or two. When you see the MSN Today window, you can click any of the pictures or headlines to read more.

If you want the rest of the newspaper, click MSN NEWS near the bottom left corner of the MSN Today window. MSN NEWS is a news service run by Microsoft.

When you finish looking at the news stories or if you want to skip the whole thing, click the Minimize button in the upper right corner of the window to shrink the window into a button on the Windows 95 taskbar (if you want to look at something later, you can click the button to see the MSN Today window again). If you're sure that you don't want to see Microsoft's daily news headlines again during this session, click the Close button.

Hello, Central?

The MSN Central window contains five options:

- ✔ **MSN Today:** Displays the MSN Today window (refer to figure 14-5).

- ✔ **E-mail:** Displays the Microsoft Exchange window, which you use for sending and reading e-mail (see the section "Sending Love Letters to Bill," later in this chapter).

- ✔ **Favorite Places:** Opens your own personal Favorite Places window, in which you can create icons to take you directly to MSN services you use frequently. To create an icon for a place to which you want to return, choose File⇨Add to Favorite Places from the menu. If you have displayed the toolbar in your MSN window, you can also click the Add to Favorite Places icon.

✔ **Member Assistance:** Takes you to the Members Lobby (see the section "Getting help," later in this chapter).

✔ **Categories:** Displays the Categories window, with icons for the major topics covered by MSN (see Figure 14-7).

The MSN Central window is the key window when you use MSN: When you close the MSN Central window, MSN figures that you want to log off MSN. It's also a good place to begin when you're looking for information about MSN.

To choose one of the options, just click it. MSN displays another window, which contains the information you chose.

Getting around

Many MSN windows look like the Categories window, as shown in Figure 14-7. You see lots of little icons, and you double-click an icon to see what's inside. When you double-click icons, MSN downloads information that may appear in the MSN window or in a new window or that may run a program. You never know what's going to happen when you ask for some information from MSN — if MSN sends a word-processing document, for example, MSN automagically runs Microsoft Word (if it's available) to display the document.

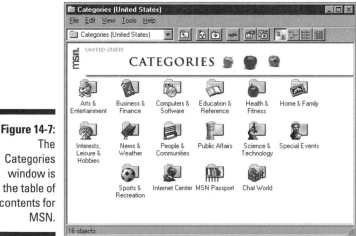

Figure 14-7:
The Categories window is the table of contents for MSN.

Choose View➪Toolbar from the menu of any MSN window. A useful toolbar appears just below the menu bar (look just below the menu bar in Figure 16-8, for example). There are icons for moving up one level, returning to MSN Central, returning to your Favorite Places window, and signing out, in addition to a drop-down list of MSN windows. When you give the command to display the toolbar, it's displayed in most MSN windows.

Making more space

If you don't like the large, space-consuming icons that usually appear in MSN, you can ask MSN to display its information in different formats. You can click one of the four rightmost icons on the toolbar, which display smaller icons in various formats, or choose the commands View➪Large Icons, View➪Small Icons, View➪List, and View➪Details, which do the same things. Figure 14-8 shows the way the Members Lobby looks after clicking the rightmost icon on the toolbar, the Details button.

What's in a name?

Every MSN window has a name, which MSN calls a *Go word.* If you know the Go word of the window you want to see, choose Edit➪Go to➪Other Location from the menu, type the Go word, and click OK. To find out the Go word of the current window, click the Properties icon on the toolbar or choose File➪Properties from the menu.

Figure 14-8:
The Details icon on the toolbar lists more information about the items available from MSN.

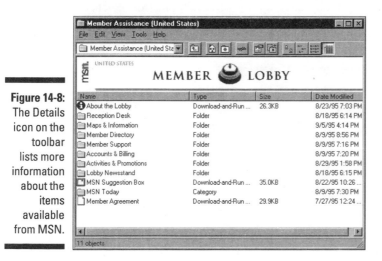

Getting home

It's easy to get back to the MSN Central window whenever you're logged on to MSN. Choose Edit⇨GoTo⇨MSN Central from the toolbar in any MSN window. If you have displayed the toolbar in your MSN windows, an icon that looks like a tiny house is displayed. Click it to return to MSN Central.

Occasionally, you may close all your MSN windows and still be connected to MSN. What's a user to do? See that tiny MSN logo at the right end of the taskbar on your Windows 95 desktop? Click it and you see the MSN Central window. Whew!

Finding stuff

A fun (but perhaps expensive) way to find things in MSN is to wander around to see what you stumble across. From the MSN Central window, click Categories to see the Categories window, and then double-click on likely-looking icons until you find out what information MSN has about the subject you're looking for.

You may not have the time, however, to perform information by wandering around. Instead, you can choose Tools⇨Find⇨On the Microsoft Network from the menu, to display the Find All MSN Services window, as shown in Figure 14-9.

Type a word or phrase in the Containing box to describe the topic you're looking for, and click Find Now. MSN expands the window to include a list of the windows it found that contain references to the topic. Double-click an item to go to its window.

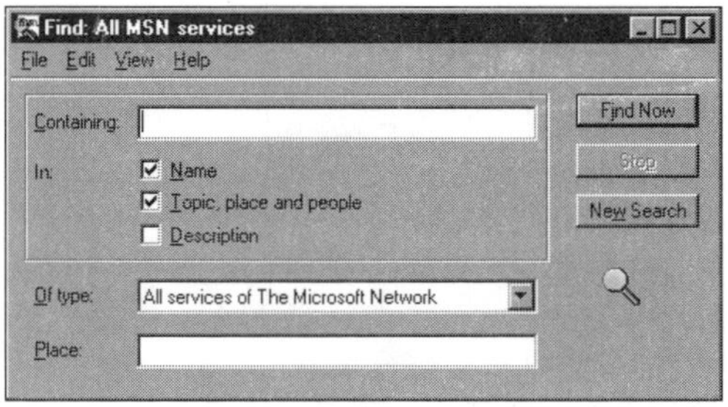

Figure 14-9:
Search for information in MSN by entering a word or phrase in this box.

Pay what?

Occasionally, clicking an MSN icon displays a little message saying that there is a charge for using the service. The message tells you what the charge is — it can be as little as a dime. Click Yes to continue, and the charge is added to your MSN bill. Or click No if the information isn't worth the charge.

Getting help

Lots of help is available on-line. For information about your MSN account, click Member Assistance in the MSN Central window. You see the Member Lobby. It contains icons for your account, billing, and how to find things.

For help with using MSN e-mail, bulletin boards, and other things, choose Help➪Help Topics from the menu in the MSN window.

Here's a list of commands you may need in order to deal with problems with your account, password, or billing:

- ✓ To change your password, choose Tools➪Password from the menu in any MSN window. You have to type your current password once and your new password twice. If you've forgotten your password, call MSN Customer Service at (800) 386-5550 to ask them to change it.

- ✓ To review how you're paying for your MSN account or how much you've spent this month, choose Tools➪Billing from the menu in any MSN window. You can see your billing statement on-line in addition to which extra-cost services you've subscribed to.

- ✓ To control the way MSN displays information in the MSN window in addition to how many minutes of inactivity MSN should wait before logging you out, choose View➪Options from the menu of any MSN window.

If you run into bigger trouble than you can handle on-line, call MSN customer service at (800) 386-5550. Choose Help➪Member Support Numbers from the menu for other phone numbers to call.

So Where's the Internet?

Microsoft made a big deal about how MSN provides lots of Internet services, and it's largely true. MSN lets you use these Internet services:

- ✔ **E-mail:** See the following section, "Sending Love Letters to Bill," to learn how to send and receive e-mail.

- ✔ **The World Wide Web:** MSN provides a separate Web browser program called the Internet Explorer.

- ✔ **Usenet newsgroups:** Double-click the Internet Newsgroups icon to read any newsgroup. Many MSN windows also list the Usenet newsgroups that relate to the topic in the window. See the section "Reading Usenet Newsgroups," later in this chapter.

To see a round-up of Internet services, go to the Internet Center. From the Categories window, double-click the Internet Center icon. From any MSN window, choose Edit⇨Go to⇨Other Location and enter **internet** as the Go word. You see the window shown in Figure 14-10.

Double-click the Getting on the Internet icon to get lots of help about using MSN's Internet services.

Figure 14-10: The Internet Center contains icons for the World Wide Web and Usenet newsgroups as well as info about using the Internet from MSN.

Sending Love Letters to Bill

E-mail is everyone's favorite Internet service, and many people use it for sending messages other than love letters to Microsoft's CEO. Windows 95 comes with a nifty program called Microsoft Exchange, which you can use for sending and receiving e-mail from various services, including MSN and your local-area network.

To run Microsoft Exchange, click the Start button on the Windows 95 taskbar, and then choose Programs⇨Microsoft Exchange. Or double-click the Inbox icon on your desktop. When you connect to MSN, if you have unread mail, MSN asks whether you want to run Microsoft Exchange to read it. The Microsoft Exchange window looks like Figure 14-11.

You can use Microsoft Exchange to handle e-mail from many different sources, including CompuServe, AOL, and other on-line services, and even faxes. You have to refer to the Windows 95 documents to set this up this program, and you may want to get a friendly computer nerd to help you because it's confusing.

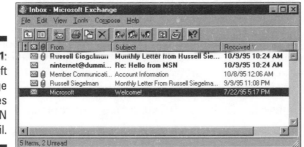

Figure 14-11:
Microsoft
Exchange
handles
your MSN
e-mail.

Reading your mail

The Microsoft Exchange window lists your incoming mail. If you haven't read it yet, the line of information about the message appears in bold. To read a message, just double-click it. The message appears in a new window and looks like Figure 14-12.

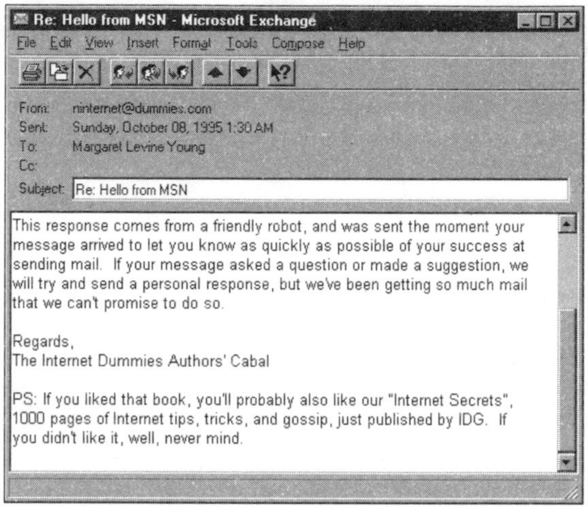

Figure 14-12:
A message
displayed in
Microsoft
Exchange.

Here are some things you can do when you're looking at an e-mail message:

- ✔ **Reply to the message:** Click the Reply to Sender icon or press Ctrl+R or choose Compose⇨Reply from the menu. If you want to address the message to everyone who received the original message (including people who were cc'd on the original message), click the Reply to All icon on the toolbar or press Ctrl+Shift+R or choose Compose⇨Reply to All from the menu. See the section "Take a letter!" later in this chapter, to learn how to type the text of the reply and send it.

- ✔ **Forward the message:** Click the Forward icon on the toolbar.

- ✔ **Delete the message:** Click the Delete icon on the toolbar or press Ctrl+D or choose File⇨Delete from the menu.

- ✔ **Print the message:** Click the Print icon on the toolbar or press Ctrl+P or choose File⇨Print from the menu.

- ✔ **File the message:** Choose File⇨Save As from the menu.

- ✔ **Display the next message in your inbox:** Click the Next button on the toolbar or press Ctrl+>. To see the preceding message, click the Previous button or press Ctrl+<.

When you finish looking at the message, close the window by clicking the Close button in the upper right corner of the window.

Take a letter!

So you're ready to write that love letter to Bill Gates or perhaps some other type of letter to someone else? Click the New Message icon on the toolbar of the Microsoft Exchange window or press Ctrl+N or choose Compose⇨New Message from the menu. You see the New Message window, which looks like Figure 14-13. You also use the New Message window when you reply to or forward an e-mail message (as described in the preceding section, "Reading your mail").

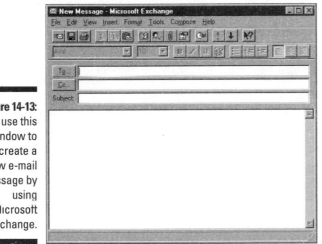

Figure 14-13:
You use this window to create a new e-mail message by using Microsoft Exchange.

Here's how to use the New Message window to send an e-mail message:

1. **Type in the To box the address to which you want to send the message.**

   When you reply to a message, Microsoft Exchange fills in the address of the person whose message you are responding to.

   You can enter several addresses, separated by commas. To send a message to another MSN user, type the member ID. To send a message to someone on another commercial on-line service or with an Internet account, type the person's Internet address. (See Table 6-1 in Chapter 6 to learn how to figure out the Internet address of someone who uses an on-line service.)

   If you want to use your address book to enter the address for the message, see the section "Using the address book," later in this chapter.

2. **If you want to send a copy of this message to someone, type the person's address in the Cc box.**

   To send copies to several people, separate the addresses with commas.

3. Type the subject of the message in the Subject box.

When you reply to or forward a message, Microsoft Exchange fills in the subject of the original message.

4. Type the text of your message in the big text box.

If you're replying to or forwarding a message, the text of the original message appears in the message text box so that you can quote parts of it in your response. Be sure to delete the boring parts.

If you're sending a message to another MSN user, you can dress up the text with all kinds of formatting. Use the icons on the second toolbar to make text boldface or italicized or to change the font. Don't bother using fancy formatting in messages to be sent to the Internet, however, because the formatting will be lost.

If you're forwarding a message, the text of the original message appears, including the headers that show whom it was from. You can add your own notes at the beginning of the message, perhaps explaining why you are forwarding it.

5. Check the spelling of your message by pressing F7 or choosing Tools⇨Spelling from the menu.

The spell checker works just like the one in Microsoft Word (it must be a coincidence). When the spell checker finds a word it doesn't recognize, you can ignore it for this message only, add it to your dictionary (so that it isn't flagged ever again), or correct it. When the spell checker is done, it tells you so.

6. Click OK to thank the spell checker.

Politeness never hurts!

7. Send your message by clicking the Send icon on the toolbar (the leftmost icon) or pressing Ctrl+Enter or choosing File⇨Send from the menu.

The MSN program sends the message to MSN and onward to its destination. The New Message window is displayed.

If you decide not to send the message after all, just close the window without sending the message.

Here's a file, too

You can attach a file to a message so that the person receives the file in addition to the message. If you are sending the file to an MSN user, it works great and you don't have to know anything about how attachments work behind the scenes. To send a file to an Internet user, however, or a user on another commercial on-line service, attachments use a system called *uuencoding.* (See Chapter 7 for a description of uuencoding.) Before you send a file, check with the people you want to send the file to and ask whether uuencoding works for them.

Note: As of this writing, MSN doesn't allow e-mail messages to Internet addresses to contain attachments, but Microsoft plans to support uuencoding, and eventually it may also add support for the standard method of attaching files, called MIME. Try it and see whether it works!

To attach a file to an e-mail message, click the Attach File icon on the toolbar (the one that looks like a paper clip) or choose Insert⇨File from the menu. Either way, you see the Insert File dialog box, in which you choose the file to insert. When you click OK, an icon for the file appears in the text of your e-mail message. Then send the message as usual.

What's this icon doing in my message?

Someday you'll receive a message with an icon in it, as shown in Figure 14-14. An icon in a message is an attached file — a document, a picture, or even a program. The icon in Figure 14-14 is a shortcut to an MSN window. When you double-click it, MSN displays the MSN Accounts and Billing Information window.

If someone you don't know sends you e-mail with an icon, don't be in a big hurry to double-click it. How do you know what the icon does? In the worst case (unpleasant but entirely possible), it could be a virus that attacks your machine and leaves your hard disk in shreds. A word of caution: Don't double-click with strangers!

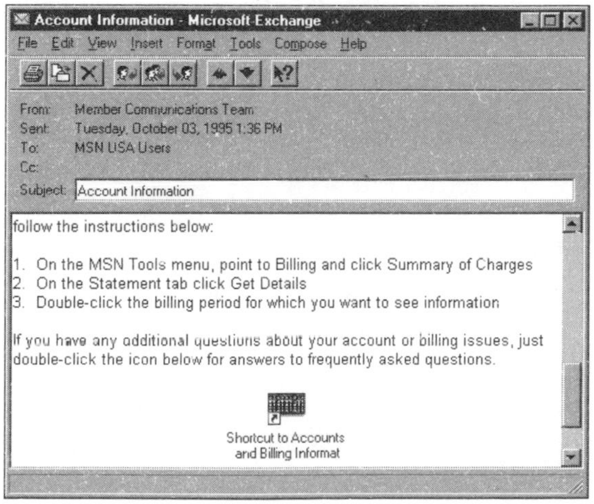

Figure 14-14:
Waiter, there's an icon in my soup!

Account Information - Microsoft Exchange

File   Edit   View   Insert   Format   Tools   Compose   Help

From: Member Communications Team
Sent: Tuesday, October 03, 1995 1:36 PM
To: MSN USA Users
Cc:

Subject: Account Information

follow the instructions below:

1. On the MSN Tools menu, point to Billing and click Summary of Charges
2. On the Statement tab click Get Details
3. Double-click the billing period for which you want to see information

If you have any additional questions about your account or billing issues, just double-click the icon below for answers to frequently asked questions.

Shortcut to Accounts
and Billing Informat

Using the address book

When you are addressing a message, you can click the To or Cc button to see your personal address book. Or you can click the Address Book icon on the toolbar or choose Tools➪Address Book from the menu or press Ctrl+Shift+B whenever you want to refer to the address book. The Personal Address Book window is displayed.

To add a name to your address book:

1. Click New on the Address Book dialog box.

You see the New Entry dialog box, as shown in Figure 14-15.

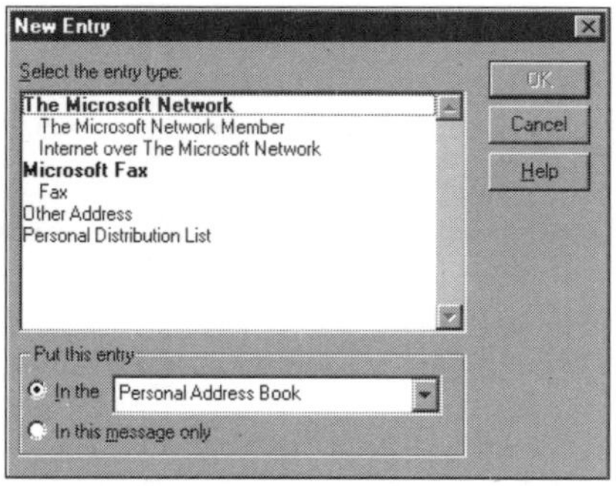

Figure 14-15: How do you send messages to this person?

2. For the entry type, choose the way in which messages can reach this person.

For people with MSN accounts, for example, choose The Microsoft Network Member. For other people with Internet addresses, choose Internet over The Microsoft Network (that is, send the message to MSN for delivery over the Internet).

3. Click OK.

You see the New Properties dialog box, as shown in Figure 14-16. The exact name of the dialog box, and the entries it contains, depends on the entry type.

4. Fill in the blanks.

For an entry for someone with an Internet address, for example, fill in the person's e-mail address, domain name, and real name. For E-mail address, it wants the part of the e-mail address that comes before the @. (In the address ninternet@dummies.com, for example, it's ninternet). For Domain name, type the part of the e-mail address that comes after the @ (such as dummies.com). We don't know why Microsoft Exchange makes you split up e-mail addresses like this.

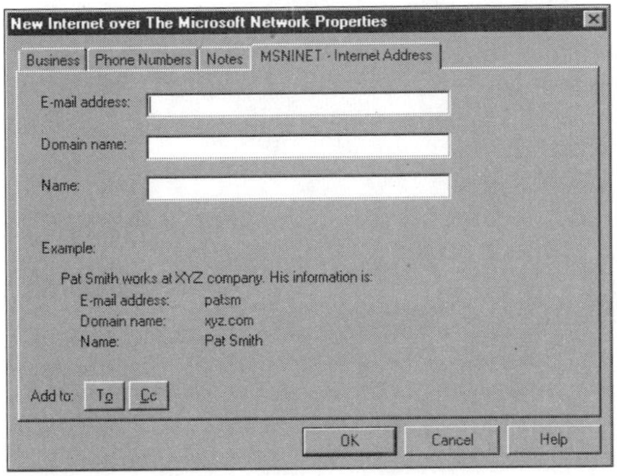

Figure 14-16:
Enter your
corre-
spondent's
personal
information.

If you want to enter other information about the person, you can click the Business, Phone, or Notes tabs to see the other parts of the dialog box.

5. To add this person to your address book, click OK.

To address a message to someone in your address book, select the name and press the To button. When your address book appears, choose the name of the person you want to send the message to and click the To button to add the person to the list of people in the To box. Click OK to make the address book disappear and return to the message you're composing.

Working off-line

You can read and compose e-mail even when you're not connected to MSN (you have the luxury of being able to think without the meter running).

Just run Microsoft Exchange as usual, and compose and read your messages as usual. The messages you create are stored in your Outbox. You can send them the next time you're connected to MSN.

In Microsoft Exchange, to see the messages in your Outbox, click the Show/Hide Folder List icon on the toolbar (the second from the left). The Microsoft Exchange window splits so that the left side lists your folders and the right side lists the messages in the chosen folder.

Aha! Unbeknownst to you, you have been looking at the messages in your Inbox all this time. To see the messages in your Outbox, choose it from the list.

To send the messages in your Outbox, choose Tools⇨Deliver Now Using⇨All Services (or press Ctrl+M). If you have defined other services for delivering your mail, you can choose Tools⇨Deliver Now Using⇨The Microsoft Network. Quick as a bunny, Microsoft Exchange logs you in to MSN, sends your mail, checks for incoming mail, and logs you off.

To make the list of folders in your Microsoft Exchange window go away, click the Show/Hide Folder List icon on the toolbar again.

Webward, Ho!

To browse the World Wide Web, you use the Internet Explorer, a separate program provided by MSN. Internet Explorer comes with MSN access software version 1.05 and with Microsoft Plus!

If your Windows 95 desktop has an Internet icon, click it — if you aren't logged in to MSN, it calls MSN first and then loads the Internet Explorer. (Installing Microsoft Plus! is one way to get that Internet icon onto your desktop.) If you don't see an Internet icon on your desktop, you have to install it. No big deal: MSN can download and install it with just a few mouse clicks.

For general information about the World Wide Web and how to browse it, see Chapters 4 and 5.

Getting your Internet Explorer

This section shows you how to download and install the Internet Explorer. Be sure that you have your Windows 95 installation disks or CD-ROM because you'll need them. Be warned: This process can take a half an hour, so be prepared to go out for a cup of latté (the official caffeine beverage of western Washington, where Microsoft lives):

1. **Double-click the World Wide Web icon in the Internet Center window. Or choose Edit⇨Go To⇨Other Location from the menu and type www as the Go word.**

   Either way, you see information about getting on the Internet.

2. **Click the Upgrade Instructions button.**

   You see step-by-step instructions for upgrading your MSN software to include the Internet Explorer.

3. **Follow the instructions, and click where indicated to check whether there is a local access number for you to use when you connect to the Internet.**

MSN downloads the list of phone numbers you can use when you connect to MSN if you also want to be able to access the Internet. If no MSN phone number is a local call, you may want to connect to the Internet through some other service because the telephone toll charges really mount up.

4. In the MSN Getting on the Internet window, click where indicated to download the new software.

This step can take a while, especially if you don't have the world's fastest modem. When the download is done, MSN hangs up on you and displays the same screen you saw when you originally signed up for MSN. "What's going on?" you may ask.

5. Click OK.

A window titled Upgrade to Full Internet Access is still open and displays messages about what it's doing, mainly setting up the MSN Internet Access Kit, which includes the Internet Explorer. This step takes a couple of minutes too. Hmm...latté's getting cold. Go nuke it.

MSN asks for your area code and telephone exchange, just as it did when you first installed it.

6. Enter your area code and exchange, and then click OK.

MSN tells you which phone number it plans to use to call MSN.

7. Click Connect.

MSN displays the regular Sign-On window.

8. Type your password and click Connect.

MSN gets the list of phone numbers it can use to connect you to MSN and the Internet. You see the window that lets you change the phone numbers you use to connect (refer to Figure 14-2).

9. Click OK.

The Internet Setup Wizard displays a message for you, warning that you are about to need your Windows 95 disks or CD-ROM. There they are — right under your latté.

10. Click OK to continue.

Lots of copying takes place. Finally, you see a message telling you that you have to restart your computer.

11. Exit from all programs. Then click OK in the Upgrade to Full Internet Access window.

You exit from Windows 95 and reenter. A new Internet icon is displayed on your desktop.

12. Double-click the Microsoft Network icon on your desktop and connect as usual.

Now you're connected to MSN and, through MSN, to the Internet. You're ready to surf!

Ready to browse

To run the Internet Explorer, double-click the World Wide Web icon in the Internet Center window or choose Edit⇨Go To⇨Other Location from the menu and type **www** as the Go word. This time, rather than boring instructions about how to upgrade your MSN software, you see the Internet Explorer, displaying MSN's home page, as shown in Figure 14-17.

Figure 14-17: It's the Internet Explorer, but it looks just like every other Web browser you've ever seen.

To use the Internet Explorer:

- ✔ Click an underlined blue word or phrase — they're hypertext links to other documents.

- ✔ Type a URL in the Address box and press Enter to see the Web page at that URL.

- ✔ Click the My Favorites icon on the toolbar (the yellow folder with the asterisk in it) to open a folder of your favorite places. To go to one of the favorite places, just double-click its icon.

- ✔ To add the current Web page to your folder of favorite places, click the Add to Favorites icon on the toolbar (the icon to the right of the My Favorites icon).

- ✔ To return to the preceding Web page, click the Back icon on the toolbar (the left-pointing arrow).

- ✔ You can see a list of pages you've seen since you started the Internet Explorer. Choose File from the menu, and look at the bottom of the menu that appears — it includes the last few pages you saw. To see the History window, a list of the other pages you've visited, choose File⇨More History from the menu.

When you finish browsing the Web, close the Internet Explorer window or choose File➪Exit from the menu. You may have to close the Favorites window and the History window, too, if you opened them.

Reading Usenet Newsgroups

Usenet newsgroups are the Internet's hub of gossip and news. There are tens of thousands of newsgroups, and you can read them from MSN.

Newsgroups Central

If you double-click the Internet Newsgroups icon in the Internet Center window, you see the newsgroups window, which offers you general information about Usenet newsgroups (alias *Net news*). If you double-click the Usenet Newsgroups icon, you see a window with an icon for each of the seven top-level Usenet hierarchies (comp, rec, soc, talk, misc, news, and sci). Double-click one of the icons to see the newsgroups in that hierarchy. To read the misc.forsale newsgroup, for example, double-click the misc icon. From the list of newsgroups that appears, double-click the newsgroup you want to read. For newsgroups with multipart names (more than two parts, separated by dots), you may be offered additional newsgroups from which to choose.

After you have chosen a newsgroup to read, you see the newsreader window. See the section "Reading newsgroup messages," later in this chapter, to learn how to use it.

If you want to read only one of the most popular newsgroups, click the Most Popular Newsgroups icon in the Newsgroups window. You have your choice of the top ten or so newsgroups, including news.announce.newusers (a must for new Usenet folk) and the ever-popular rec.humor.funny (now under new management).

Finding newsgroups about a particular topic

Throughout MSN, many windows about specific topics include an icon which lets you read the Usenet newsgroups that discuss topics related to the topic of the window. An easy way to read Usenet newsgroups is to click the Related Newsgroups icon in any MSN window.

A newsgroup window appears: See the section "Reading newsgroup messages," later in this chapter, to learn how to read a newsgroup after you've found it.

Smut me, please!

When you sign up for MSN, your account won't let you access the, er, um, dirty parts of the service, or the dirty Usenet newsgroups. If you want access to the adult portions of MSN and Usenet, choose the How To Access All Newsgroups item in the Newsgroups window.

You receive instructions for sending a form by e-mail to MSN, requesting that your account be unlocked.

For more information about blocking adult content, see Chapter 3.

Finding a newsgroup if you know its name

If you want to read a particular newsgroup, though, there's a quicker way than wandering around MSN to find the window that contains the topic you want to read about. If you know the exact name of the newsgroup you want to read, choose Edit⇨Go to⇨Other Location, and then type **news:** followed by the exact name of the Internet newsgroup (for example, **news:rec.food.chocolate**).

You see the newsgroup window for that group. Read on to learn what to do next.

Reading newsgroup messages

When you open a Usenet newsgroup, you see the newsgroup window.

Every item listed is a *conversation,* which the rest of the Usenet world calls *threads.* To read the articles in a thread, just double-click it.

When you have read the article, you can do any (or all!) of the following:

- **Save the article in a text file on your hard disk:** Click the Save icon on the toolbar (the little disk) or choose File⇨Save from the menu or press Ctrl+S.

- **Print the article:** Click the Print icon on the toolbar (you can guess which it is) or choose File⇨Print from the menu or press Ctrl+P.

- **Move along to the next article in the newsgroup:** Click the Next Message button on the toolbar (the down arrow) or choose View⇨Next Message from the menu or press F5.

- **Skip the rest of the articles in this thread (conversation) and move to the first article in the next thread:** Click the Next Conversation button on the toolbar (the arrow pointing down to a plus sign) or choose View⇨Next Conversation from the menu or press F7.

✓ **Forward the article to a friend:** Choose Compose⇨Forward by e-mail from the menu or press Ctrl+F. MSN runs Microsoft Exchange to create the e-mail message. Edit and send it as usual.

You can also reply to the message, of course, which you find out about next.

Let me say this about that

If you feel the need to respond to a Usenet article, you have two choices: Reply by e-mail to the author of the article or post a response to the newsgroup. Post a response only if you think that everyone in the newsgroup is interested in what you have to say. Never post a response just to agree with an article.

To respond to an article by e-mail, choose Compose⇨Reply by e-mail from the menu or press Ctrl+R. MSN runs Microsoft Exchange, and you see a New Message window with an e-mail message all ready for you to edit — it's already addressed to the person who wrote the article you're responding to, and the text of the article is in the e-mail message, so you can quote it. Be sure to delete the boring parts — remember that the article's author has already read it.

To post a response to the newsgroup (called a *follow-up* in the jargon), click the Reply to BBS icon on the toolbar (the one with two tiny faces), choose Compose⇨Reply to BBS from the menu, or press Ctrl+A. You see the window shown in Figure 14-18.

Edit the subject as necessary, and type the text of the article. Check the spelling, tone down the rhetoric, and remove any sarcasm before posting the message. To post your opus, click the post icon on the toolbar (the leftmost one), choose File⇨Post Message from the menu, or press Ctrl+Enter.

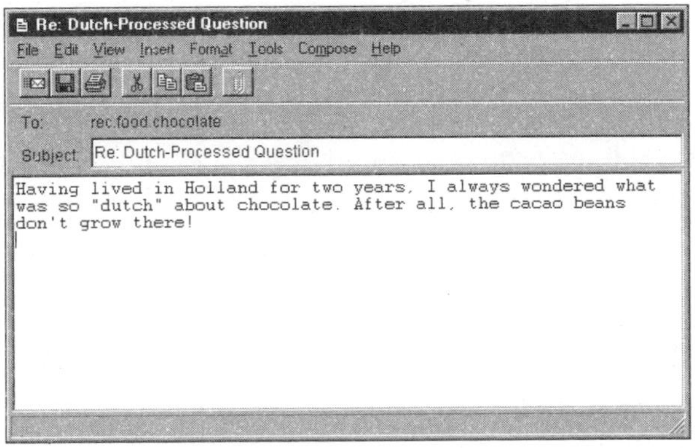

Figure 14-18: Composing a Usenet article is just like writing an e-mail message, except that tens of thousands of people may read it.

Re: Dutch-Processed Question

File   Edit   View   Insert   Format   Tools   Compose   Help

To: rec.food.chocolate

Subject   Re: Dutch-Processed Question

Having lived in Holland for two years, I always wondered what was so "dutch" about chocolate. After all, the cacao beans don't grow there!

Degibberizing gibberish

From time to time, especially in the rec.humor newsgroups, you may see an article that contains gibberish — text that is even less comprehensible than the average Usenet messages. We're talking about text that looks like words, but no words you've ever seen. The subject of the message looks fine, though, and may say something about rot 13.

What's going on? The message is potentially offensive (perhaps it's a joke about those dumb — oops, we can't say it). To prevent anyone from reading an offensive message by mistake, dirty or gross messages are frequently encrypted using a simple code called *rot 13.* If you don't want to see something yucky, skip to the article. If you want to chance it, choose Tools⇨ROT 13 Encode/Decode from the menu.

If you think better of posting a response, just close the window without posting the article.

You can compose a brand-new article, too, not in response to anything. Click the New Message icon on the toolbar (the leftmost one), choose Compose⇨New Message from the menu, or press Ctrl+N.

Doing Other Things

MSN comes with a ping program (or maybe it comes with Windows 95). Click the Start button, choose Run, and type this line in the Open box:

```
ping hostname
```

Then click OK. A nice little ping program runs.

MSN doesn't let you use telnet, finger, or other Internet services. But they are young yet — Microsoft may add other Internet services later. Check the Internet Center window for developments.

For More Information

If you like MSN, you may want to get *Microsoft Network For Dummies*, by Doug Lowe (IDG Books Worldwide). You can always choose Help from the menu in any MSN window or go to the Member Lobby (start at the MSN Central window and click Member Assistance).

Chapter 15

Using the Internet via UNIX Shell Providers

● ●

In This Chapter

▶ Signing up with a shell provider

▶ Dialing in

▶ Using UNIX commands

▶ Hanging up

▶ Welcome to the World Wide Web

▶ Sending e-mail

▶ Reading newsgroups

▶ Uploading and downloading

▶ Feeling superior to mere mortals

● ●

UNIX and You

We assume that you're choosing to connect to the Internet through a UNIX shell provider for one of the following reasons:

✔ Personal beliefs and practices make using mice impractical.

✔ Your reputation depends on it — geeks don't do Windows.

✔ It's free, or it's the cheapest thing you can find.

✔ You have no choice — it's all that's available to you.

For the purpose of this chapter, we assume that you don't know how to use UNIX already. When you use the Internet through a UNIX shell provider, the more UNIX you know, the better. So if you want to make your Internet life more fun, learn more UNIX. Get a copy of *UNIX For Dummies,* 2nd Edition, and *MORE UNIX For Dummies*, brought to you by people you know and trust (IDG Books Worldwide).

Signing Up for a Shell Account

UNIX Internet providers are widely available, and most major cities have them now (see Chapter 20 to learn how to find one). If you're a first-time user, you probably will want to call the provider and talk to a live human being to get your account set up and learn the appropriate settings for your communications software. If you've done this before, you can usually set your modem to dial in to a service, follow the instructions for new users, and sign up on-line. If this is just one more account for you, you can send e-mail to the service from your existing account to find out what you need to know to establish an account.

The Hardest Part of Using a Shell Account: Getting Connected

Unlike commercial providers that give you a disk with their software all configured and installed and ready to stick into your machine, UNIX shell providers tend to resemble secured posts with armed sentries waiting for you to provide the secret password before they blow your head off. It's not always that bad, but it can seem that way.

Shell providers assume that you have some kind of communications package installed and that you know how to set it up to dial in to an account. Maybe you do, and maybe you don't. If you're not an experienced computer user, we strongly suggest that you find a friend who is or else get help from whoever sold you your computer. Even experienced computer users sometimes have difficulty with this part.

If you don't have any friends or if you're the first kid on your block to try to do this, we highly recommend *Modems For Dummies,* 2nd Edition, by Tina Rathbone (IDG Books Worldwide). You don't need all 464 pages, but chances are that she'll answer most of your questions. The 464 pages attest to the fact that it's not so easy, and, because we have to stop writing this book at some point, we don't cover it all here.

Your modem probably came with some communications software, and that software probably came with a manual. Can you find it? We're not necessarily saying that it will help, but it probably won't hurt. Windows 3.1 users can use the Windows Terminal program that comes as a standard part of Windows. (It's not great, but it'll do.) Windows 95 users can fire up HyperTerminal (click the Start button and choose Programs➪Accessories➪HyperTerminal).

Using some combination of friends, sales support, manuals, and prayer, people really do manage to get themselves connected. You'll know you're there when:

- ✔ You press Phone⇨Dial (or your package's equivalent) and you hear your modem dialing a number (if your modem has a speaker — not all of them do).

- ✔ You see intelligible text displayed on your screen.

- ✔ When you type your response, what you think you're typing appears on-screen as you type it, with a little tolerance for typos and hidden passwords.

That's it. Congratulations — the hard part is over.

Duh, What Do I Do Now?

UNIX shell providers provide Internet access to the highly motivated. After you've successfully logged in to a shell account, nothing happens. It's up to *you* to tell it what to do. If you don't do anything for a long enough period of time, most providers will disconnect you, on the theory that you've fallen asleep and won't be back until the next morning. If you already know how to use UNIX, presumably you know what to do. If you don't, this section discusses some of the basics about UNIX commands to get you started.

The pros and cons of UNIX shell accounts

UNIX shell accounts tend to be the cheapest kind of Internet access available. Because a great deal of early Internet development was done in UNIX environments, places that have been using the Internet for a long time (more than three years, in this case) generally still use UNIX to access the Net. These places include many corporations and universities that have no major incentive to move away from UNIX.

On the other hand, compared to a Macintosh or a PC using Windows, UNIX is difficult to use.

When you access a UNIX environment through a dial-in shell account, what you get is a text-based system that requires you to learn a command for everything you want to do.

On the third hand, after you learn UNIX commands, navigating on the Net is much quicker, without the overhead of menus and graphical interfaces. Your Internet provider may have a system of menus to get you started, so you don't have to deal with UNIX commands right away. But don't expect it.

Command Performance

UNIX commands tell UNIX which program to run. To run a particular program, you type its name and press the Enter key. Most programs you use to access the Internet are described elsewhere in this book. To use e-mail, for example, you run the Pine program, as described in Chapters 6 and 7. To read Usenet news, you use a newsreader such as trn, described later in this chapter.

Here are the rules that apply to typing UNIX commands:

- If you make a typing mistake, press the Backspace key (or try Delete or Ctrl-H).
- To cancel the entire command before you press Enter, press Ctrl-U (occasionally Ctrl-K). The command disappears.
- When you finish typing a command, press Enter.
- If you type a command that UNIX doesn't know, it displays a message saying that it couldn't find the command. What probably happened is that you mistyped the command.
- UNIX cares about capitalization. Enter commands as they appear here, or else UNIX won't recognize them. UNIX considers ls and LS to be two totally different commands. Most UNIX commands are in all lowercase. When you're typing filenames, upper- and lowercase matter too: FROG, Frog, FrOg, and frog are four different names and may be four different files. (We didn't say that this would be easy.)
- Don't stick any extra spaces in the middle of commands. Do, however, type a space after a command and before any other information you type on the command line.
- If you're stuck, type **help**. Not all UNIX providers have a help command, but you never know.
- Many providers have files set up with lots of useful information for new users. Make sure that you read everything your provider suggested that you read before you take the next step.
- If you're really stuck, send an e-mail message to staff. If you're even stucker than that, call your provider on the phone and pose your question to a real person.

Hanging Up

When you're ready to leave, type **exit** or **logout**. Your provider logs you off and hangs up the phone.

If you don't slip, TIA

To get Netscape and other cool graphical programs to work with a traditional shell dial-in account, some providers support TIA (The Internet Adapter), a program that makes your connection act like a SLIP or PPP account without actually being one.

Providers vary in their support of TIA. Some feel that it's a perfectly adequate solution to their users' request for graphics. Providers that offer real SLIP or PPP accounts may be less than excited about offering something functionally equivalent at a lower price. Check with your provider regarding TIA availability on your system. That famous book we wrote, *Internet SECRETS*, (IDG Books Worldwide), has a whole chunk about TIA for Mac users.

Welcome to the World Wide Web

You can indeed get to the World Wide Web from your regular dial-in account on a UNIX shell provider. You use Lynx, a text-based Web browser described in Chapters 4 and 5. Lynx isn't as nice as Netscape (nor as famous), but it provides 80 percent of the useful stuff that Netscape does and is much faster. You might even be able to use Netscape or another graphical browser if your provider supports TIA (see the sidebar "If you don't slip, TIA").

Sending and Receiving Mail

In Chapters 6 and 7 we talk about everything you need to know about mail. We talk about Pine, a nice mail program that should be installed somewhere on your shell provider's system. If you can't find it, ask your provider where it is, and, if it's really not there, insist that it be installed. It's free; it's flexible; it's what you want.

Your e-mail address is the combination of your username and your provider's address, just as described in Chapter 6. If you know other people on your provider's system, you can send mail directly to the user without including the provider's address.

Subscribing to Mailing Lists

Because e-mail is a standard UNIX feature, getting on mailing lists from a UNIX account is easy. Follow the instructions in Chapter 8.

Reading Newsgroups

Usenet was born in a UNIX environment. If you haven't already read all about newsgroups, turn to Chapter 9. When you're ready to test them out, this section tells you what to do.

Because all newsreading programs do pretty much the same thing (they let you read news — what did you expect?), most of them work in more or less the same way, give or take some differences in the appearance of the screen and a few command letters. All news programs are written to be more or less full screen, although, as you will see, some of them take advantage of the screen better than others do. They're all designed to enable you to flip though news as quickly as possible (because there's so much of it), so they all use single-letter commands, which are a pain to remember, of course, until you get used to them.

In nearly all newsreading programs, you don't have to press Enter after typing single-letter commands. Some commands, however, require that you type a line of text after the letter, such as a filename or a newsgroup name. In that case, you *do* press Enter to tell the program that you're finished with the line of text.

This section describes trn, which is probably the most widely distributed newsreader. There are others, but trn is as good a program to start with as any, for the usual reasons: It works, and it's free. If your system doesn't have trn, it may well have rn, an older, less powerful newsreader.

Start the newsreading program by typing **trn** (or, if that doesn't work, **rn**). You should soon see something like this:

```
% trn
Trying to set up a .newsrc file
running newsetup...
Creating .newsrc in /usr/johnl to be used by news programs.
Done. If you have never used the news system before, you may
        find the articles in news.announce.newusers to be
        helpful.
There is also a manual entry for rn. To get rid of newsgroups
        you aren't interested in, use the "u" command.
Type h for help at any time while running rn.
Unread news in general                        14 articles
(Revising soft pointers — be patient.)
Unread news in ne.food                        47 articles
Unread news in ne.forsale                   1177 articles
Unread news in ne.general                    268 articles
Unread news in ne.housing                    248 articles
etc.
********  14 unread articles in general — read now? [+ynq]
```

If the program complains that it cannot find either trn or rn, you have to ask for help to find out what the local newsreader of choice is. Even if you're using a different news program, it's worth your while to look through the rest of this chapter because what you do with news is the same even if the exact keys you type are different.

Assuming that you manage to start trn or rn, it tells you that it sees that you've never used news, so it's creating a file called .newsrc (yes, it starts with a dot, and you really don't want to know why), which it uses to keep track of which articles you've already seen. Then, in a fit of wild optimism, it guesses that you want to subscribe to every single newsgroup available on your system. Naturally, the list of newsgroups it shows depends on what's available on your system.

First things first: When you're tired of reading news, you leave it by pressing **q** (for quit). Depending on where you are, you may have to press it two or three times, but you can always q your way out.

Assuming that you're not ready to give up yet, trn or rn then goes through all the newsgroups. For each group, you have basically three choices: Look at its articles now, choose not to look now but maybe come back later, or unsubscribe so that you never see that newsgroup again unless you specifically resubscribe. Press **y** to say yes, you want to read the newsgroup; **n** to skip it for now; or **u** to unsubscribe and never see the group again. (Of course, there's also **q** to quit trn or rn.)

If you press y, trn displays the first screen of the first unread article in the newsgroup general, which is the group for articles that are theoretically of interest only to users of your machine. (In practice, the newsgroup general tends to fill up with junk.) The screen looks something like this:

```
general #6281
From: fred@glooble.net (Fred)
            [1]
[1] swell new net book
Organization: Glooble Net Global Access
Date: Sat Aug  7 06:48:03 1996
+
Hey, I just read the new edition of Internet for Dummies. I
wouldn't have believed that they could make the book even
better, but they did. It's incredibly fantastic, better than
food or sex.

I've ordered 4000 copies to mail to all of our subscribers,
but you might want to pick up a few extras, just in case.
—
Fred Glooble, system manager
End of article 6281 (of 6281) — what next? [npq]
```

While you're looking at an article, you again have a bunch of choices. If the article is more than one screenful, pressing the spacebar advances you to the next screen, much like the `more` and `pg` commands. If you're done looking at the article, press **n** to go on to the next article or **q** to leave the newsgroup and go on to the next newsgroup. If you find an article to be totally uninteresting, you can skip both the rest of that article and any other articles in the newsgroup that have the same boring title, by pressing **k** (for kill). You can arrange to have articles with known boring titles killed every time you enter a newsgroup (see the sidebar "Arrgh! It's a kill file," later in this chapter).

After you get the hang of it, you mostly press the spacebar to go to the next article or newsgroup, **n** to skip to the next article or newsgroup, and **k** to skip a group of articles. Until you prune down to something reasonable in the set of newsgroups you've subscribed to, you probably will press **u** frequently to get rid of the majority of groups you don't want to read.

Where do newsgroups come from? Where do they go?

There are two things you need to know that are related to getting rid of newsgroups. The first is that new newsgroups appear several times a week because Usenet is still growing like crazy. Every time you run rn or trn, you have the opportunity to subscribe to any new newsgroups that have appeared. The trn or rn program asks a question like this:

```
Checking active list for new newsgroups...
Newsgroup alt.comp.hardware.homebuilt not in .newsrc, sub-
    scribe? [ynYN]
```

You can answer **y** if you do or **n** if you do not want to subscribe. You can also press (capital) **Y** to subscribe to all the new groups or, more likely, (capital) **N** to subscribe to none of them and go on to some actual newsreading.

UNIX more or less or pg

UNIX is in the habit of spewing forth at lightning speed much more information than is humanly cognizable. To slow it down, learn to use the `more` command, the `less` command (less is more), or the `pg` command so that your informa-tion is displayed page by page and you get to decide when you see the next page. They all do pretty much the same thing: They show you a file a page at a time and stop after each page until you press the spacebar or Enter.

If you press **y**, it asks you where in the list of newsgroups you want to see this group appear:

```
Put newsgroup where? [$^L]
```

The most likely answers to this question are $ (to put it at the end) or + followed by the name of an existing group (to put it after that group).

Eventually, you may also regret having unsubscribed to a newsgroup, in which case you want to turn it back on. If so, press **g** followed by the name of the group you want to see. If you have never subscribed to the group, rn or trn may ask you where in the list you want to put it and offer you the same choices ($ or +). You can also press **g** to go directly to a particular newsgroup to read its new articles.

Ignoring articles faster with trn

If you're using trn rather than rn, you have a better way to choose which articles you want to see and which ones you don't. The important difference between trn and rn is that trn supports *threads* (that's what the *t* stands for), which are groups of related articles. You can choose or ignore a thread at a time rather than an article at a time.

If you press the spacebar or + to enter a newsgroup, you see a table of contents screen like the following, which shows the titles of the unread messages in the group:

```
general                              14 articles
a 0000-uucp(0000)    3  New mail paths
b 0000-Admin(0000) 10  backup
c Chet Arthur        1  System down to clean hamster cages

Select threads — All [Z>]
```

Again, this newsgroup is called `general`, the group that exists on every machine for local messages that don't belong anywhere else. This example has 14 unread articles. To make it easier to choose what to read, trn groups together related articles based mostly on the titles. In this case, 3 articles are called `New mail paths`, 10 are called `backup`, and 1 is about hamsters. The letters in the left column are key letters you press to choose articles to read. You press **c**, for example, to see the article about the hamsters.

After you finish choosing interesting-looking articles, you have a few choices. You can press the spacebar to go on to the next page of the table of contents, if any, and begin reading selected articles if you've seen all the titles. Or you can

Arrgh! It's a kill file

In most newsgroups, a bunch of running discussions go on, and some of those discussions are much more interesting than others. You can arrange to permanently ignore the uninteresting ones by using a *kill file*. When you're reading along and encounter a hopelessly uninteresting article, press K (capital *K,* for *KILL!*) to kill all current articles with the same title and to put the title in the kill file for the current newsgroup. In the future, whenever you enter that newsgroup, rn or trn checks for any new articles with titles in the kill file and automatically kills them so that you never see any of them. Using kill files can save a great deal of time and lets you concentrate on discussions that are actually interesting.

Just so you know it, you're wandering into advanced territory here. We're about to talk about editing files, and you may not know how to do that yet. If you want to do much other than read what comes your way on the Internet, you have to learn to use some kind of text editor. We don't have the room to go into it here, but if you don't know a text editor, we highly recommend our very own books *UNIX For Dummies* and *More UNIX For Dummies,* which give you volumes about the subject. Now that we've gotten that off our chests, we can continue.

You can edit kill files to remove entries for discussions that have died down or to add other kinds of article-killing commands. If you press Ctrl-K while you're reading a newsgroup, it starts the text editor (usually vi or emacs on UNIX machines) on the group's kill file. Kill files look like this:

```
THRU 4765
/boring topic/j
/was Paul McCartney in another
   band before Wings?/j
```

The first line notes how many articles have been scanned for killable topics (to save time by not rescanning the entire group each time). Subsequent lines are topics you don't want to read. You remove a topic by deleting its line in the kill file. After you're finished, save the file and leave the editor, and you're back where you were, reading news.

Sometimes you may also find that *certain people* write articles you never want to read. You can arrange to kill all the articles they write! Press Ctrl-K to edit the newsgroup's kill file, and at the end add a line like this:

```
/Aaron Burr/h:j
```

Between the slashes, type the author's name as it appears in the From: line at the beginning of his articles. You don't have to type the entire contents of the From: line — just enough of it to uniquely identify the person. At the end of the line, after the second slash, place the magic incantation h:j. Then save the kill file and exit the editor, and you're set. Sayonara, pal.

press **D** (uppercase) to read the selected articles and kill any unselected articles on the screen (**d** is for delete). Or you can press **Z** (uppercase) to read any selected articles and *not* kill the unselected ones.

Binary files and groups of files

Sometimes an article contains a binary file (most often a program or a picture or a group of files). The binary files are disguised as text by *uuencoding* them, which makes the message look like this:

```
section 1/1    file zarkon.gif    [ Wincode v2.6.1 ]

begin 644 zarkon.gif
M1&\@<&50<&&QE(&%%C='5A;;&QY('('1Y<('4&&<V97&<:@=97AA;7!L;97&
:<V5E('=H870@@290&>=2!C96;97&2:D-?#$OH_
'
end
sum -r/size 15557/71
```

Trn knows all about uuencoded files. Press **e** and Enter to decode them. The decoded file is stored in your `News` directory on the UNIX system. Some uuencoded files are sent in several parts; use **e** in turn on each of them to reconstruct the original.

These files are packed up as *shell archive,* or *shar,* files. When these UNIX shell (command language) scripts are executed, they re-create the desired files. Shar files usually start something like this:

```
—cut here—
# This is a shar file created on 4 Jul 1826 ...
```

You can also extract shar files with the trn or rn **e** command, just as you do with uuencoded messages. (It's smart enough to figure out which kind of message it is.)

Be aware that shar files are a horrendous *trojan horse* loophole (a way for a bad guy to run his program but make it act as though you had done it) because a shar file can contain any command you can type from the terminal. In the worst case, it can delete all your files, send obscene e-mail with your signature, and so on. In the past, prank shar files haven't been much of a problem, but it's worth it to be a little skeptical. For the acutely apprehensive, shar-sanitizing programs are available (your system administrator should have one handy that comes with the news system software) that can scan a shar article and look for suspicious commands.

Just a few notes for our files

Now and then an article is so interesting that you want to save it for posterity. You save it with the s (for save) command. To save an article, press **s** followed by the name of the file in which you want to save it. If the file doesn't already exist, rn or trn asks you whether it should format the file as a plain file or as a *folder* (a special kind of file that usually contains mail messages). Usually, you should make the save file a folder. If you save several articles in the same file and make it a folder, you can later use mail programs such as Pine (see Chapter 6) to review and change the contents of the folder. Saved files (or folders) are put in your News directory, unless you give a different directory to the s command.

You can also save an article and pass it to a program. To do so, press | (vertical bar) rather than s and follow it with the command you want to execute. This choice is most often useful for printing a message by making the command lpr or lp or whatever your local print command is. UNIX *pipelines,* which pass the results of one program as input to the next, are also permitted, as in

```
|pr -h "An important message" | lpr
```

Don't say that we didn't warn you

You may occasionally find an article that is just plain gibberish, neither uuencoded nor a shar file. These types of articles use the infamous *a cipher. Rot13* is a simple-minded scheme that replaces each letter of the alphabet with the letter that is 13 places ahead of or behind it. For example, *A* turns into *N* and vice versa, *B* turns into *O,* and so on. This isn't a very secure code (we believe that it was cracked about 2,000 years ago by the Carthaginians), but it's not supposed to be.

The point of rot13 is to warn you that a message contains rude words or something else gross and offensive, so you shouldn't read it if you think that you may be offended. If you want to read it anyway, press X (uppercase) to get rn or trn to unscramble it.

Don't expect much sympathy if you complain about an offensive rot13 message. After all, you didn't have to read it.

A trn and rn Cheat Sheet

By now you've probably lost track of all the keys that control trn and rn. This section presents a summary of the keys described in this chapter, along with a few others you might want to try. The rn program can be in two different states: *newsgroup state* (see Table 13-1), in which you pick which group to read, and *article state* (see Table 13-2), in which you're in a particular group and are looking at articles. The trn program adds a third state, the *table of contents state* (see Table 13-3), in which you're looking at a list of titles of unread articles in a group.

Table 13-1	Newsgroup State
Key	*Meaning*
Spacebar	Enter the next group that has unread news
y	Same as spacebar
n	Skip this group
u	Unsubscribe from this group so that you won't see it anymore
g	Go to a group and type the group name after the g; if you're unsubscribed to the group, it resubscribes you
q	Quit, leave news
p	Go to the preceding group with unread news
h	Show extremely concise help
^L	Redraw screen

Table 13-2	Article State
Key	*Meaning*
Spacebar	Read the next page of the current article or the next unread article
n	Skip to the next article
k	Kill this article and any others with the same title
K	Same as k; also enters the title in the kill file so that the title is rekilled every time you enter the group
q	Leave this group

(continued)

Table 13-2 (continued)

Key	Meaning
c	Catch up and pretend that you've read all articles in this group
u	Unsubscribe
spdq	Save article to file pdq
/xyz	Find the next article whose title contains xyz
=	Show titles of unread articles
^L	Redraw screen
^R	Restart current article (redraws first page)
X	Unscramble rot13 message (not for the squeamish)
e	Extract uudecoded or shar file
edir	Extract into directory dir
h	Show extremely concise help
q	Leave this group

Table 13-3 **Table of Contents State**

Key	Meaning
Spacebar	Read the next page of the table of contents or begin reading selected articles if there's no more TOC
d	Begin reading selected articles and mark unselected articles as read
z	Read selected articles
/xyz	Select articles whose titles contain xyz
c-g	Select articles c through g in the current TOC
h	Show extremely concise help
q	Leave this group

Most letters and digits are used to mark articles to select.

The quick-reference manual entry for trn is 25 pages long, so it has many more commands. But you should be able to get along with just these. To see the on-line manual, type this line at the shell prompt:

```
man trn
```

Taking a Turn with trn

When you're ready, you can send e-mail by pressing **r** or **R**. In either case, rn or trn pops you into a text editor, where you can compose your message. The file you're given to edit contains header lines for the e-mail message, notably `Subject:` and `To:`, which you can edit if you want. The difference between r and R is that the uppercase R command also puts a copy of the text of the article into the message so that you can quote parts of it. Edit out irrelevant parts of the quoted article, and keep in mind that the author already knows what she said.

When you leave the editor, rn or trn asks whether it should send the message (s), edit it again (e), or abandon it (a). Press **s**, **e**, or **a** as appropriate. (Some versions of trn give you additional, less useful, options you can ignore.)

All New News

To post an all-new article to a newsgroup, you use the *Pnews* command. You can either run Pnews directly from the UNIX command line or press period and then F when trn asks you something like `1 unread article in rec.food.restaurants — read now? [+ynq]`. When you run Pnews, it asks you a few questions. The first, if you ran it directly rather than from inside trn, is the name of the newsgroup or newsgroups. (You can post a single article to several groups at a time if it's appropriate.) Type the name of the group or groups (separate them with commas). It asks for the subject of the message and then for the distribution (see Chapter 9) with a suggested default you can use if you haven't yet figured out distributions. Then it asks once more whether you're absolutely, positively certain that you want to post an article. If you say yes, it puts you in the text editor. From then on, it's just like when you're sending a follow-up article (as discussed earlier in this chapter).

Uploading and Downloading

One of the toughest ideas to get used to when you're connecting to the Internet from your very own computer is *where in the world your information is*. When you read mail or news on a UNIX shell account, mail and articles you save get saved in an area assigned to your account on the *provider's computer*. After you've disconnected from that account, you can no longer read whatever you left there until you dial back in.

The process of transferring files from your provider's account to your home computer is called *downloading*. The process of transferring files from your home computer is called *uploading*.

Uploading and downloading tend to frustrate most of us until we've done it several zillion times and are more sure of what we're doing.

Here are the basics:

To upload and download, you use the communications software that connects your Mac or PC to your UNIX shell provider. What gets tricky is who's sending and who's receiving. In reality, you're almost always sending — it's more a matter of where you're sending from.

Down the hatch

To send files from your UNIX shell provider to your Mac or PC, type the following command:

```
sz filename
```

where filename is the name of the file you want to send to your computer. Some communications packages, such as MicroPhone, display a reassuring window that shows you exactly how many bits are flying across the wire. Others keep you in suspense until you finally get a message back on the UNIX side saying that it's finished.

Up and down the staircase

To send files from your PC or Mac to your shell provider, you have to find the send command in your communications software package. When you have a choice of which protocol to use to send, choose Zmodem. When you have a choice of file format, choose binary. When the transfer is complete, you should be able to see the file in your directory on the UNIX system when you type ls to list the files you have.

Every communications package is different, but they all do the same thing. If you're lucky enough to have a manual that describes your software, consult it for details about uploading or downloading.

Part V
The Part of Tens

In this part . . .

Some things just don't fit anywhere else in the book, so they're grouped into lists. By the strangest coincidence, exactly *ten* facts happen to be in each list. (*Note to the literal-minded:* You may have to cut off and/or glue on some fingers to make your version of ten match up with ours. Perhaps it would be easier just to take our word for it.)

Chapter 16

Ten Frequently Asked Questions

● ●

*W*e get lots of questions in our e-mail every day. We picked some of the common questions in the hope that the answers can help you.

It also means that now, when someone asks us one of these questions, rather than answer it, we can tell them to get a copy of the book and read this chapter. Heh, heh.

If you have more than ten questions, run out and get our book *Internet FAQs* (IDG Books Worldwide, 1995). It has the answers to more than 300 frequently asked questions in addition to some rarely-asked questions.

Can I Change My E-Mail Address?

Usually no, but as is most often the case, the answer is more complicated than that. Your e-mail address is normally, but not always, your username on your provider's system. A few large providers (notably CompuServe, Prodigy, and InterRamp) simply assign you a meaningless username that you're stuck with, but most Internet providers let you choose any username you want, as long as it's not already taken. If you want to be called SnickerDoodles, that's OK with them, and your e-mail address will be something like `snickerdoodles@furdle.net`.

Later, when it occurs to you that you're going to have a great deal of explaining to do if you put SnickerDoodles on your business card, you might want to change your mail address. If you're using a small, local provider, you can probably call up and ask politely, and they'll grumble and change it. If they won't, or if you like being SnickerDoodles to your friends, you can usually get a mail *alias.* There's no law that says that each address corresponds exactly to one mailbox, and it's quite common to have several mail addresses that put all the mail in one mailbox. For example, John's true mailbox name is `john1`, but mail addressed to `john, john1, jlevine,` and a couple of other misspellings all are aliased to `john1` so that the mail is delivered automatically. (He's the system manager, so he can have all the aliases he wants.) Ask your provider whether it will give you a mail alias. Most will — it's just a line in a file full of mailing addresses. After it does that, you can set your return address (in Eudora, for example) to the alias so that your address is, as far as anyone can tell, your new alias.

If your provider can't or won't give you a mail alias, there are some third-party e-mail alias services. One is PoBox, which likens itself to a post-office-box service. It gives you any addresses you want at `pobox.com`, for a modest fee, which it then forwards to your true mail address. Contact PoBox at `http://www.pobox.com`, or you can send mail to `pobox@pobox.com`.

America Online (AOL) is a special case because it lets its users change their e-mail addresses with wild abandon at a moment's notice. When you sign up for AOL, you choose a *screen name,* which is your username and e-mail address. But each AOL user can choose as many as four extra screen names, ostensibly for other family members, and can change them at any time. The good news is that AOL users can have any addresses they want (as long as they don't conflict with any of the five million AOL addresses already assigned), but the bad news is that it's practically impossible to tell who's sending any particular piece of mail from AOL.

Prodigy lets you define additional names for your account, but you don't have much control over what they're called. If your Prodigy account name is ABC123A, you can create additional names ABC123B through ABC123F. Big deal!

How Realistic Is the Scenario Portrayed in the Movie The Net?

(If you haven't seen it, Sandra Bullock's character spends so much time on-line that, when records of her identity are wiped out, nobody can identify her.) Frankly, we've never seen a hacker who looked like that or, for that matter, anyone who ordered pizza every day and never went outside who looked like that and, trust us, we know plenty of hackers and pizza-eaters. It also occurs to us that it's hard to believe that someone with such nice teeth wouldn't have been to the dentist recently. Every hacker we know comes up for air occasionally.

We've never met bad guys on the Net, though we've definitely seen offensive material. On the other hand, we *are* living with an electronic shadow. Data about each of us is being accumulated every day. Who has access to that data and how it will be used should be of concern to all of us. Frankly, we find the idea of a monopolistic software company disturbing.

Where Do I Type the Finger Command?

In this one little question lies the concept for this all-new third edition of the *Internet For Dummies*. When we wrote the first edition in 1993, virtually all access to the Internet was through UNIX shell accounts. Last year, when we updated it for the second edition, personal users had begun to sign up for Internet access but, again, dialing in primarily to commercial UNIX shell accounts.

In this past year, most people getting on the Net for the first time are choosing either SLIP/PPP accounts or commercial providers (such as CompuServe or AOL) that provide an environment of their own and no easy access to a UNIX command. We're sorry for the disappointment and frustration this has caused many of you.

Oh, in answer to your question, if you have a shell account, you type the finger command at the UNIX shell prompt. SLIP/PPP users have to run a finger program. (See Chapter 15 for suggestions about where to find one.) If you're using a commercial on-line service, you probably can't finger, but check Table 2-1, in Chapter 2.

Is It Safe to Send My Credit-Card Number through E-Mail?

Everyone's idea of what is safe is different. Some people say that using a credit card is a lousy idea — period. Others think that the Net is full of people trying to steal credit-card numbers, so in no case should you ever send your card number across the Net.

But wait: Do you ever order anything from a catalog and give your credit-card number from your cordless or cellular phone? Have you ever thrown away a receipt from a credit-card purchase without shredding it? Have you ever left a restaurant or store with only your receipt, leaving the carbon behind? Yes, in theory it is possible for some ambitious and highly talented person to grab your unencrypted account number off the Net. And some encryption today is embarrassingly easy to break. But we don't consider credit-card transactions on the Net to be any more dangerous than most other credit-card transactions. If we were in a mood to steal credit-card numbers, we wouldn't waste time on the Net. We'd go dumpster diving.

How Important Is This Internet Stuff?

We think of the Internet as being like other media, such as the telephone and television. It was difficult, when each was new, to begin to comprehend its impact on our lives. Now we live in a world in which these devices are commonplace, and it's difficult to imagine living without them (although we confess that neither John nor Carol owns a TV).

It's difficult to know what all the ramifications will be, but we already see Internet technology weaving itself into homes and business at a rapid pace. Over the last several years, what was highly technical and only for nerds has become widely available to people in all walks of life. Every day it gets easier to use, more powerful, and more available, and every day more people are using it.

What's the Best Internet Provider?

That depends. Who's asking the question? What do you mean by "best"? For many people, it means cheapest. But right now, what's cheap are shell accounts and freenets. For people who aren't computer-savvy, these accounts might be a difficult place to start.

What do you plan to do on the Internet? If all you want is e-mail and access to the World Wide Web, almost any account will do, but the price ranges vary widely, and how easy it is to get started may be the deciding factor for you. Look closely at Table 2-1, the comparison of provider services in Chapter 2. If you've never, ever used a computer in your life and think that you might get easily frustrated, we recommend choosing a commercial service that's putting a great deal of effort into making your life easier. If you're more patient, think that you might have latent hacker tendencies, and want to save money, you can try a SLIP/PPP or shell account. Depending on where you live, you might not have that much of a choice. If you do have a choice, find out how much help is available from your provider. Talking to a service before you begin can give you valuable insight into which service is best for you.

How Can I Make Money on the Net?

We can't remember exactly how many trillions of dollars of business opportunities the Internet represents according to the people who claim to know about these things. But we do see that businesses rely on communication. As a new medium of communication, the doors of the Internet are being flung open for new ways of doing business. We recommend that, rather than try to figure out how to make money in the Internet business, you spend time getting to know the Net extensively — by checking out newsgroups and mailing lists in addition to exploring the World Wide Web. The more you see, the more you can think about organic ways in which your business can use the Net. Follow your loves: Find newsgroups and mailing lists that excite you. You'll meet all kinds of interesting people and get new ideas. We think that what you can learn from the Net can help you find for yourself where your unique opportunities lie.

(We've found that the best way to make money on the Net is to write books about it! But then again, we were writing books when dirt was two days old and playing with the Internet for longer than that.)

What Kind of Computer Should I Buy to Use the Internet?

You can guess what we're going to say, right? We're going to say, "It depends." For many people, the Internet is the first good reason they have for buying a computer. Which kind of computer you buy depends on who you are and how you expect to use it.

If you're purchasing a new computer primarily to surf the Net, buy a reasonably fast computer, a 486 of some sort with a color screen, which will cost between $1,000 and $1,500. The World Wide Web is a colorful place; to get the real effect, you have to see it in color.

On the other hand, if you already have a computer, get a modem if you don't already have one (less than $100 in most places) and try it out with what you have. By the time you really get started on the Net, you'll have a much better idea about which features are important to you. Not only that, but technology is constantly changing, and prices tend to go down the longer something is on the market.

Pardon our limited vision, but we're going to talk about only two categories of computers: Macintoshes and IBM PC clones. Which one is for you? Our experience, which includes all the stories we hear from first-time computer users, leads us to conclude the following: Macintoshes are significantly easier to use; IBM clones are significantly cheaper to buy. Here's where you have to assess your own abilities and your own resources.

When you're talking to other people and asking them what to buy, talk to people who do the same kinds of things you do, not just people who have computers. If you're a chimney sweep, find out what other sweeps use and like and why. Computers are not fair. They're more difficult to use than they should be. Some are easier to use than others. Life is not fair. Some people can afford to pay more for a machine than others can. Try as best as you can to determine which machine you will like using better — chances are that you can try them out in a computer store. When you evaluate price, try to factor in the value of your own time spent learning how to set up and use a computer and its software, and your own nature when it comes to mechanical devices.

Incidentally, if you have some other kind of computer, such as an Amiga or other "niche" machine (boy, are we going to get some angry mail from Amiga users about that), try to find a local users' group and find out which kind of Internet software is available for your machine. More likely than not, there'll be something cheap or free you can use.

How Do I Send E-Mail to Usenet?

You don't. Usenet is one thing and e-mail is another, even though they both pass messages around the Net. To add to the confusion, some programs (such as Agent and Netscape, which we mention in Chapters 6 and 9) can handle both mail and Usenet news, but underneath they're different. Some systems just provide mail without providing news, and if you're on one of them, you're out of luck news-wise.

Turn to Chapter 9 and read all about Usenet newsgroups and then, if you're using a commercial or shell provider, look at the chapter in Part IV about your Internet provider for the nitty-gritty.

What's Your Favorite Web Page?

`http://dummies.com`, of course. We never said we weren't vain.

Chapter 17
Ten Ways to Find E-Mail Addresses

* *

In This Chapter

▶ How to find an address

▶ On-line directories

▶ Lots and lots of mail systems

* *

Where in Cyberspace Is Everyone?

As you've probably figured out, one teensy detail is keeping you from sending e-mail to all your friends: You don't know their addresses. In this chapter, you learn lots of different ways to look for addresses. But we save you the trouble of reading the rest of the chapter by starting out with the easiest, most reliable way to find out people's e-mail addresses:

> Call them on the phone and ask them.

Pretty low-tech, huh? For some reason, this seems to be absolutely the last thing people want to do (see the nearby sidebar, "Top ten reasons not to call somcone to get an e-mail address"). But try it first. If you know or can find out the phone number, it's much easier than any of the other methods.

They won't mind if you give them the finger

One of the most useful commands, if you generally know where someone receives mail, is `finger`. On most shell provider systems, you can use `finger` to find out who is logged in right now and to ask about particular users. If you aren't using a shell provider, check Table 2-1 back in Chapter 2 to see whether the service you use supports a finger service.

Whaddaya mean, you don't know your own address?

It happens frequently — usually it's because a friend is using a private e-mail system that has a gateway to the outside world that provides instructions for how to send messages to the outside but no hint about how outsiders send stuff in. Fortunately, the solution is usually easy: Tell your friend to send you a message. All messages have return addresses, and all but the absolute cruddiest of mail gateways put on a usable return address. Don't be surprised if the address has a great deal of strange punctuation. After a few gateways, you always seem to end up with things like this:

```
"blurch::John.C.Calhoun"%farp@
  slimemail.com
```

Usually, if you type the strange address back in, it works, so don't worry about it.

You can find out your own address this way by sending a message to our ever-vigilant mail robot at ninternet@dummies.com, which will send you back a note telling you what the return address in your message was. (The human authors see those messages as well, so feel free to add a few words telling us whether you like the book.)

Top ten reasons not to call someone to get an e-mail address

- You want to surprise a long-lost friend.

- You want to surprise a long-lost *ex*-friend who owes you a large amount of money and thinks that he's given you the slip.

- You or your friend don't speak English. (Actually happens because many Internauts are outside the U.S.)

- You or your friend don't speak at all. (Actually happens — networks offer a uniquely friendly place for most people with handicaps because nobody knows or cares about the handicaps.)

- It's 3 a.m. and you need to send a message right now or you'll never get to sleep.

- You don't know the phone number and, because of an unfortunate childhood experience, you have a deathly fear of calling directory assistance.

- The phone takes only quarters; nobody around can break your $100 bill.

- The company installed a new phone system, no one has figured out how to use it, and no matter what you dial, you always end up with Dial-a-Prayer.

- You inadvertently spilled an entire can of soda into the phone and can't wait for it to dry out to make the call.

- You called yesterday, didn't write down the answer, and forgot it. Oops.

Fingering from UNIX

To run `finger` from a shell prompt, simply type **finger** *username@hostname* and press Enter. To finger someone whose e-mail address is `elvis@ bluesuede.org`, for example, you type this line:

```
finger elvis@bluesuede.org
```

You get back something like the following:

```
Login name: elvis                In real life: Elvis A.
                                 Presley
Directory: /usr/elvis            Shell: /bin/sh
On since Jun 30 16:03:13 on vt01  1 day 9 hours Idle
                                 Time
Project: Working on " Hound Dog"
Plan:
Write many songs, become famous.
```

The exact format of the response varies a great deal from one system to another because fiddling with the `finger` program is a bad habit of many UNIX system hackers.

Fingering with a SLIP/PPP account

But what if you don't have a UNIX shell account and have nowhere to type the finger command? Have no fear, because the Windows and Mac version of Eudora can finger people for you. In Eudora, choose Window⇨Ph (or press Ctrl+U) to see the Finger window. Type in the Command box the address you want to finger and click Finger. The results are displayed in the big text box. Press Ctrl+F4 to close the Finger window.

If you use Windows, an intrepid programmer out in Netland named Lee Murach has created a WinSock program called WS Finger just for you. You can get WS Finger via FTP from `sparky.umd.edu` in the `/pub/winsock` directory, among other places.

Using finger works only if the fingeree's Internet provider runs a program called (intriguingly enough) a *finger server*. It doesn't hurt to try — the worst that will happen is that you'll see a `Connection refused` message.

Project that plan! (Or is it plan that project?)

On UNIX systems, the response to the `finger` command comes back with a *project* and a *plan*. If you have a shell account, you too can have a project and a plan so that you look like a well-informed, seasoned network user (appearances are everything).

Your project is a file called `.project` (yes, it begins with a dot), and your plan is a file called `.plan` (it begins with a dot too). You can put in them anything you want. The `finger` command shows only the first line of the project but all of the plan. Try not to go overboard. Ten lines or so is all people are willing to see, and even that's stretching it if it's not really, *really* clever.

The industrial-strength finger

Some places, universities in particular, have attached their `finger` programs to organizational directories. If you finger `levine@bu.edu` (Boston University), for example, you get the following response:

```
[bu.edu]
 There were 55 matches to your request.

   E-mail addresses and telephone numbers are only displayed
   when a query matches one individual. To obtain additional
   information on a particular individual, inquire again with
   the index_id
```

The finger program lists all the matches. When you see a listing you want to check further, use the `index_id`:

```
finger Nxxxxx@bu.edu
```

where `Nxxxxxx` is the `index_ID` you saw listed when you first fingered your friend.

Other universities with similar directories include MIT and Yale. It's worth a try — the worst that can happen is that it will say `not found`.

Who zat?

Quite a long time ago (at least, a long time ago in the *network* frame of mind — 15 or 20 years), some of the network managers began keeping directories of network people. This, of course, was when Men were Men and Internet

Hey, Ms. Postmaster

Sometimes you have a pretty good idea what machine someone uses, but you don't know the name. In that case, you can try writing to the postmaster. Every *domain*, the part of the address after @ (the at sign) that can receive Internet mail has the e-mail address postmaster, which contacts someone responsible for that machine. So if you're pretty sure that your friend uses my.bluesuede.org, you might try asking (politely, of course) postmaster@my.bluesuede.org what the address is. (We assume that, for some reason, you can't just call your friend and ask what the e-mail address is.)

Most postmasters are overworked system administrators who don't mind an occasional polite question, but you shouldn't expect any big favors. Also keep in mind that the larger the mail domain, the less likely it is that the postmaster knows all the users personally. Don't write to Postmaster@ibm.com to try to find someone's e-mail address at IBM. (Fortunately, for people who want to find correspondents in the Blue Zone, IBM has a whois server — see the next section, "Who zat?")

Postmaster is also the appropriate place to write when you're having trouble with mail to or from a site. If your messages to someone are coming back with a cryptic error message which suggests that the mail system is fouled up or if you're receiving a flood of mechanically generated junk mail from a deranged automatic mail server (see Chapter 7), the postmaster at the relevant site is the one to write to.

connections were UNIX. The shell command that lets you look up people in these directories is called whois. Some systems have a whois command so, in principle, you can type this line:

```
whois Smith
```

and it should contact the whois database and tell you about all the people named Smith. In practice, however, it isn't quite that simple. For one thing, around the end of 1992 the main system that keeps the Internet whois database moved, and some whois commands still haven't yet been updated to reflect that move. The old standard server some whois programs contact now holds only the names of people who work for the Department of Defense. Fortunately, you can tell the whois program to use a particular server, as in

```
whois -h whois.internic.net Smith
```

because the civilian Internet service is now at whois.internic.net. The -h stands for *host*, as in the host where the server is located. But keep in mind that it still lists only network managers and administrative contacts. Here at Internet For Dummies Central, for example, whois will find John because he's the network manager (see the discussion of duct tape in Chapter 2), and Margy, who manages some name domains; but you won't find Carol, who, instead of being a network manager, has a life.

For systems that don't have the `whois` command, you can use telnet instead. You can telnet to `whois.internic.net`; then at the prompt, type `whois whoever`. For European Net people, try typing `whois.ripe.net`. A large list of `whois` servers (lots of organizations run their own `whois` service for their own employees) is in a file you can FTP (see Chapter 7) from `sipb.mit.edu`, filename `/pub/whois/whois-servers.list`.

Know what?

One more address-finding system worth trying is *knowbot*. It's at `http://info.cnri.reston.va.us/kis.html` on the Web. Just type the person's name, click the Search button, and wait, sometimes for as long as several minutes, as it looks through a bunch of directories and tells you what it finds. Knowbot has access to some directories not otherwise easily accessible, including the one for MCI Mail, so it's worth checking.

Compatible Mail System — a Contradiction?

A zillion different networks are spliced into the Internet in one way or another. With many of them, you can barely tell that it's a different network. Most UNIX systems, for example, have arranged to register standard Internet addresses, so you can send mail to them in the same way as you send mail to any other Internet mailbox.

But many other mail systems are out there, and several of them are in fact connected to the Internet. Most of the connections seem to have been assembled with spit and baling wire, however, so you have to type something strange to get the mail through. In this section, we talk about how to send mail to the most popular systems.

X.400: Just as friendly as it sounds

A great deal of international mail uses a pretty unpleasant addressing system. If you want to know how this happened, read the sidebar "We're from the government, and we're here to help you." Otherwise, we'll just cut to the chase.

OK, how do I find people at big companies?

We thought that you would never ask. IBM has a mail server that lets you look up people's names. Send a message to nic@vnet.ibm.com that contains a line like this:

whois Watson, T

It lists any users with e-mail addresses whose names match. Although nearly all IBM employees have internal e-mail addresses, only a fraction can receive mail from the outside, and you can see only those addresses. (Makes sense — no point in telling you about mail addresses you can't use.)

Many other companies have a straightforward addressing system that gives everyone at the company an alias such as Firstname. Lastname. This works at AT&T, so mailing to this address:

Theodore.Vail@att.com

finds someone pretty reliably. This technique also works at Sun Microsystems (sun.com). It's always worth a try because the worst that can happen is that you get your message back as undeliverable. If several people have the same name, you usually get a mechanical response telling you how to figure out which of them you want and what the correct address is.

An X.400 address isn't just a name and a domain: It's a bunch of attributes. The official specification goes on for dozens, if not hundreds, of pages, but we spare you the details (which would have been fascinating if we had had the space, you can be sure) and report on the bare minimum. The attributes that are usually of interest and the codes used to represent them are the following:

Surname (S): Recipient's last name

Given name (G): Recipient's first name

Initials (I): First or middle initial (or initials)

Generational qualifier (GQ or Q): Jr., III, and so on (these folks think of everything)

Administration Domain Name (ADMD or A): More or less the name of the mail system

Private Domain Name (PRMD or P): More or less the name of a private system reached via a public ADMD

Organization (O): The organization with which the recipient is affiliated, which may or may not have anything to do with the ADMD or PRMD

Country (C): A two-letter country code

Domain-Defined Attribute (DD or DDA): Any magic code that identifies the recipient, such as username or account number

You encode these attributes in an address, using / (a slash) to separate them and writing each attribute as the code, an equal sign, and the value. Is that clear? No? (Can't imagine why.)

Here's a concrete example: Suppose that your friend uses Sprint's Sprintmail service (formerly known as Telemail, the ADMD), which has an X.400 connection to the Internet. Your friend's name is Samuel Tilden, he's in the United States, and he's with Tammany Hall. His attributes would be

G: Samuel

S: Tilden

O: TammanyHall

C: US

Because the Internet domain for the gateway is `sprint.com`, the address would be

```
/G=Samuel/S=Tilden/O=TammanyHall/C=US/ADMD=TELEMAIL/
                @sprint.com
```

We're not making up this syntax. Sorry. Notice that a slash appears at the beginning of the address and just before the @. The order of the slash-separated chunks doesn't matter.

Exactly which attributes you need for a particular address varies all over the place. Some domains connect to only a single country and ADMD, so you don't use those attributes with those domains. Others (such as Sprintmail) connect to many, so you need both. It's a mess. You have to find out for each X.400 system which attributes it needs. In theory, redundant attributes shouldn't hurt, but in practice, who knows?

One minor simplification applies to the hopefully common case in which the only attribute necessary is the recipient's actual name. If the user's name is Rutherford B. Hayes, the full attribute form is

```
/G=Rutherford/I=B/S=Hayes/
```

But instead you can write

```
Rutherford.B.Hayes
```

Pretty advanced, eh? You can leave out the given name or the initial if you want. You can hope that most X.400 addresses can be written this way, but you are probably doomed to disappointment.

In most cases, the easiest way to figure out someone's X.400 address is to have your recipient send you a message and see what the `From:` line says. Failing that, you have to experiment.

X.500: We're from the government, and we're back

An official *white pages* directory-service model to look up people's e-mail addresses called *X.500* is brought to us by the same people who brought us X.400. Not surprisingly, considering who defined it, X.500 organizes its data like a shelf full of phone books (or in a large X.500 system, like a library of shelves organized by country). For any particular person, you have to tell X.500 which book or books to look in.

(Another true fact: If you're in one country, country A, and you want the phone number of someone in country B, the official ITU-T directory-assistance procedure is to connect you to someone in country A in a room full of old phone books from all over the world, in which they attempt to find the appropriate country B phone book and look up the person. If they can't find the number — because their country B phone books are all 15 years old and your friend moved 12 years ago, for example — tough. The scheme used in the U.S. in which they connect you to an actual directory operator in country B who is likely to have current phone numbers is in complete violation of standards. We feel that a moment of breathless admiration is appropriate for people who can invent standards like that.)

Note: It looks like X.500 will be widely used for two reasons. One reason is that it is somewhat more usable than X.400, and the other reason is that no other competing candidates exist. (We'll give you one guess about which is the more important reason.)

You can search a variety of X.500 directories via the World Wide Web. Point your browser at `http://www.hq.nasa.gov/x.500.html` to get started.

A Parade of Mail Systems

Here is a short (well, *pretty* short) list of major mail and on-line systems that are connected to the Internet and how to send mail to people on that system.

America Online

An AOL user's mail address is the "screen name," usually his full name. To send mail to a user named Aaron Burr, you type

```
aaronburr@aol.com
```

Some AOL users prefer their "stage name," such as `dickhmr@aol.com`. If you can't find your friend on AOL after trying the obvious, call your friend and ask.

AOL makes it extremely easy to change your screen name, and a single user can have several screen names, so AOL addresses change frequently.

For more information about using AOL, see Chapter 14. For even more information, see *America Online For Dummies,* by John Kaufeld (IDG Books Worldwide).

AppleLink

AppleLink users typically use their last name as their usernames:

```
reinhold@applelink.apple.com
```

AT&T Mail

AT&T Mail users have arbitrary usernames. To send mail to a user whose username is `blivet`, type

```
blivet@attmail.com
```

Note: AT&T Mail provides gateways to some companies' internal mail systems. In these cases, you may have an address like this:

```
argle!bargle!blivet@foocorp.attmail.com
```

BITNET

BITNET is a network of mostly IBM mainframes. Each system name is eight characters long or fewer. System names often contain the letters *VM,* the name of the operating system used on most BITNET sites. Usernames are arbitrary, but they are usually also eight characters or fewer. Many BITNET sites also have Internet mail domain names, so you can send mail to them in the regular Internet way.

If the mailer you use is well configured, it probably has a BITNET support setup to handle BITNET systems not directly on the Internet. So you can send mail to `JSMITH` at `XYZVM3`, for example, by typing

```
jsmith@xyzvm3.bitnet
```

Failing that, you have to address mail directly to a BITNET gateway. Here are addresses using two gateways that tolerate outsiders' mail:

```
jsmith%xyzvm3.bitnet@mitvma.mit.edu
jsmith%xyzvm3.bitnet@cunyvm.cuny.edu
```

These two gateways are provided by MIT and the City University of New York (CUNY), respectively, as a courtesy to the Net community.

BIX

BIX is a commercial system formerly run by *Byte* magazine and now run by Delphi. Usernames are arbitrary short strings. To mail to user xxxxx, type

```
xxxxx@bix.com
```

CompuServe

CompuServe is a large on-line service. For ancient, historical reasons, CompuServe usernames are pairs of *octal* (base eight) numbers, usually beginning with the digit 7 for users in the U.S. and 10 for users overseas. If a user's number is 712345,6701, the address is

```
712345.6701@compuserve.com
```

Note: The address uses a *period,* not a comma, because Internet addresses cannot contain commas.

Because CompuServe used to charge its users for *incoming* Internet mail, many users have set their accounts to refuse mail from the Net.

To find out how to use CompuServe to use Internet services, see Chapter 12. To find out how to use CompuServe's other services, see *CompuServe For Dummies,* 2nd Edition by Wallace Wang (IDG Books Worldwide).

Delphi

Delphi is an on-line service from the same people who run BIX, although the services are separate (Rupert Murdoch, the media baron, recently bought both of them and we hear that Delphi is about to be merged into MCI's Internet service.) Delphi usernames are arbitrary strings, most often the first initial and last name of the user. To send to user support, type

```
support@delphi.com
```

Digital's Easynet

Users on the Digital Equipment Corporation internal Easynet network have internal addresses of the form HOST::NAME, which correspond to:

```
name@host.enet.dec.com
```

Some users still use the old All-In-1 mail system, with addresses such as Ken Olsen@PDQ. These correspond to:

```
Ken.Olsen@pdq.mts.dec.com
```

Easylink

Easylink is a messaging service formerly run by Western Union and now run by AT&T. Users have seven-digit numbers beginning with 62. To mail to user 6231416, type

```
6231416@eln.attmail.com
```

FIDONET

FIDONET is a very large, worldwide BBS network. On FIDONET, people are identified by their names, and each individual BBS (called a *node*) has a three- or four-part number in the form 1:2/3 or 1:2/3.4. To send a message to Grover Cleveland at node 1:2/3.4, type

```
grover.cleveland@p4.f3.n2.z1.fidonet.org
```

If a node has a three-part name, such as 1:2/3, type

```
grover.cleveland@f3.n2.z1.fidonet.org
```

GEnie

GEnie is an on-line service run by General Electric. It's the consumer end of GE's commercial on-line service, which dates back into the 1960s. Each user has a username, which is an arbitrary and totally unmemorable string, and a mail name, which is usually related to the user's name. You have to know a user's mail name, something like J.SMITH7:

```
J.SMITH7@genie.geis.com
```

MCI Mail

MCI Mail is a large, commercial e-mail system. Each user has a seven-digit user number guaranteed to be unique and a username that may or may not be unique. You can send to the number or the username or to the person's actual name, using underscores rather than spaces:

```
1234567@mcimail.com
jsmith@mcimail.com
john_smith@mcimail.com
```

If you send to a username or an actual name and the name turns out not to be unique, MCI Mail thoughtfully sends you a response listing the possible matches so that you can send your message again to the unique user number. MCI user numbers are sometimes written with a hyphen, like a phone number, but you don't have to use the hyphen in your address.

Microsoft Network (MSN)

Microsoft Network is a commercial on-line service run by the software giant Microsoft. You have to use Windows 95 to connect to MSN. It's described in more detail in Chapter 14 and in gory detail in *Microsoft Network For Dummies,* by Doug Lowe (IDG Books Worldwide).

If your account name is *Bill Gates* (for example), your Internet-mail address is

```
BillGates@mns.com
```

Prodigy

Prodigy is a large on-line system run by IBM and Sears. (We hear that it can have upward of 10,000 simultaneous users.) It has a hard-to-use (for Prodigy users — it's a snap from the Internet side) mail gateway; see *Prodigy For Dummies,* by Gus Venditto (IDG Books Worldwide) for information about what else you can do with Prodigy.

Keep in mind that users pay for incoming mail and that the gateway can't handle long messages. Users have arbitrary usernames such as KS8GN3. Send mail to

```
KS8GN3@prodigy.com
```

Sprintmail (Telemail)

The Sprintmail e-mail system is provided by Sprintnet. Sprintmail used to be called Telemail because Sprintnet used to be called Telenet before Sprint bought it. (It was a technological spinoff of the original ARPANET work that led to the Internet.) Sprintmail is the major X.400 mail system in the United States. As mentioned in the section that disparages X.400, to send a message to a user named Samuel Tilden who is with Tammany Hall in the United States, you type:

```
/G=Samuel/S=Tilden/O=TammanyHall/C=US/ADMD=TELEMAIL/@sprint.com
```

Many corporate and government e-mail systems are attached to Sprintmail. Each has a distinct organization (O=) name and sometimes a private mail domain (PRMD=) name also that have to be entered in the address.

UUCP

UUCP is an old and cruddy mail system still used by many UNIX systems because (how did you guess?) it's free. UUCP addresses consist of a system name and a username, which are both short, arbitrary strings. The system here at Internet For Dummies Central, for example, for historical reasons has a UUCP address — iecc — in addition to its normal Internet address, so you could address mail to iecc!idummies. (The ! is pronounced "bang," and this is called a *bang path address.*) Multihop UUCP addresses also exist: world!iecc!idummies says to send the message first to the machine called world, which can send it to iecc, where the address is dummies. (Think of it as e-mail's Whisper Down the Lane.) Most often, UUCP addresses are written relative to an Internet host that also talks UUCP, so you could address mail to this address:

```
world!iecc!idummies@uunet.uu.net
```

(although it gets here faster if you send it to ninternet@dummies.com, because that avoids the UUCP nonsense). This address means to send the message to uunet.uu.net by using regular Internet mail, then by UUCP to world, and another UUCP hop to iecc, and from there to the mailbox called idummies. If you think that this is ugly and confusing, you're not alone.

UUNET Communications is a large, nonprofit outfit that, among other things, brings e-mail to the UUCP-speaking masses, so it's the Internet system most often seen with UUCP addresses. Most of UUNET's customers also have regular Internet addresses that internally are turned into the ugly UUCP addresses. If you know the Internet address rather than the UUCP address, use it.

Chapter 18

Ten Kinds of Files and What to Do with Them

In This Chapter

▶ Graphics files!

▶ Document files!

▶ Compressed files!

▶ How to unscramble and otherwise make sense of them

*N*ow that you know how to use the Web and Gopher and FTP and you know how to download, you've probably already retrieved zillions of files (well, maybe three or four). But when you look at them with your text editor, you may notice that they're garbage. In this chapter, we consider the various kinds of files on the Net, how to tell what they are, and what to do with them.

How Many Kinds of Files Are There?

Hundreds, at least. Fortunately, they fall into five general categories.

- Text files (files that contain text, believe it or not)
- Executable files (files you can execute, or run; in other words, programs)
- Archives, ZIP files, and other compressed files
- Graphics and video files
- Data files (any other kind of file)

Macs are different too

Macintosh files, regardless of what's in them, usually come in two or three chunks, one of which is the data file. You don't see the chunks on your own Macintosh, but you do see them if you try to upload them to a non-Mac server on the Net. In the Macintosh world, the three files are all pieces of one file and are referred to as *forks* — the data fork, the resource fork, and the information fork. When you upload what you think is one file from the Macintosh, it often appears as three separate files with the extensions .data, .resc, and .info appended to the filename. Various schemes exist, which we discuss later in this chapter, to glue the forks back together for transportation through the Net.

Just Plain Text

Text files contain readable text (what did you expect?). Sometimes the text is actually human-readable text (such as the manuscript for this book, which we typed into text files the first time we wrote it). Sometimes the text is source code to computer programs in languages such as *C* or *Pascal.* And occasionally the text is data for programs. PostScript printer data is a particular kind of text file discussed later in this chapter.

On PCs, text files usually have the file extension TXT. You can look at them by using Windows 3.1's Notepad, Windows 95's WordPad, or any word processor.

There isn't much to say about text files — you know them when you see them. As mentioned in Chapter 10, because the way text is stored varies from one system to another, you should FTP text files in ASCII mode to convert them automatically to your local format.

A few text documents are really archives or nontext files in drag. See the discussions of shar and uuencoded files later in this chapter.

Any Last Requests before We Execute You?

Executable files are programs you can run on a computer. Executable programs are particularly common in archives of stuff for PCs and Macs. Some executable programs are also available on the Net for other kinds of computers, such as various workstations. Any single executable file runs on only a particular kind of computer: A Mac executable is useless on a Windows machine, and vice versa.

It's a program that draws a picture

If you encounter a text file that starts out something like the following, you have a PostScript document:

```
%!PS-Adobe-2.0
%%Title: Some Random Document
%%CreationDate: Thu Jul 5 1996
/pl transform 0.1 sub round 0.1
  add exch
 0.1 sub round 0.1 add exch
  itransform bind def
```

A PostScript document is a program in the PostScript computer language that describes a document. Unless you are a world-class PostScript weenie, the only sensible thing to do with this type of document is to run the program and see the document. And the normal way to do that is to send it to a PostScript printer. PostScript interpreter programs, such as *GNU Ghostscript,* are also available that can turn PostScript into other screen and printer formats for users without PostScript printers.

The most commonly found executable programs are for DOS and Windows. These files have filenames such as FOOG.EXE, FOOG.COM, or (sometimes for Windows) FOOG.DLL. You run them in the same way as you run any other DOS or Windows program — double-click its filename in Windows 3.1's File Manager or Windows 95's My Computer or Explorer.

Some chance always exists that any new PC or Mac program may be infected with a computer virus. (Because of the different ways in which the systems work, it's much less likely for UNIX programs to carry viruses.) Stuff from well-run FTP servers such as the SimTel archives (see Chapter 10) are unlikely to be infected; if you run a random program from a random place, however, you deserve whatever you get. We don't belabor the issue of safe-software practices here; for more details, see *DOS For Dummies,* 2nd Edition, by Dan Gookin, and *Macs For Dummies,* 3rd Edition, by David Pogue (both published by IDG Books Worldwide).

Executable programs for workstations don't have easily recognizable filenames, although any file whose filename contains a dot is unlikely to be an executable. Even though nearly every kind of workstation runs UNIX, the executables are not interchangeable. Code for a SPARC, for example, doesn't work on an IBM RS/6000, or vice versa. Several different versions of UNIX run on 386 PCs, with different executable formats. Newer versions of PC UNIX generally run executables from older versions, but not vice versa.

Packing It In

Often a particular package requires a bunch of related files. To make it easier to send the package around, the files can be glommed together into a single file known as an *archive.* (Yes, the term "archive" also refers to a host from which you can FTP stuff. Sorry. So sue us. In this chapter, at least, archive means *a multifile file.*) After you retrieve an archive, you use an *unarchiving program* to extract the original files.

Some files are also *compressed,* which means that they're encoded in a special way that takes up less space but that can be decoded only by the corresponding *uncompressor.* Most files you retrieve by anonymous FTP are compressed because compressed files use less disk space and take less time to transfer over the Net. In the PC world, archiving and compression usually happen together by using utilities such as WinZip to create *ZIP files.* In the Mac world, the Stuffit program is very popular. In the workstation world, however, the two procedures — compression and archiving — are usually done separately; the programs *tar* and *cpio* do the archiving, and the programs *compress*, *pack,* and *gzip* do the compressing.

If you retrieve many files from the Net, you have to learn how to uncompress stuff. The four main compression schemes are

- ✔ ZIP
- ✔ compress
- ✔ gzip
- ✔ Stuffit

Later in this chapter, we describe UNIX compression and archiving programs.

ZIPping it up

The most widely used compression and archiving program for Windows and DOS are the shareware programs WinZip and PKZIP. Zipped files all end with the extension *.ZIP.*

Windows users all use the excellent shareware WinZip program mentioned in Chapter 10. It not only handles ZIP files but also knows how to extract the contents of most of the other kinds of compressed files you run into on the Net.

Non-Windows DOS users can use the original shareware PKZIP and PKUNZIP programs to create and extract ZIP files.

Compatible UNIX zipping and unzipping programs called *zip* and *unzip* (the authors are creative programmers but not creative namers) are available at ftp.uu.net and elsewhere. For situations in which the shareware nature of PKUNZIP is a problem, a DOS version of UNIX unzip is available, although it's only about half as fast as PKUNZIP.

Some ZIP files you encounter on the Net are *self-extracting*, which means that the ZIP file is packaged up with an unzipping program; even if you don't already have an unzipper, you just run the archive and it extracts its contents. (PKZIP and WinZip themselves are distributed in this way.) Because self-extracting archives are programs, they end with EXE rather than with ZIP. If you *do* have an unzipper already, use it to extract the files; tell it to open the archive in the same way you would open any other archive. This lets you be sure that the archive contains what it says it does and also lets you use WinZip's installation-assist feature.

Compression classic

Back in 1975, a guy named Terry Welch published a paper about a swell new compression scheme he had just invented. A couple of UNIX programmers implemented it as the program *compress*, and it quickly became the standard compression program on UNIX systems. Better compressors are available now, but compress is still the standard.

You can easily recognize a compressed program because its name ends with *.Z*. On UNIX systems, you recover the original file with *uncompress* (which is actually the same program as compress running in a different mode), as shown in this example:

```
uncompress blurfle.Z
```

This line gets rid of blurfle.Z and replaces it with the original blurfle. Sometimes uncompress is unavailable, in which case you can do the equivalent by using compress:

```
compress -d blurfle.Z
```

On PCs, compressed files often have names ending with *Z*, such as BLURFLE.TAZ. A UNIX-compatible version of compress is available in the SIMTEL archive in the directory /msdos/compress as COMP430D.ZIP, but it's easier for Windows users to use WinZip.

UNIX files are frequently archived and compressed and have names such as blurfle.tar.Z. In that case, you first uncompress to get blurfle.tar and then unarchive. If you want to see what's in a compressed file without uncompressing the whole thing, you can use *zcat*, which sends an uncompressed copy of its input to the screen. Any file big enough to be worth compressing is longer than one screenful, so you should run it through a paging program, such as *more:*

```
zcat blurfle.Z | more
```

It's patently obvious

Something that the people who wrote compress didn't realize is that Welch not only published the scheme that compress uses but also patented it. (Two other guys at IBM named Miller and Wegman independently invented the same scheme at the same time and also got a patent on it, something that's not supposed to happen because only the first person to invent something is allowed to patent it. But the patents are definitely there.) UNISYS, which employs Welch, has said from time to time that it might someday begin to collect royalties on compress. They've done so for other things that use the same compression scheme, notably CompuServe GIF files, but never compress itself.

So the Free Software Foundation, which runs the GNU free software project, wrote *gzip,* which uses 100 percent nonpatented algorithms. Files that are gzipped end with `gz` and are uncompressed with the command `.gunzip:`

```
gunzip blurfle.gz
```

It turns out that although compress's compression is patented, the *de*compression technique is unencumbered, so gunzip can also decompress `.Z` files from compress as well as from some other earlier and less widely used schemes. It can even uncompress a ZIP archive as long as only one file is in it. If you have a mystery compressed file, try feeding it to gunzip and see what happens. There is also *gcat,* which, like zcat, sends its output to the screen. A good way to peek inside a mystery file on a UNIX system is to enter this command:

```
gcat mysteryfile | more
```

UNIX versions of gzip and gunzip are available in the GNU files at `ftp.uu.net` and elsewhere, and a DOS version is in the SimTel repository (described in Chapter 21) as GZIP123.ZIP in `/msdos/compress`. Again, Windows users can use WinZip.

Just StuffIt!

The favorite Macintosh compression and archiving program is a shareware program, by Raymond Lau, known as StuffIt. It comes in many flavors, including a commercially available version called StuffIt Deluxe. StuffIt files of all varieties generally end in `.SIT`.

For decompression you can use the freeware programs UnStuffIt or StuffIt Expander or Extractor, widely available on Macs.

Other archivers

Dozens of other compressing archivers are out there with names such as *LHARC, ZOO,* and *ARC.* DOS and Mac users can find unarchivers for all of them in the SIMTEL repository. The only other one that's widely used is the Japanese LHA because it compresses well and is completely free of charge. Look for LHA213, the most recent version.

In the Archives

Two different UNIX archive programs are *tar* and *cpio.* They were written at about the same time by people at two different branches of Bell Laboratories in different parts of New Jersey. They both do about the same thing; they're just different.

An important difference between UNIX-type archives and ZIP files is that UNIX archives usually contain subdirectories; ZIP files rarely do. You should always look at a UNIX archive's *table of contents* (the list of files it contains) before extracting the files so that you'll know where the files will end up.

The tar pit

The name *tar* stands for *Tape ARchive.* Although tar was designed to put archives of files on old reel-to-reel tapes, it writes to any medium. Files archived by tar usually have filenames ending with .tar, and the frequent combination of tar archiving followed by compress compression is .tar.Z or .TAZ. Windows users can, as usual, unscramble either with WinZip. On a UNIX system, to see what's inside a tar archive, enter the following command:

```
tar tvf blurfle.tar
```

The tvf stands for *Table of contents Verbosely from File.* Verbosely in this case means that tar tells you what it's finding by echoing the files to your screen. If you don't use the v, tar gets the table of contents, but you'll never know.

To extract the individual files, use this command:

```
tar xvf blurfle.tar
```

Copy here, copy there

The name *cpio* stands for *CoPy In and Out*. The program was also intended to copy archives of files to and from old reel-to-reel tapes. (It was a pressing issue back then because at the time the disks on UNIX systems failed about once a week — tape was the only hope for getting your work back.) Files archived by cpio usually have filenames ending with `.cpio`. Cpio was never as popular as tar, which is why WinZip doesn't handle it. To get stuff out of a cpio archive, you need a UNIX shell account.

To see what's in a cpio archive, type the following:

```
cpio -itcv <blurfle.cpio
```

Note the < (left bracket) before the name of the input file. (If you wonder why it's needed, see *UNIX For Dummies,* 2nd Edition, which we wrote and IDG Books Worldwide published. The answer is pretty technoid.) The `-itcv` means *Input, Table of contents, Character headers* (as opposed to obsolete *octal* headers), *Verbosely.*

To extract the files, enter this line:

```
cpio -icdv <blurfle.cpio
```

The letters here stand for *i*nput, *c*haracter headers, *v*erbosely, and create *d*irectories as needed.

PAX vobiscum

Modern versions of UNIX (versions since around 1988) have a swell new program called *.pax* (for *Portable Archive eXchange*). It speaks both tar and cpio, so it should be able to unpack *any* UNIX archive. (Pretty advanced, huh? Took them only 20 years to think of it.) If your system has pax, you'll find it easier to use than either tar or cpio. To see what's inside an archive, enter this command (the v is for *verbose* listing):

```
pax -v <tar-or-cpio-file
```

To extract its contents, enter this line:

```
pax -rv <tar-or-cpio-file
```

(that's *r*ead, *v*erbose output).

Some files are not text, executable, archived, or compressed. For lack of a better term, we refer to them as *data files*. Programs often arrive with some data files for use by the program. Microsoft Windows programs usually come with a data file that contains the help text.

For the Artistically Inclined

A large and growing fraction of all the bits flying around the Internet is made up of increasingly high-quality digitized pictures. About 99.44 percent of the pictures are purely for fun, games, and worse. But we're sure that you're in the 0.56 percent of users who need them for work, so here's a roundup of picture formats.

The most commonly used graphics formats on the Net are GIF and JPEG. You almost never find GIF or JPEG image files compressed or archived. That's because these formats already do a pretty fair job of compression internally, so compress, zip, and the like don't help any.

I could GIF a . . .

The most widely used format on the Internet is CompuServe's *GIF* (*Graphics Interchange Format*). The GIF format is well-matched to the capabilities of the typical PC computer screen — no more than 256 different colors in a picture and usually 640×480, 1024×768, or some other familiar PC screen resolution. Two versions of GIF exist: *GIF87* and *GIF89*. The differences are small enough that nearly every program which can read GIF can read either version equally well. GIF is well standardized, so you never have problems with files written by one program being unreadable by another.

Dozens of commercial and shareware programs on PCs and Macs can read and write GIF files. On UNIX, under the X Window system, are quite a few free and shareware programs, probably the most widely used of which are ImageMagick and XV, both of which require the X Window system, so you can't use them from a dial-up account, only on a workstation or an X terminal (if you have one, you'll know).

GIF files use the same patented compression as the UNIX compress program, and in 1995 UNISYS began collecting royalties from CompuServe and anyone else it could find who sells software that uses the patented technique. As a result, a group of Net graphics users came up with a patentfree replacement for GIF called PNG. We expect to see GIF fade away over the next year or two and PNG and JPEG (see the following section) replace it.

The eyes have it

A few years back, a bunch of digital photography experts got together and decided that a.) it was time to have an official standard format for digitized photographs and b.) none of the existing formats was good enough. So they formed the *Joint Photographic Experts Group (JPEG),* and, after extended negotiation, the JPEG format was born. JPEG is designed specifically to store digitized, full-color or black-and-white photographs, not computer-generated cartoons or anything else. As a result, JPEG does a fantastic job of storing photos and a lousy job of storing anything else.

A JPEG version of a photo is about one-fourth the size of the corresponding GIF file. (JPEG files can be *any* size because the format allows a trade-off between size versus quality when the file is created.) The main disadvantage of JPEG is that it's considerably slower to decode than GIF, but the files are so much smaller that it's worth it. Most programs that can display GIF files now also handle JPEG. JPEG files usually have filenames ending in .jpeg or .jpg.

The claim occasionally has been made that JPEG pictures don't look anywhere near as good as GIF pictures do. What is true is that if you take a full-color photograph and make a 256-color GIF file and then translate that GIF file into a JPEG file, it doesn't look very good. So don't do that. For the finest in photo-graphic quality, however, demand full-color JPEGs.

A trip to the movies

As networks get faster and disks get bigger, people are starting to store entire digitized movies (still rather *short* ones at this point). The standard movie format is called *Moving Photographic Experts Group (MPEG).* MPEG was de-signed by a committee down the hall from the JPEG committee and — practi-cally unprecedented in the history of standards efforts — was actually designed by using the earlier JPEG work.

MPEG viewers are found in the same places as JPEG viewers. You need a reasonably fast workstation or a top-of-the-line power-user PC to display MPEG movies in anything like real time.

Let a hundred formats blossom

Many other graphics-file formats are in use, although GIF and JPEG are by far the most popular ones on the Internet. Other formats you'll run into include the following:

- ✔ **PCX:** This DOS format is used by many paint programs — it's also OK for low-resolution photos.

- ✔ **TIFF:** This enormously complicated format has hundreds of options — so many that a TIFF file written by one program often can't be read by another.

- ✔ **TARGA:** (Called TGA on PCs.) This is the most common format for scanned, full-color photos. In Internet archives, TARGA is now supplanted by the much more compact JPEG.

- ✔ **PICT:** This format is common on Macintoshes because the Mac has built-in support for it.

- ✔ **BMP:** This Windows bitmap format is not used much on the Net because BMP files tend to be larger than they need to be.

None of the Above

Another type of information that files can contain is sound, such as clips from radio shows. Sound files tend to have the filename extensions WAV, AU, or AIF. MPLAYER, which comes with Windows 3.1, can play WAV files. You can download sound players from many FTP software archives (see Chapter 21).

You also occasionally find formatted word-processor files to be used with programs such as WordPerfect and Microsoft Word. If you encounter one of these files and don't have access to the matching word-processor program, you can usually load them into a text editor, where you see the text in the file intermingled with nonprinting junk that represents formatting information. In a pinch, you can edit out the junk to recover the text. Before you resort to that, however, try loading them with whatever word processor you have. A great deal of word-processing software can recognize a competitor's format and make a valiant effort to convert it to something usable by you so that you aren't tempted to buy the other product.

The most commonly used text-processing program on the Net remains the elderly but serviceable TeX. It takes as its input plain-text files with formatting commands in text form, something like this:

```
\begin{quote}
Your mother wears army boots.
\end{quote}
```

If you want to know more about TeX, see the Usenet newsgroup `comp.text.tex`. Free versions of TeX are available for most computers, described in a monthly posting on the newsgroup. Another, even more elderly, text processor called troff (pronounced "tee-roff," and we used it to write the first edition of this book, so don't make too many smart-alecky comments) is also in moderately wide use, and free versions of troff are available as well. For details, read the FAQ posted to `comp.text.troff`.

A few words from the vice squad

We bet you're wondering whether any public on-line archives contain, er, exotic photography but you're too embarrassed to ask. Well, we'll tell you — they don't. Nothing in any public FTP archive is any raunchier than fashion photos from *Redbook* or *Sports Illustrated*.

That's for two reasons. One is political. The companies and universities that fund most of the sites on the Internet are not interested in being accused of being pornographers nor in filling up their expensive disks with pictures that have nothing to do with any legitimate work. (At one university archive, when the *Playboy* pictures went away, they were replaced by a note which said that if you could explain why you needed them for your academic research, they would put them back.)

The other reason is practical. From time to time someone makes his (almost always *his,* by the way) private collection of R- or X-rated pictures available for anonymous FTP. Within five minutes, a thousand sweaty-palmed undergraduates try to FTP in, and that corner of the Internet grinds to a halt. After another five minutes, out of sheer self-preservation, the pictures go away. (If you don't believe us, see *Sex For Dummies* [IDG Books Worldwide, 1995] where Dr. Ruth says the same thing.)

If someone you know is in desperate need of such works of art (not you, of course, but, er, someone down the hall needs it for sociology research — that's it), you might direct him to the Usenet group `alt.binaries .pictures.erotica`. But the last time we looked there for *our* sociology research, we found that the pictures are almost entirely gone, and what's there now are ads for paid-access WWW sites. He might also look at the free sites `www.playboy.com` and `www.penthousemag.com`, which usually contain a few of the milder pictures from the current issues of the magazines.

Chapter 19

Ten Ways to Avoid Looking like a Klutz

· ·

In This Chapter

▶ Tips for suave, sophisticated Net usage

▶ Some bonehead moves not to make

· ·

Gosh, using the Internet is exciting. And gosh, it offers many ways to make a fool of yourself — heaven forbid that you should act like a *clueless newbie*. We'll round up the usual suspects of unfortunate moves so that you can be the coolest Web surfer on your block.

Read before You Write

The moment you get your new Internet account, you may have an overwhelming urge to begin sending out lots of messages right away. *Don't do it!*

Read Usenet newsgroups, mailing lists, Web pages, and other Net resources for a while before you send anything out. You'll be able to figure out where best to send your messages, which will make it both more likely that you'll contact people who will be interested in what you say and less likely that you'll annoy people by bothering them with irrelevancies because you sent something to an inappropriate place.

Particularly if you're going to ask a question, look for a Usenet newsgroup (see Chapter 9) related to your question and see whether it has a Frequently Asked Questions (FAQ) posting that answers it. You might think that this advice is obvious, but we can report from experience that it's not — on the Usenet group that John moderates (a technoid one called `comp.compilers`), he gets at least two messages a day from clueless newbies asking the same old questions that have been in the FAQ for the past five years. Don't let yourself be one of them.

Netiquette Matters

On the Net, you are what you type. The messages you send are the only way that 99 percent of the people you meet on the Net will know you.

Speling kounts

Many Net users feel that because Net messages are short and informal, spelling and grammar don't count. Some even think that strange spelling makes them COOL DOODZ. Wel, if you feel that wey, theirs' not much we can do abowt it. But we think that sending out a sloppy, misspelled message is sort of like showing up at a party with big grease stains on your shirt. Your friends will know that it's you, but people who don't know you will tend to conclude that you don't know how to dress yourself.

Many mail programs have spell checkers. Eudora Pro (the commercial version of Eudora) checks your spelling when you click the dictionary icon (the one with the letter *A*) on the toolbar, and in Pine you check it by pressing Ctrl-T. Spell checkers aren't perfect, but at least they ensure that your message consists of 100 percent genuine words.

DON'T SEND YOUR ENTIRE MESSAGE IN CAPITAL LETTERS. It comes across as shouting and is likely to get you some snappy comments suggesting that you do something about the stuck Shift key on your keyboard. Computer keyboards have handled lowercase since about 1970, so avail yourself of this modern technical marvel and aid to literate writing.

now and then we get mail from someone who says "i dont like to use capital letters or punctuation its too much work." Uh-huh.

If you don't have anything useful to say, don't say it at all

Avoid trying to sound smart. When you do, the result is usually its opposite. One of the stupidest things we saw recently was on the mailing list TRAVEL-L. Someone posted a legitimate request for information about some travel destination. Then came the edifying comment "Sorry, Bud, Can't Help You." Now, we would have thought that people who don't know anything could keep their mouths shut, but apparently we were wrong. Each message you post to a list goes to the entire list. Each list member is there on a voluntary basis. If other members are like us, they often have conflicts about mailing-list subscriptions.

Does the good content of the list outweigh the noise and inanity? The more that inanity flourishes, the more that sensible subscribers will unsubscribe and the list itself will deteriorate. This entire issue is of major concern to the Usenet community, which has been opened to millions and millions of new users. If you're going to participate, find a constructive way to do so.

Keep your hands to yourself

Another stupidity we witnessed involved someone subscribing his archenemy to a list against his wishes. OK, folks. This is not kindergarten. When you start to abuse public lists, they go private. Lists that are unmoderated turn moderated. Moderated lists become "by invitation only." Look around; there are lists that thrive on juvenile behavior, but it's not the norm, and it's not welcome on most lists.

Subscription inscription

Signing up for a mailing list is a cool thing. We tell you all about how to do it in Chapter 8. Still, however, or maybe this is just for people who didn't read our book, one of the most common ways of looking like a klutz is to send to the list itself a message asking to be added to a list, where all the people on the list can read it but it doesn't actually get the sender subscribed. Subscription requests go to the list server program in a particular format, or in the case of lists that are not automated, to the list owner. Read Chapter 8 carefully please, lest you be the next person impressing every list member with your newbieness.

Read the rules

When you first subscribe to a mailing list, you usually get back a long message about how this particular list operates and how to unsubscribe if you want. Read this message. Save this message. Before you go telling other people on the list how to behave, read the rules again. Some officious newbie, newly subscribed to JAZZ-L, began flaming the list about the off-topic threads. Well, JAZZ-L encourages this kind of discussion. It says so right in the introduction to the list. Can't say as how she made herself real welcome with that move.

Edit yourself

When you're posting to a Usenet group or mailing list, remember that your audience will be the entire world, made up of people of all races, speaking different languages and representing different cultures. Work hard to represent yourself and your culture well. Avoid name-calling and disparaging comments about other peoples and places. It's all too easy to be misunderstood. Read whatever you intend to post several times through before you send it. We've seen inadvertent typos change the intended meaning of a message to its complete opposite.

Discretion is the better part

Sooner or later you will see something that cries out for a cheap shot. Sooner or later someone will send you something you shouldn't have seen and you're going to want to pass it on. Don't do it. Resist cheap shots and proliferating malice. The Net has plenty of jerks — don't be another one. (See the suggestion later in this chapter about what to do when you're tempted to flame.)

Keep it private

OK, someone makes a mistake, such as sending a message that says "subscribe" to the entire mailing list or posting a message that says "Gee, I don't know!" in response to a request for help on a newsgroup. Yes, it's true, someone made a dumb move, but don't compound it by posting additional messages complaining about it. Either delete the message and forget about it or respond privately, by e-mail addressed only to the person, not to the mailing list. The entire mailing list or newsgroup probably doesn't want to hear your advice to the person who blew it.

For example, you could send a private e-mail message saying, "In the future, send subscription and unsubscription messages to `eggplants-request`, not `eggplants`, OK?" or "This is a list for discussing domestic laying hens, so could you post your message about cats somewhere else?"

Signing off

All mail programs let you have a *signature*, a file that gets added to the end of each mail or news message you send. It's supposed to contain something to identify you. It quickly became common to put in a snappy quote, to add that personal touch. Here's John's signature, for example:

```
Regards,
John R. Levine, Trumansburg NY
Primary perpetrator of "The Internet for Dummies"
and Information Superhighwayman wanna-be
```

But some people's signatures get way out of hand, going on for 100 lines of "ASCII art", long quotations, extensive disclaimers, and other allegedly interesting stuff. This type of signature may seem cute for the first time or two, but it quickly gets tedious and marks you as a total newbie.

Keep your signature to four lines or fewer. All the experienced Net users do. If you want to see some examples of truly absurd signatures, visit the Usenet group alt.fan.warlord, named after the Warlord of the West, possessor of one of the most excessive signatures of all time.

Flame Off!

For some reason, it's easy to get VERY, VERY UPSET ABOUT SOMETHING SOMEONE SAYS ON THE NET. (See, it even happens to us.) Sometimes it's a Usenet posting with which you strongly disagree, sometimes it's something you find on the Web, and sometimes it's personal e-mail. You'll be tempted to shoot a message right back telling that person what a doofus he is. And guess what? He'll almost certainly shoot back. This kind of overstated outrage is so common that it has its own name: *flaming*. Now and then it's fun (if you're certain that the recipient will take it in good humor), but it's always unnecessary. For one thing, e-mail messages always come across as crabbier than the author intended, and, for another, crabbing back is hardly going to make the person more reasonable.

A technique we often find helpful is to write the strongest, crabbiest response possible, full of biting wit and skewering each point in turn. Then we throw it away rather than send it.

Spam, Chain Letters, and Other Antisocial Mail

We mentioned this in Chapters 7 and 9, but it's worth mentioning again: There are a few kinds of messages you should never, ever, send. They're not illegal (at least not in most places), but you'll quickly find your mailbox filled with displeased responses, and your provider will soon cancel your account.

The chain gang

It's easy to send a chain letter on the Net: Just hit the *Forward* button, type a few names, and send it off. But it's a lousy idea. A bunch of classic chain letters have been circulating around the Net for a decade (see Chapter 7 for details about the boy who doesn't want cards, the phantom good-times virus, the nonexistent modem tax, the overpriced recipe that isn't, and a way that you won't make money fast). But regardless of where they come from, please just throw them away.

Some of the on-line chain letters started as paper letters. We once got a paper version of the "Make Money Fast" chain letter from, of all places, Guam. We did the same thing with it that we do with computer chain letters—into the trash.

Spammety-spam, horrible spam

One of the least pleasant Usenet innovations in recent years is *spamming*, or sending lots and lots of copies of a message — usually selling something that was pretty dubious in the first place — to as many Usenet groups as possible. It's annoying, and in many cases the spammer is liable for her provider's expenses in cleaning it up. It's also ineffective because automatic systems identify and cancel most spams within minutes after they occur. For more information about this topic, see the sidebar "Spam wars" in Chapter 9.

Don't Be a Pig

You'll find unbelievable amounts of material on the Net: programs, documents, pictures, megabyte after megabyte of swell stuff, all free for the taking. You could download it all. Don't. Go ahead and take whatever you're likely to use, but don't download entire directories full of stuff "just in case."

Your Internet provider sets its charges based on the resources a typical user will use. A single user can use a substantial fraction of the provider's Net connection by sucking down files continuously for hours at a time. Providers typically "overcommit" their Net connection by a factor of three or so: If every user tried to transfer data at full speed at the same time, it would require three times as fast a connection as the provider actually has. But because real users transfer for a while and then read what's on their screen for a while, it works out OK to share the connection among all the users. (The provider is not cheating you when it does this; it's a sensible way to provide access at a reasonable cost. You can get guaranteed connection performance if you want it, but you'll be horrified at the price.) If users begin using several more connections than the provider budgeted for, the prices will go up.

Hang up, already!

This advice applies particularly to providers who offer unlimited connect-time per month. Don't leave your computer connected if you're not using it. Most Net software packages have a time-out feature that hangs up if no data is transferred to or from the Net for a given period. We leave ours set to 20 minutes on our dial-up connections. Otherwise, other users will get a busy signal when they try to connect.

Audio and video pigs

Internet Phone and the like present a particular problem on the Net because they put a much, much heavier load on both the local provider and the Net in general than do other Internet services. When you're transferring voice information over the Net, you're pumping data through as fast as your connection will let you. Video connections are even worse: When sites with fast Net connections begin sending video programs around to each other, the entire Net slows down.

For the moment, few enough people are using Internet Phone that it hasn't become a big problem, but if it becomes popular enough, providers will have to provide "no phone" and "phone" accounts, with the latter costing much more, to keep reasonable access for all their users.

Some Web Wisdom

Most Internet providers let you put your own private pages up on the World Wide Web. Again, what you put in your Web page is all that most people will know about you, so this section provides a few suggestions.

Small is beautiful, Part I

Most people who look at your Web page are connected by using a dial-up line and a modem, which means that great-big pictures take a long time to load. If your home page contains a full-page picture that takes $12\frac{1}{2}$ minutes to load, you might as well have hung out a Keep Out sign. Keep the pictures small enough that the page loads in a reasonable amount of time. If you have a huge picture that you think is wonderful, put a small "thumbnail" version of it on your home page, and make it a link to the full picture for people with the time and interest to look at the big version.

Small is beautiful, Part II

Small pages that fit in a screen or two work better than large pages. They're easier to read, and they load faster. If you find that you have 12 screens full of stuff to put in your Web page, break it up into five or six separate pages with links among them. A well-designed set of small pages makes it easier to find stuff than does one big page because the links can direct the readers to what they want to find.

If we want the White House, we know where to find it

No Web page (or set of Web pages, as we just suggested) is complete without some links to the author's other favorite pages. But for some reason every new user's Web page seems to have a link to http://www.whitehouse.gov and maybe to Yahoo, Netscape, and a few other sites that every Net user already knows about. Cool Web sites give us links to interesting pages we *don't* already know about.

Let a hundred viewers blossom

When you create a new Web page, look at it with as many Web browsers as possible. Sure, most people use some version of Netscape, but Prodigy and AOL users (close to 10 million possible visitors to your site) use the browsers that come with those services, and users with dial-up shell connections use the text-only browser Lynx. So take a look at your pages to make sure that they're at least legible regardless of which browser people are using.

Don't be dumb

Don't put on your Web page any information you don't want everyone in the world to know. In particular, you might not want to include your home address and phone number. We know at least one person who received an unexpected phone call from someone she met on the Net and wasn't too pleased about it. Why would Net users need this information, anyway? They can send you e-mail!

Part VI
Resource Reference

In this part . . .

*N*ow that you're an Internet expert, only one tiny detail remains: How do you get on in the first place? These last three chapters list places that provide access, places that provide software you need to use that access, and, finally, some points of departure for continuing on your Internet journey.

Chapter 20

Finding a Public Internet Service Provider

• •

In This Chapter

▶ How to find a provider

▶ A bunch of places that can provide Internet access

▶ Some places that can even provide access free of charge

• •

Gimme Gimme

All this talk about the Internet is well and good, but it's sort of like sitting by the edge of the pool and thinking, "Wouldn't it be nice to know how to swim?" To learn about the Internet, you have to dive in!

Consider (as best you can, given what we've told you so far) whether you want to connect to the Internet through a commercial on-line service such as America Online or CompuServe, or whether you want a simple Internet service provider. If you've chosen "simple Internet service provider," read on. If you've chosen a commercial on-line service, turn back to your provider's chapter in Part IV and follow the instructions there. One thing in favor of using a commerical on-line service is that most of them give you some free time to start with so that you can try before you buy. On the downside, depending on your geography, the closest commercial provider's access number might be a toll call away. Also, if you spend much time on-line, a commercial on-line service usually charges much more per hour (about $3 per hour) than an Internet service provider does. If you can find a local Internet provider, you're probably better off, at least costwise.

How to Find a Local Service Provider

An important topic to consider in choosing your provider is the cost of the phone call because calls to on-line systems tend to be long ones. Ideally, you want to find a provider which has a phone number that's a local call for you — either a direct number or by way of a network such as Tymnet or Sprintnet or CompuServe's network.

A few providers have 800 numbers, but their hourly rates have to be high enough to cover the cost of the 800 call. It's almost invariably cheaper to dial direct and pay for the call yourself than to use an 800 access number; someone has to pay for the 800 call, and that someone is you. Access to an 800 number is attractive to people who travel frequently. (Many local providers have local numbers for day-to-day use and a more expensive 800 number to use while traveling, which is what we use.)

Here are the best ways we know to find a provider close to home:

- Check the business pages of your local newspaper for advertisements from local access providers.
- Ask your public library's research librarian or on-line services staff.
- Look in your local Yellow Pages under "On-line service providers."
- Use a friend's Internet account or a trial account from a commercial provider to access the World Wide Web. Search for "Internet service providers." You'll find numerous lists of them that you can then search for something close to home. The Web page http://thelist.com has an excellent list of providers, grouped by area code.
- Ask anyone you know who already has access what she's using.

Signing Up

Many dial-in services list two numbers: a voice number and a modem number. If you're new at this (some of us are new at this for *years* — don't take it personally), we think that it's useful to call and talk to the human beings on the other end of the voice line to get their helpful guidance. Talking to a person enables you to ask the questions you have and in many cases goes a long way toward calming the trepidation that often accompanies this step. If you are signing up for a SLIP or PPP account, talk to your provider about what software you plan to use or ask what software they can provide you with.

If you're an old pro or would rather talk to a machine, set up your communications software to dial the modem number and follow the instructions that appear on your screen. If your modem is dialing the correct number but you're not getting anything usable on your screen, try calling the voice line to verify the modem settings and to get any other useful advice from this service you're about to begin paying for. If you *really* don't want to talk to a person, check out *Modems For Dummies,* by Tina Rathbone (IDG Books Worldwide), to see whether you can find some help there.

Sign-up generally involves providing your name, address, and telephone number, along with billing information, such as a credit-card number. Often access is granted immediately, or the service may call you on the phone to verify that you are who you said you were.

National Providers

The space available to us in this book is severely limited, so in this section we focus on national providers in English-speaking countries.

We know that you're sick of hearing us suggest that you buy another book, but if you use Windows and decide to go with a national provider, an easy way to do it is to buy our book, *The Internet For Windows For Dummies Starter Kit* (IDG Books Worldwide). The book comes with a free trial version of Internet Chameleon (described in Chapter 21) that will cost you $15 to register on-line if you decide to use it after the trial period. It also comes with a program called Automatic Internet, which can sign you up with a SLIP or PPP account with one of five national providers; it automagically configures your software to work with your account. The software also works with local SLIP/PPP providers if you later decide to switch.

U.S. providers

BBN Planet Corporation

E-mail: net-info@bbnplanet.com
Phone: (800) 472-4565
URL: http://www.bbnplanet.com

DELPHI

E-mail:	info@delphi.com (automatic response)
	service@delphi.com (personal response)
Phone:	(800) 595-4005
	(800) 695-4002, for sign-up only; log in as JOINDELPHI; password DUMMIES)
URL:	http://www.delphi.com

Note: A free, ten-hour test drive usually is available when you sign up.

Global Enterprise Services, Inc.

E-mail:	info@jvnc.net (automatic response)
	info-moderator@jvnc.net (personal response)
Phone:	(800) 358-4437
URL:	http://www.jvnc.net

HoloNet

E-mail:	info@holonet.net (automatic response)
	support@holonet.com (personal response)
Phone:	(510) 704-0160
Modem:	(510) 704-1058
URL:	http://www.holonet.net

Netcom Online Communication Services

E-mail:	info@netcom.com
Phone:	(800) 501-8649
Modem:	Many modem numbers are available. Call for the number nearest you. Free Netcruiser software is available.

Novalink

E-mail:	info@novalink.com (for automatic response)
	support@novalink.com (for personal response)
Phone:	(800) 274-2814
Modem:	(800) 825-8852 for access; dial-ups in major U.S. cities

The Portal System

E-mail:	info@portal.com (for automatic response)
	sales@portal.com (for personal response)
Phone:	(800) 433-6444
Modem:	(408) 973-8091H, 408-725-0561M (log in as info)
URL:	http://www.portal.com

UUNET Communications

E-mail: info@uunet.uu.net
Phone: (800) 4-UUNET-3

Available in major U.S. and Canadian cities, UUNET intends to have, by December 1995, most major European cities, including Paris, London, and Amsterdam in addition to Hong Kong, Singapore, and Sydney.

The WELL (Whole Earth 'Lectronic Link)

E-mail: info@well.sf.ca.us
Phone: (415) 332-4335
Modem: (415) 332-6106 (log in as *new*)

IBM Internet Connection

Phone: U.S.: (800) 821-4612
    Canada: (800) 821-4612
    Australia: 131-426
    Hong Kong: 2515-4511
    Ireland: 1-800-553175
    New Zealand: 0800-801-800
    South Africa: 011-7001370 or 0800117888
    United Kingdom: 0800-963949

Modem (sign-up only):   U.S.: (800) 933-3997
    Canada: (800) 463-8331
    Australia: 1800-811-094
    Hong Kong: 2515-2434
    Ireland: 1-800-709-905
    New Zealand: 0800-105765
    South Africa: 0800-998128
    United Kingdom: 0800-614012

URL: http://www.ibm.net

Canadian providers

Communications Accessibles Montreal

E-mail: info@cam.org
Phone: 514-923-2102
Modem: 514-281-5601H, 514-466-0592H, 514-738-3664 (Telebit)
URL: http://www.cam.org

HoloNet

E-mail:	info@holonet.net (automatic response)
	support@holonet.com (personal response)
Phone:	510-704-0160
Modem:	510-704-1058
URL:	http://www.holonet.net

Internex Online Toronto

E-mail:	vid@io.org
Phone:	416-363-8676
Modem:	416-363-3783 (log in as *new*)
URL:	http://www.io.org

IBM Internet Connection

See the "U.S. providers" section.

Australian providers

access one

E-mail:	info@aone.net.au
Phone:	03-9580-5581
URL:	http://www.aone.net.au/

apanix.apana.org.au

E-mail:	adrian@apanix.apana.org.au (log in as *guest*)
Phone:	08 373-5485
URL:	http://www.act.apana.org.au/

interconnect.com.au

E-mail:	info@interconnect.com.au
Phone:	03-9528-2239
URL:	http:/www.interconnect.com.au/

OZ e-mail

E-mail:	sales@ozemail.com.au
Phone:	02 391 0480, Fax 02 437 5888
URL:	http://www.ozemail.com.au

IBM Internet Connection

See the "U.S. providers" section.

U.K. providers

CityScape Internet Services Ltd

E-mail: sales@cityscape.co.uk
Phone: 01223 566950

Pipex (Public IP Exchange Limited)

E-mail: sales@pipex.com
Phone: 01223-250120
URL: http://worldserver.pipex.com

UK PC User Group

E-mail: info@ibmpcug.co.uk
Phone: 0181-863-1191
URL: http://www.ibmpcug.co.uk

Demon Internet Systems

E-mail: internet@demon.net
Phone: 0181-371-1234
Modem: 0181-343-4848
URL: http://www.demon.co.uk/

Total Connectivity Providers Ltd.

E-mail: sales@tcp.co.uk
Phone: 01703 393392
URL: http://www.tcp.co.uk

IBM Internet Connection

See the "U.S. providers" section.

Irish providers

Cork Internet Services, Ltd.

E-mail: info@cis.ie
Phone: 021 277124
URL: http://www.cis.ie/

Homenet

E-mail: info@Homenet.ie
Phone: 01-6707355
URL: http://www.HomeNet.ie/

Eirenet

E-mail: ron@eirenet.net
Phone: 021 274141

IBM Internet Connection

See the "U.S. providers" section.

New Zealand providers

Internet Company of New Zealand

E-mail: info@iconz.co.nz
Phone: 09-358-1186
URL: http://www.iconsz.co.nz

IBM Internet Connection

See the "U.S. providers" section.

South African providers

Commercial Internet Services / Worldnet Africa

E-mail: info@cis.co.za
Phone: 012 841-2892
URL: http://www.cis.co.za, http://africa.cis.co.za

Internet Africa

E-mail: info@iafrica.com
Phone: 021 683 4370
URL: http://www.iafrica.com/iafrica/home.html

IBM Internet Connection

See the "U.S. providers" section.

Singapore providers

Pacific Internet

E-mail: info@pacific.net.sg
Phone: 1800-872-1455
URL: http://www.pacific.net.sg

Singapore Telecom

E-mail: sales@singnet.com.sg
Phone: 730-8079
Fax: 732-1272
URL: http://www.singnet.com.sg/

It's Free!

Three years or so ago, a bunch of civic-minded people at a university in Cleveland got together and created what they called a *freenet*. People in the community use this free system to share information and to take advantage of the Internet. It was quite successful (the Cleveland Freenet now consists of three machines, each supporting many users), and freenets have appeared all over the United States and Canada.

Freenets provide lots of local community information and offer limited telnet and FTP, which allows general access to libraries and other public-interest kinds of hosts. It's not full Internet access by any means, but it's interesting in its own right. And, after all, it's *free*. Because you can telnet from one freenet to another, if you can get to one of them, you can get to all of them.

Freenets really are free (except in Los Angeles), but to get full access you have to register so that they have some idea of who's using the system. They all allow on-line registration.

Freenets all allow incoming telnet access, so if you have Internet access elsewhere, drop into a freenet and look around.

How can freenets really be free?

Most freenets are run by unpaid volunteers who borrow facilities from a local college or university. Many of them have managed to acquire charitable-foundation money too because they're community-based and educational.

Most of them welcome contributions from users, although they aren't pushy about it.

Akron Free-Net
Akron, OH
Modem: (216) 434-2736
(log in as *visitor*)
Telnet: freenet.akron.oh.us

Cleveland Freenet
Cleveland, OH
Modem: (216) 368-3888
Telnet: freenet-in-a.cwru.edu
freenet-in-b.cwru.edu
freenet-in-c.cwru.edu

Youngstown Freenet
Youngstown, OH
Modem: (216) 742-3072
(log in as *visitor*)
Telnet: yfn.ysu.edu

Heartland Freenet
Peoria, IL
Modem: (309) 674-1100
(log in as *bbguest*)
Telnet: heartland.bradley.edu

Lorain County Freenet
Lorain County, OH
Modem: (216) 277-2359 (Lorain);
(log in as *guest*)
(216) 366-9753 (Elyria)

Medina County Freenet
Medina County, OH
Modem: (216) 723-6732

Denver Freenet
Denver, CO
Modem: (303) 270-4865
(log in as *guest*)
Telnet: freenet.hsc.colorado.edu

Tallahassee Freenet
Tallahassee, FL
Modem: (904) 488-5056
(904) 488-6313
(log in as *visitor*)
Telnet: freenet.fsu.edu

Victoria Freenet
British Columbia, Canada
Modem: 604-595-2300
(log in as *guest*)
Telnet: freenet.victoria.bc.ca

National Capital Freenet
Ottawa, Ontario, Canada
Modem: 613-780-3733

Terminals are available in Ottawa and Nepean public libraries. Log in as *guest*.

Telnet: freenet.carleton.ca

Big Sky Telegraph
Dillon, MT
Modem: (406) 683-7680
　　　　 (log in as *bbs*)

Buffalo Free-Net
Buffalo, NY
Modem: (716) 645-6128
　　　　 (log in as *freeport*)
Telnet: `freenet.buffalo.edu`

St. Johns InfoNet
St Johns N.F. Canada
Modem: 709-737-3425 & 3426
　　　　 (log in as *guest*)
Telnet: `infonet.st-johns.nf.ca`

Stay Tuned

Groups throughout the world are in the process of setting up community freenets. Check with your local university or library to see whether your town has one.

The 5th Wave By Rich Tennant

"We met on the Internet and I absolutely fell in looove with his syntax."

Chapter 21

Sources of Internet Software

● ●

In This Chapter

▶ Software for your PC

▶ Software for your Mac

● ●

What Kind of Nerds Do You Take Us For?

When it comes to installing software, there are two kinds of people: those who dislike doing it and those who just plain won't. We expect that you're probably in the latter category, unless you're a PC user or a Mac user. If you use a different kind of computer or a workstation, it's somebody else's job to acquire software, negotiate contracts, handle installation and maintenance, and other wise keep things running smoothly. But for a PC or a Mac, who knows? With luck, someone is supposed to handle all that, but maybe not. This is particu-larly true in an office with a bunch of workstations, all of which are on the Internet as a matter of divine right, except that you have a PC you want to connect — even if only to avoid running around with floppies.

Software for Commercial On-line Services

Good news! If you use America Online (AOL), CompuServe, Prodigy, or Microsoft Network (MSN), you get all the software you need free of charge. If you're like us, you get another disk for your AOL Disk Coaster Set every day or so in the mail.

For instructions for installing the CompuServe and AOL software, see Chapters 12 and 13, respectively. The MSN software comes with Windows 95.

Software for UNIX Shell Accounts

To use a UNIX shell account, all you need is a terminal program. Windows 3.1 comes with Windows Terminal, and we also like ProComm, a commercial terminal program. Windows 95 comes with HyperTerminal. Mac users can get Mac Terminal, Microphone, or something like it. Most modems come with a disk containing a terminal program.

Make sure that your terminal program can do the following:

- ✔ Upload and download files by using Xmodem, Zmodem, or Kermit.

- ✔ *Emulate* (pretend to be) a VT100 terminal. Lots of UNIX systems like to talk to VT100 terminals. It doesn't matter that none of us has seen an actual VT100 in decades.

- ✔ Store the phone number and communications settings of your provider so that you don't have to set them every time.

DOS and Windows Software for SLIP/PPP Accounts

More than a dozen Internet software packages are available, but only a few that are widely used by individuals. These packages include the TCP/IP stack that lets your computer connect to the Net, an e-mail program, a Usenet newsreader, a Web browser, an FTP program, telnet, and maybe some other useful Net programs, such as ping and finger.

Windows users can mix and match their Internet software packages. Because everyone supports WinSock, you can use any WinSock application with any underlying TCP/IP package and expect it to work. (You may occasionally be disappointed, but our experience has been good.) If you use a WinSock-compatible Internet package, for example, you can run Netscape rather than the Web browser that comes with the package. There's no such standard for DOS, so what comes with a particular package is all you can use.

Many Windows Internet applications, such as Eudora and Netscape, have commercial versions that come bundled with a TCP/IP package. Even when you can get the applications free of charge over the Net, for the modest price they cost it can be worth it to get the whole thing on a few floppies that you can just install.

Trumpet WinSock

Trumpet WinSock is a shareware WinSock-compatible TCP/IP package for Windows. It comes with a few simple applications, but most people just use the basic TCP/IP package to connect to their SLIP or PPP account and add other applications such as Netscape. The most recent version is v2.0b. Many Internet providers hand out a disk with Trumpet WinSock to their new customers. (Remember to send in your shareware fee if you use it, because your provider hasn't paid for the software.)

You can FTP Trumpet WinSock from `ftp.utas.edu.au`, directory `/pc/trumpet/winsock`, files `twsk20b.zip` and `winapps2.zip`. It's also available at `biochemistry.bioc.cwru.edu`, in the directory `/pub/trumpwsk`, and many other places on the Net, and it's widely available on dial-up bulletin-board systems:

> Trumpet Software International Pty Ltd.
> Lower level, 24 Cambridge Road
> Bellerive, TAS 7018, AUSTRALIA

Chameleon and the Chameleon Sampler

Chameleon is one of the most popular commercial Internet packages. The Chameleon Sampler is a subset of an older version of Chameleon that Netmanage, the vendor, makes available free of charge. It's bound into the back of some Internet books and is available from some Internet providers. You can FTP it from `ftp.netmanage.com`, directory `/pub/demos/sampler`, file `sampler.exe`. The Sampler isn't as good as the more recent versions, but at that price it's hard to complain.

Internet Chameleon is a low-cost version of Chameleon. (You can get a 30-day demo license for free or a permanent license for $15.) It's available directly from Netmanage for a handling fee or from books such as our *Internet For Windows For Dummies Starter Kit* (IDG Books Worldwide).

Some commercial versions of Chameleon support Ethernet networks, remote files, and other fancier features not of interest to most individual users:

> NetManage, Inc.
> 10725 North De Anza Blvd.
> Cupertino, CA 95014
> Phone: (408)973-7171
> Fax: (408) 257-6405
> E-mail: `support@netmanage.com`
> Web home page: `http://www.netmanage.com`

Microsoft

Windows 95 comes with built-in Internet support, which was mentioned in Chapter 14. Microsoft gives away a WinSock software package for Windows for Workgroups 3.11 and Windows NT (but *not* for Windows 3.1). You can FTP it from `ftp.microsoft.com`, in the directory `/peropsys/windows/Public/tcpip`.

Internet in a Box

Internet in a Box is a package of Windows Internet software that includes AIR Mosaic and costs about $100. It's similar to the NetLauncher package that CompuServe provides to its users (not coincidentally, CompuServe owns the company that sells Internet in a Box):

> Spry, division of CompuServe
> 1319 Dexter Avenue North
> Seattle, WA 98109
> E-mail: `sales@spry.com`

Other freeware and shareware

This section lists some other freeware and shareware packages for DOS and Windows.

NCSA Telnet

NCSA Telnet is a good freeware package for DOS. It's available via anonymous FTP from SimTel mirrors, such as `wuarchive.wustl.edu` or `oak.oakland.edu` in the directory `pub/msdos/ncsaelnet`.

CUTCP

This TCP/IP package is available from Clarkson University. FTP from `sun.soe.clarkson.edu`, or e-mail for info to `cutcp@omnigate.clarkson.edu`.

QVT/Net

Both DOS and Windows versions are available for this shareware package. FTP from `ftp.winsite.com`, and send inquiries to `djp@troi.cc.rochester.edu`.

KA9Q

This shareware or freeware (depending on usage) DOS package was designed originally for amateur radio users. It works well, but it comes with almost no documentation. FTP from `ucsd.edu` in `pub/ham-radio/packet/tcpoip/ka9q`.

For a modified version, FTP or gopher to `biochemistry.bioc.cwru.edu`.

Other vendors of PC TCP/IP software

Many vendors will sell you commercially supported suites of software for DOS or Windows, and most of them sell primarily to businesses with large networks of PCs to connect to the Net. They won't turn down individual orders, but it's not their primary market.

FTP Software
2 High Street
North Andover, MA 01845
E-mail: `sales@ftp.com`

Distinct
P.O. Box 3410
Saratoga, CA 95070-1410
E-mail: `mktg@distinct.com`

Frontier Technologies
10201 N. Port Washington Road
Mequon, WI 53092
E-mail: `tcp@frontiertech.com`

The Wollongong Group
1129 San Antonia Road
Palo Alto, CA 94303
E-mail: `sales@twg.com`

Beame and Whiteside
P.O. Box 8130
Dundas, Ontario L9H 5E7 Canada
E-mail: `sales@bws.com`

Getting free and shareware programs from the Net

Most of the programs listed in this section are available on the Net by using the World Wide Web (see Chapters 4 and 5) and FTP (see Chapter 10).

WWW sources

Windows users should run, not walk, to Forrest Stroud's Consummate WinSock Applications page at `http://cwsapps.texas.net`, which is a large, well-organized set of reviews of WinSock software available over the Net. There are links to all the archives, so you can download with a click or two anything that looks interesting. (Expect a somewhat long wait because some of those suckers are BIG.)

FTP servers with software archives

Lots of FTP servers have huge archives of freeware and share programs, including lots of WinSock-compatible software. Table 21-1 lists some popular servers.

Table 21-1   FTP Servers with Windows Software Archives

Server Name	Directory to Use	Physical Location
ftp.winsite.com	pub/pc/win3/winsock	Indiana
wuarchive.wustl.edu	mirrors2/win3	Missouri
grind.isca.uiowa.edu	msdos/win3	Iowa
gatekeeper.dec.com	/.2/micro/msdos/win3	California
polecat.law.indiana.edu	/pub/mirror/cica/win3/pc/win3	Indiana
alpha.cso.uiuc.edu	/pub/Mirror/win3	Illinois
sunsite.unc.edu	/pub/micro/pc-stuff/ms-windows/winsock	North Carolina
vmsa.technion.ac.il		Israel
nic.switch.ch		Switzerland
ftp.cc.monash.edu.au		Melbourne, Australia
nctuccca.edu.tw		Hsinchu, Taiwan
src.doc.ic.ac.uk		London, England

Telling you about SimTel

SimTel is a particularly well-maintained library of PC software that was originally stored at the White Sands Missile Base in Mew Mexico. It includes software for DOS, Windows, Windows NT, Windows 95, and OS/2. Because of the huge demand for the software, the SimTel archive is available from almost 100 different sites, called *mirrors* (because they exactly "mirror" the contents of the SimTel archive). SimTel's primary site is `ftp.coast.net`, but the SimTel archive is available at (in addition to other places) the sites listed in Table 21-2.

Table 21-2 FTP Servers that Mirror the SimTel Archive

Server Name	Directory to Use	Location
ftp.cdrom.com	/pub/simtel	California
uiarchive.cso.uiuc.edu	/pub/systems/pc/simtel	Illinois
oak.oakland.edu	/SimTel	Michigan
wuarchive.wustl.edu	/systems/ibmpc/simtel	Missouri
ftp.uoknor.edu	/mirrors/SimTel	Oklahoma
ftp.orst.edu	/pub/mirrors/simtel	Oregon
ftp.pht.com	/pub/mirrors/simtel	Utah
archie.au	/micros/pc/SimTel	Australia
ftp.unicamp.br	/pub/simtel	Brazil
ftp.pku.edu.cn	/pub/simtel	China
ftp.demon.co.uk	/pub/mirrors/simtel	England
ftp.funet.fi	/mirrors/simtel.coast.net/ Simtel	Finland
ftp.grolier.fr	/pub/pc/SimTel	France
ftp.unl-mainz.de	/pub/pc/mirrors/simtel	Germany
ftp.cs.cuhk.hk	/pub/simtel	Hong Kong
ftp.technion.ac.il	/pub/unsupported/simtel	Israel
ftp.saitama-u.ac.jp	/pub/simtel	Japan
ftp.nic.surfnet.nl	/mirror-archive/software/ simtel-msdos/mirror-archive/ simtel-win3	Netherlands
ftp.vuw.ac.nz	/simtel	New Zealand
ftp.sun.ac.za	/pub/simtel	South Africa
ftp.nectec.or.th	/pub/mirrors/SimTel	Thailand

To get a list of other sites that mirror the SimTel archive, send an e-mail message to listserv@simtel.coast.net with the text *get simtel-download.info*. You can also buy CD-ROM software from SimTel, which may be cheaper and certainly faster if you plan to download a large number of programs — see its Web site at http://www.coast.net/SimTel/.

Gopher sites

Gopher users can look at gopher.cica.indiana.edu, where there's Gopher access to the large CICA archive of software.

Mac TCP/IP Software

Nearly every Mac Internet application requires MacTCP, which is included in Mac System 7.5. If you're still running an older version of Mac software, you can get a copy from APDA (phone [800] 282-2732 or [716] 871-6555). Generally, you should have your Macintosh dealer order it from APDA. The order numbers and list prices are as follows:

M8113Z/A	TCP/IP Connection for Macintosh ($59)
M8114Z/A	TCP/IP Administration for Macintosh ($199)

Many universities and large corporations have inexpensive site licenses; check before you shell out the bucks for your own copy. Send e-mail to apda@applelink.apple.com.

Dial-up connections

MacTCP provides the guts of the Internet software, but you need an add-on package to handle dial-up SLIP or PPP. Several good programs are listed in this section.

MacSLIP

MacSLIP is a commercial SLIP (dial-up Internet connection) as a MacTCP extension from TriSoft. Send e-mail to info@hydepark.com or call (800) 531-5170.

InterSLIP

InterSLIP is a SLIP extension to MacTCP from InterCon. It's available as part of the TCP/Connect II package or at no charge via FTP from ftp.intercon.com in InterCon/sales.

Mac Network Applications

MacTCP provides only low-level support and a control panel. If you really want to do something, you have to have applications. Many applications are freeware or shareware and can be retrieved by FTP. The major Mac FTP archives are shown in this list:

- mac.archive.umich.edu (Also provides files by e-mail. Send a message containing the word *help* to mac@mac.archive .umich.edu.)

- ftp.apple.com (This is the official Apple archive for free Apple-provided software.)

✔ `sumex-aim.stanford.edu` (Because it's the best-known archive, it's badly overloaded — try others first.)

✔ `wuarchive.wustl.edu` (Copies of sumex files are in `mirrors/infomac`; copies of umich files are in `mirrors/archive.umich.edu.`)

NCSA Telnet

NCSA Telnet, the oldest and most widely used Mac telnet program, provides incoming and outgoing FTP. It's available via FTP. Unlike every other application listed here, it runs with or without MacTCP. While running without MacTCP, NCSA Telnet contains its own SLIP (dial-up) package.

Comet (Cornell Macintosh Terminal Emulator)

Features telnet and TN3270. Available via FTP from `comet.cit.cornell.edu` in `pub/comet`.

Hytelnet

Hytelnet is a Hypercard version of telnet. Send e-mail to Charles Burchill at `burchil@ccu.umanitoba.ca`.

Eudora

Eudora is the most widely used mail package: It's flexible and complete, and the shareware version is free. What more could you ask? FTP from `ftp.cso.uiuc.edu` in `mac/eudora`, or inquire by e-mail to `eudora-info@qualcomm.com`.

NewsWatcher

NewsWatcher, a free Usenet news program, is available by FTP. Nerds can get the source code by FTP from `ftp.apple.com`.

Nuntius

Nuntius is a popular graphical Usenet reader. Contact the author, Peter Speck, at `speck@dat.ruc.dk`.

SU-Mac/IP

This suite of network applications (telnet, FTP, remote printing, and more) is from Stanford University. It's available only to "degree-granting institutions of higher education," at little or no cost. Call (415) 723-3909 or send e-mail to `macip@jessica.stanford.edu`.

TCP/Connect II

This full-featured commercial suite (telnet, FTP, news, and more) of Internet applications is available from InterCon Systems. Call (703) 709-9890 or send e-mail to `sales@intercon.com`.

VersaTerm

VersaTerm, a commercial package from Synergy Software, provides flexible versions of telnet and FTP. SLIP (dial-up) is also available. Call (215) 779-0522.

Chapter 22
I Want to Learn More

*T*he Internet is growing so fast that no single human can keep up with it all. This chapter suggests some resources to help keep abreast of what's new.

On-line Guides

The Net is its own best source of information. Here are a few places to look for what's new.

Everybody's Guide to the Internet

Everybody's Guide is an introduction to the Net, written and updated by Adam Gaffin. It's available both on-line and in book form, published by MIT Press. A monthly Everybody's Internet Update is published by the Electronic Frontier Foundation.

Updates are posted to the Usenet group alt.internet.services. If you miss one or want to see back issues, they're archived in the same places as the main document.

FTP: Connect to ftp.eff.org and go to directory pub/Net_info/ EFF_Net_Guide/Updates. There are different versions for different kinds of computers (PostScript, Windows Help, and so on), but the file netguide.eff is the generic text version.

Gopher: Look in gopher.eff.org and choose Net Info and then EFF Net Guide. For updates, choose Updates.

WWW: Point your Web program at `http://www.eff.org/pub/Net_info/EFF_Net_Guide`.

Note: Everybody's Guide used to be called the Big Dummy's Guide to the Internet. They changed the name to avoid confusion with, er, certain books.

Special Internet Connections

Scott Yanoff, at the University of Wisconsin, twice a month publishes a list of "Special Internet Connections" to services all over the world. It's posted in the Usenet groups `alt.internet.services`, `comp.misc`, `alt.bbs.internet`, `news.answers`, and `comp.answers`. It's also available in a zillion ways:

FTP: Connect to `ftp.csd.uwm.edu` and get `/pub/inet.services.txt`.

Gopher: Connect to `gopher.csd.uwm.edu` and choose Remote Information Services.

E-mail: Send an empty message to `bbslist@aug3.augsburg.edu`, and it'll automatically mail you the list.

WWW: Connect to `http://www.uwm.edu/Mirror/inet.services.html`.

Global Network Navigator

GNN is an on-line Web magazine published on the World Wide Web by America Online (AOL), which recently acquired it from publisher O'Reilly and Associates. There's no charge to use it (it's supported by advertising), but you have to register on-line. AOL also has a somewhat related GNN on-line service, but you don't have to subscribe to the on-line service to use the Web side.

WWW: To register, connect to `http://gnn.com/`.

Cool Site of the Day

The Cool Site of the Day on the World Wide Web highlights a new cool site every day. Check it daily! On one typical day, it gave us the Frog Page at Yale University with pictures, sounds (digital "ribbit," for example), stories, and much more about our friends the Ranidae.

WWW: Connect to `http://cool.infi.net/`.

Newsletters

There are lots of on-line newsletters. Here are a few that we read. You can find more by searching for `Magazines` in Yahoo or Infoseek.

The Scout Report

The InterNIC publishes a weekly Scout Report that lists interesting new sources of information on the Net. It has mostly WWW sources, but also always has a few Gopher, telnet, and e-mail resources.

The report is available in just about every form possible on the Net:

By e-mail: To get on the e-mail list, send a message to `majordomo@ lists.internic.net`, and make sure that the message text contains this line:

`subscribe scout-report`

To unsubscribe to the list, repeat this procedure and substitute the word *unsubscribe* for *subscribe*.

WWW: Point your Web program at `http://rs.internic.net/ scout_report-index.html`.

Yahoo Picks

This weekly newsletter from the Yahoo people describes their favorite new Web pages of the week. It sort of resembles the Scout Report.

To subscribe, send e-mail to `yahoo-picks-request@yahoo.com` with a one-line message containing `subscribe your-address`. (Use *your* e-mail address, not `your-address`.)

WWW: Connect to `http://www.yahoo.com/picks/`.

WEBster

This weekly newsletter discusses the Web in particular and the Internet in general. In theory you have to pay for it, but they're pretty liberal with free trial subscriptions.

For a trial subscription, send e-mail to `4free@webster.tgc.com`.

WWW: Connect to `http://www.tgc.com/webster.html`.

IWatch Digest

The Digest is another newsletter that looks at interesting new stuff on the Net.

Send e-mail to `listserv@garcia.com` with a line that contains `SUBSCRIBE IWatch your Full Name`.

Online Business Today

This weekly newsletter covers Internet business. It's available as both plain text and uuencoded PDF (which is beautifully typeset but considerably larger and readable only if you have an Adobe Acrobat reading program).

To subscribe to the text version, send e-mail to `obt.text@hpp.com`; for the PDF version, send e-mail to `obt.pdf@hpp.com`.

Net Happenings

The Net Happenings mailing list has lots of new Web pages and other interesting Net stuff. The volume is ferocious — frequently three or four digests per day.

Send a message to `majordomo@lists.internic.net` with a one-line message containing `subscribe your-address`. (Use *your* e-mail address, not `your-address`.)

Publications

Magazines and newsletters abound to track the growth and use of the Net. Two of these publications are available either on paper or in electronic versions over the Net.

I*Way

I*Way is a new, glossy bimonthly aimed at nontechnical Internet users. One editor's name may seem suspiciously familiar to readers of this book. Contact I*Way, Business Computer Publishing, 86 Elm St., Peterborough, NH 03458; phone: (800) 349-7327.

WWW: Connect to `http://www.cciweb.com/iway.html`.

Internet World

This bimonthly, glossy magazine is for Internet users. Articles include tips, case histories, interviews with notable Internauts, and product and service reviews. Contact Internet World, P.O. Box 713, Mt. Morris, IL 61054. Phone: (800) 573-3062 (U.S. and Canada); e-mail: `iwsubs@kable.com`.

WWW: Connect to `http://www.mecklerweb.com/mags/iw/iwhome.html`.

Matrix News

Matrix News, a monthly newsletter about networks, including but not limited to the Internet, is available on paper or by e-mail. The price is $25 per year delivered on-line; $30 per year on paper; and $10 less for students. Contact Matrix Information and Directory Services, 1106 Clayton Lane, Suite 500W, Austin, TX 78723. Phone: (512) 451-7602; e-mail: `mids@tic.com`.

Internet Business Report

This newsletter tracks business use of and opportunities on the Internet. It's well focused but expensive. Contact Internet Business Report, Jupiter Communications, 627 Broadway, New York, NY 10012. Phone: (800) 488-4345; fax: (212) 780-6075.

WWW: Connect to `http://www.jup.com`.

Internet Business Journal

The Journal covers business issues on nascent commercial Internet, with case histories, studies, and the like. It's available both on-line and on paper. Contact Michael Strangelove, Publisher, *The Internet/NREN Business Journal*, 1-60 Springfield Road, Ottawa, Ontario, CANADA, K1M 1C7. Phone: (613) 747-0642; fax: (613) 564-6641; e-mail: `441495@acadvm1.uottawa.ca`.

Scott and Gregg's The Internet Novice

Two brothers publish this newsletter for Internet novices. Scott is the DOS guy; Gregg does Macs. The price is $17.50 per year (U.S.) and $25 per year (elsewhere). Contact CompuTate, Inc., Box 3474, Arlington, VA 22203. E-mail: `tates@access.digex.net`.

Inside the Internet

This monthly newsletter has Internet tips and tricks. The price is $69 per year in the U.S. and $89 per year elsewhere. Contact Inside the Internet, The Cobb Group, Customer Relations, 9420 Bunsen Parkway, Suite 300, Louisville KY 40220. Phone: (800) 223-8720 or (502) 493-3300; e-mail: `ineteditor@merlin.cobb.ziff.com`.

The Cook Report

The Cook Report on-line newsletter looks at developments on the Internet, particularly political and infrastructure issues and considerable investigative reporting. Individual subscriptions cost $85. The Cook Report on Internet, 431 Greenway Ave, Ewing, NJ 08618. Phone: (609) 882-2572; e-mail: `cook@cookreport.com`

WWW: Connect to `http://www.netaxs.com/~cook`.

Wired

The trendy, glossy, magazine of the cybergeneration. If you can claw your way though the stupendously ugly graphics in the front, some of the articles are actually interesting. It also has an on-line version called HotWired, which you have to sign up for but that is free.

WWW: Connect to `http://www.hotwired.com`.

Organizations

Each of the following organizations also publishes a magazine.

The Internet Society

The Internet Society is dedicated to supporting the growth and evolution of the Internet. It supports development and evolution of Internet standards to keep the Net working as it grows. The society publishes an interesting glossy magazine and holds conferences, and it has many on-line resources. Both individual and organizational memberships are available. Contact Internet Society, Suite 100, 1895 Preston White Drive, Reston, VA 22091. Fax: (703) 620-0913; e-mail: `membership@isoc.org`.

WWW: Connect to `http://www.isoc.org`.

The Electronic Frontier Foundation (EFF)

The EFF works at the electronic frontier on issues of free speech, equitable access, and education in a networked context. It offers legal services in cases in which users' on-line civil liberties have been violated.

It publishes a magazine, has a Usenet group, keeps on-line files, and maintains human resources. Contact Electronic Frontier Foundation, P.O. Box 17, San Francisco CA 94117. Phone: (415) 668-7171; fax: (415) 668-7007; e-mail: `ask@eff.org`; Usenet: Contact `comp.org.eff.news` and `comp.org.eff.talk`.

WWW: Connect to `http://www.eff.org`.

The Society for Electronic Access (SEA)

The SEA works to promote civil rights and civilization in the networked digital world, primarily through research and education. Contact The Society for Electronic Access, P.O. Box 3131, Church Street Station, New York, NY 10008-3131; e-mail: `sea-member@sea.org`.

Glossary

● ●

account   Just like at a bank, computers used by more than one person use accounts to keep track of (and bill) who's doing what on their system. When you sign up with an Internet service provider, you're given an account name that allows you access.

address   Secret code by which the Internet identifies you so that people can send you mail. It usually looks like `username@hostname`, where `username` is your username, login name, or account number, and `hostname` is the Internet's name for the computer or Internet provider you use. The hostname can be a few words strung together with periods. The official *Internet For Dummies* address, for example, is `ninternet@dummies.com` because its username is `ninternet` ("new Internet," for this new edition of the book) and it's on a computer named `dummies.com`.

See Chapter 6 for more information about addresses, including yours, and Chapter 17 to learn how to find out other people's addresses.

alt   Type of newsgroup that discusses alternative-type topics. The alt groups are not official newsgroups, but lots of people read them anyway. We particularly like `alt.folklore.urban` and `alt.folklore.suburban`. See Chapter 9 to learn how to read Usenet newsgroups.

America Online (AOL)   A public Internet provider. If you have an account on AOL, your Internet address is `username@aol.com`, where `username` is your account name. See Chapter 13 to learn how to use America Online to access the Internet.

anonymous FTP   A method of using the FTP program to log on to another computer to copy files, even though you don't have an account on the other computer. When you log on, you enter `anonymous` as the username and your address as the password, and you get access to publicly available files. See Chapter 10 for more information about FTP-ing in general and anonymous FTP in particular.

Archie   A system that helps you find files located anywhere on the Internet. After Archie helps you find the file, you use FTP to get it. Archie is both a program and a system of servers (computers that contain indexes of files). See Chapter 11 for more information.

archive   A file that contains a group of files which have been compressed and glommed together for efficient storage. You have to use an archive program to get the original files back out. Commonly used programs include compress, tar, cpio, and zip (on UNIX systems) and PKZIP (on DOS systems). See Chapter 18 to learn how to use them.

ARPANET   A computer network started in 1969 (the original ancestor of the Internet) and funded by the U.S. Department of Defense; it was dismantled several years ago.

article   A posting to a newsgroup. That is, a message someone sends to the newsgroup to be readable by everyone who reads the newsgroup. See Chapter 9 for general information about newsgroups.

ASCII   *A*merican *S*tandard *C*ode for *I*nformation *I*nterchange. Basically, the code computers use to represent letters, numbers, and special characters.

AT&T Mail   A commercial mail system that connects to the Internet. If you have an AT&T Mail account, your Internet address is `username@attmail.com`, where `username` is your account name.

AUP   Acceptable *use* *p*olicy; a set of rules describing which sorts of activities are permitted on a network. The most restrictive AUP was the one on the NSFNET that prohibited most commercial and nonacademic use. The NSFNET AUP is no longer in force anywhere, although many people erroneously believe that it is.

automatic mailing list   A mailing list maintained by a computer program, usually one named LISTSERV or Majordomo. *See also* mailing list. Chapter 8 provides information about how to use mailing lists.

bang path address   An old-fashioned method of writing network addresses. UUCP, an old, cruddy mail system used to use addresses that contained bangs (exclamation points!) to string together the parts of the address. Forget about them.

baud   The number of *symbols* per second that a modem sends down a phone line. Baud is often incorrectly confused with bps (bits per second). A 14,400 bps modem transmits at 2,400 baud, because each of the modem symbols represents 6 bits.

BBS   Bulletin-board system; a system that lets people read each other's messages and post new ones. The Usenet system of newsgroups is in effect the world's largest distributed BBS.

BFN   '*B*ye *f*or *now*. An inanity adopted by the acronym lovers.

binary file   A file that contains information which does not consist only of text. For example, a binary file might contain an archive, a picture, sounds, a spreadsheet, or a word-processing document (which includes formatting codes in addition to characters).

bionet   A type of newsgroup that discusses topics of interest to biologists. If you're not a biologist, don't bother reading them (see Chapter 9).

bit   The smallest unit of measure for computer data. Bits can be turned on or off and are used in various combinations to represent different kinds of information. Many bits form a byte. Bytes form words. Do you care? Also, a type of newsgroup that is a BITNET mailing list in disguise.

BITFTP   The most widely available FTP-by-mail server. *See also* FTP-by-mail.

bitmap   Lots of teeny, tiny, little dots put together to make a picture. Screens (and paper) are divided into thousands of little, tiny bits, each of which can be turned on or off. These little bits are combined to create graphical representations. *GIF* and *JPG* files are the most popular kinds of bitmap files on the Net.

BITNET   A network of mostly IBM mainframes that connects to the Internet. If you have an account on machine `xyzvm3` on the BITNET and your username on the machine is `abc`, your Internet mail address is `abc@xyzvm3.bitnet`; or if your system isn't well-informed about BITNET, `abc%xyzvm3.bitnet@cunyvm.cuny.edu`. See Chapter 17 for more information about BITNET.

BIX   A commercial system formerly run by *Byte* magazine and now run by Delphi. If you have a BIX account, your Internet address is `username@bix.com`, where `username` is your account name.

biz A type of Usenet newsgroup that discusses business and commercial topics. Most other types of newsgroups are supposed to stay away from commercial messages. See Chapter 9.

bps *B*its *p*er *s*econd, a measurement used to describe how fast data is transmitted. Usually used to describe modem speed (not quite the same as *baud*).

bridge Something that connects two networks so that they appear to be a single larger network.

broadband network A network that can handle many separate signals at the same time. Broadband networks use different channels to transfer different forms of information, such as data, voice, and video.

browser A super-duper, all-singing, all-dancing program that lets you read information on the World Wide Web. Netscape Navigator is the best known (see Chapter 4).

BTW *B*y *t*he *w*ay. E-mail and newsgroups foster their own silly acronyms.

bulletin-board system An electronic message system that enables you to read and post messages. *See also* BBS.

byte A series of bits of a particular length, usually eight. Computer storage is usually measured in bytes.

Cello A program, written at the Cornell Law School, that enables you to access the World Wide Web from your PC running Windows. Obsolescent compared to Mosaic and Netscape.

CERFnet One of the regional networks originally set up to work with the NSFNET; its headquarters are in California.

Chameleon Commercial Windows software that enables you to connect directly to the Internet by way of a SLIP/PPP Internet provider (see Chapter 21).

chat To talk live to other network users from any and all parts of the world. To do this, you use Internet Relay Chat (IRC).

CIX The Commercial Internet Exchange, an association of Internet providers who agree to exchange traffic without *AUP*-type restrictions.

ClariNet Usenet newsgroups that contain various categories of news, including news from the AP newswire, distributed for a modest fee. Not all systems carry the ClariNet newsgroups because they cost money. You can also subscribe to some of them yourself — send mail to info@clarinet.com for information.

client A computer that uses the services of another computer (such as Usenet or Gopher or FTP or Archie or the World Wide Web). If your computer is a PC or Macintosh and you dial in to another system, your computer becomes a client of the system you dial in to.

client/server model A division of labor between computers. Computers that provide a service other computers can use are known as servers. Servers provide such services as FTP or Archie or the World Wide Web. If you don't have these services on your very own machine, you can connect to these machines and use these services and thereby become a client.

com When these letters appear in the last part of an address(ninternet@dummies.com, for example), it indicates that the host computer is run by a company rather than by a university or governmental agency. It also means that the host computer is probably in the United States.

communications program   A program you run on your personal computer that enables you to call up and communicate with other computers. It's a rather broad term, but most people use it to mean a program that makes your computer pretend to be a terminal (that's why they're also known as *terminal programs* or *terminal emulators*). The most commonly used communications programs on PCs are Windows Terminal (because it's free with Windows), Crosstalk, and Procomm, though there are lots of others.

comp   A type of newsgroup that discusses topics about computers, such as `comp.lang.c` (which discusses the C programming language) and `comp.society.folklore` (which covers the folklore and culture of computer users). See Chapter 9 for lists of interesting newsgroups.

compression program   Software used to squeeze files together so that they take up less room and are easier to transfer from one location to another. Popular compression programs include ZIP and Stuffit. The opposite of compression is expansion.

CompuServe   An on-line information provider that gives you some Internet access. Jeez, everyone must have heard of it by now. It provides lots of forums, which are similar to newsgroups, including many that provide excellent technical support for a wide range of PC and Mac software. If your CompuServe account number is `7123,456`, your Internet address is `7123.456@compuserve.com` (notice the period in the account number). Chapter 12 tells you how to use CompuServe's Internet services.

country code   The last part of a geographic address, which indicates which country the host computer is in. An address that ends in `ca` is Canadian, for example, and one that ends in `us` is in the United States.

daemon   A mysterious little program that runs while you're not looking and takes care of things you would rather not know about.

DARPA   Defense Advanced Research Projects Agency, the funding agency for the original ARPANET, the precursor of today's Internet.

Delphi   An on-line information provider that includes access to lots of Internet services. If you have an account on Delphi, your Internet address is `username@delphi.com`, where `username` is your account name. See Chapter 5 of our *MORE Internet For Dummies* (IDG Books Worldwide) to learn how to use Delphi to access the Internet.

digest   A compilation of the messages that have been posted to a mailing list over the past few days. Many people find it more convenient to receive one big message than a bunch of individual ones (see Chapter 8).

directory   A structure, sort of like a file folder (and called a folder in the Macintosh world). A special kind of file used to organize other files. Directories are lists of other files and can contain other directories (known as subdirectories) that contain still more files. UNIX, DOS, and Windows systems all use directory structures. The more stuff you have, the more you need directories in which to organize it. Directories enable you to organize files hierarchically.

domain   The official Internet-ese name of a computer on the Net. It's the part of an Internet address that comes after the @. Internet For Dummies Central is `ninternet@dummies.com`, for example, and its domain name is `dummies.com`.

domain name server   (Or just *name server* or abbreviated as *DNS.*) A computer on the Internet that translates between Internet domain names, such as `xuxa.iecc.com`, and Internet numerical addresses, such as `140.186.81.2`.

download   To bring software from a remote computer "down" to your computer.

dumb terminal   A screen and a keyboard and not much else. It sort of resembles a PC without the computer. Dumb terminals connect to other computers and use their data and their computing. When you use your computer to dial in to another computer (ignoring SLIP and PPP connections for the moment), your computer generally acts like a dumb terminal and relies on the computer you've dialed in to for processing the requests you make.

dynamic routing   A method of addressing information on the Internet (not just mail messages, but all information) so that if one route is blocked or broken, the information can take an alternative route. Pretty darned clever. The U.S. Department of Defense built this method into the design of the Internet for the benefit of the military, to resist enemy attack. It's also useful when nonmilitary networks are attacked by errant backhoes.

e-mail   Electronic mail (also called *e-mail* or just *mail*) messages sent by way of the Internet to a particular person. For the basics of sending and receiving e-mail, see Chapter 6.

Easylink   An e-mail service formerly run by Western Union and now run by AT&T. (It's not widely known to the public, but it's bigger than AOL.) If you have an Easylink account, your Internet address is 1234567@eln.attmail.com, where 1234567 is your account number.

edu   When these letters appear in the last part of an address (for example, in info@mit.edu), it indicates that the host computer is run by an educational institution, probably a college or university. It also means that the host computer is probably in the United States.

elm   An easy-to-use UNIX mail reader, which we vastly prefer over mail. Another good one is Pine.

environment variable   Values that can be set to help get your computer automatically into a state ready for you to use. Environment variables are part of your operating system's machinations and are specific to the operating system you run.

Ethernet   A cable that connects pieces of a local area network in a particular pattern. Developed by Xerox, it is sometimes called IEEE 802.3, which refers to the standard that defines it.

Eudora   A mail-handling program that runs on the Macintosh and under Windows. Originally a shareware program, it is now sold by Qualcomm. See Chapter's 6 and 7 in this book and Chapter 10 in *MORE Internet For Dummies* to learn how to get and use it.

expansion program   Software used to expand a file that has been compressed. Popular expansion programs include UNZIP and Unstuffit.

FAQ   *F*requently *a*sked *q*uestions. This regularly posted Usenet article answers questions that come up regularly in a newsgroup. Before you ask a question in a newsgroup, make sure that you have read its FAQ because it may well contain the answer. People get annoyed if you ask questions that are answered in the newsgroup's FAQ, because they probably have already answered the question 150 times.

FAQs are posted regularly, usually once a week or once a month. To read all the regularly posted FAQs for all newsgroups, read the newsgroup news.answers. To read an entire book of frequently asked questions about the Internet, get Margy's *Internet FAQs* (IDG Books Worldwide, 1995).

FAX modem   Modems (really should be fax-*data* modems) that enable you to send and receive faxes in addition to ordinary computer-type data. Fax is short for fac-simile or exact copy, and fax technology uses ordinary phone lines to send copies of printed material from place to place. If you stick fax technology on your computer, what you send may never touch paper. It can go from your computer to theirs or to their fax machine if they don't have a computer.

FIDONET   A worldwide network of bulletin-board systems (BBSs). Each individual BBS is called a *node* on FIDONET and has a three- or four-part numeric address in the form *1:2/3* or *1:2/3.4* (who the heck thought of this?). To send Internet mail to someone on FIDONET, address it to `firstname.lastname @p4.f3.n2.z1.fidonet.org` (for nodes with four-part names) or `firstname.lastname@f3.n2.z1` (for nodes with three-part names), substituting the addressee's username for `firstname.lastname`.

file   A collection of information (data or a software program, for example) treated as a unit by computers.

file-transfer protocol   A method of trans-ferring one or more files from one computer to another on a network or phone line. The idea of using a protocol is that the sending and receiving programs can check that the information has been received correctly. The most commonly used dial-up protocols are Xmodem, Ymodem, Zmodem, and Kermit. The Internet has its own file-transfer protocol, called FTP (clever name, huh?), to transfer files among computers on the Net (see Chapter 10).

finger   A program that displays information about someone on the Net. On most UNIX systems the command tells you who is logged on right now. On most Internet hosts, it tells you the actual name and perhaps some other information, based on the person's Internet address and the last time she logged on. See Chapter 17 to learn how to use it.

firewall   A system has a firewall around it if it lets only certain kind of messages in and out from the rest of the Internet. If an organization wants to exchange mail with the Internet, for example, but it doesn't want nosy college students telnetting in and reading everyone's files, its connection to the Internet can be set up to prevent incoming telnets or FTPs.

folder   A structure, sort of like a file folder, used to group items of a like nature. E-mail programs enable you to store your mail in folders for easy retrieval.

freenet   A free on-line system. Wow! The first one, created at the University of Cleveland, is called the Cleveland Freenet, offering local community information and limited access to the Internet. Lots of other freenets have sprung up, and because you can telnet from one to another, if you can access one, you can access them all. For a list of freenets, see Chapter 20.

FTP   *F*ile-*t*ransfer *p*rotocol; also the name of a program that uses the protocol to transfer files all over the Internet. For instructions on how to use FTP, see Chapter 10.

FTP-by-mail   A method by which you can send a mail message to a server computer to request that a file be mailed to you by way of e-mail. This is a way to get files over the Net, slowly, if you have access only to e-mail (see Chapter 10 for more information).

FTP server   An Internet host computer that stores files which can be retrieved by FTP. FTP servers also accept uploads of files. Chapter 10 tells you how to use FTP.

gateway   A computer that connects one network with another when the two net-works use different protocols. The UUNET computer connects the UUCP network with the Internet, for example, providing a way for mail messages to move between the two networks. For more information about how gateways work, see Chapter 2 of *MORE Internet For Dummies.* Also an older name for what's now called a *router.*

GEnie   An on-line service run by General Electric. If you have an account on GEnie and your mail name (not your username!) is ABC, your Internet address is ABC@genie.geis.com.

GIF   A type of graphics file originally defined by CompuServe and now found all over the Net (GIF stands for Graphics Interchange Format). See Chapter 18 for suggestions about how to handle GIF files.

global kill file   A file that tells your Usenet newsreader which articles you always want to skip. This file applies to all the newsgroups to which you subscribe.

Gopher   A system that lets you find information by using menus (lots of menus). To use Gopher, you usually telnet to a Gopher server and begin browsing the menus.

Gopherspace   The world of Gopher menus. As you move from menu to menu in Gopher, you are said to be "moving around Gopherspace."

gov   When these letters appear in the last part of an address (cu.nih.gov, for example), it indicates that the host computer is run by some part of a government body, probably the U.S. federal government, rather than by a company or university. (Your tax dollars at play!) Most gov sites are in the United States.

hardware   The actual, physical computer and all its wires and friends, such as the printer, the disk drive, and the modem. Pretty useless without software.

HGopher   A cool Microsoft Windows program that helps you view Gopher information, including seeing graphics right on the screen. It's described in detail in Chapter 12 of *MORE Internet For Dummies.*

home page   The primary Web page for an individual, software application, or organization. Home pages link visitors to other pages related to the site. To visit the *. . .For Dummies* home page, point your Web browser to http://dummies.com (see Chapter 4).

host   A computer on the Internet you may be able to log in to by using telnet, get files from by using FTP, or otherwise make use of.

HTML   *H*ypertext *m*arkup *l*anguage, used in writing pages for the World Wide Web. It lets the text include codes that define fonts, layout, embedded graphics, and hypertext links. Don't worry: You don't have to know anything about it to use the World Wide Web (see Chapters 4 and 5).

HTTP   *H*ypertext *t*ransfer *p*rotocol, which is the way World Wide Web pages are transferred over the Net (see Chapters 4 and 5). Also see Chapter 8 of *MORE Internet For Dummies* for more details about how to read the World Wide Web from a PC with Windows.

hypermedia   *See* hypertext, except think about all kinds of information, such as pictures and sound, not just text.

hypertext   A system of writing and displaying text that enables the text to be linked in multiple ways, to be available at several levels of detail, and to contain links to related documents. Hypermedia can also contain pictures, sounds, video — you name it. The World Wide Web uses hypertext. Both are discussed in Chapters 4 and 5.

ICMP *I*nternet *c*ontrol *m*essage *p*rotocol, an exceedingly uninteresting low-level protocol that Internet computers use. Used by ping.

icon A little picture intended to represent something bigger, such as a program or a choice of action or object.

IMO, IMHO *I*n *m*y *o*pinion; *i*n *m*y *h*umble *o*pinion.

InfoSeek A service that searches the World Wide Web for pages that mention a word or phrase you specify (see Chapter 11).

Internet You still don't know what it is, and you're way back here in the glossary! Yikes — we must have done a terrible job of explaining this stuff. It's an interconnected bunch of computer networks, including networks in all parts of the world.

Internet Explorer Microsoft's Web browser. If you have a Microsoft Network account, you can download it or you can buy it as part of Microsoft PLUS! (see Chapter 14).

Internet Protocol *See* IP.

Internet Relay Chat (IRC) A system that enables bored undergraduates and, occasionally, other Internet folks to talk to each other in real time (rather than after a delay, as with e-mail messages). Chapter 19 of *MORE Internet For Dummies* describes how to get in on the action.

Internet Society An organization dedicated to supporting the growth and evolution of the Internet. You can contact it at isoc@isoc.org.

InterNIC The Internet Network Information Center, a repository of information about the Internet. It is divided into two parts: Directory Services, run by AT&T in New Jersey, and Registration Services, run by Network Solutions in Virginia. It is funded partially by the National Science Foundation and partially by fees that are charged to register Internet domains.

To find out more about it, point your Web browser at http://rs.internet.net. To FTP information from InterNIC, try ftp.internic.net.

interrupt character A key or combination of keys you can press to stop whatever is happening on your computer. You might find that you have started something and don't want to wait for it to finish. Common interrupt characters are Ctrl-C and Ctrl-D. Telnet's usual interrupt character is Ctrl-].

IP Internet Protocol, a scheme that enables information to be routed from one network to another as necessary (you had to ask). Don't worry: You don't have to know about it. For a long and tedious discussion, see Chapter 2 of *MORE Internet For Dummies*.

IRC *See* Internet Relay Chat.

Jughead A program that helps you find information in Gopher by searching Gopher directories for the information you specify; sort of like Veronica (see Chapter 11).

k12 A type of Usenet newsgroup that contains information for elementary through high school students and teachers.

Kermit A file-transfer protocol developed at Columbia University and available for a variety of computers, from PCs to mainframes. See Chapter 4 of *MORE Internet For Dummies* for more information about file-transfer protocols.

kill file A file that tells your newsreader which newsgroup articles you always want to skip. See Chapter 15 in this book to learn how to make kill files by using trn.

link   A connection. Two computers can be linked together. Also can refer to a pointer to a file that exists in another place. Rather than have a copy of a particular file reside in many places, for example, some file systems (the ones in UNIX, for example) enable a filename to point to another file. Finally, a link can refer to a hypertext link in a Web page that connects one page to another.

link-level protocol   One of the seven layers of protocols defined by ISO. Sometimes referred to as the data link layer. You really, really don't care.

list server   A program that automatically manages mailing lists. *See also* LISTSERV.

LISTSERV   A family of programs that automatically manage mailing lists, distributing messages posted to the list, adding and deleting members, and so on without the tedium of someone doing it manually. The names of mailing lists maintained by LISTSERV usually end with -1 (that's an el, not a one). See Chapter 8 for information about how to get on and off LISTSERV mailing lists.

Lynx   A World Wide Web client program that works with plain old terminals, which means that it's generally available on shell provider accounts (see Chapters 4 and 5).

MacTCP   TCP/IP for the Macintosh. Not very interesting except that you can't put your Mac on the Internet without it.

mail   Pieces of paper stuffed in envelopes with stamps on the outside. This old-fashioned type of mail is known among Internauts as *snail-mail,* casting aspersions on your local letter carrier. Other types of mail include *voice mail,* which you probably already know and hate, and *e-mail* (or electronic mail), which is a powerful service the Internet provides. For an introduction to e-mail, see Chapters 6 and 7.

mail server   A computer on the Internet that provides mail services. A mail server usually sends mail out for you (using a system called SMTP) and may also enable you to download your mail to a PC or Mac by using a protocol called POP. See Chapters 6 and 7 in this book and Chapter 10 of *MORE Internet For Dummies* to learn how to use Eudora to grab your mail from a mail server.

mailing list   A special kind of e-mail address that remails any incoming mail to a list of *subscribers* to the mailing list. Each mailing list has a specific topic, so you subscribe to the ones of interest (see Chapter 8).

mainframe   A large computer usually sold complete with all its peripherals and often a closed architecture (meaning not friendly to other vendors' products). Often refers to large IBM machines.

Majordomo   Like LISTSERV, a program that handles mailing lists. See Chapter 8 in this book.

MBone   The multicast backbone. A special subnetwork on the Internet that supports live video and other multimedia.

MCI Mail   A commercial e-mail system linked to the Internet. If you have an MCI Mail account, you have both a username and a seven-digit user number. Your Internet address is `1234567@mcimail.com` or `username@mcimail.com`, substituting your username or number.

Watch out when you're addressing mail by name on MCI Mail — more than one person may have the same name! Numbers are safer. If a name is ambiguous, MCI Mail returns a message that gives some hints about how to find the user you want.

MERIT   A regional network in Michigan. Affiliated with ANS.

message   A piece of e-mail or a posting to a newsgroup.

Microsoft Network (MSN)   A commercial on-line service run by Microsoft and usable only if you have Windows 95. If your MSN username is `BillGates`, your Internet e-mail address is `billgates@msn.com`. See Chapter 14 to learn how to use MSN's Internet services.

mil   When these letters appear in the last part of an address (`wsmr-simtel20@army.mil`, for example), it indicates that the host computer is run by some part of the U.S. military rather than by a company or university.

MIME   *M*ultipurpose *I*nternet *m*ail extension used to send anything other than straight text through e-mail. Eudora and Pine and other hip e-mail programs support MIME.

mirror   An FTP server that provides copies of the same files as another server. Some FTP servers are so popular that other servers have been set up to mirror them and spread the FTP load on to more than one site (see Chapter 21).

misc   A type of newsgroup that discusses topics which don't fit under any of the other newsgroups types, such as `misc.forsale`, `misc.jobs.offered`, and `misc.kids`. See Chapter 9 for lists of interesting newsgroups.

modem   A gizmo that lets your computer talk on the phone. A modem can be internal (a board that lives inside your computer) or external (a box that connects to your computer's serial port). Either way, you need a phone wire to connect the modem to your phone jack. For tons of information about modems and how to use them, get *Modems For Dummies,* by Tina Rathbone (IDG Books Worldwide).

moderated mailing list   A mailing list run by a moderator (*q.v.,* or for you non-Latin speakers, check out the definition of moderator). See Chapter 8 for the details.

moderated newsgroup   A newsgroup run by a moderator (go ahead, *see* moderator). Check out Chapter 9 for more information.

moderator   Someone who looks first at the messages posted to a mailing list or newsgroup before releasing them to the public. The moderator can nix messages that are stupid (in his opinion, of course), redundant, or inappropriate for the list or newsgroup (wildly off the topic or offensive, for example). Yes, this is censorship, but the Internet is getting so big and crowded that nonmoderated discussions can generate an amazing number of uninteresting messages. *See also* moderated mailing list and moderated newsgroup.

Monsterboard   A giant Web resource for job-hunting.

Mosaic   A super-duper all-singing, all-dancing program that lets you read information on the World Wide Web. Comes in Windows, Mac, and UNIX flavors. See Chapter 14 in *MORE Internet For Dummies* to learn how to get, install, and use it. Similar to Netscape.

Motif   A graphical user interface for UNIX computers, sort of like Windows for the PC. Claimed to be ugly. See *UNIX For Dummies* if you really care.

MSN   *See* Microsoft Network.

MUD   *M*ulti-*u*ser *d*ungeon; a "dungeons and dragons" type of game that many people at a time can play. These games can get so complex and absorbing that players can disappear into their computers for days and weeks at a time. For information about how to join a MUD, consult the newsgroup `rec.games.mud.announce` or send a request to be added to the mailing list to `mudlist@glia.biostr.washington.edu`.

name server   *See* domain name server.

NetLauncher   CompuServe's software package that enables yout to connect to your CompuServe account as a PPP account. NetLauncher includes Spry Mosaic, a Web browser.

Netscape   The first company to scare Microsoft. Netscape's world-class World Wide Web browser has taken the planet by storm. Read all about it in Chapters 4 and 5.

network   Don't get us started. Lots of things are called networks, but for our purposes we're talking about lots of computers that are connected together. Those in the same or nearby buildings are called *local area networks,* those that are farther away are called *wide area networks,* and when you interconnect a large number of networks all over the world, you get the Internet!

For more than you want to know about how networks are connected together into the Internet, see Chapters 2 and 3 in *MORE Internet For Dummies.*

news   A type of Usenet newsgroup that contains discussions about news-groups themselves, such as `news.announce.newusers` (announcements of interest to new users). Also used to refer to Usenet itself.

news server   A computer on the Internet that not only gets Usenet newsgroups but also lets you read them. Programs such as Free Agent, Trumpet, and Cello use a news server to get the articles for the newsgroups you request. See Chapter 9 in this book for

Free Agent; see Chapter 11 in *MORE Internet For Dummies* to learn how to install Trumpet to read the news provided by a news server.

newsgroup   A distributed bulletin-board system about a particular topic. The Usenet news (also known as *Net news*) system distributes thousands of newsgroups to all parts of the Internet.

See Chapter 9 and the chapters in Part IV for a description of how to read newsgroups and for lists of interesting newsgroups. While you're at it, check out Chapter 11 of *MORE Internet For Dummies* to learn how to read newsgroups by using Windows programs.

newsgroup kill file   A file that tells your newsreader which articles you always want to skip. This file applies to only a specific newsgroup (*see also* global kill file). See Chapter 15 in this book to learn how to make kill files by using trn.

newsreader   A program that lets you read the messages in Usenet newsgroups and respond if you are absolutely sure that you have something new and interesting to say. See Chapter 9 in this book and Chapter 11 of *MORE Internet For Dummies* to learn how to use the Trumpet newsreader on your PC; see Chapter 14 to learn how to use two UNIX newsreaders, trn and nn.

NIC   Network Information Center. The address of the one for the U.S. part of the Internet is `internic.net`. An NIC is responsible for coordinating a set of networks so that the names, network numbers, and other technical details are consistent from one network to another.

NIS   Formerly known as the *Yellow Pages,* before some trademark lawyer in the United Kingdom complained. The NIS is a facility used on some TCP/IP networks to administer a group of computers (usually UNIX workstations and PCs) as through they were one big computer. For Internet purposes, who cares? Well, NIS sorts incoming e-mail on some UNIX systems and can cause peculiar-looking mail addresses.

NNTP server   *See* news server.

node   A computer on the Internet, also called a *host.* Computers that provide a service, such as FTP sites or places that run Gopher, are also called *servers.*

NSFNET   The National Science Foundation's former network, a part of the Internet devoted to research and education and funded by government money. It has gone away, replaced by pieces of commercial networks. ANS, which formerly ran the NSFNET, now belongs to America Online.

Open Book Repository   A collection of on-line text, including the text of books, journals, and other reference materials, maintained by the Online Book Initiative at obi.std.com.

packet   A chunk of information sent over a network. Each packet contains the address it's going to, the address of who sent it, and some other information. For more than you ever wanted to know about how the Internet handles packets, see Chapter 2 of this book and Chapter 2 of *MORE Internet For Dummies.*

packet driver   A small program used on DOS and Windows PCs to connect network software to a particular kind of network card. Similar to NDIS or ODI driver.

page   A document, or hunk of information, available by way of the World Wide Web. To make information available on the World Wide Web, you organize it into one or more pages. Each page can contain text, graphics files, sound files — you name it. Don't worry: You don't have to create WWW pages — you can just read them.

pager   A feature in *Archie* (and other programs) that breaks up the data Archie displays into chunks that fill up only one screen at a time, enabling you to read what's there before it scrolls off the screen.

parameter   A value a computer program needs to know in order to behave correctly.

password   A secret code used to keep things private. Your account on the system that connects you to the Internet is no doubt protected by a password. Be sure to pick a code that is not obvious, preferably combining numbers and letters so as to thwart any untoward activity.

password file   The file in which all the passwords for a system are stored. Most systems are smart enough to keep passwords encoded so that even if someone gains access to this file, it isn't of much value.

pine   A UNIX-based mail program based on elm. (It stands for *pine is not elm.*) Pine is easy to use, at least for a UNIX program; it's described in Chapters 6 and 7.

ping   A program that checks to see whether you can communicate with another computer on the Internet. It sends a short message to which the other computer automatically responds. If you can't "ping" another computer, you probably can't talk to it any other way either.

Chapter 8 of *MORE Internet For Dummies* describes how to get and use a program called Pingw for Windows systems connected to the Internet by using SLIP.

Pipeline   An Internet provider in New York City (`pipeline.com` is its address) that works with a special Windows communications program, also called Pipeline. It uses its own protocol to talk to this program, which enables it to display everything in a nice Windows-y way. Several other providers around the country use the Pipeline program, giving it different names to avoid consistency.

PKZIP   A file-compression program that runs on PCs. PKZIP creates a *ZIP file* that contains compressed versions of one or more files. To restore them to their former size and shape, you use PKUNZIP. *PK,* by the way, stands for Phil Katz, who wrote the program. PKZIP and PKUNZIP are shareware programs available from many FTP sites. If you use the programs, you are honor-bound to send Mr. Katz a donation (the program will tell you the address).

If you use a Windows computer, you will probably prefer WinZip, which has nice Windows-y menus and buttons. You can get it via FTP from `ftp.winzip.com` in the `/winzip` directory (see Chapter 18).

POP   Post Office Protocol, a system by which a mail server on the Internet lets you pick up your mail and download it to your PC or Mac. See Chapters 6 and 7 in this book and Chapter 10 in *MORE Internet For Dummies* to learn how to install and run Eudora, which requires POP.

port number   On a networked computer, an identifying number assigned to each program that is chatting on the Internet. The program that handles incoming telnet sessions uses port 23, for example, and the program that handles some other service has another number. You hardly ever have to know these numbers — the Internet programs work this stuff out among themselves.

posting   An article in a Usenet newsgroup.

PPP   *Point-to-point protocol,* a scheme for connecting two computers over a phone line (or a network link that acts like a phone line). Like *SLIP,* only better. See Chapter 2 of *MORE Internet For Dummies.*

Prodigy   A large on-line system run by IBM and Sears. If you have a Prodigy account, your Internet address is `username@prodigy.com` (substitute your username for `username`).

protocol   A system two computers agree on. When you use a file-transfer protocol, for example, the two computers involved (the sender and the receiver) agree on a set of signals that mean "go ahead," "got it," "didn't get it, please resend," and "all done."

The Internet involves tons of different protocols for the many different types of computers on the Net that interact.

pseudoterminal   A fake terminal. On most systems, telnet uses a pseudoterminal to log you in and run your commands.

public-service provider   A time-sharing or SLIP service that enables you to use the Internet on a paying (by the month or hour) basis. Chapter 20 lists some of them.

RCP   *Remote copy,* a UNIX command that lets you copy files from one computer to another. Like FTP, only different (see our *UNIX For Dummies,* published by IDG Books Worldwide).

rec   A type of newsgroup that discusses recreational topics, such as `rec.humor.funny` (jokes that are sometimes funny) and `rec.gardens` (guess). See Chapter 9 for lists of interesting newsgroups.

regex method   Search criteria for the advanced geek. *See* regular expression.

regular expression   Not what one would usually think of as regular. For UNIX hackers and those who love to encode the ordinary into arithmetic representation. Many kinds of conditional searches (meaning, under these conditions, "do this") can be represented by using mathematical expressions. If you haven't studied much math or logic, forget about it.

router   No, not a power tool used for finish work on fine cabinetry (that's pronounced "rowter"). This system, pronounced "rooter" in most countries, connects two or more networks, including networks that use different types of cables and different communication speeds. The networks all have to use IP (the Internet Protocol), though. If they don't, you need a gateway.

RTFM   *R*ead *t*he *m*anual. A suggestion made by people who feel that you have wasted their time asking a question you could have found the answer to another way.

A well-known and much-used FTP site named `rtfm.mit.edu` contains FAQs for all Usenet newsgroups, by the way. Read the, uh, friendly FAQ.

sci   A type of Usenet newsgroup that discusses scientific topics.

search engine   Software used to find stuff, particularly on WAIS and the World Wide Web.

security   In the computer world, a means to allow access to only those who should have it. Security includes the use of passwords to protect your account.

serial line   A connection between computers using the serial protocol.

serial port   The place on your computer where you can plug in a serial line.

serial protocol   The simplest way to send data over a wire — one bit at a time.

server   A computer that provides a service to other computers on a network. An Archie server, for example, lets people on the Internet use Archie.

service provider   An organization that provides access to the Internet. Your service provider might be a commercial on-line service such as America Online or CompuServe, a shell provider, or your school or workplace.

shareware   Computer programs that are easily available for you to try with the understanding that if you decide to keep the program you will pay for it and send the requested amount to the shareware provider specified in the program. In this honor system, a great deal of good stuff is available, and voluntary compliance makes it viable.

SimTel   A computer that used to contain an amazing archive of programs for MS-DOS in addition to Macintosh and UNIX. Run by the U.S. Army in New Mexico, it was shut down in 1993. Fortunately, its files live on in mirror (duplicate) archives at `oak.oakland.edu` and `wuarchive.wustl.edu`. For more information, see SimTel's Web page at `http://www.coast.net/SimTel`.

See Chapter 10 for other top spots for FTP-able files.

SLIP   Short for Serial Line Internet Protocol, a software scheme for connecting a computer to the Internet over a serial line. For example, if you can run SLIP on your personal computer and you call up an Internet provider that does SLIP, your computer is *on the Internet;* it's not just a terminal — it's right on it. You can telnet and FTP to other computers; when you get files, they arrive back on your PC, not on the Internet provider's computer.

For instructions about how to run SLIP on your computer, see Chapter 8 of *MORE Internet For Dummies.*

SMTP   Simple Mail Transfer Protocol, the optimistically named method by which Internet mail is delivered from one computer to another.

soc   A type of newsgroup that discusses social topics, covering subjects from soc.men to soc.religion.buddhist to soc.culture.canada. See Chapter 9 for lists of interesting newsgroups.

socket   A logical "port" a program uses to connect to another program running on another computer on the Internet. You might have an FTP program using sockets for its FTP session, for example, while Eudora connects by way of another socket to get your mail.

software   Computer programs that make computers usable as something other than a paperweight. Compare to *hardware.*

spam   Originally a meat-related, sandwich-filling product. The word now refers to the act of posting inappropriate commercial messages to a large number of unrelated, uninterested Usenet newsgroups (see Chapter 19). See the sidebar "Spam wars," in Chapter 9, and the sidebar "I don't like Spam!" in Chapter 18 of *MORE Internet For Dummies.*

Sprintlink   One of the large commercial networks in the Internet, run by Sprint (the telephone company).

SprintMail   An e-mail system provided by Sprintnet and formerly named Telemail. Believe it or not, if you have a SprintMail account, your Internet address is /G=firstname/S=lastname/O=company/C=countrycode/A=TELEMAIL/@sprint.com. Substitute your first name, last name, company name, and country code (us for United States folks).

string   A bunch of characters strung together, such as "Internet For Dummies." Strings are composed of any characters available in the character set being used, typically all letters, digits, and punctuation.

StuffIt   A compression program for the Mac.

subdirectory   A directory within a directory.

substring   A piece of a string; *see also* string.

SURAnet   One of the regional networks originally set up to work with the NSFNET; its headquarters are in Florida.

SurfWatch   A program that censors your Internet account. Used by parents who want to control what their kids see on the Net (see Chapter 3).

System 7.5   The latest, most feature-laden, Macintosh operating system.

talk   A type of newsgroup that contains endless arguments about a wide range of issues, such as talk.abortion and talk.rumors. See Chapter 9 for lists of interesting newsgroups.

TCP/IP   The system that networks use to communicate with each other on the Internet. It stands for Transmission Control Protocol/Internet Protocol, if you care. See Chapters 2 and 3 of *MORE Internet For Dummies* for the gory details.

telnet   A program that lets you log in to other computers on the Net.

terminal   In the olden days, a terminal was a thing that consisted of a screen, a keyboard, and a cable that connected it to a computer. These days not many people (not many people *we* know) use terminals, because personal computers are so cheap. Why have a brainless screen and keyboard when you can have your own computer on your desk?

Of course, there are still many times when you want to connect to a big computer somewhere. If you have a personal computer, you can run a program that makes it *pretend* to be a brainless screen and keyboard — the program is called a *terminal emulator, terminal program,* or *communications program.*

terminal emulator   *See* communications program and also terminal.

terminal program   *See* communications program and also terminal.

text file   A file that contains only textual characters, with no special formatting characters, graphical information, sound clips, video, or what-have-you. Most computers other than some IBM mainframes store their text by using a system of codes named *ASCII,* so this type of file is also known as an *ASCII text file* (see Chapter 18).

third party   Sometimes you buy your computer from one place and your operating software from somewhere else, but you find that you still need other hardware or software pieces to make it all work. The people from whom you buy those other pieces are known as third-party vendors.

thread   An article posted to a Usenet newsgroup, together with all the follow-up articles, the follow-ups to follow-ups, and so on. Organizing articles into threads makes it easier to choose which articles in a newsgroup you want to read. See Chapters 9

and 15 in this book and Chapter 16 in *MORE Internet For Dummies* for descriptions of newsreaders that enable you to choose which threads to read.

threaded newsreader   A newsreader that enables you to choose articles by thread. See Chapter 9 for a description of Free Agent; Chapter 12 of *MORE Internet For Dummies* for a description of vnews, a threaded newsreader for Windows; and Chapter 15 in this book for more information about trn, a threaded newsreader for UNIX.

TIA   The Internet Adaptor, nifty software that makes your regular dial-up account look like a SLIP or PPP account. Also *t*hanks *i*n *a*dvance, for you acronymophiles.

Trumpet   A moderately cool newsreader program that runs on computers which run Windows. Chapter 11 of *MORE Internet For Dummies* tells you all about it. We like Free Agent better. Trumpet is only slightly related (in that it was written by the same guy) to Trumpet *WinSock,* a separate program that provides TCP/IP connections for Windows PCs.

UNIX   An operating system everyone hates. No, an operating system everyone ought to love. No, it's both! It's an operating system that can be confusing to use, but it sure is powerful. Internet users are likely to run into UNIX if they use a shell provider as their Internet provider or when they telnet to UNIX computers. For the complete truth about UNIX, get a copy of *UNIX For Dummies,* 2nd Edition.

upload   To put your stuff on somebody else's computer (see Chapter 14).

URL   Uniform Resource Locator, a way of naming network resources and originally for linking pages together in the World Wide Web. Luckily, you don't have to know much about them — only the people who *write*

WWW pages really have to fool with them (see Chapters 4 and 5).

Usenet A system of thousands of distributed bulletin boards called *newsgroups*. You read the messages by using a program called a *newsreader*. See Chapter 9 for an introduction to newsgroups and a list of some interesting ones.

UUCP An elderly and creaky (but cheap) mail system still used by many UNIX systems. UUCP stands for *UNIX-to-UNIX-copy*. UUCP uses mail addresses that contain exclamation points rather than periods between the parts (and they are in reverse order), a method known as *bang path addressing*. Whenever possible, use regular Internet addresses instead.

uuencode/uudecode Programs that encode files to make them suitable for sending as e-mail. Because e-mail messages must be text, not binary information, *uuencode* can disguise nontext files as text so that you can include them in a mail message. When the message is received, the recipient can run *uudecode* to turn it back into the original file. Pretty clever. For more information, see Chapter 18.

UUNET A formerly nonprofit organization which, among other things, runs a large Internet site that links the UUCP mail network with the Internet and has a large and useful FTP file archive. You may encounter it in addresses that contain `uunet.uu.net` at the end. The organization also runs Alternet, one of the larger commercial network providers.

V.32 The code word for a nice, fast modem (one that talks at a speed of 9600 bits per second). Even faster modems (that talk at 14,400 bits per second) are called V.32bis, which is French for V.32-and-another.

V.34 The code word for really fast modems that talk at 28,800 bps.

VAX/VMS Digital Equipment's major computer line over the past 15 years was the VAX; its proprietary operating system is known as VMS. (Vaxen are now passé, replaced by DEC's new Alpha line.)

Veronica A program that helps find things in Gopherspace (see Chapter 11); a friend of Archie's.

version creep A problem that occurs when lots of people add features to programs that people are already using. Unless care is taken to keep programs compatible, sooner or later the program you're using doesn't talk to its "new and improved cousin" until you get the latest and greatest version that should make everybody happy 'til they add more features again.

viewer A program used by Gopher, WAIS, or World Wide Web client programs to show you files that contain stuff other than text. For example, you might want viewers to display graphics files, play sound files, or display video files.

virus Software that infects other software and causes damage to the system on which the infected software is run. You should download software only from reputable servers. Safe software is everyone's business. Viral infection can be deadly. Don't let it happen to you.

VT100 The part number of a terminal made about 15 years ago by the Digital Equipment Corporation. Why do you care? Because many computers on the Internet expect to talk to VT-100-type terminals, and many communications programs can pretend to be (emulate) VT-100 terminals. See Chapters 2 and 15 for more information about communications programs and terminals. The VT102 was a cheaper version that for most purposes acted exactly the same.

WAIS   Wide Area Information Servers (pronounced "ways," not "wace"), a system which lets you search for documents that contain the information you're looking for. It's not supereasy to use, but it gets there. See Chapter 11 in this book to learn how to use WAIS, and see Chapter 13 of *MORE Internet For Dummies* for even more info about it.

Web   The World Wide Web. "The Web" is a term of endearment used by those intimate with the World Wide Web.

Web page   The basic building block of the World Wide Web. Information displayed on a Web page can include highly sophisticated graphics, audio and video, the locus of contemporary creativity. Web pages are linked together to form the World Wide Web.

Web server   An Internet host computer that stores Web pages and responds to requests to see them. Web servers talk to Web browsers by using a language named HTTP (see Chapter 5).

Web site   A location on the World Wide Web. It means the same as a Web page or Web server, depending on whom you ask.

WELL   The WELL (the Whole Earth 'Lectronic Link) is a public Internet provider in Sausalito, California. You can contact it at info@well.sf.ca.us.

whois   A command on some systems that tells you the actual name of someone, based on the person's username. *See also* finger. You can use whois by way of the World Wide Web — see Chapter 17 in this book.

Windows   An operating system for the PC that includes a graphical user interface; also a religion.

Windows 95   A new instance of an operating system for the PC that includes a graphical user interface. Quietly introduced in the summer of 1995, it includes built-in support for TCP/IP, the Internet's networking scheme. Originally code-named Chicago.

WinGopher   A Windows program that lets you see Gopher pages. See Chapter 8 of *MORE Internet For Dummies* to learn how to get, install, and use it.

WinSock   WinSock (short for *Windows Sock*ets) is a standard way for Windows programs to work with TCP/IP. You use it if you connect your Windows PC directly to the Internet, either with a permanent connection or with a modem by using SLIP or PPP. Chapter 21 lists a bunch of WinSock packages and programs that run by using WinSock. *The Internet For Windows For Dummies Starter Kit* (IDG Books Worldwide) comes with a free trial version of an entire set of WinSock software, including programs for e-mail, the Web, Gopher, FTP, and telnet.

WinWAIS   A Windows-based program that lets you use WAIS to search for information about the Internet. See Chapter 14 in *MORE Internet For Dummies* about both WAIS and WinWAIS.

WinZip   A Windows-based program for zipping and unzipping ZIP files in addition to other standard types of archive files. WinZip is shareware, so you can get it from the Net from http://www.winzip.com. See Chapter 10 in this book and Chapter 9 of *MORE Internet For Dummies* to learn how to get WinZip and install it.

workstation   Although this term gets bandied about in a bunch of different contexts, we generally mean high-powered microcomputers with big screens, somewhat overkill for the average PC user. We mean such things as SPARCstations and other typically single-user but very powerful machines, generally running UNIX.

World Wide Web (WWW) A hypermedia system that lets you browse through lots of interesting information. See Chapters 4 and 5, and then check out Chapter 14 of *MORE Internet For Dummies* for the latest in PC programs that make the WWW even niftier. The best-known WWW client is Netscape; Mosaic is a close second.

X.25 A protocol that defines packet switching. You shouldn't care. The thing that TCP/IP is much better than.

X.75 The way you splice together X.25 networks, which shouldn't interest you either.

X terminal A terminal that uses the X graphical user interface. This interface enables you to open lots of windows on your screen and do all kinds of things at the same time. Popular in the UNIX world.

xarchie A version of *Archie* that runs on UNIX under X Windows. If you use a UNIX workstation and Motif (or another windowing system), try typing **xarchie** to see whether you have a copy. See Chapter 11 for info about Archie.

xgopher A version of Gopher that runs on UNIX under X Windows. If you use a UNIX workstation and Motif, try running xgopher.

Xmodem A file-transfer protocol developed ages ago (1981?) by Ward Christiansen to check for errors as files are transferred. It has since been superseded by Ymodem and Zmodem, but many programs (especially Windows Terminal) still use it. See Chapter 15 in this book and Chapter 4 in *MORE Internet For Dummies* for information about transferring files.

xwais A version of WAIS that runs on UNIX under X Windows. If you use a UNIX workstation and Motif, try running xwais.

Yahoo An index to the World Wide Web, at `http://www.yahoo.com` (see Chapter 11).

Yellow Pages *See* NIS.

Ymodem A file-transfer protocol that's faster than Xmodem but not as powerful (nor as complicated) as Zmodem (see Chapter 4 of *MORE Internet For Dummies*).

ZIP file A file that has been created by using WinZip, PKZIP, or a compatible program. It contains one or more files that have been compressed and glommed together to save space. To get at the files in a ZIP file, you usually need WinZip, PKUNZIP, or a compatible program. Sometimes you may get a self-extracting file, which is a ZIP file that contains the unzipping program right in it. Just run the file (type the name of the file at the command line), and it unzips itself.

For information about how to get and set up WinZip on a Windows computer, see Chapter 10 in this book and Chapter 9 in *MORE Internet For Dummies*.

Zmodem A fast file-transfer protocol defined by Chuck Forsberg, used by many programs. With Zmodem, you can transfer several files with one command, and the names of the files are sent along with them. Some communications programs (such as ProComm) can detect when a Zmodem transfer has begun and automatically begin receiving the files. Nifty. See Chapter 4 of *MORE Internet For Dummies* for more info.

Index

IDG BOOKS WORLDWIDE REGISTRATION CARD

RETURN THIS REGISTRATION CARD FOR FREE CATALOG

Title of this book: The Internet For Dummies, 3E

My overall rating of this book: ❏ Very good [1] ❏ Good [2] ❏ Satisfactory [3] ❏ Fair [4] ❏ Poor [5]

How I first heard about this book:

❏ Found in bookstore; name: [6]

❏ Advertisement: [8]

❏ Word of mouth; heard about book from friend, co-worker, etc.: [10]

❏ Book review: [7]

❏ Catalog: [9]

❏ Other: [11]

What I liked most about this book:

What I would change, add, delete, etc., in future editions of this book:

Other comments:

Number of computer books I purchase in a year: ❏ 1 [12] ❏ 2-5 [13] ❏ 6-10 [14] ❏ More than 10 [15]

I would characterize my computer skills as: ❏ Beginner [16] ❏ Intermediate [17] ❏ Advanced [18] ❏ Professional [19]

I use ❏ DOS [20] ❏ Windows [21] ❏ OS/2 [22] ❏ Unix [23] ❏ Macintosh [24] ❏ Other: [25]_____
(please specify)

I would be interested in new books on the following subjects:
(please check all that apply, and use the spaces provided to identify specific software)

❏ Word processing: [26]

❏ Data bases: [28]

❏ File Utilities: [30]

❏ Networking: [32]

❏ Other: [34]

❏ Spreadsheets: [27]

❏ Desktop publishing: [29]

❏ Money management: [31]

❏ Programming languages: [33]

I use a PC at (please check all that apply): ❏ home [35] ❏ work [36] ❏ school [37] ❏ other: [38] _____

The disks I prefer to use are ❏ 5.25 [39] ❏ 3.5 [40] ❏ other: [41]_____

I have a CD ROM: ❏ yes [42] ❏ no [43]

I plan to buy or upgrade computer hardware this year: ❏ yes [44] ❏ no [45]

I plan to buy or upgrade computer software this year: ❏ yes [46] ❏ no [47]

Name: _____ Business title: [48] _____ Type of Business: [49] _____

Address (❏ home [50] ❏ work [51]/Company name: _____)

Street/Suite# _____

City [52]/State [53]/Zipcode [54]: _____ Country [55] _____

❏ **I liked this book!** You may quote me by name in future
IDG Books Worldwide promotional materials.

My daytime phone number is _____

IDG BOOKS
®
THE WORLD OF
COMPUTER
KNOWLEDGE

❏ YES!

Please keep me informed about IDG's World of Computer Knowledge.
Send me the latest IDG Books catalog.

BUSINESS REPLY MAIL
FIRST CLASS MAIL   PERMIT NO. 2605   FOSTER CITY, CALIFORNIA

IDG Books Worldwide
919 E Hillsdale Blvd, STE 400
Foster City, CA 94404-9691